❧ HAWLEY ❧
HALLEY ❧ HOLLEY

and
Families of Similar Surnames
Found in the Early Records of Maryland and Virginia,
Whose Descendants Migrated to Alaska, Arkansas,
California, Connecticut, Ohio, Florida, Georgia,
Iowa, Kansas, Kentucky, Missouri, Nebraska,
New York, North Carolina, Ohio,
South Carolina, Texas, Washington
and West Virginia

A Resource Book

Laura Hawley

HERITAGE BOOKS
2012

HERITAGE BOOKS
AN IMPRINT OF HERITAGE BOOKS, INC.

Books, CDs, and more—Worldwide

For our listing of thousands of titles see our website
at
www.HeritageBooks.com

Published 2012 by
HERITAGE BOOKS, INC.
Publishing Division
100 Railroad Ave. #104
Westminster, Maryland 21157

Copyright © 2001 Laura Hawley

Other Heritage Books by the author:

*Hawley, Halley, Holley and Families of Similar Surnames Found in the
Early Records of England, Maryland and Virginia: A Resource Book*

*Hawley, Halley, Holley and Families of Similar Surnames Found in the
Early Records of Maryland and Virginia, Whose Descendants Migrated to
Alaska, Arkansas, California, Connecticut, Ohio, Florida, Georgia, Iowa,
Kansas, Kentucky, Missouri, Nebraska, New York, North Carolina, Ohio,
South Carolina, Texas, Washington and West Virginia: A Resource Book*

*Traxel, Trexel, Trexler, Trissler, Trostle, Troxel and Similar Surnames Beginning with the
Letters T and D Found in the Early Records of Georgia, Indiana, Kansas, Kentucky,
Louisiana, Maryland, New Jersey, New York, North Carolina, South Carolina, Ohio,
Pennsylvania, Virginia, West Virginia and Wisconsin: A Resource Book*

International Standard Book Numbers
Paperbound: 978-0-7884-1804-4
Clothbound: 978-0-7884-9127-6

for now,

to my precious daughter

Susan Marie Dovel
December 10, 1970 - February 25, 1999

TABLE OF CONTENTS

A.   INTRODUCTION

The research that led to the publication of this book began 30 years ago with my desire to learn more about my ancestors.

My ancestor John Hawley married Hester Burch, in Accokeek, Maryland, on March 4, 1712. This was his first appearance in the Maryland records. My initial pursuit was to determine where John Hawley originated. The Accokeek, Maryland area is north of the 17th-century settlement in Maryland and directly across the Potomac River from the 17th-century settlement in Virginia. Possibly, was he born in Maryland? Possibly, did he come from Virginia? Possibly, was he the first of his line in the colonies? I have studied the existing early records of England, Maryland and Virginia, and there is not a specific family or individual I can match with John Hawley.

Family legend says that three Hawley brothers came from England to the colonies. One settled in Massachusetts, one in the Middle Atlantic Region, and one in the Carolinas. The northern branch of the Hawley family is well documented by the Hawley Family Society and in The Hawley Record, compiled by Elias S. Hawley in 1890. My area of research concentration has been England, Maryland and Virginia. I have not researched the Carolinas.

Jerome Hawley, a Roman Catholic gentleman, was from a prominent English family. He was a close friend of George Calvert, Lord Baltimore, and had an 1/8 interest in the colony of Maryland. He was one of the commissioners who worked with the Calverts in settling the colony, and he arrived there on March 3, 1634 in the ship Dove. He built a brick home, which he named St. Peters, in St. Maries City, Maryland. In 1637, he was appointed Royal Treasurer of Virginia by the King of England. He commuted between his home in Maryland and his post in Jamestown, Virginia, while his family remained at St. Maries. He died testate in July of 1638 at his Maryland seat, St. Peters. His will was presented in England.

Another Hawley Family member who settled in Maryland, was William Hawley, brother to Jerome Hawley. From the records it is clear that William Hawley moved around a great deal. It is most probable that he had a residence in Virginia as well as Maryland. He is found in the Virginia records as early as 1640. He served as Deputy Governor of Barbados while his brother Governor Henry Hawley was away on leave, and he was Deputy Governor of the Carolinas in 1640 for Lord Maltravers. He received title to St. Jerome's Manor, in St. Maries Co., Md., in 1648, following Jerome Hawley's death. The court records show that he made his residence there for a time. He signed the Protestant Declaration in St. Maries, Md., in 1650 and he was a resident of Virginia in March of 1652. He died c. 1654, at his seat on St. Jerome's Creek, Md. His Maryland will, which is referenced in the Chancery Records of the Provincial Court of Maryland, has never been found. Is it possible William Hawley married and had descendants? Is it possible there is a will in England?

Family legend of the Maryland Hawleys implies that my ancestor, John Hawley who married in 1712, descends from Jerome Hawley through a son named Gabriel Hawley who was born in 1602. A Bible record on page 264, discovered by Mrs. J. Stanford Halley in 1915, shows a different lineage. Family legend of the Virginia Hawleys implies that this branch of the family descends from the same English family as Jerome Hawley, but through a son named Thomas Hawley who was born in Wales in 1662. Information on this lineage was presented by Eugene Fairfield MacPike, the prominent English genealogist in 1933, and it is furnished on page 263. Both of these legends have been referenced in numerous published articles on the families Halley and Hawley. I have been unable to prove either the Maryland or the Virginia legend or to prove a clear ancestor for either family.

In the Maryland and Virginia colonies, the Hawley surname took the form of Hailey, Haily, Hale, Haley, Halley, Hally, Haly, Haulin, Healley, Healy, Holey, Holley, Holly, Hoslly, and similar forms. Members of families I studied branched off under variations of the above surnames. Their descendants are found in the contemporary records of Alaska, Arkansas, California, Connecticut, Ohio, Florida, Georgia, Iowa, Kansas, Kentucky,

Missouri, Nebraska, New York, North Carolina, Ohio, South Carolina, Texas, Washington, and West Virginia, as well as many other areas, under these surnames.

This effort is the second time in genealogical research that I have encountered frequency of surname change for the same individuals. I have labeled this occurrence the *surname distortion factor*. Being of the same family but found in the records under many different surnames. Because of this, I have researched all possible surnames the individuals are found under. I have consistently found that there are often several variations of the surname contained in a single document, as well as throughout the records, for each individual.

The Hawley surname is English and denotes a habitation of various places so called. One is in Kent, the name of which is from the old English "Halig," which comes from combining "Holy" (meaning wood) with "Leah," (clearing). One is in Hants, and has for its first element, "Oeh(e)all," (hall, manor) or the homonymous "h(e)all," (rock, stone). The surname is common mainly in South Yorkshire and Nottinghamshire and is derived from a lost place called Hawley, near Sheffield, which is from ON (Old Norse) "haugr" (mount), plus OE "leah," (clearing).

During my research in the records from the 17th, 18th, and later centuries, I identified a total of 138 families and individuals with identical or similar surnames as Hawley. These comprise the foundation for this book. Included are the descendants of John and Hester, (nee Burch) Hawley, as well as the Virginia family, and many are supplemented by contributions from descendants. The actual source records, containing the surname variations, are furnished in sections D through S (see further).

I have denoted each of the 138 families and individuals by a Unit number. These numbers bear no weight but simply reflect the numerical order in which I identified each of them through my research. When conclusive evidence was not found to tie a particular individual to a family group, but a match is possible, I have recorded that individual with a question mark (?) before the given name. This will indicate to a fellow researcher that more research is needed for definitive proof. When proof of the parents of a family group's male head is proved, in the supplemental resource records or by contributions from direct descendants, I have documented the parents through the use of a corresponding number.

The source records are found in sections D through S, and include Birth Records, Cemetery Records, Census Records, City Directory Records, Church Records, Court and Legal Records, Early Settlers Records, Land Records, Marriage Records, Mercantile Claims, Merchants Records, Military Records, Rent Rolls, Tax Records, Slave Records, Wills and Probate. Section T contains descendants of female Hawleys.

The source records are grouped under each heading by geographic locality, followed by the name of the record, and then by the name of the individual in the record. These records reflect the path of my individual research and are by no means complete in all areas. They include evidence of many individuals with the subject surnames that I could not connect with one of the 138 groups presented here. I have included the names of many individuals with whom the subjects were interacting in everyday life with the hope of providing clues for future research.

I researched both the Maryland and Virginia early records because the two colonies were separated by the Potomac River. The river runs southeast from above Washington, D.C., and empties into the Chesapeake Bay at Point Lookout, Maryland. It is narrow at some points, which facilitated easy travel between the two colonies by sail or rowing. The early settlers used the Potomac River on a daily basis for social as well as economic pursuits. There is evidence of many families having members living on both sides of the river, as well as throughout the two colonies. Roads were almost non-existent in the early period of both colonies. There were crude rolling roads which were used by the planters for little more than to roll hogsheads of tobacco to the Potomac River to load on ships bound for foreign ports. Almost all personal and economic travel was done by water. Water was to the early settlers what our super highway is to us today, a convenient means of traveling from one location to another.

My purpose in publishing this book is to help other individuals working on the surnames of Hawley, Halley, Holley and similar surnames to identify target Maryland and Virginia individuals easily, regardless of the surname or geographic locality changes. Because of this I have not included extensive family histories. A researcher interested in a particular family or individual will be able to quickly eliminate a great deal of background research and concentrate on the particular geographic area in which his subject is found, the variations in surname spelling under which they are found, and the path of their migration. The information furnished with each Unit will serve as a foundation for individuals to add their own family history, seek additional information, or add to information previously collected.

Section U is comprised of research data on the families of Bridwell, Burch, Colvin, Davis, Dickerson, Dillard, Downs, Emerson, Gilbert, Hutchison, Oden, Perkins, Trexler and Woolridge. A member of each of these families married a Hawley or was found in the Hawley descent. Each of these families is found in both the Maryland and Virginia records reviewed.

Of importance to Americans of African descent, I have included all the references that I found in the records, for each of the families researched, that refer to free and bonded slaves. These are recorded in the Census Records, Court and Legal Records and in Section R, Slave Records.

I am most grateful to the many research facilities that allowed me access to their records, as well as the family historians who furnished me data on their personal lineage. I have endeavored to always give credit for individual contributions.

I would like to give special thanks, to my Cousin, Mr. Charles Wirt Hawley, President Emeritus of The Hawley Family Society, and a fellow descendant of John and Hester (nee Burch) Hawley, for his steadfast encouragement over the years.

Laura Hawley
St. Jerome's Creek, Maryland
March 7, 2001

B. Abbreviations

ac.	acre
adj.	adjacent
adm.	administrator
b.	born
c.	circa
CSL	California State Library
bapt.	baptised
bur.	buried
cos.	counties
DAR	Daughters of the American Revolution, Washington, D.C.
d.	died
dau.	daughter
dec'd	deceased
est.	estate
exr.	executor
Inv.	Inventory
Gov.	Governor
LC	Library of Congress, Washington, D.C.
m.	married
MdHR	Maryland Hall of Records, Annapolis, Md.
nee	maiden name
NA	National Archives, Washington D.C.
P.G.,Co.	Prince George County, Md., Upper Marlboro. Md.
VSL	Virginia State Library, Richmond, Va.
vs.	versus

C.   RESEARCH UNITS

Rsh.1 John Hawley, Holly, Haly, Haley, Holey, Halley, Hally, Holley, Gentleman, Planter, Colonial Militia Soldier, m. Hester Burch on March 4, 1712, in Prince George Co., Md. Hester Burch was the dau. of John and Elizabeth Burch. His Will probate, August 4, 1757, is in Charles Co., Md. John Hawley is shown on the tax list for Piscattaway Hundred of P.G. Co., Md., in 1719. In 1722 he received a survey for a 173 acre tract of land called *Exeter* to be held of Calverton Manor. In 1733 he received a survey for a tract of land in Charles Co., Md. In 1735 he received a survey for a tract called *Costly* held of Zachia Manor, Charles Co., Md., and in 1748 he received a survey for a tract of land called *Costly Addition,* held of Zachia Manor. In 1752 he purchased *Fellowship* in Frederick Co., Md. In 1746, 1747 and 1749 he served in the Colonial Militia in Charles Co., Md. His Will dated September 20, 1755, in Charles Co., Md., leaves the three tracts of land above to his three sons, Rsh. 2, Rsh. 3, Rsh.9, known children:

> Thomas Hawley, (Rsh.2) b. 1713 m. Elizabeth Emerson
> Nathaniel Hawley, (Rsh.3) m. Mary Thompson
> John Hawley, (Rsh.9) b. 1739 m. Mary Ann Downs

Rsh.2 Thomas Hawley, Hally, Holly, Hailey, Holley, Gentleman, Planter, (son of Rsh.1) was b. on December 17, 1713, and he m. Elizabeth Emerson, dau. of John Emerson, of Prince George Co., Md. They lived at *Carrick*, Pomonkey Neck, and later on Calverton Manor, at *Exeter*, which he inherited from his father. Thomas Hawley's Will, probate June 16, 1769, P.G. Co., Md., known children:

> Elizabeth Hawley, bapt. in 1761
> John Hawley, (Rsh.4) bapt. April 17, 1768,
> > P.G.Co., Md., Church Records, m. Elizabeth Price
> Samuel Hawley, (Rsh.5) m. Barbara, widow of John
> > Sheridine, Fairfax Co., Va., after Samuel Hawley's
> > death she m. John Radcliff in Fairfax Co., Va.
> James Burch Hawley, (Rsh.6) m. Margaret, son James
> > Burch Hawley, b.1772, lived Hardy Co., W. Va.
> Bathsheba Hawley, m. William Hawley, he was the child
> > of Nathaniel (Rsh.3) and Mary Thompson Hawley
> Sarah Hawley, m. Robert Gordon, April 1769

1

Rsh.3 Nathaniel Hawley, Holly, Holey, Hoslley, Gentleman, Planter (son of Rsh.1) m. Mary Thompson, dau. of Robert Thompson. He inherited *Costly* and *Costly addition*, from his father, in Charles Co., Md. He was Assistant Inspector at Colchester, Virginia Tobacco Warehouse. In 1790 he purchased land on the line of Fairfax and Loudoun Cos., Va. His estate account is found in Fairfax Co., Va., in 1791, known children:

> William Hawley, (Rsh.7) b. January 19, 1747
> Mary Eleanor Hawley, b. November 21, 1752, m. William Smith and moved to Kentucky, child Robert Thompson Smith m. Harriet Wright, they had child William Halley Smith who m. Ann Elizabeth Duerson, they had child Jefferson Wright Smith who m. Fannie Alice Kiser, they had child Harry Rodes Smith who m. Mary Ingels Ranson and they had child Robert T. Smith; John m. Elizabeth Lyle, moved to St. Charles, Mo.; Elkanah m. Fanny Botts and Sarah Green; Elizabeth m. Micajah McClenny; Sarah m. Richard Crump, moved to Mo., Nancy m. Ira Nash; Mary; Lidia
> Elizabeth Hawley, b. 1755, never m., d. 1827
> Thomas Hawley, Halley, (Rsh.8) b. August 23, 1762 m. Penelope Stone
> Ierusha Hawley, m. Thomas Barker, moved to Mt.Sterling, Ky., children Elizabeth m. Willoughby Newton Lane; Silas, Thomas d. prior to 1829 w. heirs
> Susannah Hawley, b. June 28, 1765 m. Francis Stone, brother of Penelope Stone

Rsh.4 John Hawley, Holley, Halley, Holey, Hale, Gentleman, Planter, Revolutionary War Soldier (son of Rsh.2), b. c. 1739, m. Elizabeth Price, a widow, and they lived in Charles Co., Md., and at *Exeter*, Prince George's Co., Md., known children:

> Mary Hawley, b. 1762 m. William A. Athey who was b.1742. They lived in Prince William Co., Va., and Fairfax Co., Va., in 1764. He was a member of the Colonial Militia of Fairfax Co., Va., 1770. Their home was near "Ravensworth" in Fairfax Co., in 1772. William Athey d. August 21, 1819, known children: James Birch Athey b. 1773, d. 1809; Susan Athey b. 1781; William Athey Jr., b. 1783 d.

1830 and Violinda Athey
Thomas Hawley, bapt. February 9, 1766, m. January 29,
    1800 to Amy Downs, child Maria b. November 8,
    1805, Prince George Co., Md.
John Burch Hawley, Jr., bapt. April 17, 1768 m. Ann, child
    Nathaniel b. October 4, 1805, Prince George Co.,
    Md.
Samuel Hawley, b. March 23, 1772
Ama (Aimy) Hawley, b. January 2, 1774, King George
    Parish Records, m. Pyle
Nathaniel Hawley, (Rsh.95) b. February 9, 1776 m. Martha
    Jacobs, 11 children
Pennellopy Hawley, m. William Peacock, on June 28,
    1792
Mildred E. Hawley, m. an Emerson
Elizabeth Price Hawley, m. William Pumpheny
?Amos Pyle, possible stepson

note: His Will bequeaths a sum to Hillary Hanson Wade, alias
Halley, and Elizabeth Meeks Emerson, ?possibly granddaughters.

Rsh.5 Samuel Hawley, Hally, Holly, Halley, (son of Rsh.2) m.
Barbara, who was the widow of John Sheridin. They lived on part
of the Ravensworth Tract in Fairfax Co., Va., Parish of Truro. The
lease term was for the lives of Samuel Hawley, Barbary Hawley,
his wife, and (Rsh.6) James Burch Hawley, his nephew. His Will,
presented in Fairfax Co., Va., on May 17, 1779, names his
beloved wife Barbery, and his brother-in-law William Halley,
Barbara later m. John Radcliff and d. c. September 19, 1796 She
left money to the Baptist Church at Backlick, in Fairfax Co., Va.,
additional information not known.

Rsh.6 James Burch Hawley, Hally, (son of Rsh.2) m. Margaret___
___.He d. c. 1796, known children:
        James Burch Hawley, Jr., b. August 29, 1772, lived
            in Hardy Co., W.Va.

Rsh.7 William Hawley, Halley, Hally, Holly (son of Rsh.3) was b.
on January 19, 1747. He m. Bathsheba Hawley, dau. of Rsh.2,
his first cousin, when Bathsheba Hawley d., he m. Esther Morgan.
In 1787 and 1788 he was a Juror at the Court of Fairfax County,

Va. In 1787 he was appointed Inspector at the Alexandria, Virginia Tobacco Warehouse, Fairfax, Co., Va. He reportedly moved to Marietta, Ohio. Esther d. in 1831 and left a Will in Alexandria, Va., in which she bequeathed money to the Baptist Church in Alexandria, Va., and Nancy Bridwell. A land sale in 1802 was witnessed by a Robert Halley. William Hawley's estate records are filed in Loudoun Co., and Fairfax Co., Va., and reportedly in Fayette Co., Ky. His Will was written December 5, 1802, only known children were by 1st wife:

> Eleanor Hawley, b. March 21, 1774
> Samuel Hawley, b. November 8, 1775

Rsh.8 Thomas Hawley, (son of Rsh.3), was b. August 23, 1762. He m. Penelope Stone. They lived in Fairfax Co., Va., and Alexandria, Va., additional information not known.

Rsh.9 John Hawley, Holly, Holley, Hally, Gentleman, Planter, Revolutionary War Soldier, (son of Rsh.1) was b. in 1739. He m. Mary Ann Downs, dau. of Benjamin and Mary Downs. On October 6, 1761, John Hawley sold *Fellowship*, in Frederick Co., Md., which he inherited from his father. They lived in Montgomery Co., Md., and Loudoun Co., Va. His Revolutionary War Service was with the Lincoln Militia, State of Virginia, under the Command of George Rogers Clark, where he served along with his Loudoun Co., Va., neighbor Thomas Oden, who was the father of his future dau.-in-law, Mary Ann Oden. He served in the attack on Ruddle's Station. He also served with the Lincoln Militia, under Col. Benjamin Logen, where he aided in building a Fort at the Falls of the Ohio River. John Hawley built a home in 1779 in Loudoun Co., Va., on 198 acres adjoining Difficult Run at the border of Fairfax and Loudoun Cos., Va. The home has been restored and an addition added to the rear. It is believed he is bur. in the family grave yard there, known children:

> Absalom Hawley, (Rsh.10) b. c. 1757, m. Charity Eulich
> William Hawley, (Rsh.11) b. c. 1759, m. Bathsheba
>   Hutchison
> Amos Hawley, (Rsh.12) b. c. 1763, m. twice, first wife's
>   name is unknown, second wife Elizabeth
> Abraham Hawley, (Rsh.13) b. c. 1773, m. Mary Ann Oden
> Tabitha Hawley, m. Elijah Legg, known children, Zephania
>   Legg, Willis Legg

4

Barton D. Hawley, (Rsh.14), m. Catherine Heath, then
Hannah James
?adopted: Winifred m. Fielding Turner, she had an
unborn child in 1794, James Hawley Turner,
orphan in 1813, whose grandfather is John
Hawley

Rsh.10 Absalom Hawley, Halley, Holley, Holly, Gentleman,
Planter, (son of Rsh.9) was b. c 1757. He m. Charity Eulich. He
took the Oath of Fidelity at Bladensburg, Md., P.G. Co., in March
of 1778. In August of 1783 he is found in Cameron Parish,
Loudoun Co., Va., on a list of Tithables, and he remains on this
list through 1806. In March of 1791 he purchased 198 acres in
Loudoun Co., Va., and he witnessed the estate papers of
Benjamin Jordan there in June of 1804, known children:
Barton Hawley, (Rsh.15) b. November 14, 1791 m.
Harriett Mount
Tabitha Hawley, m. Richard Applegate on July 27, 1827
Elizabeth Hawley, m. Taliaferro Shanks on April 8, 1829

Rsh.11 William Hawley, Holly, Holy, Holey, Hally, Gentleman,
Planter, (son of Rsh.9) was b. c. 1759 and d. in 1829. He m.
Bathsheba Hutchison, dau. of Jeremiah and Keziah, nee Settle,
Hutchison. Bathsheba d. before 1815. In 1778 he was in Prince
George's Co., Md., and he later lived in Fairfax and Loudoun
Cos., Va. His Will was written on September 30, 1827, and
presented October 20, 1829, in Fairfax Co., Va., known children:
Susan Hawley, m. William Ambler, Jr.
William Hawley, Jr.,(Rsh.27)
Jeremiah Hawley, (Rsh.28) b. c. 1795
Nancy Ann Hawley, m. James M. Hutchison, known
children, John Hutchison, Joshua Hutchison,
Barbara (Bathsheba) Hutchison, William
Hutchison and they were in Morgantown, W.V., in
August 21, 1841
Mary (Molly) Hawley, m. Thomas Davis
Elizabeth (Betsy) Hawley, m. Jacob Zinn on May 6, 1833,
Jacob Zinn was from Preston, W.Va., and they
had pre-nuptial agreement, in Loudoun Co., Va.

Rsh.12 Amos Hawley, Hally, Halley, Holley, Gentleman, Planter

(Son of Rsh.9), was b. c. 1763, d. prior to 1830. He m. twice, and the name of his 1st wife is unknown, she probably d. in Loudoun Co., Va. His second wife was named Elizabeth, possibly a Hawkins or a Squires. Amos Hawley is found on the Tax and Tithable lists in Loudoun Co., Va. He migrated to Preston Co., W.Va., when he accompanied Col. John Fairfax for whom he was an Overseer, see additional information, known children by first wife, her name unknown:

> Margaret Hawley, m. John Samuel Welch, and moved to
>> Iowa
> Nancy Ann Hawley, m. William Carroll
> Elizabeth Hawley, b. July 1, 1805, d. March 24, 1892, m.
>> Benjamin Freeling, Freeland, in 1841 they settled
>> in Preston Co., W.Va. Benjamin was b. 1809, the
>> son of John and Mary, nee McCann, Freeland of
>> Pennsylvania, he d. 1875
> John Hawley, (Rsh. 29)
> by 2nd wife:
> Barton R. Hawley, (Rsh. 30) b. 1808 m. Jemima Pyles
> Amos Hawley, b. 1820 (Rsh.32) m. May Salona Black
> Abraham Hawley, b. 1825 (Rsh.31) m. Phebe Garner
> Thomas Hawley, (Rsh.33)
> Sarah Hawley, m. Anthony Poling
> Melinda Hawley, m. Henry Mincer, Meanear, child Amos
>> b. 1836, then Melinda Hawley Mincer, m. Lewis
>> Wright

Rsh.13 Abraham (Abram) Hawley, Holly, Halley, (son of Rsh.9) Gentleman, Planter, Lime Kiln Owner, Soldier in the War of 1812, was b. c. 1773. He m. Mary Ann Oden (Polly), the dau. of Thomas and Martha Oden of Loudoun Co., Va. Abraham Hawley d. c. February 1836 in Albermarle Co., Va., where they had moved c. 1804 with Jeremiah and Mary Ann Hutchison. Jeremiah Hutchison was the brother of Bathsheba Hawley (Rsh.11). Abraham Hawley purchased a Lime Kiln from President Thomas Jefferson, of Monticello, who retained lifetime rights to the lime from the kiln for Monticello's own use in the Deed of Sale. Abraham Hawley and William Hawley were at the Estate Sale of Mr. Jefferson at Monticello on January 17, 1827. Abram Hawley's War of 1812 service was in the 8th Regt., Virginia Militia, known children:

Thomas Hawley, (Rsh.52) m. Lucy Ann Woolridge

Mary Elizabeth Hawley, b. March 31, 1799, m. Henry M.
Harlow, on January 6, 1824, she d. after February
17, 1871, known children: A. Hustin M. Harlow;
Mary Jane Harlow; Anne E. Harlow; Benjamin
Franklin Harlow; George William Harlow; Martin
Van Buren Harlow

James Overton, (?Oswald) Hawley, (Rsh.53) m. Mary M.
Jones

William Hawley, (Rsh.54) m. Mary Ann Gillium

George Washington Hawley, (Rsh.55), m. Mary Waldridge
then Elivra Crooks

Amanda F. Hawley, b. 1826 m. William Holmes Bridwell
on September 1, 1841 in Culpeper Co., Va., (see
Section T. for her descendants)

Rsh.14 Barton D. Hawley, Holly, Halley, Hawly (son of Rsh.9)
was b. c. 1763. He m. Catherine Heath, on April 8, 1779, the
dau. of Andrew Heath of Loudoun Co., Va. She d. on April 17,
1813. After her death Barton D. Hawley m. Hannah James, who
was possibly the widow of William James, known children by
Catherine Heath Hawley:

Andrew H. Hawley, (Rsh.66) b. April 19, 1812 m. Delialah
Bucklew and lived in Preston Co., W.Va.

Louisa Hawley, m. E.P. Church

Sarah Hawley

Lucinda Hawley, m. Chapin H. Harris

Lamech Hawley

Malinda Hawley, m. John Shoff

Rsh.15 Barton Hawley (son of Rsh.10) was b. on November 14,
1791 and d. July 9, 1833. He m. Harriet Mount on January 20,
1823. She was b. on May 11, 1798 and d. on September 30,
1870, known children:

Milton Harvey Hawley, (Rsh.16) m. Amelia Doggett

Pauline A. (Pliny) Hawley, b. February 20, 1825 d. April 6,
1849, m. James F. Storts on December 11, 1845,
known children, Mary Paulina Storts and Harriet
Storts, b. July 13, 1848, d. July 23, 1848

Mary J. Hawley, b. January 28, 1830 d. August 27,1841

William Absalom Hawley, (Rsh.17) m. Lucy Stonestreet

Rsh.16 Milton Harvey Hawley (son of Rsh.15) was b. on
September 26, 1823, and he d. on April 6, 1908. He m. Amelia
Doggett on November 2, 1848. Amelia Doggett Hawley was b.
on April 2, 1825 and she d. on February 6, 1908, known children:
Mary Thomas Hawley, b. September 28, 1849, d.
December 4, 1940, m. Isaac Shelby Hunter on
February 27, 1879, he was b. November 13, 1845
and d. July 9, 1932. Mary Hawley and Isaac
Hunter had the following children: Blanche Hunter
b. September 3, 1884 m. David Isiah Cooper, they
had child Mary Thomas Cooper b. August 21,
1919
William Absalom Hawley, b. on May 5, 1852, d. May 28,
1868
Leonidas Barton Hawley, (Rsh.22) m. Janey Higdon
Rochester Atkerson Hawley, (Rsh.23) m. Mary Frances
Duncan
Harriet Levica Hawley, b. February 21, 1860 d. January 6,
1943 m. Claude Dayton Moody on December 19,
1883, he was b. October 9, 1860 and d. October
20, 1951, known children, Jennie Lee Moody, b.
October 27, 1884 and Amelia Rebecca Moody, b.
May 11, 1895

Rsh.17 William Absalom Hawley (son of Rsh.15) was b. in 1827
and d. 1908. He m. Lucy Stonestreet who was b. 1837 and d.
1914, known children:
William Absalom Hawley, (Rsh.18) m. Christie A. Barnhill
Mary Hawley, b. April 22, 1876 m. Elmore Clore, known
children: John Clore, b. May 19, 1898 and d.
December 15, 1947 m. Mae Spear: Joe Clore, b.
July 3, 1906 m. Deliah Platt; Roger Clore, b. May
6, 1904 m. Frances Dale Hawley on November 5,
1955; William Clore, b. January 6, 1901; Ernest
Clore, b. October 9, 1911
Addie Hawley, d. April 23, 1950, m. Charles Rankin
who was b. May 22, 1863 and d. November 2,
1936, known children: Murray Rankin b.
November 11, 1897 and d. March 7, 1928 m.

Forest Arnold; Anna Mae; Lucille b. April 14, 1892
Charles W. Hawley, (Rsh.20) m. Mollie Baird
Robert M. Hawley, (Rsh.21) m. Ida M. Davis and then
  Mollie Davis
John M. Hawley, (Rsh.25) m. Lula Taylor

Rsh.18 William Absalom Hawley (son of Rsh.17) was b. on May
12, 1859 and d. February 19, 1934. He m. Christie A. Barnhill on
February 1, 1888, she was b. on November 23, 1860 and she d.
on July 18, 1927, known children:
> Sallie Lee Hawley, b. June 12, 1889 and m. John G.
>> Theiss, June 5, 1912, he d. December 4, 1918,
>> known children: Mary Christine Theiss, b. March
>> 15, 1913 m. Cathcart Wilhoyte Kemp on August
>> 26, 1935, known children Lida Lee Kemp, b.
>> August 27, 1937 and Mildred Theiss Kemp, b.
>> February 12, 1940
> Charles William Hawley, (Rsh.19) m. Brownie C. Hodges

Rsh.19 Charles William Hawley (son of Rsh.18) m. Brownie C.
Hodges, additional information not known.

Rsh.20 Charles W. Hawley (son of Rsh.17) m. Mollie Baird,
additional information not known.

Rsh.21 Robert M. Hawley (son of Rsh.17) b. in 1854, m. Ist Ida
M. Davis who was b. in 1857, and then Mollie Davis the sister of
Ida, known children:
> Evelyn Hawley m. Courtnay Karman, known children,
>> Mary Ann Karman m. Dr. C.E. Quaife
>> Robert Hawley Karman

Rsh.22 Leonidas Barton Hawley (son of Rsh. 16) was b. on
September 24, 1854, and d. on February 22, 1925. He m. Janey
Higdon on September 2, 1885. She was b. on February 9, 1859,
and d. on December 2, 1943, known children:
> Rochester Manly Hawley, b. December 30, 1886 and m.
>> Edith Mary Crum on March 21, 1908. Edith Crum
>> was b. December 21, 1885, known children,
>> Harriet Lee Hawley, b. February 13, 1909 and
>> Pauline Higdon Hawley, b. February 28, 1913.

Pauline m. Edward Frisbee Coleman on August 6,
1938. Edward Coleman was b. July 30, 1900 and
he d. December 18, 1944, known children,
Edward Frisbee Coleman, Jr. b. October 1, 1942
Edward Sheppard Hawley, b. on March 23, 1890, and
m.1st Virginia Wood on May 10, 1919, and 2nd
Lula Gray on January 22, 1944

Rsh.23 Rochester Atkerson Hawley (son of Rsh. 16) was b. on
July 10, 1857, and d. on April 1, 1930. He m. Mary Frances
Duncan on November 7, 1883, known children:
Lonnie Duncan Hawley, b. August 8, 1884 and d.
February 8, 1885
Wm. Huston Hawley, b. March 5, 1886 m. Anna Mae
Crum on October 6, 1907, she was b. on March
15, 1888
Ida Hawley, b. November 17, 1888 m. John Lewis on May
6, 1908, known children, Mary Elizabeth Lewis, b.
February 15, 1920 who m. Franklin Walker,
August 15, 1944 and they had Brenda Kay
Walker, b. July 1, 1952
Clifton Harvey Hawley, (Rsh.24) m. Selina Powell
Mary Alice Hawley, b. July 7, 1893, m. Herbert Clore on
November 23, 1918

Rsh.24 Clifton Harvey Hawley (son of Rsh. 23) was b. on July
26, 1891 and m. Selina Powell on November 28, 1911, known
children:
Frances Dale Hawley, b. February 23, 1913 d.
February 24, 1958 she m. Roger H. Clore on
November 5, 1955
Clifton Harvey Hawley, Jr., (Rsh.26) m. Martha Setzer

Rsh.25 John Merritt Hawley (son of Rsh.17) m. Lula Taylor,
known children:
John Merritt Hawley, Jr.
Mildred Hawley
Margaret Hawley
Catherine Hawley

Rsh.26 Clifton Harvey Hawley, Jr., (son of Rsh.24) was b. on

September 19, 1915. He m. Martha Setzer in 1945, known children:
> Clifton Harvey Hawley, III, b. April 8, 1947
> Vickey Hawley, b. January 4, 1949

Rsh.27 William Hawley, Jr. (son of Rsh.11), was deeded land in Fauquier Co., Va., in 1824 and 1830, and Fairfax Co., Va., in 1830, additional information not known.

Rsh.28 Jeremiah Hawley (son of Rsh.11) b. c. ?1795, was deeded land Fairfax Co., Va., in 1830, additional information not known.

Rsh.29 John Hawley (son of Rsh. 12) was b. in Loudoun Co., Va. He moved with his family, at an early age, to Preston Co., W.Va., additional information not known.

Rsh.30 Barton R. Hawley, Farmer (son of Rsh.12) was b. on March 18, 1808, on the Alex D. Squires Farm, Preston Co., W.Va., and d. on August 23, 1892. He m. Jemmima Pyles in 1832, she was b. on April 14, 1811 and d. on August 9, 1885. They lived near Manown, W.Va. They are bur. in Bethlehem Methodist Church Cemetery, Preston Co., W.Va., known children:
> William Carl Hawley, (Rsh. 34)
> Solomon P. Hawley, (Rsh.35)
> Elisha Hawley, (Rsh.36)
> Caleb Fortney Hawley, (Rsh.37)
> Rebecca Jane Hawley, twin to Elizabeth Ann, b. May 14, 1853 at Mt. Phoebe Section, Preston Co., W.V., m. Elias Hawkins from Marion Co., W.V., known children: John A. Hawkins, Curtis Hawkins, Estella Hawkins, Harry B.Hawkins, Emma Hawkins
> Elizabeth Ann Hawley, twin to Rebecca Jane, m. John H. Fortney, Preston, Co., W.Va., family of five boys and four girls, she d. August 23, 1923, he d. October 24, 1926, one child, Okey Fortney lived in Lead Mines, W.Va.
> Joshua F. or A. Hawley, (Rsh.38)

Rsh.31 Abraham Hawley (son of Rsh.12) was b. in 1825, in Preston Co., W.Va. He m. Phebe Garner, who was b. in 1826, she was from Barbour, Virginia. An Elizabeth Hawley b.1790 and Amos Mincar b. 1836 are shown in the 1850 Census as living with them, additional information not known.

Rsh.32 Amos Hawley (son of Rsh.12) was b. in 1830. He m. May Salona Black, and they lived in Barbour Co., Va., known children:
> Sylvinius Hawley
> Sarah Hawley
> Margaret Hawley
> Eldridge Hawley

Rsh.33 Thomas Hawley (son of Rsh. 12) was b. Preston Co., W.Va., additional information not known.

Rsh.34 William Carl Hawley (son of Rsh.30) was b. on October 18, 1837, in Preston Co., W. Va., he was a Farmer, and a Methodist. He served in the Civil War as a Cpl., in the Union Army. He m. Caroline Sharps of Preston Co., W.Va., and moved to Granville, Iowa, then Gresham, Nebraska. Caroline d. July 13, 1912 and is bur. beside her husband, who d. February 23, 1923, in Blue Ridge Cemetery, Gresham, Nebraska, known children:
> Emory Judson Hawley, (Rsh.39) m. Lucy Samuels, then Mary Mcmahon
> John E. Hawley, b. May 9, 1859 d. October 15, 1865
> Barton L. Hawley, (Rsh.41) m. Cora L. Rags then Louise Elliott
> Alonzo Amos Hawley, (Rsh.42) m. Mary E. Hibbard
> Phillip Sheriden Hawley, (Rsh. 43) m. Mary H. Marsden
> Charles Wesley Hawley, (Rsh. 44) m._____
> Hosea Manown Hawley, d. age 17
> Estella V. Dell Hawley, b. April 9, 1876, m. William J. Robertson, on February 4, 1894 in York Co., Nebraska, known child, Burniece Robertson, b. November 13, 1894 m. Norman Moomey; Vera May Robertson, b. September 19, 1896 m. Evan Edgar Miller on May 5, 1920 in Gresham, York Co., Nebraska; Herchel Hawley Robertson, b. October 9, 1903 m. Winona M. Henderson July 21, 1928; Audrey Robertson b. September 17, 1908 m. Miller E. Barnes

Rsh.35 Solomon P. Hawley, (son of Rsh.30) was a Civil War Soldier, and a Methodist Minister. He was b. on September 24, 1841, at Phoebe Station Section, in Preston Co., W.Va., and d. on November 22, 1911, in Preston Co., W.Va. He m. Emma Fortney at Bethlehem Church on December 1, 1864. Following Emma's death he m. Jennie E. Ervin, the dau. of Jacob Ervin, on May 20, 1890. Jennie Hawley d. June 6, 1936. His Civil War Service was in 3rd W.Va., Vol. Unit. He served as Pastor of Bethlehem Community Church, known children by 1st wife:

> Ulric D. Hawley
> Lucy May Hawley

2nd wife

> Custer W. Hawley
> Rufus W. Hawley, d. March 28, 1936
> Okey S. Hawley

Rsh.36 Elisha Hawley (son of Rsh.30) was b. in 1846 at Mt. Phoebe Section, Preston Co., W.Va. He m. Sarah A. Roice, who was from Kingwood, W.Va. After Sarah Hawley's death he m. Hannah Stemple, known children:

1st wife

> John Hawley, b. 1870, resided in Bridgeport, Ohio
> Alvah Hawley
> Elmer Hawley
> Elbert Hawley
> Barton Hawley
> Grover Hawley
> Minnie Hawley, b. 1874
> Kate Hawley, b. 1872
> Lona Hawley

2nd wife

> George Prentice Hawley, m. Lucille Pratt, and they lived in Tunnelton, W.Va., he d. June 9, 1963, and she d. June 9, 1963, a son James Prentice was b. February 13, 1930, James P. Hawley m. June Ruggles on January 27, 1951

Rsh.37 Caleb Fortney Hawley, (son of Rsh.30) was a Logger and Foreman for Standard Oil Company. He was b. on April 10, 1850 at Mt. Phoebe Section, in Preston Co., W.Va., and he m. Elizabeth Ellen Keister on January 24, 1876. He d. on January 5,

1905, at Parkersburg, W.Va. Elizabeth Ellen Keister was b. on June 26, 1850 in Cox Mills, W.Va., and she was the dau. of George and Sarah (nee Probst) Keister. Caleb and his family were Methodists, known children:

    Harry Herbert Hawley

    Wirt Garfield Hawley, b. December 9, 1879 in Burning Springs, W.Va., d. September 14, 1956 in Parkersburg, W.V., never m.

    Arthur William Hawley, (Rsh.45) b. March 9, 1882

    Maude May Hawley, b. October 27, 1884 at Burning Springs, W.Va., d. October 26, 1967 in Parkersburg, W.V. m. 1908 to Horace D. Leach, known children, Kenneth Eugene Leach, b. June 13, 1909 and lived in Bradford, Pa.; Marvin Hawley Leach, b. June 6, 1914, and lived in Parkersburg, W.Va.; second Maud May m. M.C. Cremer and the known children are, Harry Herbert Cremer, b. March 29, 1887 m. September 17, 1908 to Dora D. Welch in Marietta, Ohio, d. December 7, 1971 in Akron, Ohio, known child Evelyn N. Cremer

Rsh.38 Joshua A. (or H.) Filmore Hawley, (son of Rsh.30) was b. on April 10, 1856, and he d. on February 25, 1928. He m. Mary Alice Riggleman of Gladesville, Preston Co., W.Va., on September 8, 1878. Alice Riggleman was b. 1857 and d. 1936. He was a Farmer and lived on part of the old home place, known children:

    Audie Elma Hawley, b. January 5, 1881, d. March 24, 1944 m. Charles Eiseman, on December 20, 1902, he was b. November 7, 1877 and d. December 30, 1960, child, Grace Edna Eiseman, b. September 28, 1904, Athens, W.Va., taught school, m. on January 1, 1926 to Boyce Leslie Gumm who was b. November 8, 1894 and d. December 30, 1978, he was a Naval Cmdr., WW II Vet., and was a Professor at Athens College

    Lattie L. Hawley, b. October 3, 1887 m. Clarence Shaffer, (see Section T. for her descendants)

    John A.M. Hawley, (Rsh.50) m. Eva Faber

    Henry Lloyd Hawley, (Rsh.48) m. Retta Miles

    Fannie J. Hawley, (see Section T. for her descendants)

Enos A. Hawley, (Rsh.49) m. Agnes Pratt
Lula M. Hawley, (see Section T. for her descendants)

Rsh.39 Emory Judson Hawley (son of Rsh.34) was b. on June
28, 1857, in Preston Co., W.Va., and nicknamed Judd. He d. on
October 24, 1898. He m. Lucy Samuels on October 3, 1881, and
then Mary McMahon, additional information not known.

Rsh.40 Robert Hawley, Holy, Holly, (son of Rsh.90) transported
himself to Maryland in 1648, and he received land in the area
below Annapolis, Md., on the South River. A Robert Hawley is
found in Cecil Co., Md., 1650. Additional information not known.

Rsh.41 Barton Luther Hawley, (son of Rsh.34) was b. on June
18, 1861, in Preston Co., W.Va., and d. August 20, 1929. He m.
Cora L. Rags on September 14, 1882, then m. Louise Elliott,
additional information not known.

Rsh.42 Alonzo Amos Hawley, (son of 34) was b. on December
23, 1863, in Preston, Co., W.Va., and nicknamed Lon. He d.
February 1, 1948. He m. Mary E. Hibbard on October 29, 1885,
then Maymie Gilbert, on June 6, 1906, then Mary E. Nibart on
March 19, 1924, known children by 1st wife:
> Bruce P. Hawley, b. February 14, 1888, d. May 31, 1965
> Hazel G. or S. Hawley, b. May 7, 1889 d. March 14, 1911
> by 2nd wife:
> Glenwood W. Hawley, b. August 13, 1907

Rsh.43 Philip Sheriden Hawley, (son of Rsh.34) was b. on June
9, 1866, in Preston Co., W.Va., and nicknamed Sherd. He d. on
May 31, 1965. He m. Mary H. Marsden on December 25, 1885,
additional information not known.

Rsh.44 Charles Wesley Hawley, (son of Rsh.34), was b. in
Preston Co., W.Va., additional information not known.

Rsh.45 Arthur William Hawley, (son of Rsh.37) was b. on March
9, 1882, in Burning Springs, W.Va., and d. April 10, 1960 in
Morgantown, W.Va. He m. Ella Mae Trembly, the dau. of George
Hartman and Eva Charity (nee Smith) Trembly, on January 10,
1906, in Terra Alta, W.Va. Ella Mae Trembly was b. on October

26, 1876 in Tannery, Preston Co., W.Va., and she d. November 12, 1979 in Morgantown, W.Va. She is bur. in Oak Grove Cemetery, Morgantown, W.Va. They were Methodist and they lived in Rowelsburg, Masontown, Morgantown, W.Va. He was a Bookkeeper by profession, known children:

> Charles Wirt Hawley, (Rsh.46) b. June 18, 1907, m. Dorothy Olga Meyrowitz
> Ireta Estelle Hawley, b. May 2, 1909 in Morgantown, W.Va., m. Thomas H. Johnson on November 19, 1931, two children, she next m. Howard A. Tebay on August 7, 1954
> Eva Claire Hawley, b. March 20, 1911 in Masontown, W.V., nicknamed Dimps, m. Thomas Watson Lewis on March 25, 1939 at Morgantown, W.Va., 4 children

Rsh.46 Charles Wirt Hawley (son of Rsh.45) was b. on June 18, 1907 in Rowelburg, W.Va. He m. Dorothy Olga Meyrowitz, dau. of Russell A. and Mildred J. (nee Ambly) Meyrowitz, on May 26, 1951, in New Rochelle, N.Y. He is a Methodist and a Chemist by profession. They have lived in Parlin, NYC, NY, Stanford, CT., and Trumbull, CT. They currently reside in Iaasquah, Washington, known children:

> Stephen Clarke Hawley, (Rsh.47) b. August 8, 1953

Rsh.47 Stephen Clarke Hawley (son of Rsh.46) was b. on August 8, 1953. He m. Glenda Carolyn Brown, on May 21, 1983, in Rancho St. Park, San Diego, California, known children:

> Kevin Jonathan Hawley, b. December 31, 1985
> Michael Charles Hawley, b. June 25, 1987

Rsh.48 Henry Lloyd Hawley (Son of Rsh.38) was b. on March 14, 1898, and d. May 25, 1969. He m. Ist Retta Miles who was b. December 29, 1902 and d. July 15, 1936, and 2nd Maxine Elvia Gamble, who was b. March 27, 1918. He lived Manown, Preston Co., W.Va., and was a Coal Miner, known children, 1st wife Retta Miles:

> Harold Lloyd Hawley, b. November 13, 1923 m. Margaret Viola Dalton, served in WW II, Painter, lived Kanes Creek, Preston Co., W.Va., children Carolyn Fay Hawley b. June 4, 1949 m. Frank Street on

September 23, 1966, he was b. August 25, 1947, children Steven Franklin Street, b. July 22, 1967 m. Ann Cupp b. August 4, 1968, child Sarah Ann Street; Edward Franklin Street, b. May 19, 1971 m. Brenda George on October 18, 1991, she was b. February 9, 1971; Craig Franklin Street, b. July 1, 1974; Stephanie Fay Street, b. July 9, 1979: Phyllis Ann Hawley b. September 8, 1952 m. Kenneth Kisner, b. December 31, 1953, children Shannon Kisner, b. November 23, 1979, Ashley Ann Kisner b. October 13, 1984 and Shyla Brianna Kisner b. July 24, 1993

Charles Robert Hawley (Rsh.51) m. Mary Chedister then Velma Scott

Infant son b. and d. April 12, 1927

Wilda Pearl Hawley b. December 29, 1931 d. June 8, 1984 bur. at Arthurdale W.Va., m. Donald Bernard Holman on September 2, 1926, he retired C.& P Telephone Co., children, David Lee Holman, b. November 14, 1958, m. Martha Louise Cherry on June 10, 1978, she was b. October 16, 1958, children Jennifer L. Holman b. March 30, 1981, Bridgit Louise Holman b. April 24, 1984, Alicia Lyn Holman b. September 14, 1987; Linda Kay Holman b. May 19, 1962 m. George Allen Reith on June 11, 1983, lives in Charlotte, N.C., children, Amanda Reith, b. July 12, 1985 and Christopher Reith b. August 14, 1987

2nd wife Maxine Elvia Gamble:

Blenda Ray Hawley, b. September 19, 1940, Manager, C&P Telephone Co., lives Davidsonville, Md., m. Norman A. Martin on June 10, 1961, he was b. March 13, 1933 and is retired from Sears, children, Kevin Lee Martin, b. October 30, 1964 and d. February 1, 1965, bur. at Manown, Preston Co., W.Va., Sheri Lynn Martin b. July 27, 1966, School Teacher, lives Davidsonville, Md., m. on April 2, 1994, Douglas Arnold, b. November 19, 1967; Steven Michael Martin b. February 14, 1963, Engineer, lives in Pasadena, Md., m. Chrystal M. Gallager on September 13, 1986, she was b.

August 8, 1965, children, Joshua Michael Martin,
b. March 21, 1990 and Kyla Marie Martin b. June
23, 1994
Richard Filmore Hawley b. December 30, 1942, LTC U.S.
Army, Viet Nam, lives Anchorage, Alaska, m.
Nancy Gaida on March 24, 1973, she was b. June
19, 1950
Kermit Wade Hawley b. July 9, 1944, FmHA, USDA, Lt.
U.S. Army, lives Kanes Creek, Preston Co., W.Va.
Ronald Lee Hawley, b. September 23, 1949, C&P Tele-
phone Co., Ridgley W.Va., m. in 1971, Linda
Buda, child Mathew Lee Hawley, b. May 3, 1972,
m. 2nd Brenda Sue Alridge on May 12, 1978, she
was b. July 23, 1959, children, Krista Sue Hawley,
b. August 15, 1976, Ian Lloyd Hawley, Isaac
Lance Hawley, b. May 25, 1986

Rsh.49 Enos A. Hawley (son of Rsh.38) was b. on April 5, 1885
and d. in 1934. He m. Agnes Pratt who was b. in 1888 and d. in
1949, known children:
Sherman Hawley, b. April 17, 1909 d. April 21, 1909
Jessie Pauline Hawley, b. May 12, 1910 at Cascade,
W.Va., Painter and Artist, m. William Ray Miles b.
April 25, 1907 d. November 20, 1979, child Betty
Lois Miles b. September 10, 1930 m. William
Shepherd who was b. January 17, 1929, children,
Patricia Ann Shepherd b. January 8, 1955 m.
Jean Moise who was b. January 5, 1955, lives in
Chicago, Ill, children, Jessica Lucille Moise, b.
May 27, 1985, Michael Shepherd Moise, b.
January 22, 1987, Daniell Ashley Moise b. May 4,
1989: William Patrick Shepherd II, b. October 18,
1957, lives in Mgnt. W.Va.: Robert Joseph
Shepherd, b. May 10, 1968 lives Mgnt. W.Va.
Mary Ann Hawley, b. November 7, 1911 at Kanes Creek,
W.Va., m. Eugene Saunders, children Sandra
Stephanie Saunders m. Geon, and Robert
Sanders
Russell Hawley, b. May 17, 1913 at Reedsville, W.Va., d.
March 18, 1980, bur. Sarasota, Fla., children
David Hawley m. Jennifer Hawley; Jean Hawley

m. Annie, Jeanifer

John Hawley, b. April 10, 1928 m. Laven Sue Courtney who was b. November 2, 1924 and d. March 24, 1989, he lived in El Paso., Texas., and is retired from the U.S. Army, at the rank of Sgt. Major, children John Courtney Hawley b. July 4, 1953, El Paso, Tx., Sign Maker, m. Patricia Herrinn, who was b. 1952, children Jeremiah Hawley b. November 6, 1976 and Dawn Ann Hawley b. September 15, 1971; Melissa Hawley b. November 2, 1957 in San Antonio, Texas, m. David Herandez

Rsh.50 John A.M. Hawley (son of Rsh.38) was b. on May 17, 1890 and d. on October 13, 1917. He m. Eva Faber in 1912, she was b. on February 3, 1880, d. in 1958, and bur. in Kingwood, W.Va. He was killed in an auto accident, additional information not known.

Rsh.51 Charles Robert Hawley (son of Rsh.48) was b. on April 21, 1929 and d. on November 13, 1974. He m. Mary Chedister, then Velma Scott, known children by 2nd wife:

Donald Charles Hawley, b. June 16, 1950 m. Gladine Gibson (divorced), children Corena Dawn Hawley b. May 3, 1970, m. Terry Spiker, child, Ashley Nichole Spiker who was b. September 3, 1991 and Larry Hawley b. June 27, 1969, m. Chandel Strawser, child Kayla Hawley b. October 17, 1987

Ronald Allen Hawley, b. September 2, 1952, d. July 11, 1972

Connie Sue Hawley, b. September 2, 1952 m. Paul Joseph Greaser, who was b. November 10, 1942, children Billy Joe Greaser b. September 14, 1970 and Tammy Brelene Greaser b. February 23, 1972 m. Eugene Thiel who was b. November 27, 1970, child Steven Roy Thiel b. October 12, 1991, 2nd marriage to Barry Atkins who was b. December 5, 1968.

Rsh.52 Thomas Hawley, (son of Rsh.13) Gentleman, Planter, War of 1812 Soldier (son of Rsh. 13) was b. c. 1795/96 in

Loudoun Co., Va. He m. Lucy Ann Woolridge, in Culpeper Co., Va., on January 25, 1821. Lucy Woolridge was b. in Culpeper Co., Va., in 1802 and she was the dau. of John and Mildred Woolridge. Thomas Hawley had land holdings in Orange and Culpeper Cos., Va. His service in the War of 1812 was in the 8th Virginia Militia. He d. in Orange Co., Va., of Typhoid Fever, on April 28, 1853. Following Thomas Hawley's death, Lucy Woolridge Hawley m. Simon Wise of Culpeper Co., Va., on October 13, 1864. Mr. Wise d. on January 31, 1879. The Hawley-Wise pre-nuptial agreement is on file in the Culpeper Co., Va., C.H., known children:

> Ellen Elizabeth Hawley, b. 1823, m. William Thomas
> Martin, who was a Wheelwright, from Chesterfield,
> Co., Va., known children: John E. Martin; William
> T. Martin, Jr.; Sarah T. Martin; Martha A. Martin;
> Marian S. Martin. They lived in Culpeper Co., Va.,
> children from Census of 1850, Elva Saunders
> notes say 10 children
>
> John William Hawley, b. 1824, d. of small pox, Elva
> Saunders notes Shown in 1850 Census Culpeper
> Co., Va., as Merchant, John W. Hawley, Trustee
> Act. Book T., pg.277, December 17, 1855,
> Culpeper Co., Va., Book 12, pg.124, 1855 record
> which says "land formerly owned by James W.
> Hawley, he was a merchant, he m. Marietta
> Beasley
>
> Charles McKee Hawley, (Rsh.56) b. February 27, 1829,
> Merchant, m. Lucy Ellen Colvin Elva Saunders
> notes say 12 children
>
> Lucy Mildred Hawley, b. 1832, Orange Co., Va., m.
> February 15, 1855, to William F. Colvin, 4 children
>
> Mariah Alice Hawley, b. 1832 m. July 12, 1855, in
> Culpeper Co., Va., to James W. Rush, 4 children
>
> Marian Robin Hawley, b. 1834 m. twice, moved to Phila-
> delphia, m. first Carrie Black, 6 children, 2nd
> Mrs.Elizabeth Wick, no children, enlisted April 1,
> 1862, 6th Virginia Calvery, Payne's Brigade,
> Fitzhugh Lee's Division
>
> Savilla Benton Hawley, b. 1843, m. September 2, 1857 to
> Thomas Sherman, of Culpeper, 5 children
>
> Thomas Anthony Hawley, b. c. 1838, went to Kansas and

was never heard from, notes of Elva Saunders,
The Hawley Record says two daus.
Burgess R. Hawley, b. c. 1839 m. Margaret Ann Sherman,
August 19, 1862, no children
James Overton (?Oswald) Hawley, b. c. 1841, m. Mary
Sophia Sherman. They lived initially in the
Randolph Cottage in Culpeper County, Virginia
and later in Los Angeles, California where they
were in 1907. Their descendants, 6 children, are
listed in The Hawley Record. Discovery of the six
children was made too late for publication. They
will be included in a second book on these
families currently being researched. Hopefully
information will be forth coming on their
descendants.

Rsh.53 James Overton (?Oswald) Hawley, (son of Rsh.13) was
b. in 1823. He m. Mary M. Jones, on December 6, 1842. They
resided in Washington D.C. in 1870, additional information not
known.

Rsh.54 William Hawley (son of Rsh.13) was b. in 1805, in
Albermarle Co., Va. He m. Mary Ann Gillium, on August 18,
1829, and they lived in Albermarle Co., Va. Mary Ann Gillium was
b. in 1813. Known children:
William R. Hawley, b.1832, m. Francis, children: J.O.
Hawley and Samuel Hawley
James Oswald Hawley, twin, b. July 6, 1836 was a Canal
Boatman
Mary Elizabeth Hawley, twin, b. July 6, 1836 m. a Ladd, d.
July 12, 1933
John A. Hawley, b. 1839, served in the Confederate Army,
m. Margaret Skipp, May 10, 1862
Fleming Hawley, b. 1839
Ann Hawley, b. 1841
Schyler Hawley, b. 1844, m. Sarah Sprouse, November
26, 1877
Lucy Hawley, b. 1846
Taylor Hawley, b. 1848
Gey Hawley, b. 1852
Minn Hawley, b. 1860

Rsh.55 George Washington Hawley (son of Rsh.13) m. Mary Waldridge, then Elivra Crooks. He lived in Albermarle Co., Va., known children by Mary Waldridge:

> John Abram Hawley, a Confederate Soldier, b. 1844, m.
> Susan Pope, Madison Co., Va.

Rsh.56 Charles McKee Hawley (son of Rsh.52) a Merchant, Farmer, and Confederate Soldier, was b. on February 27, 1829 in Culpeper Co., Va. He m. Lucy Ellen Colvin on October 10, 1854. She was the dau. of John Dillard Colvin and Francis, nee Bridwell, Colvin. Charles and Lucy Ellen Hawley initially lived in Culpeper, Virginia, and the family moved to Richmond, Va., following his medical discharge from the Confederate Army. Lucy Ellen Colvin Hawley ran a boarding house in Richmond, Va. He d. on December 24, 1895. He is bur. in Riverview Cemetery in Richmond, Va., known children:

> Marietta (Mary Ellen) Hawley, b. July 1857 d. May 17,
> 1898, bur. Riverview Cemetery, Richmond, Va.
> John Thomas Hawley, b. 1859, d. October 11, 1920, m.
> Fanny Kate Gilbert of Greene Co., Va., 5 children.
> Edwin Barbour Hawley, (Rsh.57) b. May 2, 1860, d. March
> 30, 1899 m. Laura Elmore Dickerson, of Greene
> Co., Va., bur. Riverview Cemetery, Richmond, Va.
> Mollie Daniel Hawley, b. 1861, d. February 23,1928, m.
> Robert E. Chamlee of North Carolina, 2 children,
> resided in Los Angeles, California at time of
> death.
> Lillian H. Hawley, b. April 6, 1865, d. March 13,1926 m.
> Michael A. Barnett
> Sue D. Hawley, b. April 1, 1867, m. George H.
> Palmore, a Railroad Engineer whom she met at
> her mother's boarding house, 3 daus., d. 1937,
> St. Petersburg, Florida
> Lucille Green Hawley, b. July 13, 1869 d. October I, 1896,
> m. Charles I. Root, no children. Elva Saunders
> Notes (tombstone in Riverview Cemetery,
> Richmond, Va., reads: Lucille E. Root, b.
> Culpeper Co., Va., June 18, 1871, d. Richmond,
> October 31, 1896) Note Charles I. Root had
> brother who lived in California and was an
> attorney in Los Angeles.

Irene R. Hawley, b. May 1, 1872, m. Frank A. Turner, one son Dan Turner, she d. 1945 and is bur. Riverview Cemetery, Richmond, Va.

Elva V. Hawley, b. October 6, 1874, m. William O. Saunders, a Railroad Engineer, whom she met at her mother's boarding house. She d. September 5, 1961, and she is bur. in Riverview Cemetery, Richmond, Va., l dau., Frankie Saunders (named for grandmother Frances Bridwell Colvin), Frankie m. James Jefferson Camper, a widower, no children, she d. February 3, 1994 at the age of 96.

Kate Overton Hawley, b. April 10, 1876 d. March 4, 1881

Sadie Overton Hawley, b. January 1880, d. December 16, 1965, never m., bur. Riverview Cemetery, Richmond, Va.

Charles McKee Hawley, Jr., b. March 1, 1882, d. April 10, 1916, bur. Riverview Cemetery, Richmond, Va.

Rsh.57 Edwin Barbour Hawley (son of Rsh.56), nicknamed JEB, was a Farmer and a Well Driller. He was b. on May 2, 1860, in Culpeper Co., Va. He m. Laura Elmore Dickerson, the dau. of Barnett Simms Dickerson and Cornelia, nee Gilbert, Dickerson, on November 15, 1885, at Cedar Grove Church in Greene Co., Va. JEB and Laura Hawley moved to Richmond, Va., with his parents. He. d. March 30, 1899 and is bur. in Riverview Cemetery, Richmond, Va. Laura Dickerson Hawley is bur. in the Dickerson Family Plot, in Greene Co., Va., known children:

Maude Covington Hawley, b. August 1886, Monroe Dist., Greene Co., Va., Birth Records, Greene Co., Va. 1853 - 1893, m. a Mr. Sisson, child Anne Winona Sisson, Maude Sisson d. July 27, 1914

Mable Gertrude Hawley, b. September 1887, Ruckersville District, Greene County, Virginia Birth Records, 1853 - 1893, d. summer 1901

John Edward Hawley, (Rsh. 58) b. September 10, 1889

Marietta (Mary Ellen) Hawley was b. August 1892, Ruckersville Dist., Greene Co., Birth Records, 1853 - 1893.

Lucille Hawley was b. September 1893. Ruckersville Dist., Greene Co., Va., Elva Hawley Saunders notes

Rsh.58 John Edward Hawley, (Sonny), (son of Rsh. 57), was b. on September 10, 1889, in the Ruckersville District of Greene County, Virginia. He m. Margaret Ruth Perkins, who was the dau. of Egbert and Emma Perkins, of Richmond, Va., there were no children born of this marriage. They lived in La Mesa, California, where he was a Plumber and a Rancher, and they were both active in the Masonic Lodge. He returned to Richmond, Virginia when Margaret Hawley became ill with cancer. After her death he m. Daisy Adelaide Trexler, on April 8, 1939, in Stafford Co., Va. Daisy Trexler was the dau. of James Washington Trexler and Lottie May, nee Perkins, Trexler, of Richmond, Va. He then established a new business in Richmond, Va., and became the largest Mechanical Contractor in the southeast. He traded under the name of J.E. Hawley and Company, and his firm did the pipe/duct work, heating and air conditioning on major schools and government buildings in Maryland, Virginia and Washington, D.C. He d. in Richmond, Va., on November 5, 1961. He is bur. in Riverview Cemetery, known children of his second marriage:

> Laura Mae Hawley, named for grandmothers' Laura
>> Elmore Dickerson and Lottie May Trexler, b. July 23, 1941, m. Beverly Lee Perrin, of Richmond, Va., on March 17, 1957 in Emporia, Va., 2 children, Debra Lee Perrin, (named Lee for her father), b. July 7, 1958 and Kenneth Lynn Perrin, (named for his Uncle Kenneth Perrin), b. September 2, 1959; m. 2nd Errol Hermann Lillien of Brooklyn, N.Y., on August 19, 1961, in Hendersonville, N.C., one child, Anne Elizabeth Lillien, (named Anne for her grandmother Anna Murray Trexler), b. November 17, 1962; m. 3rd. Isaac Randolph Dovel, Jr., of Luray, Va., on June 8, 1968, one child, Susan Marie Dovel, (named for her grandmother Susan Sandridge Gilbert), b. December 10, 1970, d. February 25, 1999, bur. in Riverview Cemetery in Richmond, Va.
>> note: Debra Lee Perrin, Kenneth Lynn Perrin and Anne Elizabeth Lillien were legally adopted by Isaac Randolph Dovel in June of 1969, and the Dovel name became their legal name at that time.

> Betty Sue Hawley b. March 21, 1947, m. Clarence Uray

Mull of Chase City, Va., on June 19, 1964, children, John Uray Mull, b. October 28, 1965, (named Uray for his father), Michael Hawley Mull, b. March 18, 1968, (named Hawley for his mother's family), Margaret Michelle Mull, b. August 13, 1969

Rsh.59 Francis Holly, was b. in 1791, m. Mary. She was b. in 1805. They lived in Kanawah Co., Va., known children:
> Deliah Holly, b. 1823
> Joseph Holly, b. 1830
> William Holly, b. 1831
> John Holly, b. 1835
> Martha Holly, b. 1837
> Mary Holly, b. 1839
> Matelan Holly, b. 1841
> George Holly, b. 1845
> Andrew Holly, b. 1848

Rsh.60 William A. Holly, was b. in 1810, in Virginia. He m. Nancy. She was b. in 1816, and they lived in Kanawah Co., Va., known children:
> John W. Holly, b. 1833
> Mary E. Holly, b. 1835
> Emily A. Holly, b. 1837
> Elizabeth Holly, b. 1839
> Lefsse Holly, b. 1840
> Louisa Holly, b. 1842
> William F. Holly, b. 1843

Rsh.61 Jeremiah Holly, was b. 1790, in Virginia, (?son of Rsh.11, ?same as Rsh.28). He m. Edathy who was b. in 1815, they lived in Kanawah Co., Va., known children:
> Elijah Holly, b. 1833
> Bartholomew Holly, b. 1834
> Ann Holly, b. 1836
> Edathy Holly, b. 1840
> Emmilloa Holly, b. 1839
> Sarah Holly, b. 1841
> Charlotte Holly, b. 1743
> John Holly, b. 1845

Jeremiah Holly, b. 1847

Rsh.62 George Holly was b. in 1817, in Virginia. He m. Jane who was b. in 1817, and they lived in Mason Co., Va., known children:
Caroline Holly, b. 1839
Mary C. Holly, b. 1845

Rsh.63 Timothy Holly was b. 1826, in Virginia. He m. Mary who was b. in 1831. They lived in Mason Co., Va., known children:
Deliah Holly, b. 1849

Rsh.64 Thomas Holly was b. in 1812, in Virginia. He m. Nancy who was b. in 1812. They lived Mason Co., Va., known children:
William C. Holly, b. 1835
Ellen Holly, b. 1839
Mary M. Holly, b. 1841
Thomas H. Holly, b. 1844
Elizabeth Holly, b. 1847
Nancy Holly, b. 1849

Rsh.65 Samuel Holly was b. in 1827, in Virginia. He m. Janey who was b. in 1828, they lived Mason Co., Va., additional information not known.

Rsh.66 Andrew H. Hawley (son of Rsh.14) was b. on April 19, 1812, and he was a Farmer. He m. Delilah who was b. in 1816. They lived in Preston Co., W.Va., known children:
Mary R. Hawley, b. 1847

Rsh.67 Wellington A. Holley, was b. in 1813 in W. Va., he was a Farmer. He m. Mary A. Holly, who was b. in 1835. They lived in Greenbrier, W.Va., known children:
John A. Holley, b. 1855
Hannah Holley, b. 1857
William Holley, b. 1858
Ellen Holley, b. 1859
Virginia Holley, b. 1861
Mary A. Holley, b. 1863
Sophronia Holley, b. 1865
Addie Holley, b. 1867

Charles Holley, b. 1873

Rsh.68 J.C. Holly, was b. in 1840, in W.Va., he was a Farmer. He m. Elizabeth who was b. in 1841, and they lived in Kanawha Co., W.Va., known children:
> Martha Holly, b. 1865
> Malry Holly, b. 1868
> Lily Holly, b. 1872
> Rosa Holly, b. 1876
> Thomas Holly, b. 1877
> Belle Holly, b. 1878

Rsh.69 John Holly was b. in 1846, in W.Va. He m. Rebecca who was b. in 1848. They lived in Kanawha Co., W.Va., known children:
> Allen Holly, b. 1868
> Elben Holly, b. 1870
> Mandania Holly, b. 1875
> Isam Holly, b. 1877
> John C. Holly, b. 1879

Rsh.70 William Holly was b. in 1850, in W.Va. He m. Mary who was b. in 1859. They lived in Kanawha Co., W.Va., additional information not known.

Rsh.71 Thomas Hayle, Hailes, Hayles, Orley, Hales, Haies, (?son of Rsh.118) b. c. 1626, m. _____, lived Northumberland Co., Va., known children:
> John Hayles, was given bequest by John Trussel in 1651
> Thomas Hayles b. c. 1652

Rsh.72 Edward Haley, Hawley, Sr., m. Catherine, and they lived in St. Thomas Parish, Orange Co., Va., where they had 140 acres. His Will was dated December 29, 1752, known children:
> Edward Haley, Jr., m. Mary, he d. before 1728, children,
>> Sarah, Mary
> James Haley m. Susanna
> Benjamin Haley
> William Haley, plantation called William Haleys
> Thomas Haley
> David Haley

Elizabeth Haley m. a Christopher
John Haley m. Mary (Rsh.73)
Ambrose Haley
Sarah Haley m. Oakes
Valentine Haley m. James Herndon

Rsh.73 John Haley (son of Rsh.72) m. Mary. He left a Will in
Louisa Co., Va., in 1777, known children:
    Tabitha Haley, m. James Dyches, November 8, 1773
    Ursuly Haley, m. a Crews
    Sarah Haley, m. Will Dyches on September 28, 1778
    William Haley, m. Elizabeth Clark on January 1, 1773
    Benjamin Haley, (Rsh.74) m. Judith Dyches, a widow, on
        February 2, 1779
    Randolph Haley, m. Agnes Clark
    John Haley, Jr., m. Martha Flucher of Hanover, March 17,
        1779
    Bartlett Haley, m. Jane Statham on August 16, 1770
    Delia Haley, m. Henry Dyches on January 10, 1799

Rsh.74 Benjamin Haley (son of Rsh.73) m. Judith Dyches, a
widow, with a child named James Dyches, known children:
    John Haley

Rsh.75 George W. Halley m. Sally. He had a Will, in Fairfax Co.,
Va., dated, September 15, 1823, mentions children but not
named, additional information not known.

Rsh.76 James Hawley, Halley, Holley, (?son of Rsh.107, or
?grandson of Rsh.71), was b. in England on June 14, 1707. His
Will was written in Fairfax Co., Va., and proved on July 6, 1792.
He m. Elizabeth Simpson, the dau. of Richard Withers Simpson.
He d. July 6, 1792 at his home *Pleasant Green*, near Fairfax Court
House, leaving a parcel of land to the Baptist Society and their
Successors, known children:
    William Halley, (Rsh.77)
    James Halley, Jr. (Rsh.100) m. Frances Hereford
    John Halley, m. Susan Anne Hart, settled Boonsboro, Ky,
        where he established the first store, planted the
        first orchard, and was the first to ship a cargo of
        tobacco to New Orleans in 1783 and to England.

He imported goods from England and France. No known children.

Richard S. Halley, b.c. 1750, Fairfax, Va., d. Winchester, Ky., June 30, 1833, ?or 1816, m. Lydia, children: Henry m. Polly Patton; James m. N. Dunn and B. Valiandingham, Richard S., Jr., m. Nackie Dunn, and Elizabeth Stevens; William Halley, Sibela m. John Patton; John; Polly m. Reason Ridgeway, George, Elizabeth m. Benjamin Blackwell, Lydia Halley, wife of John Roberts, Minerva Halley, wife of Jacob Lindsay, ?Dinwiddie Halley

Francis Halley, d. Richmond, Ky, 1817, m. Francis, last name unknown then Nancy Calk, moved to Kentucky in 1782, known children: Elizabeth (Betsy) Halley b. March 14, 1799, m. Wesley Green in 1818; Pressley W. Halley, (Rsh.102) b. February 3, 1801, Madison Co., Ky.

Henry Simpson Halley, b. May 18, 1762 (Rsh.78)

Sarah, Sallie Hawley, Haney, Hanigane, b.c. 1739, d. 1819, about 80 years, old. m. lst William Wilkerson, then William Haynie, child., Sibel Haynie b. November 20, 1783, d. March 20, 1843, m. Matthew Thompson, April 16, 1891, child, Harrison Thompson, m. Joyce Quisenberry, child, Annie Maria Thompson, m. William Boone Moon; Henry b. December 6, 1768; Richard b. April 1771; Betsey b. June 1773; Sally b. August 1775 m. George Cleveland Kirtley; Nancy b. July 1777, m. Edward Whaley; Richard b. September 1779; Betsey b. 1781 m. William Smith; Anna b. 1785 m. Joseph Thompson

Sybill Halley, m. William Harrison Peake and ?Jesse Peake

Mary Mountjoy Halley m. Richard Crump and Smith King, children Turner Crump, Thompson Crump, Richard Crump m. Sarah Smith; James Crump, Benedict Crump; Lucy Crump m. John Biggs; Sally Crump m. James Dunlop; Mary Crump; Lidia Ann Crump

Susannah Halley m. William Said, and then Alex Smith, lived in Ohio and Ky., children: Anna Said m. Mr.

Campbell; Sarah Said m. John Ramsay, January
5, 1796; Susan Said; Libby Said; Lydia Said m.
John Heryford, April 23, 1798; Elkanah Said m.
Sarah; William Said; Simpson Said m. Elizabeth
Presley; James Said m. Nancy Higgins; Jesse
Hawley Said, Sr., b. March 15, 1791 d. May 1876,
Effingham Co., Ill, m. Nancy Eubanks, dau. of
Thomas Eubanks, August 4, 1817, children:
Susan Said b. September 17, 1818, Delaware Co.,
Ohio, d. April 17, 1891 m. John Henry Loveless,
November 19, 1835; Jesse Hawley Said, Jr., b.
about 1820 m. Susan Thompson, m. December 7,
1847 and Nancy Eubanks; Sarah Said b.
September 2, 1824, m. Leroy Bell, August 1,
1846; Lydia Said, b. about 1826; William Said b.
June 28, 1829 d. 1831; Harriet Said b. 1832, m.
Lewis Smith, November 15, 1853; Harvey Said b.
September 28, 1835, d. February 19, 1919, m.
Almenda Turner, 12 chidren, 5 d. early

Rsh.77 Wm. Hawley, Hally, Holly, (son of Rsh.76) was b. c. 1731
and d. on April 22, 1806. He m. Catherine Jeffries, on February
9, 1758, and they had one son, Henry Simpson Halley, who was
lost in shipwreck. Wm. Hawley's Will was dated January 17,
1798, and presented on April 22, 1806, in Fairfax Co., Va. It
names brothers Henry Simpson, James, son of James, Wm.,
brother Richard, sons of Henry Simpson, Henry and James, sister
Tuckery Laid, her son Elkanah Laid, sister Mary, sister Tibble
Peake, brother John, sisters Sarah Haynei, sons Richard and
Henry Haynie, sisters Mary Crump, Suckey Said, no known
children survived.

Rsh.78 Henry Simpson Hawley, Halley, Sr., (son of Rsh.76), was
b. on May 18, 1762, in Fairfax Co., Va. He m. Elizabeth
Hampton, on July 8, 1786, dau. of John Hampton and Margaret,
nee Pierce, Hampton. Elizabeth d. on September 24, 1824. His
Will, was written in Fairfax Co., Va., on February 18, 1835, and
was presented December 5, 1838. Henry and Elizabeth Hawley
lived at *Pleasant Green* and were neighbors of President George
Washington. At the age of 16, he was with General Washington
at the surrender of Cornwallis at Yorktown, Va., known children:

John Hampton Halley, b. June 5, 1788 m. Catherine
    Coffin, he d. a year after his marriage in 1826.
Henry Simpson Halley, Jr., b. October 2, 1789, Jr., m.
    Elizabeth Reid, Reed, dau. of James Reid, Reed,
    on September 26, 1816, in Culpeper Co., Va.
Mary M. Halley, b. March 3, 1791, m. John Reid on
    January 11, 1816, children Martha Ann Reid, Mary
    Elizabeth Reid, Catherine Frances Reid, Lucretia
    Reid
James Madison Halley, b. November 25, 1792, m.
    Elizabeth Simpson, July 24, 1821, in Fairfax, Va.
Catherine Templeton Halley, b. July 29, 1794, nickname
    Killey, m. Edmund Payne on October 11, 1816 in
    Fairfax Co., Va.
Frances Halley, b. June 16, 1796, m. John DeBell and
    second a Wilcoxen
Samuel Halley, b. (Rsh.94) April 29, 1798, in Fairfax Co.,
    Va., m. Mariam Elkin, May 8, 1827, in Fairfax Co.,
    Va., d. July 30, 1872, Fayette Co., Ky.
Tammy Halley
Elizabeth Halley, m. Newman Burke
Margaret Halley, m. Allan Elkins
Thomas Jefferson Halley

Rsh.79 Clement Haley, Haly, Hely, Helly, Hales, Holey, Holley,
Helly, Hly, Hey, Planter, received 50 acres of land due for his time
of service performed in the Province, under Mark Bloomfield, in
St. Mary's Co., Md., on May 4, 1675. The time of his service was
not stated. Clement Haley m. ?possibly John Robert's daughter,
then _____Turner, dau. of Edward Turner, and then Mary
Connery, widow of Edward Connery. John Roberts, in his May 4,
1671, St. Mary's Co., Will, leaves his leasehold estate to Clement
Haley, his heirs and assigns. A witness to the Will was Edward
Connery. On May 17, 1676, Mary Connery asked the Court that
Clement Haley be appointed to appraise her late husband
Edward Connery's estate. She stated that "she was a stranger in
these parts," at that time. By April 20, 1677, Mary Connery had
m. Clement Haley. Clement Haley d. c. 1694, in St. Mary's Co.,
Md., at which time he was one of the largest land holders in the
Chaptico area. Clement Haley, in his 1694 Will, leaves land and
other bequests to his two daus., along with other individuals. The

children's estate was managed by John Long who in his Will
dated November 19, 1697 stated that if his wife Eleanor Long d.
in the girls minority their grandfather Edward Turner should
handle their estate. Edward Turner also mentions the children in
his Will dated December 28, 1693. After John Long's death the
widow Eleanor Long m. George Ayrs. Guardianship of the girls
estate was passed to George Ayrs in Charles Co., Md., and in
1699 the estate was referred to the Colonial Court for review,
known children:
> Mary Haley
> Elizabeth Haley

Rsh.80 William Haley, Halley, of the County of Accomac, Va.,
wrote his last Will and Testament there on November 24, 1799.
He d. in November of 1813. He m., but his wife's name is not
known, and had the following children:
> James Haley, d. before father, never m.
> William Haley
> Leah Haley
> Benjamin Haley
> George Halley, b. September 1800
> Jesse Halley, b. March 11, 1805
> John Halley, b. November 9, 1809

Rsh.81 James Hawley, Hawlye, was b. c. 1628. He m. Ann, and
they lived in Northumberland Co., Va., in the area between
Potomac and Rappahannock Rivers, known as Nominie, known
children:
> Mary Hawley, m. James Lucas, b. c. 1641, children
> > James Lucas, Elizabeth Lucas, b. before 1673,
> > Charles Lucas, John Lucas, ?Henry Lucas
> Anne Hawley m. Peter Knight, children Elizabeth Knight,
> > Mary Knight, James Knight, Leonard Knight m.
> > Anne
> ?Edward b. c. 1645, m. Sarah

Rsh.82 Edward (Edmund) Hawley, Haley, Haly, Hally, (son of
Rsh.83), was b. c. 1640. He m. Sarah c. 1697, and lived in
Westmoreland Co., Va. He served as Juror and Escheat
Commissioner, and he d. there in 1702. His estate was adm. by
Jacob Lucas and Henry Hawley as "next of kindred," known

children:

      John Haley, b. December 19, 1701

      Elizabeth Haley, b. August 11, 1699 ?m. Peter
      Walker

Rsh.83 James Hawley, Hawly, Hauley, Haule, Haly, was b. c. 1615, and he m. Ann. He was granted land in Isle of Wight Co., Va., on April 22, 1641 for transport of himself and his family. They lived on the Wicomico River in Virginia. James Hawley was named a Juror and a Commissioner in Northumberland Co., Va., in the year 1654. In 1655 he was named a Vestryman in Wiccomico Congregation and he served as a Justice in 1657. A 700 acre land grant was made to him in 1662. This was near the head of the Nominy River. He received the land for transporting 14 people into the Colony. There is a notation in the records that James Hawley and his son are living out of the County on October 8, 1662. He is not found in the records of Westmoreland Co., Va., until March 1663. In 1664 John Paine purchased 300 acres from James Hawley. In 1666 James Hawley was issued a patent for the 700 acres at the head of the Nominy River by Herring Point in Copley Parish. In the Warrants and Assignments, Provincial Court Records of Maryland, in the year 1664, James Hawley of Virginia, John Williams and John Paine, warrant 500 ac. in Maryland, from the records it appears he d. c. 1677, known children:

      Henry Hawley, (Rsh.85), b. c. 1643

      Edward Hawley, (Rsh.82)

      Francis Hawley b. before 1641

      Ann Hawley b. before 1641

      Alice Hawley b. before 1641

Rsh.84 Raleigh, Rolly, Rawleigh, Hawley, Holly, Halley m. Mary Colvin, on December 26, 1788, in Fauquier Co., Va. On a land Deed, that bears the original transfer date of September 23, 1772, to Raleigh Holly, a sale was made in Stafford Co., Va., on February 28, 1803. He received a grant for 200 acres in 1783 for his Revolutionary War Service. He is on the Bedford Co., Virginia Census in 1800, known children:

      Liddy George Halley m. Richard Colvin in Fauquier Co.,
      Va.

Rsh.85 Henry Hawley, Hayley, Haly, Haley, Hallige, Hawly, Sr., (son of Rsh.83), was b. c. 1643. He m. Mary. In 1693 he lived in Westmoreland Co., Va., on a land patent of Col. Nicholas Spencer, which was partitioned by George Brent. In 1671 he gave a gift to Elizabeth Lucas, dau. of Jacob Lucas, (Jacob Lucas m. Mary Hawley, dau. of James Hawley). He adm. Edward Hawley's estate along with Jacob Lucas. He is in the county records until c. 1718, known children:

> Henry Hawley, Jr., (Rsh. 107)
> William Hawley, b. c. 1685, lived in Westmoreland and
> > later Stafford Co. where he owned 520 acres in
> > 1723.
> Sarah Hawley b. c. 1686, m. William Harrison, children,
> > Capt. William Harrison, b. 1703, m. Isabella
> > Triplett; Sybil Harrison b. 1705, m. Col. Hugh
> > West; Sarah Harrison b. 1708, m. Thomas Triplett,
> > and John Manley; George Harrison b. 1707, m.
> > Martha Price; Mary Harrison b. 1714, m. John
> > Brown and John Peake; at age 54, Sarah Hawley
> > Harrison m. Thomas Lewis
> Edward Hawley
> ?Ann Hawley b. after 1670

note: the Brent Family was Catholic and moved to Virginia from Maryland.

Rsh.86 Abel Hawley m. Sarah, and they lived in Accomac-Northampton, Va., where he d. in 1796. He was a Silver Smith and left his tool chest and silver smith tools to his minor son Henry in his Will. Known children:

> Henry Hawley, a minor October 1795

Rsh.87 Jerome Thomas Hawley, Jeremy, (son of Rsh.88) was b. in Boston, near Brentford, County Middlesex, England, and d. in 1593. He m. Rynburgh Saunders, dau. of Valentine Saunders, of Sutton Court, County Middlesex, England. Rynburgh Hawley d. in February of 1575, known children:

> James Hawley, (Rsh.89) b. Boston, Middlesex, England,
> > d. there c. 1622
> William Hawley
> Kynborough Hawley, m. Richard Wroth of Younges Herts

note: descendants listed here are from previous researchers' efforts and have not be proved by author.

Rsh.88 James Hawley m. Dorothy, who was a sister of William Walnot of Shopwick, England. They lived in Boston, near Brentford, County Middlesex, England, known children
> son
> Jeremy Hawley, (Rsh.87)

Rsh.89 James Hawley (son of Rsh.87), was b. Boston, England in 1558, and d. there c. September of 1622. There is indication of a Will probate on May 4, 1624. He m. Susannah, dau. of Richard Tothill of Amersham, Devonshire, England. Susanna Hawley d. in 1610, and he m. Elizabeth Burnell. Elizabeth Burnell Hawley d. c. 1621. His Will, written in 1622, names his son Jerome Hawley as sole exr. and his cousin Valentine Saunders, known children:
1st wife Susanna Tothill Hawley
> son, Jeremy Hawley, Jerome b. 1580 (Rsh.90)
> son, Henry Hawley, (Rsh.91) d.c. 1676
> son, William Hawley, (Rsh.92) d. 1654
> son, James Hawley, reportedly d. childless in England
> > in 1667
> Gabriel Hawley, b. c. 1601, Delegates Examination, Vol. 2,
> > <u>Baltimore vs. Leonards</u>, Public Record Office,
> > London, year 1635, Gabriel Hawley of London,
> > Gent., aged 34, has lived there 5 years; before
> > that in Virginia 10 months; and before that in
> > London 5 years or more. He lived in Virginia c.
> > 1630 for 10 months, lived in London c. 1624-1630,
> > and he was Surveyor General of State of Virginia.
> > He d. c. March 1637/8, at which time Robert
> > Evelin was appointed Surveyor of Virginia in place
> > of Gabriel Hawley who was dec'd.
> son,
> dau., Katherine Hawley
> dau., Susanna Hawley
> dau.
2nd wife Elizabeth Burnell Hawley
> son, Henry Hawley

son, Thomas Hawley
son, Valentine Hawley, (Rsh.93)
dau., Susanna Hawley m. Sir Richard Pier, Peer, went to
    Barbados. Sir Richard Pier, was deputy Governor
    of Barbados in 1633. His Will dated December
    18, 1659 and proved April 2, 1661, names Col.
    Henry Hawley of Barbados and Capt. James
    Hawley of New Brainford Co., Middlesex

note: five of these children reportedly came to America,
descendants listed here are from previous researchers' efforts
and have not been proved by author.

Rsh.90 Jerome Hawley, Hawlye, Halley, Hally, (son of Rsh.89) a
Roman Catholic Gentleman, was b. in 1580. He was a member
of the Royal Court and one of the "sewers" of the banquets and
entertainments of the Queen Consort, Henrietta Maria, dau. of
Henry IV of France. He m. Lady Judith Hawkins, she d. and then
he m. Elinor Brereton de Courtney, widow of Thomas de
Courtney and mother of Sir William de Courtney. Jerome Hawley
had a close friendship with George Calvert, Lord Baltimore, and
he took an eighth interest in Calvert's project to settle Maryland.
He was a Commissioner, assisting Leonard Calvert in the
settlement of Maryland, along with Thomas Cornwallis. Jerome
Hawley arrived in Maryland on March 3, 1633/4 and landed on St.
Clements Island on March 25, 1634. This was the first day of the
year (old style). In June 1635 he appeared before the Privy
Council in London, England and remained there for about a year.
During this time he corroborated with John Lewger, Esq., in the
preparation of <u>A Relation of Maryland; Together with a Map of the
Country, The Conditions of Plantation, His Majesties Charter to
the Lord Baltimore</u>. This was translated into English on
September 8, 1635 with the objective of selling Maryland to
prospective British settlers. On January 5, 1636 Jerome Hawley
was appointed Royal Treasurer of Virginia by King Charles I. He
had an audience with the King on June 27, 1636, and in August
he sailed in the Ship Black George for Virginia. The Ship leaked
and he returned to England. He arrived in Virginia for his post as
in August of 1637 in the Ship Friendship. On November 28,
1637, when the Maryland government was re-organized, Jerome
Hawley was made a member of the Council of the Province. He

built a town home in St. Mary's City, Maryland known as *St. Peters*, and his family remained there while he was away in Virginia as Royal Treasurer. The records indicate that he returned frequently to St. Mary's City to be with his family. On the 4th day of the Assembly in Maryland, February 8, 1638, Jerome Hawley was present and his name was recorded next to the Governor's name. On the 12th day of February 1638 he signed a proclamation by the Maryland Governor announcing his intention of invading Kent Island and reducing its inhabitants to obedience, by military if necessary. He remained in Maryland at least through February 26, 1638. He wrote to the Secretary, Sir Francis Windebanke in England, from Jamestown, Va., on March 20, 1638 and on May 8, 1638. Because of his prominence in the Maryland project, Jerome Hawley was granted 6,000 acres, surrounding a creek named St. Jerome in his honor, in St. Mary's Co., Md. This grant was referred to as the manor of *St. Jerome*. A second grant, of unknown acreage and location, was made named *St. Helen*. These grants were made prior to leaving England in 1633 and he never took title. His brother William Hawley lived on *St. Jerome*, after receiving title to 6,000 acres, after Jerome Hawley's death. William Hawley proved his brother's claim to this land in the Provincial Court of Maryland. Jerome Hawley's Will was written October 20, 1633 in England, and he d. July 1638, at his residence in St. Mary's City, Maryland. He never moved his family to Virginia. From the surgeons bills an inference may be drawn that his death was caused by some unexpected injury or illness. His estate papers were active in the English Records, under the name of Jeremiah Hawley, as late as January of 1651. Thomas Cornwallis, as principal creditor, was granted administration of the estate and could not prove his claims of money owed him by Jerome Hawley to the satisfaction of the Court. A Court battle, brought by Jerome Hawley's brother James Hawley, ensued in the English records regarding Thomas Cornwallis's claims. The Court called the claims frivolous. Jerome's widow, Eleanor Hawley, d. prior to 1655, in England. She returned to England following Jerome's death. Jerome Hawley is bur. in the Catholic Chapel graveyard at St. Mary's City, Maryland, known children:

> Robert Hawley, (Rsh.40), arrived in Maryland 1648
> Gabriel Hawley, b. c. 1609, Draper Co., London,

January 22, 1636, Gabriel (?Francis) Hawley, of
St. Martin in Fields, Middlesex, apprentice pavier
to William Hawley for 9 years, free of Company
July 6, 1636, takes apprentice, July 11, 1636,
John Boroughs. In a case Baltimore vs. Leonards
in London, it is stated that Gabriel Hawley "did
bespeak and provide beer and victuals for the
ship Ark. Reportedly Gabriel Hawley had a son
Clement Hawley named for St. Clements Island.
Judith Hawley, was in Brabant (Belgium) in 1649

note: descendants listed here are from previous researchers'
efforts and have not been proved by author. St. Jerome's Creek
is directly off the Chesapeake Bay, on the western shore, under
Point no Point Light, which is north of Point Lookout, in southern
Maryland.

Rsh.91 Henry Hawley, Sr., (son of Rsh. 89) m. Kinborough. He
was in Barbados as early as July of 1628, and was officially sent
there as Governor in June of 1630. On March 27, 1639,
Kinborough, wife of Capt. Henry Hawley, "who is now in
Barbados," made a petition in England asking that her husband
be allowed to enjoy his estate in Barbados. The population of
English in Barbados was 6,000, in September of 1636, as stated
in a petition by Capt. Sir Thomas Warner of St. Christopher. On
July 11, 1639, Henry Hawley had been elected Governor, even
though the Crown was sending a new Governor to Barbados.
Correspondence reveals that Henry Hawley was making
preparations to go to Florida in 1639. On December 16, 1639 he
was ordered, by the government, to yield up the Governorship.
On July 23, 1640 he had resigned his position and was being
sent home in custody. On January 17, 1641 an order was issued
for his sequestered estate to be restored to him. Henry Hawley
and Major Valentine Hawley were named as guardians of the
children of Reynold Alleyne on June 14, 1652. His Will was
written on January 24, 1676. Known children:
 Henry Hawley, Jr., m. Jane, and he is listed as the sole
  heir of James White in Barbados in July of 1668.
  Henry and Jane Hawley had two daus., Susanna
  Hawley, Mary Hawley, bapt. St. Michael's Parish,
  Barbados April 24, 1677, and one son Henry

Hawley. Roger Cowley, was named guardian of daus. Susanna and Mary, and both were sent to England to be educated, while there Anthony Thomas and wife Anna Thomas shall be the guardian of Susannah. Col. Henry Hawley is listed as a most eminent planter in Barbados in 1673 with 300 acres. Henry Hawley's Will was written June 8, 1679 and he and his wife Jane d. in Barbados.

Rsh.92 William Hawley, Halwy, Haly, Haley (son of Rsh.89), was in Virginia as early as 1640. He acted as Deputy Governor of Barbados while his brother Henry Hawley was away on leave, and was Deputy Governor of the Carolinas in 1640 for Lord Maltravers. On April 11, 1640 he received an order from the Court to give liberty to such as should be willing to accompany him to the Province of Carolina. He signed the Protestant Declaration, in St. Mary's Co., Md., in 1650. He was a resident of Virginia in March of 1652, as stated in a letter written by his brother James Hawley. On March 24, 1652, St. Jerome's Manor, consisting of 6000 acres, in St. Mary's Co., Md., was surveyed for him following proof of his brother Jeromes Hawley's interest. He d. c. 1654, at his seat on St. Jerome's Creek. His Maryland Will, which is referenced in the Chancery Records of the Provincial Court, has not been found, additional information not known:

Rsh.93 Major Valentine Hawley, (son of Rsh.89) m. Mary. They lived in Barbados, and he is found there on July 20, 1651. Henry Hawley and Major Valentine Hawley were named as guardians of the children of Reynold Alleyne on June 13, 1652 in Barbados. His Will proved February 10, 1651/2 in Barbados names his brother Thomas Hawley, additional information not known.

Rsh.94 Samuel Halley, (son of Rsh.78) was b. on April 29, 1798, in Fairfax Co., Va. He moved to Kentucky in 1824 and d. in Lexington, Kentucky, on July 30, 1872. Samuel Halley m. Mariam Elkin, dau. of Zachariah Elkin on May 8, 1827, Zachariah Elkin was the son of Rev. Robert Elkin, a Baptist Minister and Mary, nee Fletcher, Elkin. Known children:

    Elizabeth Thomas Halley, b. February 20, 1828, at
        Pleasant Green, Va., m. Andrew J. Tribble, May 1,

1850, Madison Co., Ky, d. childless, February 20, 1910
Mary Margaret Halley, b. August 10, 1829, Boonesboro, Ky, m. Rufus Lisle of Lisland, near Lexington, Ky, January 18, 1849, son of James Lisle of Clark Co., Ky, known children; Samuel Lisle b. November 5, 1853, James Lee Lisle, b. January 12, 1856, Rufus Lilse, II, b. September 22, 1857, Lizzie Lisle, b. September 4, 1859, Fannie Lisle, b. May 4, 1861, Henry Edward Lisle, b. October 16, 1863, Virginia Hampton Lisle, b. October 16, 1869, Nancy Lisle, b. July 30, 1871, Miriam Lisle, b. September 1872, Hampton Lisle, b. March 7, 1877
Catherine Frances Halley, b. January 24, 1831, d. February 23, 1834
Samuel Halley, II, b. September 19, 1832 d. March 12, 1834
Fanny Debell Halley, b. December 19, 1834, d. August 27, 1837, m. John H. Payne on December 15, 1857
Robert Samuel Halley, b. August 8, 1836, d. August 27, 1837
Edmund Payne Halley, (Rsh.103)
Henry Simpson Halley, (Rsh.104)
Virginia Hampton Halley, b. November 10, 1841, m. Sidney S. Moore, June 5, 1880, children, Miriam Moore, b. June 29, 1882, m. William R. Nevins, June 29, 1882, child, Virginia Halley Nevins, b. August 16, 1910

Rsh.95 Nathaniel Hawley, Halley, (son of Rsh.4), was b. on February 9, 1776, in Prince George Co., Md. He was a School Teacher, in Georgia. He wrote several school texts. Nathaniel Hawley m. Martha Jacob, dau. of Benjamin Jacob, on March 19, 1800, she was b. in Prince George Co., Md. They moved to Georgia and then later moved to Texas, known children:
Samuel Hawley, b. January 29, 1801, became a doctor, with the power of laying on hands.
Jermima Jacob Hawley, b. October 5, 1802, m. William Merritt
Benjamin Jacob Hawley, b. December 31, 1804, m.

Rebecca Lumpkin, and lived in Buena Vista and
Tazewell, Georgia
Elizabeth Price Hawley, b. March 1, 1808, m. John U.
Moore
Martha Ellen Hawley, b. May 31, 1812, m. Samuel James
Fulford
Mordicai Jacob Hawley b. July 12, 1810
Nathaniel Thomas Hawley, b. February 10, 1815, m.
Nancy Ingrahm, children: Samuel; William;
Francis Asbory m. Susan A. Sharp; Mordecai;
Virginia m. Wilson; Nathaniel Thomas; Nathaniel
then m. Emily Kirkland and then Rachael Johnson
Eleanor Hawley b. January 6, 1817
John Cook Hawley, b. February 9, 1819
William Woodward Hawley (Rsh.96) b. January 26, 1821,
m. Susan Parker
Robert Bonner Hawley (Rsh.111) m. Lydia A. Ederington

note: The sons in this family, other than Benjamin Jacob Hawley,
reportedly moved to Arkansas

Rsh.96 William Woodward Halley, Hawley, (son of Rsh. 95), was
b. on January 26, 1821 and he d. on December 16, 1852. He m.
Susan Parker, and the family lived in Prince George Co., Md.
They moved to Tazewell, Georgia, known children:
James Madison Halley, (Rsh.97) m. Sarah E. Oatts
Elizabeth Jemima Halley
William Nathaniel Halley
Martha Victoria Halley

Rsh.97 James Madison Halley, Hawley, (son of Rsh.96), was b.
on March 3, 1847. He m. Sarah Elizabeth Oatts on January 11,
1871, known children:
Susan Elizabeth Halley
William Thomas Halley
Lura Emms Halley
James Stanford Halley, (Rsh.98)
Edgar Bruce Halley
Mitchell Halley
Ruth Halley
Mary Belle Halley

Zella Eloise Halley
Nathaniel Halley

Rsh.98 James Stanford Halley (son of Rsh.97) m. Mabel Christie
on February 4, 1907 at Austin, Texas, known children:
　　Frances Nell Halley m. Malsell P. Armstrong at
　　　　Georgetown, Texas, July 15, 1935, children:
　　　　Mable Christie Armstrong and Stanford Halley
　　　　Armstrong

Rsh.99 John Halley (son of Rsh.112) m. Nancy Douglas, their
Marriage Bond was December 28, 1801. They lived in Bedford
Co., Va., and Montgomery Co., Ky., known children:
　　Uriah Halley, b. May 9, 1810 m. Sarah Davis, children
　　　　Mary E. Halley m. Hugh Hensley; Ann E. Halley
　　　　m. Jerey Wilson; Carolina; Leora A. Halley m. F.H.
　　　　Frisby; Elizabeth E. Halley m. James L. Werh;
　　　　Nancy C. Halley; William H. Halley m. May; John
　　　　Halley m. Lottie Fields
　　Caroline Welch Halley, b. May 22, 1813 m. Robert Yocum
　　　　Welch, children Elizabeth Elinor Welch m. George
　　　　C. Smith; Nancy Jane Welch; John H. Welch;
　　　　Robert D. Welch; William Hunt Welch; Mary
　　　　Welch; Emily Welch; Caroline Welch; George W.
　　　　Welch; Laura Welch; David Hamilton Welch
　　Nancy Jane Halley, b. February 19, 1818, m. James
　　　　Franklin Jones, children, John D. Jones; William
　　　　F. Jones; Matthew T. Jones; Sally Jones m.
　　　　James Gaddie
　　John Halley, b. April 14, 1820 m. Armena Jones, children
　　　　Angelena Halley m. A.P. Stephens; Casandra
　　　　Halley; Boone C. Halley; Scott Winfred Halley m.
　　　　Stoteree Keslo; Kate Halley m. a Stroup
　　Emily Jane Halley, b. October 22, 1822, m. Jedeiah
　　　　Williams children, Mary Williams m. Fletcher Zuan;
　　　　Martha Williams; James Crettenden Williams m.
　　　　Mary Alice Bridges; Elizabeth Jane Williams m.
　　　　Henry S. Payton; George Lincol Williams m. Mary
　　　　Alice Schultz; Carolyn Williams m. James Dixon
　　Elizabeth, Betsey Halley, m. Hiram Wilkerson, children
　　　　John H. Wilkerson; Nancy D. Wilkerson; Nimrod

A. Wilkerson; Sedona C. Wilkerson; Moses
Wilkerson; Elizabeth Wilkerson; Sarah Wilkerson
Polly (Mary) Halley m. Thomas Helms, she was dec'd in
1844, children, Leah Helms m. Peter C. Helms;
Caroline Helms m. J.D. Caldwell; Thomas J.
Helms m. Linda Docaning; Nancy Helms m.
Walter C. Helms; Andrew Helms; Uriah Helms m.
Josephine Giblin

Rsh.100 James Hawley, Halley, Jr., (son of Rsh.76) was b. on
May 4, 1732, and d. on August 25, 1827. He m. Frances
Hereford, who was b. on May 21, 1737, the dau. of John and
Jane Hereford, known children:
James Halley III
William Halley
Henry Hereford Halley (Rsh.101)
Peggy Halley m. Simpson
George Halley m. Sally

Rsh.101 Henry Hereford Halley, (son of Rsh.100), was b. on
December 14, 1780 and d. in April of 1865. He m. Anna Burke,
who was b. on April 17, 1783, and d. December 30, 1862, the
dau. of James and Catherine Burke, known children:
Catherine Donne Halley, b. November 2, 1804
Sarah Ellen Halley, b. January 20, 1807
James Hereford Halley, b. July 22, 1809, went to
Breckinridge Co., Ky.
Henry Simpson Halley, b. May 22, 1812
William Francis Halley, b. March 13, 1814
Maria Mariah Halley, b. March 5, 1816
Martha Elizabeth Halley, b. June 24, 1818
Silas Burke Halley, b. July 4, 1820
John Robert Halley, b. February 6, 1822
Ann Frances Halley, b. March 30, 1824 m. Caleb Stone
Edgar Halley, b. June 7, 1826, m. Catherine Elgin
Richard Thomas Halley, b. August 24, 1828

Rsh.102 Pressley W. Halley, (grandson of Rsh.76) was b. on
February 3, 1801, in Madison Co., Ky., and d. in February 1884,
in Howard Co., Mo. He m. Ist Anne Thomas on November 18,
1827. Anne Thomas was b. on April 7, 1796 in Ky. and d. on

January 24, 1844. He m. 2nd Eunice Ann Thompson on April 6, 1845, known children
> Robert Pressley Halley, b. October 15, 1828, (Rsh.109)
> Elizabeth Halley, b. 1830, m. Dr. Jordan Hayes, then
>> William Heryford
> Susan Laura Halley, b. February 16, 1834, d. June 6,
>> 1930 m. James Reeves Collins, (see Section T. for
>> her descendants)
> William Halley, b. 1836, never m.
> Elvina Halley, b. January 19, 1846, d. April 17, 1861 m.
>> N.W. Quinn
> George T. Halley, b. December 1, 1848, m. Minne Ryan,
>> 1866, then Mary Margaret Sellenburger, July 19,
>> 1900, children, Mattie Halley; Guy T. Halley, b.
>> June 22, 1871, m. Nell H. Smith, April 7, 1919;
>> Anna Halley; Lizzie Halley

Rsh.103 Edmund Payne Halley, Sr., (son of Rsh.94), was b. on May 22, 1838. He m. Mary Theresa Combs, on October 1, 1867. Mary Combs was the dau. of James Combs, and Julia, nee Peters, Combs, of White Sulphur, Scott Co., Ky. Edmund Halley served in the Confederate Army, as 2nd Lt., known children:
> Samuel James Halley, b. September 21, 1868 m. Lilie
>> Edburg
> Edmund Payne Halley, Jr., b. March 4, 1871 m. Martha
>> Elkin, June 26, 1907, of Garrard Co., Ky.
> Henry Hampton Halley, b. April 10, 1874, m. Madge A.
>> Gillie, June 6, 1899, children: Edmund Paul
>> Halley, b. August 25, 1900; Mary Margaret Halley,
>> b. 1904, d. 1905; Julia Halley,. b. May 4, 1907
> Julia Halley, b. November 6, 1876, m. Charles Edra
>> Marvin, November 10, 1897, children: Louis Halley
>> Marvin, b. October 11, 1902; Mary Lewis Marvin,
>> b. July 9, 1908, Julia Marvin Halley, b. October
>> 12, 1909
> Fanny Payne Halley, b. March 24, 1883, m. W. Graham
>> Kerr, June 7, 1906

Rsh.104 Henry Simpson Halley, (son of Rsh. 94), was b. in Boonesboro, Ky., on March 18, 1840. He m. Alice Hunter Bell, on June 9, 1870. She was the dau. of James Franklin and Mary

Jane, nee Wilson, Bell. Henry and Alice Halley lived at *Halleywood*, in Scott Co., Ky. He served in the Confederate Army and he was shot through the mouth and neck in battle. He was a Farmer, known children:

    Samuel Hampton Halley, b. September 21, 1871, Lexington, Ky., m. Katherine Anderson Helm, November 16, 1898, dau. of James Pendleton and Pattie, nee Kennedy, Helm of Louisville, Ky., children, James Halm Halley, b. August 26, 1899, d. June 10, 1900; Katherine Anderson Halley, b. April 20, 1901, d. December 31, 1901; Alice Bell Halley, b. January 2, 1903; Pattie Helm Halley, b. March 1, 1905, d. April 23, 1910; Anne Hampton Halley, b. October 24, 1907; Samuel Hampton Halley, Jr., b. July 20, 1914

    Mary Bell Halley, b. May 4, 1873, m. Charles Wellington Burt, October 14, 1890, son of Wellington R. Burt of Saginaw, Michigan, children, Alice Annie Burt, b. August 17, 1898; Mary Bell Burt, b. March 9, 1902; Marion Stone Burt, b. February 22, 1905

    Anne Wilson Halley, b. September 29, 1880, m. Walter Lewis Vaughn, June 18, 1907

    Margaret Lisle Halley

Rsh.105 Anthony Marshall Plyer Halley, (son of Rsh.109), was b. on July 24, 1868 in Westville, Clariton Co., Mo., and d. August 17, 1944. He m. Margaret Copenhauer, of Iconium, St. Clair Co., Mo., on January 23, 1931. Margaret was the dau. of Benjamin Copenhauer and Mary Ann, nee Hudson, Copenhauer, known children:

    Lillian Verline Halley, b. May 27, 1901, m. William Ethel Head, June 5, 1921, he was son of John Calvin Head and Elizabeth, nee Pierce, Head, children: Mary Elizabeth Head, b. November 16, 1922

    Thomas Heryford Halley, b. July 22, 1903, Keytesville, Chariton Co., Mo., stillborn

    Harold Albert Halley, b. July 3, 1905, Keytesville, Chariton Co., Mo., m. Minnie Mae Bennett, December 5, 1932

    Helen Maurine Halley, b. September 14, 1907, m. Lester Milnes Oswalk, June 2, 1929

Adeline Ferne Halley, b. June 3, 1910, m. John Wesley
        Penick, April 6, 1944
Anthony Elmer Halley, b. November 11, 1912, m. Oleta
        Johnson December 25, 1933
Virgil Marshall Halley, b. March 10, 1915, m. Carmen
        Myetta, March 21, 1942 and then remarried

Rsh.106 Henry Hawley, Halley, III, (son of Rsh.107), was b. c.
1705. He m. Judith Reno, c. 1730, she was b. c. 1710 to Lewis
Reno, of Prince William Co., Va. Henry Hawley, III, d. prior to
February 24, 1756, when his children were minors. Francis Halley
was named guardian for minor children, known children:
        Margaret Hawley
        Thomas Hawley
        Mary Hawley
        Sarah Hawley

Rsh.107 Henry Hawley, Halley, Jr., (son of Rsh.85), was b. c.
1678, probably in Westmoreland Co., Va. He petitioned for land
in Stafford Co., Va., in 1710, and lived Prince William Co., Va., on
the south side of the Occoquan River. The Quit Rent roll for
Stafford Co., Va., lists a widow Hawley in 1723. He apparently d.
prior to 1723, known children:
        Henry Hawley, III, (Rsh.106) b. c. 1705
        Thomas Halley, b. c. 1710, purchased Grist Mill on
                South side of Holmes Run in northern Prince
                William Co., 1733, documentation in 1741 states
                that Thomas Halley was no longer of the County
                of Prince William, Va.
        Sibella Hawley, b. c. 1718, m. Edmond Holmes, lived in
                Prince William Co., Va., she moved to Fauquier
                Co., Va., and d. c. 1803
        Francis Hawley, b. prior to 1724, Stafford Co., Va., d. prior
                to 1733, Prince William Co., Va.
        Mary Hawley, m. Zachariah, Zacheus, Miles, Niles, Mills
        ? James Hawley, b. c. 1708 (Rsh.76)

Rsh.108 Benoni, Benjamin, Haley, Halley, Hawley, Halinge,
Haling, (?Benjamin), was b. c. 1715, and lived in Fairfax Co., and
Prince William Cos., Va. He m., and his 1st wife's name is not
known. He m. 2nd by March 1747, Mary, who was the widow of

Thomas Ellzey, Ellsley. Benoni migrated to S.C. and was alive in 1803. Benoni leased land from George Mason, and served as a chairman on a survey for William West in 1742, Fairfax Co., Va., along with James Halley, known children:
> George Hawley, alive in 1753, named as son on lease

Rsh.109 Robert Pressley Halley, (son of Rsh.102), was b. October 15, 1828 in Howard Co., Mo., and d. March 11, 1913, in Armstrong, Howard Co., Mo. He m. Sarah Heryford on February 26, 1861, at Glasgow, Howard Co., Mo., known children:
> Pressley Wilkerson Halley, b. February 13, 1862, d. January 23, 1905
> William Halley b. December 9, 1863, d. February 9, 1864
> Charles Halley, b. March 4, 1865, d. June 10, 1865
> Nellie B. Halley b. March 4, 1866 d. November 30, 1932, m. William Bozart, April 11, 1894, lived Vancouver, Washington, children, Anthony Bozart, d. infancy, Kenneth Bozart, d. infancy
> Anthony Marshall Plyer Halley, b. July 24, 1868, (Rsh.105)
> John Dennis Thomas Halley, b. December 10, 1869, d. June 24, 1891, Chariton Co., Mo.
> Susan Elizabeth Halley, b. December 9, 1870, d. December 30, 1871
> Robert Joseph Halley, b. June 4, 1872, d. June 12, 1956, Chariton Co., Mo.
> James Marshall Halley, b. October 15, 1874, d. October 9, 1930, m. Marie Bailey, June 30, 1897, two children, m. 2nd Annie Howe, June 15, 1907 from Co. Claire, Ireland (Anna Elizabeth Haugh), 2 children b. and d. in infancy, Milton James Halley, b. December 21, 1910, m. lst Patricia Gertrude Meier, children: Michael Patrick Halley, b. July 8, 1946, adopted, Susan Victoria Halley, b. April 9, 1949
> Ollie January Halley, b. January 14, 1876, Chariton Co., Mo., d. September 14, 1880
> Anna Zulu Halley, b. July 14, 1878, m. Joshua Terrill Bunton, March 29, 1899, children: Harry Heryford Terrill Bunton, b. May 23, 1904; Margarithe Lynn Bunton b. March 31, 1907

Rsh.110 Francis Halley, Hawley, Holley, Haley, m. Sarah Ann. His Will of June 28, 1808, was proved August 23, 1813, in Bedford Co., Va., known children:

> Francis Halley, Jr. m. Elizabeth Douglas
> Sabina Halley, b. February 25, 1768, Amherst Co., Va., d. 1837, Crab Orchard, Ky, (Sebia) m. John Goff, Jr., children, James Uriah, Mary, Alexander, Almira, Lucinda, Caroline, John, Nancy, Malinda, Creed Pascal, Hansford
> Prudence Halley, m. Wm. Ferrall, January 29, 1787
> Chloe Halley, m. James Thomas
> Frankey Halley, m. Littleberry Leftwich
> Suky Halley, m. James McGasson
> Doshia Halley, Eodocia m. Joel McGlasson
> Fanny Halley, m. Isarel Winfrey
> Nancy Halley, m. Robert Warnock
> James Halley, m. Ann Williamson
> William Halley, m. Rebecca Ferrill, December 12, 1785, Bedford Co., Va.
> Thomas Halley, m. Mary
> Sanford Halley, m. Betsey Turpin, January 20, 1801, Bedford Co., Va.
> Joshua Halley, m. Elizabeth Douglas, March 13, 1792, Bedford Co., Va.

Rsh.111 Robert Bonner Halley, (son of Rsh.95) was b. May 14, 1823 at Macon, Georgia. He m. Lydia Anderson Ederington on August 16, 1849, and they lived in Lanark, Arkansas and moved to San Antonio, Texas in 1853 and then to Salado, Texas, where he d. in 1875, known children:

> Minnie Halley, b. May 13, 1861 in Salado, Texas m. John Ransome Smith, one child Eugenia Halley Smith
> Augusta Fredonia Halley, m. Charles Ramsdell
> Martha Eleanor Halley, m. Sidney Wilkirson
> Emma Halley, never m.
> Robert Burns Halley, never m.
> Samuel Leroy Halley, never m.
> William Benjamin Halley, m. Velma Bailey, no children
> Herbert Horace Halley, m. Della Younger, no children

Rsh.112 John Halley, Holley, was b. c. 1732 in Prince Wm. Co.,

Va. He had moved to Bedford Co., Va., by 1765. He m. Judith Goad, c. 1765, the dau. of Abraham and Johannah Goad of Pittsylvania Co., Va. In 1778 he accompanied Daniel Boone to Blue Licks, where the group surrendered to the Shawnee Indians in order to save the Fort at Boonesborough from attack. He was rescued in November of 1782. His Will was written October 4, 1796 and proved in Bedford Country, Va., on December 27, 1802. His widow Judith moved to Montgomery Co., Ky., and she d. in 1826, known children:

>Benjamin Halley, b. prior to 1767, m. Nancy, children
>>Wesley M. Halley b. c. 1825, William M. Halley b. c. 1825, Benjamin N. Halley, b. c. 1826, John F. Halley, b. c. 1825
>Mary Halley, m. Reason Williams, she b. c. 1769
>Sarah Halley, m. Giles Halley, she b. c. 1772, children
>>Cornelius Halley, Benjamin A. Halley, James B. Halley, Samuel Halley, Caroline P. Halley, Elizabeth Halley, Sarah m. Guy Fry
>John Halley, (Rsh.99) b. c. 1773, m. Nancy Douglas
>Joshua Halley, b. c. 1775, m. ?Sally Jennings
>Susanna Halley
>Fanny Halley, b. c. 1776, m. Strode Benefield, children
>>Judah Benefield; Milly Benefield m. Wm. Willoughby; Nancy Benefield m. James Willoughby; John Benefield; Reuben Benefield; Henry S. Benefield
>Ann Halley, b. c. 1778, m. Newport Oldham, child
>>Benjamin Franklin Oldham
>Jacob Halley, b. c. 1785 a minor in 1796, m. Charlotte McGeorge, children, Smithson G. Halley m. Catharine Oxer, children John Halley, Lawrence Halley, Harrison Halley, Henry C. Halley, Daniel Halley; William M. Halley

Rsh.113 Thomas Holley m. Jane. He was transported from England in 1679. He adm. the estate of Abraham Knott in 1701. They lived in James City and Northumberland Cos., Va. He d. c. March 17, 1707, additional information not known.

Rsh.114 William Holley m. Sarah Chaseman, on August 9, 1683, at Christ Church in Lancaster Co., Virginia, additional information not known.

Rsh.115 Henry Halley, Holley, Holly, (?son of Rsh.106), m. Elizabeth, and they lived in Prince William Co., Va., then Bedford Co., Va. He d. on April 19, 1813, known children:

Giles Halley, b. August 8, 1763 m. Sarah Halley, (dau. of Rsh.112) children, Cornelius Halley m. Mary Drummond; Samuel Halley m. Lettice Thomas and then a Wood; Benjamin A. Halley m. Rachael Clark; James B. Halley m. Barbara; Caroline W. Halley m. William Carter; Sarah Halley m. Guy Fry

Samuel Halley, b. June 22, 1770

Charles Halley, b. July 16, 1772

Jane Halley, b. September 6, 1774

Augustus M. Halley, b. November 12, 1776 m. Betsey Arthur

Timothy Halley, b. December 22, 1778

Elizabeth Halley, Betsey b. March 14, 1781 m. David George

Henry Halley, Jr. m. Sarah Sharp

Bailey Halley, m. Sally Bayman and then Margaret Drummone, children, George Washington

Judith Halley

Jenne Halley, m. William Lovegrove

John Halley, m. Ann Gaddy children, Elijah Halley m. Mildred Edison; Jeremiah Halley; John Halley; Henry Halley m. Nancy Hardy; Bartholomew Halley m. Agatha Adams; Pamphylia Halley; Bertha Halley; George G. Halley; Ruth Halley

Rsh.116 John Hawle m. Christian Poole, the dau. of Thomas and Christian Poole. Thomas Poole was b. c. 1622. John and Christian Hawle lived in Isle of White Co., Va. In 1681 Thomas Poole left 100 acres, where John Hawle lives, to grandchild Poole Hawle, known children:

Poole Hawle

Rsh.117 John Hole, Gentleman, of Devon, m. Mary, and purchased 130 acres in Isle of White Co., Va., August 1688. He d. intestate, October 8, 1688, additional information not known.

Rsh.118 Thomas Orley, Orlye, Hale, Hales, Haile, Halle, Halles, Hayles, Hailes, Hayle, ?Hawley, was the son of Thomas and Anne, of Middlesex, England. His sister was Mary Hardinge, wife of George, of London, England. He was b. c. 1601-1605, and m. Rebecca. He received land from Leonard Calvert in St. Mary's Co., Md. in 1642, Archives Vol.41, pg.181. He lived at Cherry Point in Northumberland Co., Va., and he d. there. His widow m. Wm. Jollins, Jollard. Thomas's Will, was written August 11, 1662, probate October 8, 1662. Known children:
?Thomas Hayles, (Rsh.71)
?William Haylles
?Susan Orley

Rsh.119 John Halley, Hayle, Hayley, m. Elizabeth, and they lived in Stafford Co., Va., where he d. in January 1708, additional information not known.

Rsh.120 Richard Haley m. Anne. She was bur., on June 7, 1681, in James City Co., Va., additional information not known.

Rsh.121 John Hailes, Hailey, Hayles, Haile, Halle, Halls, m. Mary, and they lived in St. Mary's Co., Md. He is found in the records of St. Mary's Co., Md., from 1650 to 1675, and he owned a property called *Gallasay*. He was Juror, in the City of St. Maries, on April 14, 1674. He d. intestate January 25, 1675, and his wife's sureties were Joseph Hackney and Robert Large, additional information not known.

Rsh.122 Darbey, Darby, Haley, Hales Heley, m. widow Elizabeth Strickland, (widow of Thomas Strickland) before October 1694. They lived in Cecil and Dorchester Cos., Md. He appraised the inventory of John James in Dorchester Co., Md., additional information not known.

Rsh.123 William Holly m., and lived in Prince George Co., Md. He d. c. June 14, 1729, and his estate was adm. by Philip Lee, Esq., and Wm. Harris, known children:
William Holly b. 1721, his godfather was William Miles

Rsh.124 Roger Hales, Hailes, Hailey, m. Ann, and they lived in Kent Co., Md. He wrote his Will on July 29, 1729, naming Ann

Hailes, his exr. Richard Davis and John Williams were her sureties. Her Will was written in the Kent Co. Md., additional information not known.

Rsh.125 William Haley, Sr., was b. in Stafford Co., Va., in 1720, and he d. in Fairfax Co., Va., in 1796. He m. Anna, and he received a land grant for his Revolutionary War service, known children:

> James Haley, b. 1743 m. Mary Jane
> John Haley
> William Haley, Jr. b. 1750 d. 1818 in Fairfax, Va., m.
> > Bathsheba Dulin who was b. 1752 they m. in
> > 1771, children: William Hally, Jr. b. 1798 m. (?)
> > children: Anna, Abram, Samuel, Robert,
> > Thompson, Mary

Rsh.126 Francis Hawley, Hales, Hayles, Halley of All Hallows Staining London, Gent, d. in Va. He Will was written on June 28, 1698, and probate was September 28, 1702, London, England, known children:

> son, Francis Hawley, Halley

Rsh.127 John Haley m. Elizabeth, they lived on William Hunter's Plantation in Charles Co., Md., where he d. in 1728, intestate. Elizabeth Haley d. in 1720 leaving three minor children. Her estate was settled by John Butts and Stephen Manakin, and one of the minor children is named, known children:

> Thomas Haley
> child
> child

Rsh.128 Thomas Hawley, Sr., m. Elizabeth. They lived in James City Co., Va., in 1669. Additional information not known.

Rsh.129 William Argyle Haley m. Elizabeth Allen. They lived in Richmond, Va., and then moved to Kentucky, know children:

> James Littleberry Haley, b. c. December 6, 1832, m. Mary
> > R. Long of Spotsylvania, Va., on August 11, 1858.
> > He d. in 1917. He was a Baptist Minister

Rsh.130 Nicholas Hawley, Haile, Hailes, Hale, Sr., m., and his wife's name is unknown. He is found in the Provincial Court Records of Maryland where he sold property prior to 1649. He lived in Patapsco Hundred, in Baltimore Co., Md., on his property on the north side of the Patpasco River. He had two tracts of land, *Hale's Fellowship* for 200 acres and *Hailes Adventure*, known children:

> Nicholas Hailes, Hale, Jr., wife's name unknown, dau. Susannah m. a Green in 1745 in Baltimore Co., Md.

Rsh.131 Spencer, Hailey, Hales, Hailes, lived in Calvert Co., Md. His Will was written March 20, 1674, and he named his sister Anne Hales and her heirs. He gave her all of his land in England and Wales. He owned land in Charles and Calvert Cos., Md., additional information not known.

Rsh.132 Thomas Hallings, Haylmys, Heylmys, was b. 1642. In a deposition taken before the Grand Jury at Mattawoman, in Charles Co., Md., on August 17, 1665 and another on September 27, 1665, he testifies against an Indian named Maquamps, alias Bennett Marhegey. Also testifying were Angatha Langsworth, b. c. 1705 and Elizabeth Brumley, b. c. 1731. He stated that he was "working on a plantation next to Mr. Langsworths, where he had bought a crop, and they had well made an end of worming and fureroring when they decided to sit down a pipe it...," additional information not known.

Rsh.133 Jeremiah Hales, lived in Somerset Co., Maryland. His property was called *Tevey Neck* and consisted of 300 acres. He purchased this property on October 1, 1729, additional information not known.

Rsh.134 William Haleys, Haley, lived in Kent Co., Md., on his property The Gift. He m. Elizabeth Henrietta and she was pregnant at the time he wrote his Will in April of 1770. He states in Will that his son and all his daughters are under the age of 21. He d. in 1775, known children:

> William Haley, under 21 years of age in 1770
> Mary Elizabeth Haley, under 21 years of age in 1770

Rsh.135 Nathaniel Holley m. Jane and lived in Chrowan Co.,

N.C., in the area that was originally part of Nansemond Co., Va. He is first found in the records of Chrowan County in a Deed notation in 1719. He was a Carpenter by trade. He d. in August of 1726. Children all minors when he d., known children:

John Holly m. Elizabeth Simmons, a dau. of Edward
    Simmons, known children, son James Holly
Nathaniel Holly m. Jane Simmons, a dau. of Edward
    Simmons
William Holly

Rsh.136 John Holly, Holley, b. c. 1690, m. Sarah, who was possibly the dau. of Richard and Jane Church, of Albermarle Co., N.C. John and Sarah Holly lived in Chrowan Co., N.C., in the area that was originally part of Nansemond Co., Va. He is first found in the records there in 1717, and his Will is dated December 23, 1728. The widow m. John Gilbert, known children:

John Holly m. Rebecca, he was b. c. 1715, lived in
    Johnston Co., N.C., child Edward Holly.
Richard Holly b. before 1728, was in Duplin in 1754.
James Holly m. Sarah, his Will, Bertie Co., N.C.,
    December 19, 1761, states that his wife is
    pregnant. Children, John, James, Tamor m.
    Joseph Barks.
Jacob Holly, b. before 1728, was in New Hanover Co. in
    1747, in Duplin Co. in 1754. Moved to S.C.
Edward Holly b. c. 1741, in 1790 Census of Bertie Co.,
    N.C., wife's name not known. Children, Osbourn
    Holley, William Holley, Neddick Holley, Sherwood
    Holley, Col. John Holley, Mary Holley.

Rsh.137 John Holly m. Elizabeth. He received a land patent in Crowan Co., N.C., on March 1, 1719 which he resided on. He sold this land in Edgecomb Co., N.C., records, in November of 1733. Additional information not known.

Rsh.138 Peter Hawley, Farmer, b. c. 1809 m. Christina and lived in Pulaski Co., Va., known children:

Francis b. c. 1838; Rebecca b. c. 1840; Mamarcus b. c. 1844, Rachel b. c. 1845, Jeremiah b. c. 1846; Biem b. c. 1848; Malinda b. c. 1849. Additional information not known.

D.   **BIRTH RECORDS**

Barbados
Andrew Halley, bapt. March 21, 1682, son of James and Mary Halley

Maryland
MdHR, Birth Records, Charles Co., Md.
Mary Hawling, dau. of Wm. and Mary Hawling of Port Tobacco Way, year 1687
William Haleing, son of Wm. and Mary of Port Tobacco Way, year 1689

Prince George, Co., Md., Historical Society, King Georges Parish, I, II, St. Johns
Thomas Holly (Rsh.2) is b. December 17, 1713 to John and Hester Holly (Rsh.1), pg.248
(Rsh.3) Mary Eleinor is b. November 21, 1753 to Nathaniel Holley and Mary Holley
(Rsh.2) Elizabeth Holly, bapt. 1761, dau. of Thomas and Elizabeth
(Rsh.7) William and Bathsheba Hawley, Eleanor b. March 21, 1774, Samuel b. November 8, 1775
(Rsh.4) Nathaniel Halley b. October 4, 1805, bapt. November 10, 1805, son of John and Ann
(Rsh.4) Maria Halley b. November 8, 1805, bapt. December 22, 1805, dau. of Thomas and Amy Halley
Emma Maude Halley bapt. May 27, 1877, dau. of James E. Halley

MdHR: Prince Georges Parish (Rock Creek) 1711-1798
Thomas Holley b. February 1, 1763, son of John and Maria Holley

MdHR, Prince George Co., Md.
John Hales b. December 29, 1730, son of John and Jane
Luke Hales b. June 9, 1733, son of John and Jane
Thomas Hales b. February 26, 1728/29, son of John and Jane
(Rsh.3) Thomas Holey, b. August 23, 1762, son of Nathaneil and Mary Holey
(Rsh.3) Susanna Holey, bapt. June 23, 1765, dau. of

Nathaniel and Mary Holey
(Rsh.4) Thomas Holey, bapt. February 9, 1766, son of
John and Elizabeth Holey
(Rsh.4) John Holley, bapt. April 17, 1768, P.G. Co., Md.,
son of John and Elizabeth Holley
(Rsh.4) Samuel Halley b. March 23, 1772, son of John
and Elizabeth Halley
(Rsh.6) James Burch Halley b. August 29, 1772 son of
James Burch and Margaret Halley
(Rsh.4) Aimy Halley b. January 2, 1774, dau. of John and
Elizabeth Halley
(Rsh.7) Eleanor Halley b. March 21, 1774, dau. of William
and Bathsheba Halley
(Rsh.7) Samuel Halley b. November 8, 1775, son of
William and Shaba Halley
(Rsh.4) Nathaniel Halley b. February 9, 1776, son of John
and Elizabeth Halley

Virginia

Culpeper Co., Va., C.H.
(Rsh.56) Rowena R. Hawley, b. May 2, 1870, father C.W.
Hawley, mother Lucy
(Rsh.56) Kate Hawley, b. April 10, 1876, father Charles M.
mother Lucy E.

Goochland Co., Va., Historical Society
From The Douglas Register, births with only one parent:
Sarah Haley, son named Pleasant Wade b. June 10, bapt. July
22, 1771

1853 - 1893, Greene Co., Va., C.H.
(Rsh.57) Monroe Dist., Maud Hawley, female, 1886
August, father Ed., Farmer, mother Laura
(Rsh.57) Ruckersville Dist, M.G. Hawley, female,
September 1887, father E. Hawley, mother Laura
(Rsh.57) August 1892, Ruckersville Dist., Marietta Hawley,
father Ed. Hawley, Farmer, mother Laura

VSL, Middlesex Co., Va.
Judith Haley, b. dau. of William and Elizabeth Haley, May
18, 1750, Christ Church

<u>Warren Co., Va., C.H.</u>

Lucy Haley, female, father Cornelius, mother Susan Haley, April 20, 1857, Book 1, pg.29, line 7

CEMETERY AND DEATH RECORDS

Barbados
(Rsh.91) May 11, 1678, burial, Parish of St. Michaels, ye wife of Capt. Henry Hawley
(Rsh.91) June 8, 1679, burial of Capt. Henry Hawley

English
Gentleman's Magazine, for 1802, part 2, pp. 877, 888, London, September 1802, Obituary: July 13, 1802, in the prime of life, at Petersburg, in the State of Virginia, America, Mr. Thomas Halley, Merchant, a native of Pontefract, Yorkshire. note: other Halleys are found in Derebyshire. Petersburg, Va., is south east of Richmond.

Maryland
Shiloh M.E. Church, near Bryans Road, Tombstone, Thomas Richard Halley d. June 1892 in 85th year of life, b. 1807, on same stone second name of Maria

Virginia
VSL: Cemetery Records of Virginia
(Rsh.85) William Lewis Harrison b. 1750, d. 1830 son of Thomas and Sarah Hawley Harrison of Dougue Creek, Fairfax Co., Va.

Washington D.C.

NA Census Index of 1820 - Washington, D.C.
Hawley, Rev. William 015 Wash. D.C. 1st Ward
Holly, James 057 Wash D.C. Geotwn

NA Census Index of 1830 - Washington, D.C.
Halley, Elizabeth, 254 Alex
Halles, George W., 142 Wash Geotwn
Haley, Helen, 153 Wash Geotwn
Holly, James, Wash 062 lst wd
Holly, Lucy, Wash 079 2nd ward
Haley, Thomas, Wash 141 Geotwn
Hale, John, Wash 158 Geotwn
Hawley, William, Wash 089 2nd Ward

NA 1840 Census Index - Washington, D.C.& Maryland
Jacob Holly 246 Alex.
Francis H. Hawley 91 Caroline Co.
Ann Holly 217 Charles Co.
William Hawley 023 Wash.Dist.
Hariett Holly 189 Wash. Georgetown
Rev.Wm.Hawley 15 Washington
Hillery H. Holly 94 Frederick Co.

1870 Washington D.C. Census Index
Anderson Hawley Wash. 328 7th Ward
Ellen Hawley Wash. 758 4th Ward
H.S. Hawley Wash. 705 7th St. East of Div.
(Rsh.53) J.O. Hawley Wash 445 3rd Ward
James Hawley Wash 059 1st Ward
Virginia Hawley Wash 759 4th Ward
Catherine Holley Wash 469 7th Ward
David Holley Wash 046 1st Ward
Isaiah Holley Wash 774 4th Ward
Josephine Holley Wash 304 2nd Ward
Smith Holley Wash 611 3rd Ward
Mary Holly Wash 265 2nd Ward
Ruben Holly Wash 284 7th Ward
Sabra Holly Wash 830 4th Ward

Edward Halley Wash 762   4th Ward
Frederick Halley Wash 213   2nd Ward
Hodges Halley Wash 213   2nd Ward
James Halley Wash 336   7th Ward
Robert Halley Wash 183   1st Ward
Thomas F. Halley Wash 323   7th Ward

Maryland

MdHR:

John Halley, (Rsh.9) 1771 Federal Census, Prince
George Co., Md., St. John Parish, John Halley, b. 1739,
Mary, b. 1738, males b. 1757, 1759, 1763, 1771, 1773,
Females (name Winifred written in but name has a line
drawn through it) 36, 16, 7, 5, 1; one female slave 21,
male whites between 16 - 50 = 3, males under 16 = 3,
female whites = 6., Maryland, Box 1, Folder 18.

Nathaniel Halley, (Rsh.3) 1775-1778 Census, Pomonkey Hundred,
Md.

John Halley, (Rsh.4) 1776, Maryland Census, P.G. Co., St. Johns
Parish, John Halley, b. 1739, males 10, 8, 4, 1, Elizabeth
Halley, age 40, b. 1738, females 14, 12, 7, 2; 62, 58, Box
2, Folder 1776, P.G. Co., and St. Johns Parish

1776 Spesutia Lower Hundred, Harford Co., Md.
August 19, 1776, Wm. Hailey age 48

1778 Harford Co., Md.
William Hawey

1790 Census, Md.
(Rsh.4) John Holly, pg.95, Prince George Co., Md., John Holly,
free white males of 17 and up 3, under 16 - 2, free white
females 7, slaves 28

Joseph Holly, pg.106, St. Marys Co., Md., Joseph Holly,
all free persons 8

<u>1800 Census Index Md.</u>
Wm. Holly, Harford Co., pg.83, no twp
Matilda Holly Black, St. Marys, pg.174
Joseph Holly Baltimore Co., pg.48
Enlch Holly St. Marys, pg.231

<u>1810 Harford Co., Md., Census, Microfilm M2059-3 , pg.870</u>
J. Haley, 0 males under 10, 1 male 10-16, 0 males 16-26, 0 males
    26+, 0 males 45+, 0 females under 10, 0 females 10-16,
    1 female 16-25, 0 females 26 to 45, 1 female 45+, 0 other
    free, 0 salves

<u>1850 Maryland Census Index</u>

Andrew Hawley	Bal	079	1st wd
John Hawley	Car	167	no two
Michael Hawly	Bal	275	1st wd

Virginia
(some areas later became W.Va.)
note: some of these census records have been read and
recorded here, otherwise the numbers are the pages, in the
individual country records, on which the information is recorded.
These will hopefully serve as an index to facilitate further
individual research. 1783 Tithables are included.

<u>VSL</u>
<u>1783 List of Tithables</u>
Cornelius Holly
James Hutchison
Thomas Hutchison

<u>1785 Heads of Families Virginia</u>
Peter Halle, white members 7

<u>1787 Census of Fairfax</u>
(Rsh.76) James Halley 1063
(Rsh.100) James Halley, Jr. 1063
(Rsh.77) William Halley 1064

<u>1790 Fairfax Co., Va.</u>
Nathaniel Hawley, (Rsh.3) 1790 Census, Heads of Virginia

Families, Fairfax Co., Va., Nathaniel Hawley, 7 white souls, 1 dwelling and 7 other buildings.

1800 Accomack, Va.
Abel Holley 96 self 00239 two wheeled carr.
Francis Holly 196 self 1449 13

1800 Alexandria, Va., City, Tax
William Halley and wife, Millstone Maker, 1 child

1800 Bedford, Va.
(Rsh.115) Henry Holley 196 self 20035
(Rsh.112) John Holley, Sr. 195 self 1004 12
(Rsh.110) William Holley 195 01014 Ordinary License
William Holly 164 00027
(Rsh.84) Rauleigh Holley 273 03145
(Rsh.110) Francis Hawley 270 00036

1800 Fauquier, Va. Allen Red charged w/tax
Thomas Holley 204 self 00036

1800 Loudoun, Va.
(Rsh.10) Absolum Hawlly 61 00013
(Rsh.9) John Hawley 60 self 0104 16
(Rsh.11) William Hawley 60 00045
William Hawley 61 0522 19
(Rsh.9) Elijah Legg 894

1810 Census Index Virginia
(Rsh.13) Abraham Hawley, Alb.197
Charles Haley, Augusta 350
_____Holly, Bedford 465
(Rsh.112) Jacob Holly, Bedford 465
(Rsh.115) Jiles Holly, Bedford 466
John Hally Berkeley 584
Penelope Holly Brooke, 681
Mary Haley, Caroline 36
Meriday Haley, Caroline 36
Ambrose Haley, Charlotte 52
Humphrey Haley, Charlotte 51
John Haley, Charlotte 53

Joseph Haley, Charlotte 53
Pricilla Haley, Charlotte 53
Thomas Haley, Charlotte 53
Pleasant Haley, Charlotte 51
(Rsh.15 Barton Hawley, Frf 266
(Rsh.11) William Hawley, Frf 346
William Hawley, Frf 201
(?Rsh.14) Burton D. Hawley, Frf 201
George Halley, Fairfax 199
Henry H. Halley, Fairfax 199
(Rsh.78) Henry S. Halley, Fairfax 200
James Halley, Fairfax 199
William Halley, Fairfax 199
Ezekial Halley, Grayson G4 1 white
Joel Halley, Greenbrier E2 1
Israel Halley, Greenbrier E6 2 white
Thomas Haley, Jefferson 181
William Holly, Kanawha 210
(Rsh.9) John Hawley, Ldn 316
John Hawley, Ldn 244
(Rsh.12) Amos Hawley, Mnn 508
Sterling Holly, Mecklenburg M7 1
Joseph Holly, Mont. 7
Peter Holly, Mont. 13
William Holly, Mont. 18
William Holly, Mont. 3
Benjamin Holly, Orange 07 1 white
James Holly, Pittsylvania 18 1 white
Leonard Holly, Pittsylvania D18 1
Thomas Holly, Pittsylvania D13 (and sons) 3
William Holly, Pittsylvania D11 1
James Halley, Prince G. 288
Samuel Holly, Rockbridge 377
John Hally, Shenan 5
James Haley, Washington 219
(Rsh.9) Elijah Legg, Loudoun 283

1810 Albermarle Co., Va., Census
Abraham Holly, (Rsh.13) 1810 Census Abraham #197 head of
        household in Albermarle Co., Va., in Fredericksville
        Parish. White Males under 10 = 3; 16-20 = 1; 26-40 = 1;

45 and up = 1.: White females under 10 = 1; 10 - 16 =
1; 26 - 45 = 1; 45 and up = 1.

1820 Census of Virginia
(Rsh.13) Abram Holly, Alb, 9A
William Haley   Acc   43A
Betsey Haley   Acc   43A
Henry Holley   Acc   44A
Sally Haley   Aug   17A
David Holley   Bth   73A
John A. Holley   Bth   73A
(Rsh.110) Elizabeth Halley Bfd 39A
(Rsh.110) Francis Halley Bfd   39A
(Rsh.110) Joshua Halley Bfd   39A
(Rsh.99) John Halley   Bfd 40A
John P. Holly   Bky   87A
Edward Haylie Cam   118A
Thomas Halley Cam   110A
John Haley   Car   168A
Winston Haley Car   168A
Meriday Haley Car   168A
Ambrose Hailey Chl   13A
Susan Hailey   Chl   13A
Woodward Hailey Chl 13A
Coleman Hailey Chl   13A
Archibald Hailey Chl   14A
Benjamin Hailey Chl   14A
Humphrey Hailey Chl   14A
Joel Hailey   Chl   14A
Joseph Hailey Chl   14A
Pleasant Hailey Chl   14A
Sarah Hailey   Chl   14A
Henry Haley   Cpr   77A
Thomas Holly   Cpr   78A
Richard T. Haile Esx   41
Robert J. Haile Esx   39
William Haley   Fau   64A
David Haley   Fau   64A
Mark Haley   Fau   64A
Joseph Haley   Fau   63A
James Haley   Fau   61A

64

Marcus Hawl	Frd	22A
George Hally	Frx	51A
Henry H. Hally	Frx	60
(Rsh.78) Henry S. Hally	Frx	60
William Hally	Frx	57A
Andrew Holly	Gbr	75A
Fanny Holly	Gbr	75A
Joel Holley	Gbr	75A
Benjamin Hailey	Grn	3A
Henry Hailey	Grn	3A
Thomas Hailey	Han	31
James Hailey	Hen	31A
Ambrose Hailey	Hfx	58A
Lewis Hailey	Hfx	72
Sterling S. Hailey,	Hfx	84
Anthoney Haley	Hsn	89A
Benjamin Haley	Hco	102A
James C. Haley	Hco	102
Phillip Haley	Hco	102
Phillip Haley	Hco	102A
Stephen Haley	Hco	102A
John Holley	Kan	5
Augusta Hauly	Kan	5
Joseph Hawley	Kan	5
John Hayle	Lew	149
David Hawley	Ldn	148A
John Holly	Ldn	145A
Francis Hailey	Mat	30A
John Hailey	Mec	164
Thomas Hailey	Mec	164
Meredith Hailey	Mec	148A
Philip Hailey	Mec	161A
James Holly	Mtg	176A
Joseph Holly	Mtg	176A
William Holly	Mtg	176A
William Haley	Mtg	175A
E. Hawl	Nbo	97a
R. Hallys	Nbo	105
Benjamin Haley	Nhp	216
Robert Haley	Nhp	216
John Hayly	Ohi	18A

```
William Holly    Pit    57
James Holly      Pit    52A
Leonard Holley   Pit    56A
Joseph E. Haley  Pit    65A
Lovelace Haley   Pit    62A
William Haley    Pow    26A
(Rsh.12) Amos Hawley, Pre 233
James Hawley     PrWm   253
John Hawley      Shn    167
John Haley       Sva    63
Ezekiel Holly    Taz    249A
Sally Holly      Taz    249A
David Holly      Wtn    211A
Benjamin Holley  Wyt    215A
Richard Hailey   Yrk    159A
Thomas Hailey    Yrk    159A
```

1830 Federal Census Index Virginia

```
(Rsh.13) Abraham Holley  259    Albe
(Rsh.54) William Holly   259    Albe
Elijah Holley            128    Bedf
Henry Holley             126    Bedf
(Rsh.99) John Holley     128    Bedf
Thomas Holley            146    Bedf.
Elizabeth Holly          145    Bedf.
Benjamin Holly           285    Bote
William Holly            149    Broone - from
          Kanawah/Cabell/Logan - Ohio
Joseph Holley            016    Cabe. Western
(Rsh.52) Thomas Hawley   075    Culp.
Archibald Hawley         118    Culp.
James Holly              070    Frank
Stephen G. Holly         067    Frank
Andrew Holly             181    Greenb.
Joel Holly               182    Greenb.
John A. Holly            179    Greenb.
Augustine Hawley         196    Kawa
Elis Holley              197    Kana
(Rsh.110) Absolom Holly  194    Kana
(Rsh.59) Francis Holly   193    Kana
Hunt Holly               194    Kana
```

(Rsh.10) Absolom Holly	194	Kana
Hunt Holly	194	Kana
(Rsh.9) Mary D. Hally	006	Loud.Cameron
Wilson Halley	066	Loud.Cameron
George Halley	028	Loud.Shelburn
Margaret Halley	055	Loudoun
Julius Holly	146	Maso.
Bailey Holley	146	Madso
Joseph Holly	073	Mont.
James Holly	073	Mont
William Holly	072	Mont.
Henry H. Halley	233	Norton
Jeremiah Halley	261	Norton
John H.Halley	235	Norton
Leonard Holley	401	Pitt
Lewis Holley	371	Pitt
Williams Holley	375	Pitt.
(Rsh.12) Elizabeth Hawley	014	Preston
James Hawley	072	P.Wm.
(Rsh.9) Eli Legg	076	P.Wm. no twp
Dennis Holly	221	Rock
Elizabeth Haly Acco.	292	St. Geo.
John Hawley	063	Shen.
(Rsh.55) Washington Halley	048	Stafford
Edmund Holley	204	Tasw
Joseph C. Hawley	335	Wyth.
Barnet Holly	254	Wash
David Holly	254	Wash

1840 Census Index - Virginia

(Rsh.54) William Holly	110	Albe
(Rsh.52) Thomas Holly		Culp.
James Holly	016	Mont
Joseph Holly	016	Mont
Thomas Holly		Mont
(Rsh.9) Eli Legg	005	Nich no twp
(Rsh.9) Elijah Legg	006	Nich no twp
(Rsh.55) George W. Holly	212	Orange no twp
William Holly	196	Pulaski
Henry L. Holly	007	Rapp
Joseph Holly		Roan

Benjamin Holly   230   Roanoke

1850 Census Index Virginia
Abel Holly   Acco   098 St. George
(Rsh.52) James Hawley Albe 213 no twp
(Rsh.54) William Hawley Albe 158 no twp
Jacob Holly   Augu   432   2 1/2 Dist
William Hailey   Augu   413   2 1/2
(Rsh.13) Abram Hawley Barb 038 Dist
(Rsh.32) Amos Hawley Barb   030 Dist
Amos Hawley   Barb   030   Dist
John Hawley   Bote   066   8th Dist
Andrew Holly   Broo   264   Dist
William Holly   Broo   230   Dist
Warryton Holly Broo   279   Dist
Phillip Holly   Broo   227   Dist
Andrew Holly   Cabe   038   10 Dist.
Andrew L. Holly Cabe 037   10th Dist
James A. Holly   Cabe 037   10th Dist
Woodward Holly Cabe   037 10th Dist
William Holly   Cabe   036   10 dist
Charlotte Holley Camp   101   Lynchburg
Edmond Holly Camp 149   no twp
William E. Holly Camp 083   Lynchburg
Anna Haily   Char   010   Char
Betsey Hailey   Char   006   Charlott
James H. Hailey Char 033   Charlotte
Joel Hailey   Char   032   Charlott
John Hailey   Char   024   Char
Nancy L. Hailey Char 024   Char
Nancy P. Haily Char   026   Char
Samuel M. Hailey Char   027   Char
Thomas Haily   Char   021   Char
Manilla Hawley, 20 years old, Culp 263 no twp
James Hawley Eliz 056   Old Point
Nathaniel Hawly, Black, Fair 196, no twp L
Harcus Haly   Fauq   237   Ashby Di
Milly Haly   Fauq   218   Ashby Dist
William Holly   Faye   443   W. Dist.
James Holly   Fran   146   No twp
Joseph C. Hawly Fran 105   no twp

(Rsh.112) Smithson G. Holly Fran 110 no twp

David Holly	Fran	146	no twp
Joel Holly	Grbr	234	Dist
John Holly	Grbr	250	Dist
Elizabeth Hailey	Hali	032	Northern
Jesse R. Hailey	Hali	044	Northern
Lucy Hailey	Hail	052	Northern
Mary Hailey	Hali	109	Southern
Samuel R. Hailey	Hali	079	Southern
Susan Hailey	Hali	110	Southern
William Hailey	Hali	114	Southern
William Hailey	Hali	115	Southern
Rebecca Hawley	Hard	083	23rd Dis
Mary Hawley	Hard	084	23rd Dis
Mary Lousa Hawley	Hard	013	23rd Dist
James Hailey	Henry	022	no twp.
Jefferson Hailey	Henry	052	no twp.
Polly Hailey	Henr	020	no twp
Polly Hailey	Henry	020	no twp
Thomas Hailey	Henr	008	no twp
William M. Hailey	Hn Co.	047	no twp
William M. Hailey	Hn Co.	469	
J. Holley	HnC	339	Richmond
Charles Holly	Jack	187	27th Dist
Betsey Holly	Jack	187	27th Dist
Emily Hailey, age 20,	Kana		146 Dist
Frances Holley	Kana	027	Dist
Jeremiah Holly	Kana	127	Dist
John Holley	Kana	128	Dist
John Holley, b. Ky, age34,	Kana	129	Dist
Joseph Holly	Kana	028	Dist
William A. Holly	Kana	098	Dist
William Hailey, age 28,.	Kana		145 Dist
Samuel Hailey	Lewi	014	30th Dist
Betsy Hailey	Loud	222	no twp. l
Henry Hailey	Lune	043	no twp.
John T. Hailey	Lune	041	no twp.
William H.Hailey	Lune	047	no twp
Cornelius Holly	Maso	430	38th Dist
George Holly	Maso	370	38th Dist
George Holly W.	Maso	430	38th Dist

Greenville Holly Maso 430 38th Dist
Matilda Holley, age 14, Maso 429 38th Dist
Samuel Holly Maso 432 38th Dist
Thomas Holly Maso 430 38 Dist
Timothy Holly Maso 430 38th Dist
William Holly Maso 430 38th dist
Crockett Holley Mont 0l9 41st Dist
Boyd Hawley Mont 010 414 1st Dist
James Hawley Mont 010 41st Dist
John Holley Mont 028 41st Dist
Joseph Hawley Mont 011 41st Dist
Thomas Holly Mont 063 41st Dist
Elener Holly Nort 313 no twp
Oliver Hawley Ohio 096 44th Dis
(Rsh.56) Charles M. Hawley, 233 Oran no twp
Thomas Hawley Oran 219 no twp
Daniel Holly Page 271 40th Dist
William Holley Patr 414 Northern
Elizabeth Hawley Barb 038 Dist
James Haily Patr 380 Southern
John W. Hawley Pend 064 Franklin
Thomas Haly, fr. Ireland, Pres 385 45th Dist
        Rachael, Edward
(Rsh.66) Andrew Hawley Pres 448 45th Dist
(Rsh.14) Barton Hawly Pres 433 45th Dist
Elizabeth Holley Pitt 068 Southern
Griffieth D. Holly Pitt 078 Southern
Leonard Holly Pitt 078 Southern
Peter Hailey Pitt 139 Southern
Samuel Holley Pitt 068 Southern
Thomas Holley Pitt 209 Northern
William Holly Pitt 078 Southern
Sarah Holly P An 203 no twp
Richard Holley P Wm 157 no twp
John Hawley Pula 253 48th Dist
William Hawley Pula 253 48th Dist
William Hawley Pula 253 48th Dist
Francis Holly Putn 284 46th Dist
Anderson Hawley Rale 016 59th Dist
Benjamin Holley Roan 318 57th Dist
Edward H. Holley Roan 318 57th Dist

Jerry Holly	Rock	024	Harriso
Mary Holly	Rbrg	460	51st Dist
Nancy Holly	Rock	024	Harrison
Shedrick Holly	Rock	164	56th Dist.
Sally Holley	Russ	257	54th Dist
Harrison Haily	Scout	264	St. Luke
Holiday Haily	Scout	264	St. Luke
Holladay Haily	Spou	259	St. Luke
Betsy Holly	Taze	304	Western
Betsey Holly	Taze	305	Western
Edmund Holly	Taze	238	West
Mary Holly	Taze	250	West
Milton Holly	Taze	319	West
William Holly	Taze	263	Western
Jane Hawley	Warr	051	69th Dist
Jane Hawley	Warr	014	69th Dist
Susan Hawley	Warr	031	69th
Samuel Hawley	Warw	066	Eastern
David Hailey	Wash	134	67th Dist
Madison Holly	Wash	086	67th Dist
Harriet Holly	West	275	Cople Pa
Abijah Hawley	Wirt	085	70th Dist
Calvin Hawley	Wirt	085	70th Dist
Willard F. Hawley	Wirt	093	70th Dist

1850 Albermarle Co., Va.
        Lucy Bailey   60 F
        Catherine Bailey 30
        Jane Bailey   25
        Thomas Bailey 20
        William Bailey   18
        John Bailey   10
        James Hawley   6
        Lewis Hawley   4

1850 Barbour Co., Va.
(Rsh.32) Amos Hawley 30 M   Farmer
                Value RE 100   b. Va.
        May Salona Hawley 26 F
        Sylvinius Hawley   7 M
        Sarah Hawley   6 F

Margaret Hawley   4 F
Eldridge Hawley   2 M
pg.38
(Rsh.31) Abram Hawley 25 M Farmer
b. Va.
Phebe Hawley   24 F
Amos Mincar   14 M
(Rsh.12) Elizabeth Hawley 60 F

1850 Kanawah Co., Va.
(Rsh.59) Francis Holly 59 M
Mary Holly   45 F
Deliah Holly   27 F
Joseph Holly   20 M
William Holly   19 M
John Holly   15 M
Martha Holly   13 F
Mary Holly   11 F
Matelan Holly   9 F
George Holly   5 M
Andrew Holly   2 M
(Rsh.60) William A. Holly 40 M, Farmer
Value RE 1,200, b. Va.
Nancy Holly   34
John W. Holly   17
Mary E. Holly   15
Emily A. Holly   13
Elizabeth Holly   11
Lefsse Holly   10 M
Louisa W. Holly   8
William F. Holly 7
(Rsh.61) Jeremiah Holly, 60 M, Farmer
Value RE 300   b. Va.
Edathy Holly   35
Elijah Holly   17   Laborer
Bartholomew Holly 16
Ann Holly   14
Edathy Holly   10
Emmilioa Holly   11 F
Sarah Holly   9 F
Charlotte Holly   7 F

72

John Holly   5 F
Jeremiah Holly   3 M

1850 Loudoun Co., Va.
Betsey Hawley 63   F
        Value RE 1,000 b. Va.

1850 Mason Co., Va.
(Rsh.62) George Holly 33M   Farmer
        Value RE 200   b. Va.
        Jane Holly   33 F
        Mary C. Holly   5 F
        Caroline Holly 11 F
(Rsh.63) Timothy Holly 24 M   Farmer
                Value RE 250   b. Va.
        Mary Holly   19 F
        Deliah Holly   1 F
(Rsh.64) Thomas Holly 38 M   Farmer
        Value RE 400   b. Va.
        Nancy Holly   38 F
        William C. Holly 15 M
        Ellen Holly   11 F
        Mary M. Holly   9 F
        Thomas H. Holly 6 M
        Elizabeth Holly 3 F
        Nancy Holly   6/12 F
(Rsh.65) Samuel Holly 23 M   Laborer b. Va.
        Janey Holly   22 F

1850 Census, Nicholas Co.
(Rsh.9) Elijah Legg   45 M   Farmer
                Value RE 240, b. Va.
        Ailsy Legg   34 F
        Sarah Legg   8
        Mary Legg   14

1850 Orange Co., Va.
        James M. Jacobs 39   Miller
                Value RE 300 b. Va.
        Lucy Jacobs   39
        Ann Jacobs   6

Sarah Jacobs   5
Richard Jacobs 9
(Rsh.56) Charles M. Hawley 21 Merchant b. Va.

1850 Preston Co., Va.
(Rsh.30) Barton Hawley 42
            b. Va.
          Gemima Hawley 37
          William Hawley 13
          Solomon Hawley 8
          Elisha Hawley 3
(Next Family), Henry Fortney 67
          Value RE 1,000 b. Md.
          Hannah Fortney 46
          David Fortney 18
          Lynda Fortney 10
          Tempresanna Fortney 9
          Jacob Fortney 7
(Rsh.66) Andrew Hawley   38 M b. Va.
          Delia Hawley   23 F b. Va.

1850 Pulaski Co., Va., Dist. 148
#428, all b. Va.
(Rsh.138) Peter Hawley, age 41, m., Farmer Value RE $500
Christina Hawley, age 30, f.
Francis Hawley, age 12, f.
Rebecca Hawley, age 10, f.
Mamarcus Hawley, age 6, f.
Rachel Hawley, age 5, f.
Jermiah Hawley, age 4, m.
Biem Hawley, age 2, f.
Malinda Hawley, age 6 mos., f.
#429
Wm. Hawley, age 32, m., Laborer
Margaret Hawley, age 8, f.
Elizabeth Hawley, age 6, f.
Mary Hawley, age 4, f.
#429
William Hawley, age 68, m. Laborer
Margaret Hawley, age 60, f.
Margaret Hawley, age 27, f.

Lucretia Hawley, age 8, f.
#149
James Haley, age 45, m. Farmer
Hannah Haley, age 50, f.
Joseph T. Haley, age 18, m
James A. Haley, age 16, m.
Virgil A. Haley, age 9, m.

1855 Census Territory of Kansas
Horace Haley   20A 15th Elect Dist from Mo
J.O. Hawley   216 15th Elect Dist from Mo

1860 Virginia Census Index
note: unlike the above, the following records are alphabetized by name and not county.
Benjamin Hawley Mont. 621 Chris. P.O.
Bergus Hawley Henrico 851 Rich.East Div.
Burnett C. Hawley Pulaski 737 Newbern P.O.
Crocket Hawley Mont. 668 Christiansburg
George Hawley Rocking.828 Harris.P.O.
Henry H. Hawley Lee 928 Jonesville P.O.
Horace Hawley Culpep. 787 Fairfax P.O., shoemaker,
15 yrs. old, Margaret Hawley, age 18
Isaac Hawley   Loudoun 755 Leesburg P.O.
James Hawley   Warwick 357 Warwick P.O.
James M. Hawley Mont. 641 Child. St. P.O.
James P. Hawley Pulaski 736 Newbern P.O.
John Hawley   Pulaski 761 Newbern P.O.
John Hawley   Pulaski 782 Newbern P.O.
Joseph Hawley Mont. 654 Christi.P.O.
Samuel Hawley Warwick 359 Warwick P.O.
Stewart Hawley Pulaski 762 Newbern P.O.
William Hawley Mong. Co. 630 Snowville Pulaski Co.
Jeremiah Hawly Fairfax 953 no twp listed
Francis M. Holle Loudoun 372 Leesburg
Andrew Holly   Taze 899 Tazewell C.H.P.O.
Artemus Holly Princ Wm. 431 Groveton P.O.
Boyd Holly Floyd 479 Flat Head P.O.
Chapsvill Holly Roanoke 781 Salem P.O.
Charity Holly Rock 572 Harrisonburg
David Holly Franklin 045 Long Branch P.O.

Edmound Holly Taze 901 Tazewell C.H. P.O.
Edwin Holly Roanoke Co. 786 Salem P.O.
Elijah Holly Bedford 332 Burfords Dep P.O.
Elizabeth Holly Taze 895 Tazewell C.H.P.O.
Ezekiel Holly Taze 825 Knob P.O.
Fanny Holly Alex.Co. 697 Alexandria
Grace Holly Rockbg. 584 Harrisonburg P.O.
James Holly Rockbridge 039 Lexington
Jesse Holly Alex. 725 Alexandria
John Holly Roanoke 793 Salem P.O.
Katherine Holly Taze 896 Tazewell C.H.P.O
Madison Holly Washing.394 Saltville P.O.
Maria Holly Rockin 402 Harrisonburg
Martha Holly Campbell 411 Lynchburg
Milton Holly Tazewell 902 Tazewell C.H.
Richard N. Holly Prin.Wm.431 Groveton P.O.
Rosaline Holly Prin Wm.431 Groveton P.O.
Rufus Holly Roan 781 Salem. P.O.
Sarah Holly Wise 372 Guest's Station P.O.
Thomas Holly Mont. 683 Blacksburg P.O.
Thomas J. Holly Rock. 396 Harrisonburg
William E. Holly Campbell 358 Lynchburg
Elener Holley Nansemond 505 Suffock
Elizabeth Holley Patrick 933 Elamsville
Elizabeth Holley Pitt. 425 Whitmell P.O.
Griffith D. Helley Pitt. 395 Whitmell
Jacob Holley Rockb. 238 Lexington P.O.
John Holley Roanoke 719 Salem P.O.
Joseph Holley Pitt. 391 Whitmell P.O.
L.J. Holley Alber 411 Fredericksville PO
Leonard Holley Pitt. 391 Whitmell P.O.
Milly Holley Franklin 023 Long Branch P.O.
Nancy Holley Rocking. 570 Harris.P.O.
Paton Holley Patrick 937 Elamsville P.O.
Samuel Holley Pitt. 396 Whitmell P.O.
(Rsh.112) Smithson G. Holley Frank. 248 Hales.P.O.
W.R. Holley Albermar 412 Fred.Parish
William Holley Alber. 411 Fred. Parish
William Holley Patrick 900 Elamsville P.O.
William Holley Pitt. 391 Whitmell P.O.
John Haley Loudoun 598 Upperville P.O.

Littleberry J. Haley Louisa 870 Louisa C.H.
(Rsh.9) Eliza Legg, age 36 F. Monroe 977 Peterstown

1860 Pulaski Co., Va., Western District
#303, James O. Hawley, age 30, Merchant,
Value Personal Estate $3,000.
Leatharcne ?Cynthia Hawley, age 33
Robb H. Hawley, age 7, m.
Barnett C. Hawley, age 6, m.
Susan E. Hawley, age 4, f.
Chester C. Hawley, age 2, m.
#481,
John Hawley, age 29, Farmer, b. Va.,
Value R.E. $155
Elizabeth Hawley, age 25, f.
Stewart Hawley, age 4, m.
John Hawley, age 2, m.
Cynthia E. Hawley, age 4 1/2 female
Francis M. Hawley, age 24, Bricklayer
#418,
Henry Haley, age 59, m. Farmer
____, Haley, age 5, f.
Malcomb Haley, age 5, m.
Charles H. Haley, age 3, m.
Sanford Haley, m.
#419,
John Healy, age 24, m. Farmer, Value R.E. $300
Martha Healy
Mary Healy, f.
Harrell Healy, age 8/12, f.
#421,
John Hawley, age 57, m. Farmer, $l,000 R.E., $200, Per.
Christine Hawley, age 40, f.
Mary F. Hawley, age 15, f.
Rebecca Hawley, age 24, f.
Sarah W. Hawley, age 18
Rachael Hawley, age 14
Jermiah Hawley, age 14
Nancy Hawley, age 11
Malenga Hawley, age 9
Sockey Hawley, age 7

Rhoda E. Hawley, age 4
Amanda Hawley 3/12, f

1860 West Virginia Census Index
Peter M. Halley Preston 180 Kingswood P.O.
William Hally Wayne 733 Wayne C.H. P.O

1870 Virginia 1870 Census, name, age, place of birth, county in
which person resides
Boyd Hawley 43 Va Floy,Alum Rid1646/3
(Rsh.56) Charles M. Hawley 41 Va Culp,Catalpa1641/566
Crocket Hawley   47   Va Mont,Black/1664/76
David B. Hawley   16   Va Pulas,Wassee/1674/59
Francis M. Hawley   23   Va Floyd,AlumRi/1646/3
Henry Hawley   28   Ct Appom/Ston/1633/111, next
family...
(Rsh.11) W.L. Ambler age 60 and Mary Ambler age 52
James Hawley   79   Va Mont,Aubu,1664/71
James M. Hawley   45   Va   "   "/45
James P. Hawley   47   Va Pula, Wassee,1674/60
(Rsh.28) Jeremiah Hawley   75   Va FFX, Centv/1645/242,
R.E. $1,000, Mary E. Beach 38, keeping home
John Hawley   60   Va Pulas/1674/54
Joseph Hawley   90   Va Mont,Aubu,1664/64
Margaret Hawley   40   Va Pulas,Wassee/1674/57
Stewart Hawley   30   Va Mont,Aub,1664,70
Susan Hawley   86   Pa York, Nelson,1682,571
Tenitia Hawley   16   Va Pulaski,Wassee   1674,50
Thomas Hawley   35   Va Pulaski,Wassee,1674,37
Thomas Hawley   61   SC Pulaski,Dublin,1674/11
William F. Hawley   5   Va Carol,Bowl Gr/1639/210
Edgar Hawly   44   Va Fauq,Warr,1645/508
Benjamin Holley   94   Va CA Sp.Roan,1675,336
Edwin H. Holley   50   Va CA Sp.,Roan,1675,336
Elijah Holley   85   Va Lis Twp,Bed,16735,260
Fannie Holley   18   Va 3Wd.,Alex1632,77
James H. Holley   25   Va Whit.Pitt1671,82
Jefferson D.Holley   12   Va New.Pul,1674,68
Mildred Holley   79   Va Lis.Bed,1635,260
Richard Holley   45   Va Lis.Bed.1635,260
William Holley   36   Va East.Camp.1638,9

78

William Holley	67	Va Whit.Pitt,1671,81
Henry E. Halley	81	Va Warr.Fauq,1645,509
William R. Holly	42	Va Fred.Albe,1631,312
John Haley	62	Va Culp.Culp.1641,635
Littleberry J.Haley	37	Va Fred. Hall, Louisa, 1660,321
Rich C.D. Haley	25	Va Sou. Dist., Loud, 1659, 223
Benjamin Hailey	40	Va Augusta
Caroline Hailey	24	Va Henry
Edward Hailey	46	Va Henry
Eliza Hailey	24	Va Henry
Elvira Hailey	23	Va Halifax
John E. Hailey	36	Va Charlotte
Joseph Hailey	21	Va Henry
Julia Hailey	40	Ireland Dinwiddie
Mary R. Hailey	65	Va Henry
Sally Hailey	50	Va Henry
Stephen Hailey	28	Va Halifax
Thomas J. Hailey	59	Va Henry
William Hailey	70	Va Augusta,M593.1634.481
Ben Haily	49	Va Northampton
Emily Haily	16	Va Northampton
Hennie Haily	12	Va Northampton
James R. Hailey	37	Va Patrick
Julia Haily	58	Va Patrick
Samuel H. Haily	35	Va Patrick
Albert Haley	36	Va Charlotte
Ann Haley	59	Ireland Campbell
Ann Haley	33	Va Charlotte
Ann E. Haley	10	Va Orange
Annah Haley	37	Va Charlotte
Archibald Haley	68	Va Pitt M593,1671,324
Benjamin Haley	62	Va Spot M593,1679,418
Benj. Haley	25	Va Accomack
Bettie Haley	25	Va Loud, No.Div 593/1659/93
Charles Haley	34	Va Pitt. Chat P.O.
Charles L. Haley	68	Va Pitt, Chat.1671/35
Charles L. Haley	68	Va Pitt, Chat.1671/264
Charles W. Haley	31	Va Pittt, Whitmell
David Haley	36	Va Pitt Chat
David Haley	36	Va Pitt Chat
Elijah Haley	16	Va Augusta Staunton

Eliza Haley	66	Va Acco, St.Geo 1630/196
Elizabeth Haley	50	Va Halifax, Burch Crk
Frances Haley	19	Va Caroline, Reedy Church
Francis Haley	42	Va Charlotte, Walton
George Haley	23	Va Amherst, Elon Twp
Hannah Haley	70	Va Lee, Jones, Twp.1658/250
Harriett Haley	77	Va Fauq. Warr, 1645/521

1890 Virginia, Special Census of Vetrans, Ronald Vern Jackson, Accelerated Indexing Systems International
Henry Hawley, Culpepper Co., Va. 001, Calalpa TWP
John Haley, Eliz City 153 National Home for Disab. Vet.
Martin Haley, Eliz City, 100, National Home for Disab. Vet.
Mary C. Haley, Culpepper Co., 001, Salem
Peter Haley, Eliza City, 124, National Home for Disab. Vet.
Thomas Haley, Eliza City, 135, National Home for Disab. Vet.
William Haley, Accomack 002 Pungoliaguo Dist.

1900 Pulaski Co., Va., Dublin District, Census
#189
Samuel Holley, head of family, b. September 1858, age 41 m. 16 years
Lommia, wife, b. April 1858, age 42 years, dependents 9
#8, Hiwassee Mag., Dist.
Wilbur Hawley, Jr., head of family, b. February 1862, age 38, m. 9 years, parents b. Va.
Sallie E. Hawley, wife, b. March 1870, age 30
Mary E. Hawley, dau. b. September 1891, age 8
C. Bonnie Hawley, son., b. December 1895, age 6
Minor L. Hawley, son, b. July 1898, age 1 year
#80, (Rsh.138), Jeremiah (P. or G.) Hawley, head of family, b. May 1846, age 54, m. 29 years, parents b. Va.
Sarah V. Hawley, b. April 1850, age 50
Laura C. Hawley, dau. b. August 1879, age 20
John M. Hawley, son, b. February 1884, age 16
Irvin (P. or G.), son, b. September 1889, age 10
Earl U. Hawley, son, b. October 1896, age 3
#81, Frances M. Hawley, head of family, b. 1837, age 63, parents b. Va.
Rachael E. Hawley, sister, b. May 1844, age 56
#114, Malcum L. Haley, head of family, b. May 1835, age 65, m.

32 years, parents b. Va.
Sarah M. Haley, b. February 1842, age 58
John H. Haley, son, b. February 1869, age 31, m. 2 years
A. Emma Haley, in-law, b. April 1869, age 31, m. 2 years
#192, Jeff D. Haley, head of family, b. September 1861, age 38,
m. 17 years
Thodocine V. Haley, b. December 1859, age 40, m. 17 years
Murry J. Haley, son,. b. January 1884
George C. Haley, son, b. August 1885
Ada C. Haley, dau. b. June 1891
Willie M. Haley, dau. b. February 1893
Jesse W. Haley, son, b. December 1896
Eula G. Haley, dau., b. September 1900
Martha F. Haley, aunt, b. January 1833, age 67
Sarah Haley, aunt, b. March 1845, age 57
#13, John Hawley, head of family, b. June 1857, age 42, m. 16
years
Lucinda Hawley, b. June 1865, age 35
Alice T. Hawley, dau., b. 1887
May Hawley, dau., b. June 1889
Pearl Hawley, dau., b. June 1894
Rockford S. Hawley, b. January 1897
Lizzie P. Hawley, dau., b. 1899, 11/12
#16, Maria Hawley, head of family, b. September 1834, m. 25
years
Fannie Hawley, wife, b. June 1856, age 43, m. 25 years
John T. Hawley, son, b. March 1877
Stafford Hawley, son, b. January 1883
#24, Jackson Hawley, head of family,. b. November 1878, age
21, b. Va., single
#77, Steward Hawley, head of family, b. May 1856, age 44, m. 22
years
Leota Hawley, wife, b. April 1859, age 41, m. 22 years
Willie Hawley, son, b. October 1889, age 10

West Virginia
1870 West Virginia Census Index
A. Hawley, Wirt Co. 243 Newark P.O.
Anderson M. Hawley, Rale.Co. 1007 Shocking
Franklin Hawley, Hampshire Co. 301 Pied.
James Hawley, Brooke Co. 566 Wellsburg

James O. Hawley, Ohio Co. 152 2 W.Wheeling
James O. Hawley, Ohio Co. 186 3 W. Wheeling
John Hawley, Brooke Co. 575 Wellsburg
Joseph Hawley, Brooke Co. 583 Fowlers P.O.
Oliver Hawley, Ohio Co. 120 1 W. Wheeling
Thomas Hawley, Taylor Co. 617 Pruntytown
Thomas Hawley, Jr., Taylor Co. 617 Prutytown
Andrew Holly, Cabell Co. 140 Hamlin P.O.
Andrew M. Holly, Mason Co. 871 Apland P.O.
Charlotte Holly, Kana. Co. 177 Kanawha P.O.
Cornelius Holly, Mason Co. 872 Apland P.O.
Cornelius Holly, Mason 897 Upland P.O.
Cotholom W. Holly, Kana. Co. 128, Siss.P.O.
Elijah Holly, Kana. Co., 100 Siss. P.O.
Francis Holly, Kanawha Co., 035 Upper Falls of Coal
George C. Holly, Mason Co. 899 Upland P.O.
George E. Holly, Mason Co. 895 Upland
George W. Holly, Mason 871 Apland P.O.
Greenville Holly, Mason 895 Upland P.O.
Isabelle Holly, Marshall Co. 260 GlenEaston
J. Holly, Putnam Co. 858 Teages Valley
James Holly, Mason Co. 895 Upland P.O.
Jeremiah Holly, Kana.176 Kanawha
Joel Holly, Greenbrier Co. 291 Lewisburg
John Holly, Brooke 520 Wellsburg
John Holly, Kanawha Co. 096 Sissonsville
John A. Holly, Greenbrier 263 Lewisburg
John A. Holly, Greenbrier 284 Lewisburg
John H. Holly, Mercer 346 Princeton
John L. Holly, Kanawha Co. 041 UpFalls,Coal
Joseph Holly, Kanawha 035 UpFalls of Coal
Joseph Holly, Jr., Kanawha 036 Upper Falls
Lorenzo D. Holly, Kanawha 231 Kan.Salines
Maretta Holly, Cabel Co. 054 Cabell C.H.
Marshall Holly, Kanawha 177 Kanawha
Moses Holly, Cabell 172 Green Bottom
Nealy Holly, Mason 900 Upland
Percella C. Holly, Mason 896 Upland P.O.
Perry Holly, Kanawha Co. 036 Upper Falls
Sarah Holly, Kanawha 177 Kanawha
Thomas Holly, Mason Co. 895 Upland P.O.

Thomas Holly, Mason 899 Upland P.O.
Timothy Holly, Mason 896 Upland P.O.
W.B. Holly, Mason 871 Apland P.O.
Wellington Holly, Greenbrier 263 Lewisburg
William Holly, Cabell 145 Hamlin P.O.
William Holly, Kanawha 262 Kanawha
William Holly, Pendleton 152 Franklin
William C. Holly, Kanawha 231 Kanawha Sal.
William W. Holly, Mason 871 Apland P.O.

1880 W.Va., Census

Mary Hally, age 67 Kana. keep. hou. b. VA
John Hally, age 34 Kana. coal miner, b. VA
James Hally, age 32.Kana. coal miner b. WVA
Joseph Hally, age 25 Kana. coal miner b. WVA
(note in record says this family moved to West Virginia 32 to 34
years ago from Va.)
(Rsh.68) J.C. Holly, age 40, Kana. Farmer, b. WVA
Elizabeth Holley, age 39, keep.hou. b. WVA
Martha Holly, age 15, dau.,at home, b. WVA
Mary Holly, age 12, at home b. WVA
Lily Holly, age 8, dau, at home, b. WVA
Rosa Holly, age 4, dau., at home, b. WVA
Thomas Holly, age 3, son, at home b. WVA
Belle Holly, age 2, dau. at home, b. WVA
(Rsh.69) John Holly, age 34, Kana.farm lab., b. WVA
Rebecca Holly, age 32,wife,keep.hou.b. WVA
Allen Holly, age 12, son, at home b. WVA
Elben Holly, age 10, son, at home b. WVA
Mandania Holly, age 5, dau, b. WVA
Isam Holly, age 3, son b. WVA
John C. Holly, age 1, son b. WVA
(Rsh.70) William Holly, age 30, Kana.farm wk.b. WVA
Mary Holly, age 21, wife, keeping house. b. WVA
(Rsh.66) Andrew Hawley, age 68 Pres.Farmer b. WVA
Delilah Hawley, age 64 Pres.keeping house, b. WVA
Mary R. Hawley, age 33 Pres.at home b. WVA
(Rsh.30) B. Hawley, age 72, male Pres.Farmer, b WVA., par.b.
        VA
J. Hawley, age 79 female Pres. keeping house b. WVA par b. Va
(Rsh.36) Elisha Hawley, age 35 Pres.Farmer, b. WVA

Sallie Hawley, age 31, Pres. keeping house, b.WVA
John Hawley, age 10
Minnie Hawley, age 6
Kate Hawley, age 4
Baby Hawley, white male 8/12
Joshua H. Hawley, age 22 Pres. Farmer b.VA
Mary A. Hawley, age 23 Pres.keep. hou. b. VA
Fanny Hawley, white female 5/12, b. Jan. 1880, in VA
Mary Holley, age 72 Greenbrier b. VA
Joel Holly, age 30 Greenbrier b. VA
Mary Margaret Holley, age 29, dau., at home b. VA
Charles Henry Holley, age 26, son, b. VA
(Rsh.67) Wellington A. Holley, age 67, Greenb., Farmer, b. WVA
Mary A. Holley, age 45, Greenbrier, b. WVA
John A. Holley, age 25 Greenbrier, son b. WVA
Hannah Holley, age 23, dau. at home, b.,WVA
William Holley, age 22, son works on Farm, b. WVA
Ellen Holley, age 21, dau. at home, b. WVA
Virginia Holley, age 19, dau. at home b. WVA
Mary A. Holley, age 17, dau. at home, b. WVA.
Sophronia Holley, age 15, dau. at home, b. WVA
Addie Holley, age 13, dau. at home b. WVA
Charles Holley, age 7, son, at home b. WVA

CITY DIRECTORY NOTES

California

CSL, LaMesa, CA

(Rsh.58) 1925, 1926, 1927,1929, Spring Valley, John E. Hawley, Plumber, Rancher and Maggie, wife

(Rsh.58) 1932, 1933, 1934, 1935, 1936, 1937, John E. Hawley, Plumber, Rancher and Margaret R. Hawley, wife, 8230 Lookout Avenue

Virginia

VSL, Richmond, Va., City Directory

1883, Mayette Hawley, widow of Glover, 902 Leigh

(Rsh.56) 1891, Charles M. Hawley, Agt., 602 E. Leigh

(Rsh.56) 1896, Charles M. Hawley, Drummer, 602 Leigh, Miss Sue Hawley, Sales Lady

(Rsh.56) 1897, Edward E. Hawley, Overhauler, 506 6th, Irene Hawley, Lucy E., Hawley widow of Charles M., Miss Sue Hawley, Marietta, widow of Glover; Robert Hawley, Machinist 520 Mill, Charles M. Pump Maker 523 3rd

(Rsh.56) 1902, Charles M. Hawley, Clerk Eagle Paper Co., 518 N. 5th, Laura E., widow of J.E.B., Lucy E., widow of Charles M.; John T. Hawley, Plumber, 14 Meadowbridge Rd.

English

Parish Records, England 1583-1817, taken from Internet

Robert Hawley m. Joane Dunton, November 18, 1585, Harefield Parish

Samuel Holley m. Rebecca Whitbye, 1615, Parish Heston

Elizabeth Hawley, bur. 1618, New Brentford Parish

John Holly m. Ann Rose, April 18, 1697, Hayes Parish, groom from St. Andrews, Holburn

Joseph Holley m. Elizabeth Teoms, August 4, 1802, Ealing Parish

William Holley m. Sarah Ansley, April 16, 1809, groom widower, Ealing Parish

John Holly m. Susannah Amos, May 12, 1817, Ealing Parish

Maryland

MdHR First Parishes of the Province of Maryland

1638, Jerome Hawley, Charles Co., Catholic

1693, St. John's Parish, alias Copley Parish, Dr. Allen's minutes gives the following vestrymen in June 1693, Mr. Thomas Haley and others.

Quakerism on the Eastern Shore, The Maryland Historical Society, Kenneth Carroll 1970

James Holle, December 24, 1728, Death Record

P.G. Co. Md., Index of Church Registers 1686-1885, 1797-1878, St. Johns, comp. Helen W. Brown, Pub. P.G. Co., Hist. Soc. 1979, King Georges Parish I, II (St. Johns)

Mr. Thomas Haley, St. John Parish, June 1693, Vestryman

(Rsh.1) John Holly m. March 4, 1712 to Hester Birch

Mary Holley m. Thomas Long, July 30, 1791

Alice L. Haley, age 18, dau. of James E. Halley m. June 26, 1877 to Wm. B. Bayne, Jr., age 28, son of Wm. B. and Elizabeth

MdHR, Prince George Co., Md.

Mary Holley, m. July 30, 1791, to Thomas Long

Virginia

Encyclopedia of American Quaker Genealogy, Hinshaw, Vol. VI, Va., Geo. Pub., Baltimore, 1973
Camp Creek Monthly meeting, served Louisa, Orange and Albermarle Co., Va., Wm. Haley in 1748 later moved to Bedford Co., Va.

(?Rsh.73) Cedar Creek Monthly meeting, 1758, Judith dau. John Haley of Louisa Co., m. Wm. Diggs, 1746, Wm. John Barlett m. Ursula Haley

(Rsh.110) Silver River Monthly meeting, 1787, Wm. Ferrell m. Prudence Halley January 29, 1787, father Francis Halley, Wm. Halley surety

Goose Creek Monthly meeting, Loudoun Co., Va., Ella Haley m. Jacob W. Rees; m. contrary to discipline Margaret E. Haley, dau. of John Haley, m. Henry Madison Taylor, November 12, 1877; Campbell Co., Marriage Bonds 1804 Edmund Farthing m. Agnes Haley, dau. of Wm. Haley

note: Quakers first came to Jamestown, Va., in 1657 and were imprisoned there and then taken to Eastern Shore of Maryland and Northern part of Northampton Co., Va. Later found in Maryland, Barbados, Virginia and New England. Gov. Calvert granted each Quaker 50 acres for settling in Maryland.

VSL, Fredericksville Parish Vestry Book, Charlottesville, Va.
1742-1787, September 13, 1743, ordered that Thomas Clark and John Halley do possess all lands from Roundabout Creek to Fork Creek between the Goochland line and the River

VSL, Burton and Middleton Parishes Register, James City Co., Va.
(Rsh.120) Burials 1681, Anne Haley ye wife of Richard Haley, June 7, 1681

Virginia Baptist Ministers, George Braxton Taylor, 6th Series
(Rsh.129) James Littleberry Haley, son of William Argyle and Elizabeth Allen Haley, soon after the birth of James Littleberry Haley on December 6, 1832, in Richmond, Va., the family moved to Kentucky. He m. Mary R. Long of Spotsylvania, on August 11, 1858 and he d. 1917. He was a Baptist Minister.

VSL: St. Pauls, Fairfax Va., Parish, time period of 1810-1832, shows records for William Hawley, Alexandria, Va.

VSL: First Minute Book, Upper Beaver Dam Church, Fluvanna, Virginia
        (Rsh.55) March 12, 1837, George Washington Hawley was dismissed by letter from the Upper Beaver Dam Brethren Church

VSL, Northumberland Co., Va.
(Rsh.83) List of Vestry, August 22, 1655, Wiccomico Congregation, Mr. James Hawley, Northumberland Co.

I.   COURT AND LEGAL RECORDS

<u>VSL, Colonial Records Project</u>

English

(Rsh.90) November 1621, Petition of James Clemonts, John Herricke and John Smith against Lord Baltimore and his deputy Gabriel Hawley, Hawley now detained in the Fleet Prison, billeted men and women in the petitioners' homes intended for Maryland, but paid no rent for them.

(Rsh.90) October 16, 1633, High Court of Admiralty, Obligation signed by Leonard Calvert, Jerome Hawley, Thomas Cornwallis and John Saunders. Lord Baltimore has hired Richard Orchard to be the master of the Ship Dove for a voyage from London to Virginia. They undertake to pay the wages of Orchard and the crew including Samuel Lawson, Richard Kenton, John Conner, John Curle and Nicholas Paine.

(Rsh.90) Public Records Office, London, England, Delegates Examination, Vol. 1, <u>Baltimore vs. Leonards</u>, Year 1635, Gabriel Hawley, of London, Gent, age 34 has lived in there 5 years, before that in Virginia 10 months, and before that in London 5 years or more; Lord Baltimore, his house at the Upper end of Holborn; his brother and partner; Leonard Leonards loaded into the Ark sailing to Maryland in September 1633, divers toones of beer to the use of Lord Baltimore. There were three or four joined as partners in the said ship and her pinnace the Dove; Mr. Jerome Hally, a partner in the Ark had an eight part; (Rsh.90) Gabriel Halley, did bespeak and provide beer and victuals for the ship; Capt. Leonard Calvert, partner in the pinnace; Mr. Thomas Cornwallis, ditto, Mr. John Sandes, Saunders, ditto; John Boulter, citizen and skinner of London, of St. Batolph, Aldgate, aged 40, has lived there 3 years, and before that for 12 years in the East Indies. Was purser and steward of the ship for the said voyage under the Lord Baltimore.

(Rsh.89) June 1635, Letter from England to Governor Harvey in Virginia ordering him to appoint Capt. Francis Hook Captain of Fort at Point Comfort and Gabriel Hawley, Gent., Surveyor for assigning lands which by his instructions he is to allow to planters. Procured by Secretary Windebanke.

(Rsh.90) year 1636, Sir John Harvye, Governor of His Majesty's Colony in Virginia, age 54. In November 1634 Leonard Calvert and Mr. Jerome Hawlye, owners of the pinnace Dove came to him with a complaint against her Master, Richard Orchard, for leaving his Ship at risk and for behaving insolently. Orchard and his men had refused to return to their Ship unless their outstanding wages were paid, and Calvert and Hawlye refused to make payment unless or until the pinnace returned to Maryland.

(Rsh.90) April 11, 1636, Council of John Harvey, Governor of Virginia, found in favor of Orchard but decision overruled by Governor Harvey. Richard Orchard vs. John Baltimore. Pinnace Dove made passage to West Indies and Virginia with Orchard as master. He hired Samuel Lawson, Richard Kenton, John Curley, Nicholas Perry and John Garnes to serve on her for the voyage adding that if they failed to complete the trip within 12 months, they were to receive their wages on return to England, and, if they so wished, were to be discharged. After 13 1/2 months the men demanded their wages. Orchard said he had no money with which to pay them and told them to go to the Governor of Maryland, Mr. Leonard Calvert (brother of Lord Baltimore) and Capt. Jeremy Hawley, who were then in Virginia. Calvert and Hawley refused to pay until the Ship reached Maryland and threatened Orchard with hanging if he refused to follow their orders.

(Rsh.90) year 1636, John Games, of Ratcliffe, Middlesex, sailor, age 34 was hired by Orchard in 1631 together with Samuel Lawson, Richard Kenton, John Curle and Nicholas Perry to serve on the Dove for a voyage from London to the West Indies and Virginia. In June 1634 Leonard Calvert, Capt. Hawlye and Capt. Cornwallis send the Dove with corn from Maryland to Mathew Tewes in New England and on the way, she stayed at Virginia to take on a pilot and have her bottom refurbished. Returning from England she was forced by contrary winds to put into Point Comfort, Virginia, and, understanding that Calvert and Hawlye were then in Virginia, Orchard went to demand wages from them. Richard Kempton of Tower Wharf, London, sailor, aged 24 was hired as boatswain of the Dove and Nicholas Perry was hired as a sailor. Lord Baltimore, Leonard Calvert, Jeremy Hawley and Thomas Cornwallis had fitted out the pinnace for service in Maryland and in 1633 she was to accompany the Ark and her passengers from Gravesend to Maryland, but on passage the two vessels separated and did not meet again until they reached the West Indies. Capt. Curle d. before the pinnace reached Virginia.

In 1634 Orchard set out from Maryland in the Dove to Hackamacke in Virginia, victualled there, and went on to New England to deliver corn...

(Rsh.91) September 10, 1636, Capt. Sir Thomas Warner, Governor of St. Christopher's writes that since his recent arrival he has been pestered by the complaints of the planters. The Plough, one of the two Ships that came out, is probably lost, and on his own Ship there was such great sickness that 40 died. He called at Barbados, which is inhabited by 6,000 English, but the Governor, Capt. Henry Hawley, would not provide arms.

(Rsh.90) February 3, 1636/7, Jerome Hawley to the Lords Commissioners for the Admiralty, answer to the report, with accusations of William Smith

(Rsh.90) February 4, 1636/7, Handwriting of Edward Nicholas, business of the Admiralty. Whitehall, to consider Mr. Hawley's answer to Capt. William Smith's charge against him and Sir John Harvey touching a boat taken away from Weymouth upon pretense of the King's service and still detained.

(Rsh.90) February 9, 1636/7, handwriting of Edward Nicholas, Commission of the Admiralty, St. James. "To give order whether the Ship Black George, (being certified by the officers of the Navy to be unserviceable) shall cast and should for his Majesties advantage."

(Rsh.90) March 1636/7, Petition of Jerome Hawley to the Lords Commissioners for the Admiralty. Will go to Virginia on board the Ship Friendship of London. Requests that sailors may not be pressed from that Ship. Lists Crew.

(Rsh.90) January 5, 1637, the King appoints Jerome Hawley as Treasurer of Virginia.

(Rsh.89) mid March 1637/8, Grant for life of office of surveyor general of all royal castles, manors, lands, tenements and hereditaments in Virginia, with all fees and profits, to Thomas Evelin in place of Gabriel Hawley, dec'd. Royal pleasure signified by Secretary Windebanke.

(Rsh.90) April 1, 1637, petition of Jerome Hawley, bond to Virginia in the Ship Friendship, that his seamen may not be pressed

(Rsh.90) March 28, 1637, Admiralty, Whitehalll: Notes in the handwriting of Edward Nicholas concerning affairs of the Admiralty, "Captain Hawley desires your Lordships' order to the Treasurer of the Navy to deliver up to him the bond he gave for payment of wages to the Ship Black George's men."

(Rsh.90) April 2, 1637, William Russell to the Lords
Commissioners for the Admiralty of England, Jerome Halley has
paid the money due to the men serving in the Ship Black George.

(Rsh.90) Lords Commissioners of the Admiralty, Whitehall,
April 15, 1637. The sailors of the Ship Black George, Capt. Mr.
Smith, say that money is still owing to them. The desire that the
bond given by Sir John Harvey, Mr. Hierome Hawley and others
will not be delivered until their case has been heard.

(Rsh.90) February 26, 1638, George Reade writes from
James City, Va., to his brother Robert Reade in London informing
him that Hawley has arrived bringing no servants and is now
away in Maryland.

(Rsh.89) April 6, 1638, Westminster, Patent Roll, Charles I,
Robert Evelin is appointed officium supervisorum (Surveyor
General) over all lands and buildings in the Colony of Virginia,
replacing Sir Gabriel Hawley, lately dead.

(Rsh.91) March 27, 1639, petition of Kinborough, wife of
Capt. Henry Hawley, now in Barbados, petitions that he may
continue to enjoy his estate there without impeachment, a warrant
is granted for him to go from plantation to plantation

(Rsh.90) no date: Calendar of State Papers, Charles II,
Petition of James Neale for the office of Treasurer of Virginia.
Neale and his father, who lost severely in the rebellion, are well
acquainted with affairs in Virginia. James Hawley, Treasurer, is
now dec. note: Treasurer who is dec. is Jerome Hawley and not
James Hawley as referenced in this document.

(Rsh.91) July 11, 1639, Sgt. Major Henry Hunckes report
to the Earl of Carlisle that his passage to Barbados took 12
weeks and before he could read his commission Capt. Hawley
had settled a Parliament, been elected Governor and disputes the
Earl of Carlisle's ownership. Hawley is about to go to Florida and
the writer is at Antigua awaiting orders.

(son of Rsh.89) October 14, 1639, James Hawley vs
Thomas Cornwallis, Chancery Proceedings, Series I, Charles I:
James Hawley had an agreement with his brother Jerome to
supply the latter with goods for his voyage to Virginia in 1636.
The goods were put on board the Ship Black George at
Portsmouth. In return Jerome was to send a quantity of tobacco
within a given space of time. In 1637 Jerome left for Virginia but
d. the following year intestate in Maryland and Thomas Cornwallis

who lived in that Colony took over his goods with the intention of defrauding James Hawley of his share in the venture. Asks that a writ be issued to order Cornwallis to come into Court to answer the charges.

(Rsh.90) (son of Rsh.89) October 19, 1639, Court of Chancery, C24-C243, pg.5, Public Records Office, James Neale, Jerome Hawley, brother of James Hawley, went to Virginia in October 1637 where he met the deponent. Sent goods to Virginia in several Ships which were delivered safely and sold by Hawley. Shortly before his death Hawley took goods to Cornwallis for the latter to sell. Neale delivered business papers to the court in Virginia after the death of Hawley. This file contains estimated value of Hawley's assets.

(Rsh.90) November 28, 1639, Chancery, Defendant Thomas Cornwallis maintains he cannot put in an answer without sight of the evidence in the hands of Lord Baltimore. Now he threatens to leave the country. An immediate attachment is awarded against the defendant to make his answer.

(Rsh.90) November 29, 1639, Answer of Thomas Cornwallis: Details of the debts owed by Jerome Hawley to himself and to Lord Baltimore and to other people in Maryland. Cornwallis was granted letters of adm. by the Maryland Court to deal with Hawley's estate. He paid off the debts as far as he was able since Hawley's assets did not cover his liabilities.

(Rsh.91) December 16, 1639, Henry Hawley is ordered to yield up the Governorship of Barbados

(Rsh.90) (son of Rsh.89) February 1, 1639/40, case debated. Jeremy Hawley, brother of James Hawley, intended to take his family to Maryland; needing money to make necessary provisions for the voyage, he borrowed L200 from James in return for a security of the proceeds of the sale of goods in Maryland. Jeremy d. in Maryland, possessed of an estate worth L1500; the defendant gained letters of adm. and took possession of the estate maintaining that Jeremy owned him L44 as well as L300 to Lord Baltimore. The bill has been exhibited to discover the true nature of these debts. Defendant maintains that, as the greatest creditor of Jeremy, he was granted letters of adm. by the law of Maryland. Paid all debts as far as the estate would allow. Court believes the plea of the Defendant is 'frivolous' and orders him to put in a proper answer, March 3, 1639/40.

(Rsh.90) March 17, 1639/40, answers of Thomas

Cornwallis, adm. of the goods of Jerome Hawley to the Bill of
Complaint of James Hawley: Jerome Hawley d. in Maryland in
possession of a personal estate but of greater debts so his widow
refused to take letters of adm. which were therefore granted to
Cornwallis in August of 1638 being his greatest creditor.
Cornwallis took an inventory of the estate and with the proceeds
paid off the creditors. The letters of adm. did not extend to cover
the dealings that Jerome Hawley had with James Hawley in
England. Believes Jerome defrauded James by using goods the
latter sent over for his account or sent to Virginia to be sold by
(Rsh.89) Gabriel Hawley and James Neale.

(Rsh.90) April 22, 1640, Defendant, Thomas Cornwallis,
has made an answer. Plaintiff maintains his debt of L1200 should
be the first to be paid out of the estate. Defendant intends to go
to Maryland but before leaving he must give good security to
abide by the order of the court and to return a full answer within a
certain time.

(Rsh.90) May 18, 1640, Defendant, Thomas Cornwallis,
now employed in the King's army and does not intend to go to
Maryland. Is not to be given a time limit in which to put in a full
answer and bring in his evidence from Maryland.

(Rsh.91) June 23, 1640, Henry Ashton, Peter Hay, William
Powrey and Daniel Fletcher, the King's Commissioners in
Barbados report that Capt. Hawley has resigned the government
and is being sent home in custody

(Rsh.92) year 1640, Capt. William Hawley, brother of
(Rsh.91) Capt. Henry Hawley the late Gov. of Barbados, seized
the goods and estates of William Madison, dec'd.

(Rsh.91) January 17, 1641, order for Captain Henry
Hawleys sequestered estate to be restored to him

September 1, 1657, William Halley of London Gent aged
27 deposes that on 7 November 1654 Edward Wright of London
Merchant signed a financial obligation to Humphrey Halley of
Canning Street near Eastcheapc citizen and vintner of London.
William Leachman of London Gent, and Richard Ellis of Barbados
Merchant have been named attorneys. Depositions and
interrogatories in the Lord Mayors Court of London. Originals at
Corporation of London Record Office.

year 1660, Elizabeth Webb, wife of Thomas Webb of
Ratcliffe, Middlesex, age 34. She was formerly wife of John
Thompson who was Master of the Ship Gift of God, of New

England from 1647 to 1650. The Ship was owned by Arthur Spry. John Holle bought her in France in 1647 and her former husband sailed her from there to New England. In 1650 the Ship was seized at Barbados by Sir George Ascough

 (Rsh.91) August 2, 1660, Deposition of Thomas Paris, merchant. He arrived at Barbados with several others in July 1628 in the Ship Long and Costly, and found Capt. John Powell, the elder, had been chosen Governor 18 months previously. Wolverton afterwards came there and proposed to make a colony under the patent of Lord Carlisle, but the inhabitants refused. Capt. Henry Hawley some time after seized Governor John Powell who was taken forcibly to England.

 March 1670, Probate granted to William Hally, in the Prerogative Court of Canterbury, of Will of Lewis Phillips of Huntington, whose cousin, John Throckmorton, was in Virginia.

 Chancery Proceedings (Hamilton, England), February 12, 1675, pgs. 79, 179, proves the pedigree following: Thomas Halley, wife Elizabeth, of Peterboro, yeoman, d. c. 1642, son Robert Halley, wife Edith, d. c. 1658, son Thomas Halley b. c. 1655

 (Rsh.83) no date: Joseph Saunders of London, merchant. His factor in Virginia, Peter Knight, advised him to come to account over the lading of the Ship Flower deluce with Thomas Burbage

Maryland

MdHR, Provincial Court Judgments Index
note: some records have been read and recorded here, otherwise this is an index.

 (Rsh.79) M, 469, 170, Edward Comelry, St. Clements Manor at Mattapany

 (Rsh.79) JJ, 1669-1672, Hales to Blemfield, no folio given

 (Rsh.79) JJ, cont., Hales to Blemfield, judgment, from folio 214

 (Rsh.79) NN1675-1679, Clement Hales, Haly to Ches___, folio 368, Judgment, year 1677, as Attorney of Edward Connery, decd. against executors of Thomas Gerard, dec'd.

 (Rsh.79) folio 350, year 1677, 2500 lbs. tobacco against Thom Gerard estate, Clement Haly and Mary his wife

 (Rsh.79) folio 307, Robert Ridgely attorney of Clement and Mary Haly...against heirs of Thomas Gerard, John Gerard,

Robert Gerard, April 20, 1677

(Rsh.79) NN, 1675-1679, folio 471, year 1677, delivered by Gardrd Sly, Sheriff, to Clement and Mary Haly, witness in suit against Thom Garard, the said Clement Haly and Mary his wife hold the majority of the lands of St. Clement's Manor as their freehold to them and their assigns during the term of 99 years; Thomas Lomax, Wm. Walk, John Hoard, John Bullock, John Turner, Wm. Longworth, Thos. Stagg, Ro. Soloman, Jno Shopherd, John Upgabo, Henry Spyi, Benjamin Gurgill

folio 568, John Halls, Halles

folio 579, John Halles of Calvert Co., Year 1678

folio 579, John Halles, Halls

Hamsley, folio 664

(Rsh.79) DS#A, pg.578, 1684-1686, (Rsh.79) Clement Haly against George Newman

PL#2, pgs.550, 587, 1707-1709, Benjamin Halley, Merchant and Co., with Joshua Meachon, Judgment

TP#2, pg.19, 1711-1712, April Court 1711, Benjamin Halley and Company, D132N

MdHR, Provincial Court and General Court Index
note: some of these records have been read and recorded here, otherwise this is an index.

(Rsh.90) Provincial Court 1637-1650, Vol.4, pg.14, Jerome Hawley, in Court on behalf of Valentine Sanders, who was brother to John Saunders, now dec'd.

(Rsh.121) BB folio 191, 192, February 1663, Bonded by Provincial Court, John Hayles, Hailes, Andrew Bashaw, Anthony Bower

Hercules Hayle, October 1665, Provincial Court, Liber FF, pg. 115, declares for England

(Rsh.92) Proceedings 1667, folio 184, Court Series 8, Joseph Hackney age 40, swore April 9, 1667, 6 head of cattle given to Wm. Gwither by his godfather Capt. Wm. Hawley

(Rsh.121) John Hailey, MM, Juror, pg.173

(Rsh.92) Wm. Hailey, Def, Nehemiah Blackiston, Pltf, NN, pg.799, Nehemiah Blakiston, against Wm. Hillies, both agree

Rich. Haley, PL#5, men. pgs. 19, 21

(Rsh.131) Spencer Hales, Vol. JJ, folio 214, against John Blomfield of St. Mary's Co., February 16, 1669

(Rsh.121) John Halle, to Chas. Delaroche, NN, 1675-1679,

pg. 5, Deed, John Halle to Charles Delaracoche, indenture made 24th November 1675, by and between John Halle of St. Mary's Co., and Charles Delaroche of the same for and in consideration of 2,000 lbs. of tobacco...grand bargain and sold all that tract of land, or parcel of land formerly called Bettys' Holly but now called Gallasay, lying and being in St. Mary's Co., on the east side of a piece of land formerly laid out for Thomas Innes...in the presence of Henry Exon, Thomas Poxery, sworn in the presence of John Blonfield, Clerk.

(Rsh.79) Court 1677, pg.350, (Rsh.79) Clement Haly and Mary his wife, admx. of the goods and chattels of the said Edwin Conway.

(Rsh.121) John Halle, Pltf, John Slanesby, Def., NN, pg. 498, action continued until June Court, Jno Halle, against John Stanesby, pgs. 568, 720, same suit, judgement

pg.789, John Halls of Calvert Co., March 8, 1678, John Stansby paid Halls.

Mr. Halley, Lib. S., men. 312

(Rsh.79) Clement Haley and wife, NN, 1675-1680, adm., pg.36, signed Clement Hely, witness Jno Blomfield, Clement Hely named as attorney of Edward Conery, dec'd, pg.307, Clement Haley and Mary his wife, adm. of the goods and chattels of Edward Conery prayed, by Robert Ridgeley their attorney, against the goods and lands of Thomas Gerard in the hands of John Gerard and Robert Gerard, it is granted them by the Court the 20th of April 1677, for 5 and 20 thousand lbs. of tobacco to be recovered against the estate of Thomas Gerard, pg.469, an inquisition taken at Mattapany on St. Clement's Manor, Clement Haley and Mary his wife 25,000 lbs. tobacco, signed Thomas Lomax, William Walker, John Hoard, John Bullock, John Turner, Wm. Langsworth, Thomas Stagg, Benjamin Gurgill, Robert Soloms, John Shepherd, John Upgabo, Henry Prye.

(Rsh.79) DS#A, 1684-1686, folio 578, February Court 1686, Clement Haly against George Newman

Martha Hawley, TP#4, convict, pg.528, June 20, 1719, Evan Jones Deputy Collector of his Magistys Customs do make known to all persons who it may concern that on the 5th day of this June, Capt. Edwin Tomkyns, Commander of the Ship Worchester of London, burdened 100 mounted with 10 guns transported the following convicts, has no order of court, among others, Mary Joy, Martha Hawley, Wm. Barton, note: see Early

Settlers records.

(Rsh.92) Wm. Hawley, Halwy, reference to in, PL#3, pg.169; TP#4, 1709 - 1719, Planter pg.20, land called Barberry, St. Mary's Co., near Chesapeake Bay; Wm. Guythord land boundary, bounded by St. Elizabeth Manor, bounded Wm. Hawleys, sold by Wm. Tayard and Audrey Tayard of Annapolis to Charles Carroll of Annapolis, witness Benjamin Rawleigh, Richard Rudyard, August 7, 1710, pg.92, November 7, 1711, Charles Beckwith of St. Mary's Co., and Amas Garrett of Annapolis, several parcels of land containing 5,700 acres, lying near Chesapeake Bay at or near St. Jeromes, original taken up by Capt. Wm. Halwy, where on Charles Beckwick now living containing 200 acres, another parcel of the great tract heretofore purchased by Wm. Guither from Thomas Williams, said Guither made over to Beckwith knowth by the name of Hoggneck, 200 acres.

(Rsh.92) Capt. Wm. Hawley, reference to, Book S., pg.347, FF, reference to, pg.468, High Court of Chancery, year 1667, held at Mattapomy, September 15, 1667, 6 head of cattle given to Wm. Gwither by his god father Capt. William Hawley...sworn to by Nicholas Guither, age 16

Herculus Hayle, FF, Declaration for England, Court of October 1665, pg.115

(Rsh.121) John Hayles, BB, bonded, pgs. 191, 192, FF, cattle mark pg.740, year 1668, John Hayles of the County of St. Mary's do declare his mark of cattle to be as follows...crop on both ears, under sreeke on both ears, and still on right ear,

(Rsh.121) pg.171, Juror, John Hayles, Juror, City of St. Maries, April 14, 1674, to wit, John Blackiston, Thomas Warner, Lobard Willis, James Green, Tamor Thompson, Thomas Hallon, Nathaniel Ascomb, William King, John Slaughter, Wm. Balder, Richard Rigull, and John Hayles summonsed to Jury

(Rsh.121) John Hailey, folio 173, St. Maries Co., Juror

(Rsh.132) Year 1650, Thos. Haylmys, Heylmys, pgs. 69 to 73, before Grand Jury, Mattawomen in Charles Co., August 17, 1655, witness, Angatha Langsworth age 50 or thereabouts of St. Johns saw Maquamps alias Bennett rise upon John Landsworth son of Agatha Langasworth by force and cut off the head of John...rise upon Agatha with a tomahawk an assault did make giving her a dangerous wound in her head, witness, Angatha Langsworth, Elicabeth Brumley, age 24 or thereabouts, Lucy

Good age 21 ore thereabouts, Thomas Heylmys, Bennett Marhegey

(Rsh.132) FF, Deposit, pg.71, Thomas Hallings, age 23 or thereabouts, (b. 1642) on September 27, 1665, working on a plantation next to Mr. Langsworths, where he had bought a crop, and they had well made an end of worming and fureroring when Bennett Marchegay asked him if he would sit down and pipe it, as he did..., and ran to help Langsworths, deposition taken before Charles Calvert.

TL#2, 1699-1707, Benjamin Hatley, folio 731

PL#3, 1707-1709, Benjamin Hatley, folio 122

(Rsh.130) Nicholas Haile, DD#5, 1762-1764, Provincial Ct. 1650, reference to Nicholas Haile, pgs.149, 150, 151, 186, 194, 486, note: when read, page 149, 150, 186, 194, 486, contain nothing on Nicholas Haile.

MdHr, Testamentary Proceedings, Index #2
note: some of these have been read and recorded here, otherwise this will serve as an index.

John Halls, Hales, 1674, Book 6, pgs. 193, 194, JoAne Tyler, widow of Robert Tyler, John Hales, witness to Will, John Halls wrote testament, gave wife land in Calvert Co., on west side north Patuxent River, son Robert, dau. Elizabeth, witness Thomas Sprigg.

(Rsh.131) Spencer Hales, Gentleman, Book 7, pg.369, last Will, March 20, 1674, of Calvert County, oaths of Christopher Rowsby, Gentleman and Jane Halfhead, Spinster, loving sister Anne Hales and her heirs, all my land in England and Wales.
Ann Hales, 1675, no Co., Book 7, pg.369

(Rsh.121) Mary Hailes, Book 7, pg.212, January 24, 1675, Mary Hailes of St. Marys Co., John Hailes her husband late of said County, dec'd intestate, and prays to adm. all the goods and chattels and debts of her dec'd husband, her sureties Joseph Hackney and Robert Large to appraise goods and chattels of dec'd.

(Rsh.121) Mary Hailes, Book 7, pg.219, February 4, 1675, came Mary Hailes of St. Marys the widow and adm. of John Hailes late of the County d. intestate and exhibited an Inv. which was ordered recorded.

(Rsh.79) Clement Hales, Haly, St. Marys, Book 43, pg.18, June 6, 1675, citation given unto Clement Haly of St. Mary's Co.,

to cause Canya White of the said County, the widow of Roland White, late dec'd intestate to appear at St. Marys before the Judge for probate of the Will, to take out letters of motion, otherwise renounce her rights of motion, whereby that action may to the greatest creditor of the dec'd be given.
Spencer Hales, 1675, Calvert, Book 7, pgs. 294, 364

Oliver Haille, 1676, Baltimore, Co., Book 8, pg.413, witness to Will of James Covill, February 7, 1676

(Rsh.131) Anne Hales, 1676, no Co. recorded, Book 8, pg.58, April 25, 1676, Anne Hales by Christopher Rowsby, last Will of her brother Spencer Hales

(Rsh.79) Mary Connery, Book 8, pgs. 69, 190, May 16, 1676, came Mary the widow of Edward Connery, late of St. Marys Co., dec. intestate and prayed adm. of goods and chattels of her dec'd husband and that Clement Haly and Dorby Downing may be appointed to appraise the goods and chattels and that Joseph Pile, Gentleman, to swear them in regard. She the said Mary "is a stranger in these parts," to return Inv. by August 17, 1676

(Rsh.79) Mary Connery, Book 8, pg.190, September 1676, came Mary Connery of St. Maries the widow and adm. of Edward Connery, Inv. ordered recorded.

Mary Hailes, Hales, widow and adm. of John Hailes, dec'd 1677, Book 4C, pg.33, citations served by Sheriff of St. Marys Co., October 1677

Mrs. Hales, Hailes, see also Mrs. Bourke, 1677, St. Marys, Book 9, pg.184

(Rsh.79) Ed Connery, 1677, St. Marys, Book 4C, pg.35

(Rsh.79) Mary Haley, 1677, St. Marys, Book 9, pg.397, Mary Haley, see also Mary Connery

John Hales, no date, no Co., Book 6, pgs. 193, 194

Mary Hales, St. Marys, Book 9, pg.399, Mary Hales, see also Mary Spry

Jasper Howley, April 3, 1678, Book 10, pg.18, came Daniell Clark of Dorchester Co., with account of the last Will of Edward Savage, late proved by oaths of Jasper Howley and Robert Ellys, now present.

(Rsh.79) Clement Hely, Book 12A, pg.167, October 19, 1680, of St. Marys, adm. of all goods and chattels of Edward Connary late, exhibited his account, Judge ordered recorded. Clement Hely m. the widow Mary Connary.

Jasper Howly, Book 12B, pg.146, July 27, 1682, letter

from Robert Ellis, Attorney, Ellis to pay 163, Jasper Hawly 251 Daniel Hully, 1694, Calvert Co., Book 16, pg.64

(Rsh.122) Darbey Heley, Cecil Co., Book 15C, pg.139, October 1694, came Darbey Heley of Cecil Co., who intermarried Elizabeth the relict adm. of Thomas Strickland and entered his oath upon the adm. of the dec'd estate, ordered recorded.

(Rsh.122) Elizabeth Heley, see also Elizabeth Strickland, Elizabeth Heley, Cecil Co., Book 15C, pg.139

(Rsh.79) Clement Hely, Book 15C, pg.165, January 15, 1694, came John Long of St. Marys sole exr. of Clement Hely, Thomas Clark, Thomas Carwile, to appraise estate, pg.166, January 21, 1694, made return to the last Will of Clement Hely, ordered recorded.

(Rsh.122) Elizabeth Stickkland, Cecil Co., Book 15C, pg.139

Daniel Hully, Book 16, pg.64, May 23, 1694, estate of John Abington, London Merchant, late of Calvert Co., Daniel Hully, a surety 2000 sterling for William Turner, sister Mirrott Carney, wife of Doctor Carney, niece Merroit, godson John Abington, son of Wm. Abington

(Rsh.79) Clement Hely, Book 15C, pg.194, April 1695, Inv. exhibited Inv. of lat Clement Hely, amounting of 94-1-6, and in tobacco 3173500 debts.

(Rsh.79) Clement Holey, Heley, Book 16, pg.62, St. Marys Co., May 20, 1695, was exhibited Inv. of late Clement Holey, adm. to 139++, tobacco debts 31723++ recorded Book XIII, folio 268

(Rsh.79) Clement Haley, account, Charles Co., 1696, Book 18A, pg.51

(Rsh.122) Darby, Darbey, Haley, Hales, Book 18A, pg.62, Dorchester Co., Inv. of John James, dec'd. 5-6-6, Darby Haley appraised

(Rsh.79) Clement Haley, 1699, Charles Co., Book 18A, pgs. 48, 51, Charles Co., George Ayrs and Eleanor his wife (former wife of John Long) who was exr. of Clement Haley filed account for Halys estate, referred to Colonial Courts for adjustment of account.

(Rsh.79) Clement Heley, no date recorded, St. Marys, Book 15C, pgs. 165, 166, 194

Benjamin Haley, Book 18B, pg.16, October 29, 1700, John Hammond for Benjamin Haley of London Merchant, against adm. of late Thomas Rusmond, Planter, dec. debt of 22015 tobacco to be paid.

Mary Hailes, 1712-1713, Dorchester Co., Book 2, pgs. 95, 128, 148, 223

Joseph Hailes, 1712-1713, Dorchester Co., Book 22, pgs. 95, 128, 148, 267

James Hailey, 1714, Dorchester Co., Book 2, pg.378

Elizabeth Haley, 1718, Charles Co., Book 23, pgs. 206, 207, 294

Elizabeth Hales, 1719-20, Charles Co., Book 24, pgs.4, 272, 287

Elizabeth Haley, 1722, Charles Co., Book 25, pg.133

Elizabeth Haley, 1722, Book 26, pg.121

(Rsh.122) Elizabeth Strickland, 1722, Calvert Co., Book 26, pg.101

(Rsh.122) Elizabeth Strickland, 1724, Calvert Co., Book 27, pgs. 15, 72, 78

Mary Ann Holly, 1726, P.G. Co., Book 27, pg.359

(Rsh.124) Roger Hales, 1721, Kent Co., Book 25, pg.15

(Rsh.124) Roger Hailes, 1727-29, Kent Co., Book 28, pg.144, 396

Robert Hales, 1727-29, Kent Co., Book 28, pgs. 144, 396, 429

(Rsh.124) Ann Hailey, 1727-1729, Kent Co., Book L28, pgs. 144, 396

(Rsh.131) Spencer Hailes, Charles Co., Book 6, pg.429, appraised estate Christopher Rowsby

Margaret Haill, 1728-29, Dorchester Co., Book 28, pgs. 248, 403, 434

John Hailes, Kent Co., February 19, 1728, Jeremiah Herring his adm. bond in common form by John Hailes, his adm. with Morgan Hurt and Thomas Lewis, his sureties, 60 lbs. sterling

John Hailey, 1729, Kent Co. Book 28, pg.381

(Rsh.123) William Holly, Book 28, pg.385, June 25, 1729, Prince George Co., his adm. bond in common form by Philip Lee, Esq., his adm. with Wm. Harris, Surety, 50 lbs, June 14, 1729

(Rsh.123) Wm. Holly, Prince George Co., Infants and Orphans, 1695-1750, August 1729, Book P., pg.133, Wm. Holly, age 8 years old last day of February, bound to godfather, William Miles until age 21

(Rsh.124) Roger Hailes, July 29, 1729, Book 28, pg.396, Will and Testament in common form by Ann Hailes, his exr. with Richard Davis and John Williams, 600 lbs.

John Holly, 1729, P.G. Co., Book 28, pg.428

(Rsh.124) Roger Hailes, 1731, Book 29, pgs. 92, 161
Edward Hales, 1736, Kent Co., Book 30, pg.208
Philip Hales, 1736, Kent Co., Book 30, pg.208
John Holly, 1746, P.G. Co., Book 32, pg.45
Thomas Halley, 1750, Charles Co., Book 33, pg.146 #1
Thomas Haile, Book 30, pg.305, Charles Co., 1737,
Alexander Lashley, his adm. bond in common form by Thomas
Haile his adm. with Francis Glass and William Penn of Charles
Co., his sureties in 50 lbs., July 10, 1737
(Rsh.2) Thomas Holly, 1747, P.G. Co., Book 32, pg.68
(Rsh.1) Hester Holley, 1756-57, Charles Co., Book 36,
pgs. 277, 418
Benjamin Hales, no date, no Co., Book 18B, pg.16
Daniel Haley, no date, no Co., Book 13, pgs. 201, 203,
238
John Hails, Baltimore Co., Book 14, pg.156
(Rsh. 130) Nicholas Hailes, no co., Book 17, pg.337
Samuel Howley, no date, no co., Book 17, pg.311

MdHR, General Index to Warrants and Assignments, Liber #1,
note: when these were read the information has been recorded,
otherwise this will serve as an index.
(Rsh.90) Jerome Hawley, Esq., enters 5 rights, folio 17,
Jerome Hawley who transported Mary and Ellen Jormogan,
Thomas Jormogan, Thomas Cullamore came into providence
November 28, 1637 in Ship called Unity of the Isle of Wight.
Thomas Hales, demand and warrant 50 acres, folio 85,
Thos. Hales, year 1640, Isle of Kent, Planter, Grant of Capt. Wm.
Clayborne, bonded on west, branch of Goose Harbor called
Cedar Branch, East Creek coming out of Pine Bay called
Phillpotts Creek, 50 acres.
(Rsh.89) James Hawley to (Rsh.92) William Hawley,
Power of Attorney, folio 162, James Hawley from Brainford, to
Wm. Hawley power of attorney, July 20, 1649, "there is only one
dau. of his, (Rsh.90) Jerome Hawley, before you which said dau.
is in Brabanth and mindeth not the same". note: Is Brabanth not
Belgium
(Rsh.92) Wm. Hawley, order for warrant 6000, folio 428,
Court held at St. Maries March 24, 1652, "it is thought fit with the
government approval that for the present a Warrant be granted to
the said Capt. Hawley for 6,000 acres of land only where he now

lives..." note: the site of this grant is in the year 2000 on St. Jerome's Creek, Dameron, Maryland. A house built at the site, in 1830, sits on the original foundation of St. Jerome Manor, where William Hawley lived.

Liber #2, from old A

(Rsh.90) Jerome Hawley, adm. of his est. granted to Thom Conwallis, folio 98; Thomas Conwallis, folio 101; security, folio 102; appraisers folio 105; estate amount folio 174, granted folio 176

(Rsh.92) Wm. Hawley from Robert Sharpe, 100, folio 425; from Mary Theygo 600, folio 425; from Wm. Stone, 6 rights, folio 425, from Culhbert Fenwick, 2,000, folio 425, from Jno. folio 425, demand, folio 426, to John Sherlcliff, folio 550.

Liber #3, trans. from old A and B

(Rsh.92) Wm. Hawley to Marlyn Kwike, Deed of gift 200 ac. of land, folio 97, January 4, 1650, I Capt. Wm. Hawley do hereby give unto Martin Kirke at the north side of St. Jeromes plantation a thicket of land commonly called St. Jeromes Thicket...200 acres of land and do for me, my heirs, executer or assigns warrant the same...paying unto the Lord Prop. of this Province of Maryland his usual rent, witness, George Manneis, Friendship Tougne

Liber A.B.H. trans. from old A Blt., year 1647

(Rsh.92) Wm. Hawley from Robert Sharpe, folio 9, from Marke Pheypo, folio 9, from Robert Clarke, folio 9, from Wm. Stone, folio 9, from Gulthb Fenwick, folio 9

Liber A.B.H.

(Rsh.92) Wm. Hawley from Jno Sherlcliff, folio 10, demand and warrant, folio 10

year 1640 Thomas Hales prays confer of a parcle of land prod. thereon, folio 85

year 1643, Thomas Hales to Wm. Johnson, folio 200

(Rsh.92) Capt. Wm. Hawley, warr 6000, folio 333

Liber 7, 1664-1665

(Rsh.83) year 1664, James Hawley of Virginia, John Williams and John Paine, warrant 500 ac. folio 471

Vol. 12

1669, folio 384, December 22, 1669, Joseph Horsely of Calvert Co.

Vol.15

folio 598, December 16, 1678, Came Jasper Howley of St.

Maries and proved and claimed 100 acres for transporting himself and Ann Paritis, do hereby give same to Robert Ellis

Folio 599, Robert Ellis hereby gives to Dr. Jacob Lockaman of St. Maries, November 14, 1679, Jacob Lockerman gives to John Alford of Dorchester Co., Md., November 1679

Vol.18, 1674-1675

pg.127, James Harle of Dorchester Co., for 50 acres 12th day of July 1673, makes over to Wm. Hord, August 4, 1674, signed with mark, James (H) Harle

(Rsh.79) pg.310, Clement Helley of St. Mary's Co., Planter, for a consideration paid me in hand do hereby assign unto John Blomfield all my right title and interest to 50 acres of land due me for my time of service performed to Marke Bramfield, Bacarnfield, Bcarnfield, Blumfield, dec'd in the year 1667. In witness where to I have here unto let my hand and seal this 4th day of May 1675, Clement Helley, signed, witness Barthod Ennals, Clement Hill

(Rsh.79) pg.311, May 4, 1675, came Clement Helly of St. Mary's Co., and proved his right to 50 acres of land for his time of service performed in this Province.

Every Name Index, Charles Co., Md., Orphans Court Proceedings 1774-1778

Hally, John 646, Nathaniel 645, Nathaniel 637

Court Record Book 3, Index, 1791-1803

Halley, John a135, b376, Holley, John a424, Thomas a257, Holly, John c138

P.G. County Maryland Court Records, Upper Marlboro, Md.

(Rsh.4 or Rsh.9) AA#2, December 5, 1769, report of stray mare, John Halley states that he lives 5 miles below Piscattaway near Accokeek Chapel in P.G. Co., tract for chapel on south side Piscataway Creek, Christ Church, St. John's Parish

(Rsh.4 or Rsh.9) November 24, 1772 Court Session, P.G. Co., John Holley was appointed a Constable for the Rock Creek Hundred.

(Rsh.4) July 26, 1787, Book HH, folio 452, John Halley presented certificate for a black mare

North Carolina
<u>Crowan/Bertie Cos.,N.C.</u>

January 19, 1714, Book 1, pg. 1,2, Col. Wm. Maule brings before the Court four servant boys, Alexander Steel, age 15, John McCorkingdale, age 10, James Tyler, age 10, John Holley, age 9. John b. b. 1705

Virginia
Colonial Records
County not Recorded
<u>VSL</u>

Henry Hawley petitioned to keep a ferry at the mouth of Hampton River in Sequotan. Granted for his natural life, June 30, 1640

Counties
<u>VSL, Albermarle Co., Va.</u>

(Rsh.13 or Rsh. 54) August 26, 1841, Mary Ann Hawley of the County of Albermarle and Town of Milton of the one part, and Andrew McKee of the County and Town of Charlottesville of the other part and Thomas Hawley of the third part. Mary Ann Hawley in order to secure the payment of a debt to Thomas Hawley due by bond dated August 26, 1841 for the sum of $35.50 with legal interest thereon...and for the further consideration of the sum of one dollar in hand paid by the said Andrew McKee at the ensealing and delivery of these presents the receipt whereof is hereby acknowledged hath given, granted, bargained and sold, and by these presents doth grant, bargain and sell unto the said Andrew McKee...the following property to wit, one feather bed and furniture, five windsor chairs, one pair of flat irons, one folding table, two bedsteads, one spinning wheel, two butter pots...to have and to hold the said property unto the said Andrew McKee...that if the said Mary Ann Hawley shall ...and satisfy the said sum of money as aforesaid, then this indenture shall be null and void....but on default thereof it shall be lawful for the said Andrew McKee to sell the aforesaid property at the request of the said Thomas Hawley having duly advertised the time and place of sale for ten days or more at three or more public places signed Mary Ann Hawley, Andrew McKee, Thomas Hawley, witness Fontaine Walls, Henry M. Harlow, James C. Reiley

(?Rsh.54) Orphan Thomas Jones, Parent James W. Jones, August 7, 1843, security Lewis B. Bailey, October 1, 1845, January 6, 1851, James O. Hawley is a citizen of the County of Lewis, West, Virginia, note: B. Harlow also in Lewis, W.Va., in 1859

VSL, Alexandria, Va.
(Rsh.7) Book U, pg.362, January 21, 1793, William Halley of Alexandria frees two negro men, witness William Summers, John Butcher

VSL, Culpeper Co., Va.
(Rsh.52) Thomas Hawley land in Town of Fairfax, County of Culpeper, April 8, 1823

John A. Hawley, no Inher. Tax Report, Book 9, pg.375, January 24, 1928, (Rsh.52) John W. Hawley, Trustee Act., Book T, pg.277, December 17, 1855

(Rsh.52) John W. Halley, Book 12, pg.124, 1855

(Rsh.56) Charles M. Hawley sale made by James Barbour Trustee on April 22, 1856

VSL, Elizabeth City Co., Va.
(?Rsh.85) May 1642, Henry Hawley, Elizabeth City, Co.

(?Rsh.85) August 1642, Henry Hawley owes debt, it is ordered that an attachment shall issue against the state of Henry Hawley of the County of Elizabeth City, Co.

Fairfax Co., Va., C.H.
Court Orders, Part 2, 1754-1756, pg.501, May 18, 1756, Deed from John Halley and Mary, his wife, to Elizabeth their daughter.

(Rsh.3) 1783, Nathaniel Halley, def, vs. Thomas Stone, petition to pay 793 lbs. tobacco and costs, May 20, 1785, pg.145

(Rsh.7) September 18, 1787, William Halley, recommended Inspector at Alexandria Tobacco Warehouse. pg.448, Fairfax County Records 1783

(Rsh.7) March 20, 1787 to May 22, 1788, William Halley, Juror, Book 1783

(Rsh.5) 1795, Lib. X, pg.490, Barbara Radcliff to Edward Poller, Bond

June Court 1799, Deed from Nathan Halley, Matthew

Halley, William Halley to Alex. Smith, proved by James Keith, David Henderson, John Dundas and ordered certified to the County of Fauquier, to be recorded. June, Fairfax County Court Orders 1799-1800.

(Rsh.3) August 17, 1799, Court Records, Fairfax, Co., Va. William Hawley adm. of Nathaniel, dec'd, against Francis Stone and Daniel Lewis for 297.12.10

(Rsh.11) January 19, 1785, William Halley, Court Records Fairfax Co., Va., pg.108, paid 120 lbs tobacco by the County of Fairfax for a horse to carry a criminal to Richmond for 10 days at 12 lbs per diem.

(Rsh.11) October 20, 1785, William Halley, Fairfax Court Records 1783, pg.178, survey of road from the folks of the road below Saugsters to the mountain road by Halleys.

March 20, 1809, Elizabeth Halley, Plt. vs. John Stanhope and Coleman Lewis, two suits, Court Records Index, FFX Co., Va. NOTE: there are several other references for Elizabeth Halley that I have not recorded.

(Rsh.14), June 22, 1809, Barton D. Halley, vs. Samuel Adams, in debt to pay debt + one cent damage. Fairfax Co., Court Records, Index pg.116, Fairfax, Va.

(Rsh.11) July 21, 1829, William Hawley, Sr., Fairfax 1829 pg.87, to view way to alter the Gum Spring, Centreville Road on land of Gustavous H. Scott.

VSL, Fairfax Co., Va.

(Rsh.3) 1783 Nathaniel Hawley named in the Journals of the Council of the State of Virginia as being an Assistant Inspector at the Colchester Virginia Tobacco Warehouse. note: Colchester, Va., is across the Potomac River from Charles Co., Md.

VSL, Isle of Wight Co., Va.

December 10, 1694, Jury in the case of Mr. Robert Coleman and Malurk Hawley

August 9, 1694/95, Malluck Halley appoints Charles Chapman, his attorney, in suit with Mr. Robert Coleman, Matt Halley, signed with x

Mallachi Hawley, 1694 Deed, appt. John Giles his attorney, Isle of Wight Co.

Malcichi Hawley, November 15, 1694, Jury to settle affairs

between Robert Colman and Malcichi Hawley, Isle of Wight Co.

Malluch Hawley appoints Charles Chapman, Attorney to answer suit brought by Robert Colman, August 9, 1695, Isle of Wight Co.

Court April 9, 1694, Susanna Callaway vs. Mallucke Hawly, and Susanna Callaway vs. John Davis

Court Orders, 1695, Robert Coleman vs. Malluke Hawly

October 9, 1710, John Hole appoints Mr. Joseph Chapman as his attorney, John Hole

(?Rsh.136) March 6, 1711, Arthur Smith, John Hole and John Surley, witness, Richard Pugh, Nansemond Co., to John Gill of Isle of Wight Co., transfer of 100 acres

VSL, James City Co., Va.

(Rsh.113) Court, January 21, 1701/02, motion of Thos. Holly, Commissioner, of adm. on the estate of Abraham Knott, dec'd.

(Rsh.113) Court, March 17, 1707/08, Petition of Jane Holly, widow and relict of Thomas Holly, decd, adm. to her

Loudoun Co., Va., C.H.

(Rsh.9) August 18, 1791, Chancery Suit, M 2484, Loudoun Co., Va., year 1793, Hawley vs. Sears...John Hawley and his wife advanced in years (John was 54, old for 1793), children grown. Suit concerned purchase of black female slave named Tamor, who was purchased by Hawley from Sears, for 30 lbs, twelve shillings and 8 pence, contingent upon her living 18 months. William Bernard Sears had borrowed this amount from John Hawley and could not pay... Sears suggested the sale of slave whom he said was a house slave and well trained.... Hawley says she was a real handful, more trouble than any of his own children, and she came with one child and pregnant with another. The labor was very difficult and they had to get a midwife. She caught cold and d. leaving child 8 days old and now they have the two children to care for. Hawley requests that the two children be sold and the money applied toward settling his claim.

(Rsh.9) September 1809, Chancery M 2507, Turner vs. Turners exrs., Answer of John Hawley Executor of Fielding Turner dec'd...Fielding Turner left three children and another b. since his death...all infants under 21 years of age except Lewis Turner.

John Turner and James Hawley Turner are infants under 21 years of age by (Rsh.9) John Hawley, their grandfather and next friend, who was appointed guardian by the Court and qualified alone as Executor. Suit closed February 18, 1820, Loudoun Co., Va.

(Rsh.14), April 14, 1810, witnessed that James Turner paid money he owed John Hawley, Barton D. Hawley, Jachariah Halsey, James Turner.,LL #2, pg.332.

(Rsh.9) August 10, 1810, November 22, 1811, Chancery Record M. 1628, John Hawley sues John Hopwood regarding a promissory note for 8 lbs that Hopwood had given Hawley on August 10, 1810.

(Rsh.14), November 15, 1813, Barton D. Hawley and Coleman Lewis appointed guardian to James Turner, Orphan, Fairfax Co., Va., C.H., Liber K., pg.169

(Rsh.14), December 30, 1813, a purchase is made by Barton D. Hawley at the Public Auction of William James, Loudoun Co., Va.

(Rsh.9) October 15, 1816, Halley vs. Halley, Chancery M. 2120, Estate sale of movable property netted $1,327.72. Sale made February 12, 1816, disbursement made prior to 1816... now requests funds from sale to (Rsh.11) William Hawley, on February 24, 1819, of 105 acres for $700. Date on Jacket of this request is 1832. (Rsh.10) Absalom Halley and others vs. (Rsh.9) John Hally's exrs. Directed residue of estate be sold and proceeds divided between his children, which are named. We find each legatees part to be $447.49, total, we have examined and settled the above estate of (Rsh.9) John Hawley, dec'd, February 4, 1819, Book O. pg.488, Charles Lewis, Lewis Hutchison, Andrew Heath, James McKim and Robert Lathan

(Rsh.9) February 24, 1819, John Haley, dec'd, Executors James McKim of Loudoun Co., and Robert Latham of Prince William Co., to (Rsh.11) William Haley, of Fairfax 105 acres on west bank of Elk Licking Run for $700. Deed RR #2, F. 134, witness Wm. H. McKim, Wm. Ambler, Jr., Lewis Hutchinson, Thomas Hutchinson, Jermiah Hawley. Fairfax C.H., Fairfax, Va.

(Rsh.14) Chancery M721, November 8, 1819, Hawley et als vs. Heaths exrs., et als Loudoun Co., Va., Chancery Records, This suit involves proceeds of Andrew Heaths estate to children and grandchildren. Catherine Heath Hawley dec'd. in 1819, give and bequeath to Barton D. Hawley one dollar and no more, son Andrew, daus. Reuhannah McKim, Sarah James, and seven grandchildren by Catherine Hawley...daus. Reuhannah McKim, Sarah James and Lynda Heath, four children Andrew Heath, Reuhannah McKim, Sarah James and Lindia Heath, son in law James McKim, witness, Wm. James, Thomas Davis, Timothy Paget, Andrew Shelton Heath. It names the children of (Rsh.14) Barton D. Hawley and Catherine Heath Hawley as Andrew H. Hawley, Louisa Hawley who m. E.P. Church and survived him, Sarah M. Hawley, Lucinda Harris husband Chapin Harris, Lamech Hawley, Nelson H. Hawley, Malinda Hawley who intermarried with John Shoff and d., Andrew and Linda Heath live in the County of Loudoun as does Charles Lewis, Abel James who m. Sarah has heirs out of the state, Ames Skinner, James McKim who m. Rhuhannah departed this life and she m. Thomas Beck and they live in Warren Co., Va., personal estate of Andrew Heath $5,195.89

(Rsh.78) Chancery, M. 6759, Court August 25, 1827, Samuel Halley and John H. Hawley, Merchants and partners, trading under the firm of S. & J. H. Hawley, vs. Thomas Green, Sr., Nathan and Peter Skinner

(Rsh.9) August 1833, Bargain and Sale, (Rsh.11) Mary D. Hawley to John S. Wilson, 190 Acres. Loudoun Co., Va., C.H. Leesburg, Virginia

Note: John S. Wilson was the highest bidder at public auction held in 1833 with a bid at $604.50 for the 195 Acres, to be paid by 1/3 cash, 1/3 in 12 months, 1/3 in 18 months without interest.

(Rsh.14) M721, Hawley et. als, vs. Heaths exr., et als 1853, February 1837 pub. in newspaper, Andrew H. Hawley, Louisa Church, formerly Hawley, Lamech Hawley, John Shoff, survivor of John Shoff and Malinda his wife who was Malinda Hawley, Nelson H. Hawley and Sarah M. Hawley, vs. Jacob Summers, adm. of James McKim, dec., who was exr. of Andrew Heath dec., Abel James and Sarah his wife late Heath and others...

(Rsh.9) March 12, 1845, Chancery M 1155, Hawley vs. Hawley, Exhibit in file is as follows:
William Ambler who was to collect money from sale of 195 acres authorized to pay to the parties in suit moneys now in his hands and any that may hereafter come into his hands in the following manner to wit, 1/5 to heirs of (Rsh.11) William Hawley, 1/5 to heirs of (Rsh.12) Amos Hawley, 1/5 to heirs of (Rsh.10) Absalom

Hawley, 1/5 to heirs of (Rsh.13) Abraham Hawley, 1/5 to heirs of Elijah Legg and Tabitha his wife.

Note: evidently everyone was paid except heirs of William and Amos thus a second action in Oct. 1848 shown below.

(Rsh.9) May 30, 1845, Chanc. M1155, Loudoun Co., Va., Coleman Lewis vs. John S. Wilson, Fairfax Co., Va., Loudoun Co., Va., Chancery, Robert Ratcliff, Justice of the Peace, John S. Wilson, insolate debtor now in custody as a prisoner on a judgement against him at the suit of John Hunter, adm. of Coleman Lewis dec'd, which he is unable to discharge. He prays benefit of the act of the General Assembly made and provided for the relief of insolvent debtors...John S. Wilson. A schedule of the property of John S. Wilson insolvent debtor, real estate, (Rsh.9) "whatever interest I may have in a tract of land in this County, Fairfax, and Loudoun containing 195 acres," (original land of Rsh.9) personal property, none, mixed estate, none. To the Sheriff or Jailor of Fairfax Co... you are hereby commanded to release and set free John S. Wilson, having complied with direction of the General Assembly...The estate of Coleman Lewis was committed to the Sheriff of Fairfax at Dec. Court 1844.

(Rsh.11) July 27, 1848, M1155, wife Mary D. Hawley, William Ambler and Susan his wife and John S. Wilson

(Rsh.9) October, 1848, M 1155 orators and oratories respectfully represent to your honor that John Hawley late of the said county now dec'd by his last Will and Testament devised a certain tract of land in the County of Loudoun near the line between said County and the County of Fairfax, containing 195 acres of land to his **widow** Mary D. Hawley for her life and after her death to his heirs at law. The said John Hawley left, as his heirs at law after the death of his said widow, his five children, Absalom Hawley, Abraham Hawley, Tabitha Hawley who intermarried with Elijah Legg, Amos Hawley and William Hawley. The said William Hawley and Amos Hawley have since d..

(Rsh.11) William Hawley leaving as his heirs at law his children viz your oratories:

Elizabeth Hawley m. Jacob Zinn
Mary Hawley m. Thomas H. Davis
Ann Hawley m. James Hutchison
Jermiah Hawley
William Hawley
Susan Hawley m. William Ambler

(Rsh.12) Amos Hawley leaving as his heirs at law and representatives his widow, Elizabeth Hawley and:

> Ann Hawley m. William Carroll
> Elizabeth Hawley m. Benjamin Freeling
> Barton Hawley
> Thomas Hawley
> Amos Hawley
> Abraham Hawley
> Malinda Hawley m. Henry Minser
> Sarah Hawley m. Anthony Poling
> John Hawley
> Margaret Hawley m. John Welsh

Your orators and oratories state that after the death of the said Mary D. Hawley, in a suit between the heirs of John Hawley instituted in the County Court of Loudoun for the sale of said land, a sale was ordered at the August Court 1841. William Ambler made the sale to the said John Wilson for the sum of $604.50 1/3 in cash and 1/3 in 12 months and the balance in 18 months without interest, and the sale was confirmed by the 1845 Court. As of October 19, 1841 they have received nothing. September 18, 1858, Absalom Hawley and others (note a line is drawn through (Rsh.10) Absalom Hawley and others and this is changed to Elizabeth Hawley and others.

VSL, Lundenburg Co., Va.
(?Rsh.130) Justices of County Court of Lundenburg, Nicholas Hayle, year 1749

VSL, Middlesex Co., Va.
William Holley, son of Sarah Holley, widow, now m. Samuel Smitheman, late of Parish of Christ Church, Middlesex, by his own will put himself into apprenticeship with James Williams October 7, 1689, Book 2, pgs. 357, 359

VSL, Northumberland Co., Va.
(Rsh.92) 1641, Capt. William Hawley; March 1642, Capt. Wm. Hawley; April 1642, Capt. Wm. Hawley; May 1642, Capt. Wm. Hawley, August 1642, Capt. Wm. Hawley, July 1644, January 1643, Capt. William Hawley, Esq. of Northampton Co., Va., this bill Capt. William Hawley, Esq. of Northampton Co., to

pay or cause to be paid unto Capt. William Stone attorney of Samuel Chandler, by the last of April next ensuing in England where the said Stone shall appoint the other half in 1645, at the same time and place, I said Capt. Hawley do bind over my Negro Mingo, July 29, 1644, Signed and Sealed William Hawley, recorded November 1644, by Edwynn Conaway

(?Rsh.118) April 3, 1647, Thomas Hayles, by bill, due to James Claughton's estate

(Rsh.118) Tho Orly, who intends, God willing, to go to foreign land this shipping, gives oath, Northumberland Orders 1650-1652

(?Rsh.118) Court of 1651, Mr. John Hollowes, agt. Thomas Hailes, cause to be referred to next court

(?Rsh.118) January 17, 1651, Deposition of Thomas Hale, age 50 or thereabouts, Thomas Hale, his Mark, Thomas Shepard, age 30 or thereabouts, swear answer that what Thomas Hale doth say to be true, Thomas Shepard, his mark, witness, John Trussel, William Presly

(Rsh.118) January 21, 1651 Thomas Orlye gives deposition

(?Rsh.118) November 7, 1651, witness that I Thomas Hailes do owe John Hayney 1340 lbs. of good sound well condition tobacco...I Thomas Hayle...

(?Rsh.118) Thomas Hale, age 50 years or thereabouts, January 17, 1651, Northampton Co.

(?Rsh.118) March 10, 1652, Thomas Hailes, age 44 years, or thereabouts, said that when he lived with Mr. Trussel he heard him say...signed Tho. Hailes, his mark

(?Rsh.118) Thomas Haile, signs oath to Commonwealth of England, April 13, 1652, note: preceding entry, appears two of the same name who signed, possibly father and son, Northampton Co.

(?Rsh.118) May 1652, Thomas Hailes acknowledged unto Mr. Thomas Speake, 300 lbs. tobacco

(?Rsh.118) Lee Hugh, agt. of Thomas Hailes

(?Rsh.118) October 23, 1652, know that I Thomas Hailes, of Youcomico, in the County of Northumberland and Colony of Virginia, Planter, do give for my mark of hoggs and cattle, he made mark, that indicated a T and H together.

(?Rsh.118) September 20, 1653, deposition of Greshon Cromwell that Thomas Hailes, showing 2 heads unto passep and indian...

(Rsh.118) Thomas Orlye, November 12, 1653, gives mark for cattle

(?Rsh.118) John Hull, November 20, 1654, gives deposition about heifer going into John Hailes fence

(Rsh.83) Order Book 2, Northumberland Co., deposition in year 1662, Edward Hawley named himself as a son of James Hawley

James Hawley, Juror, July 20, 1654, Northumberland Co.

July 29, 1654, more commissioners nominated, Mr. Richard Cole, Mr. James Hawley and Mr. Wm.Reynolds, Northumberland Co.

(?Rsh.118) Thomas Hayles, Hales, judgment to Hugh Lee, signed Tho Hailes, his mark, Northumberland Co.

(?Rsh.118) Alice Shaw against Tho. Haile, Haile is ordered to pay her 50 lbs. tobacco for witness for Tho Halle against Anthony Linton, Northumberland Co.

(?Rsh.118) Thomas Hales, signs oath to Commonwealth of England, March 26, 1655

(Rsh.83) James Hawley, Market Places Appointed, July 21, 1655, Northumberland Co.

(Rsh.83) November 1655, Mrs. Hawley gives oath for abused servant age 12, Northumberland Co.

(Rsh.83) Mr. Jas Hauley, Juror, June 1655, Northumberland Co.

(Rsh.83) 1655, Mrs. Ann Hauley, age 40 years, or thereabouts, b. c. 1615, Northampton Co.

(Rsh.83) Mr. James Hauley, land in Wico River, adj. Jno Johnson, June 4, 1655, Northampton Co.

(Rsh.83) Mr. James Hauley, witness agreement Kingwell and Essex, November 20, 1655, Northampton Co.

(Rsh.83) November 1655, Mr. James Hawley took oath of Peter Knight, Northumberland Co.

(?Rsh.118) Thomas Hayles, age 50 years, or thereabouts, b. c. 1605, says upwards of 7 years ago he had 100 acres surveyed adjacent Wm. Reynolds, January 20, 1656, Northampton Co.

(Rsh.83) Mr. James Haule, transfers guardianship of Elis Perry to Abraham Joyce who m. her sister, September 20, 1658, Northampton Co.

(Rsh.83) Mr. James Hauley, gift to grandchild Elizabeth

Knight, February 15, 1660, Northampton Co.

George Hale, above 60 years, exempt from levy, July 22, 1661, Northampton Co.

(Rsh.83) Mr. James Hauley and his son Edward live out of the county, Mr. Peter Knight to take their depositions, October 8, 1662, Northampton Co.

(Rsh.118) George Harding of London, Citizen and Grocer, September 22, 1664, with wife Mary, dau. of Thomas Orley of London and his wife Anne, late of Cherry Point in Potomack, ..to demand from Rebecca Orley, late wife and exr. of the Will of said Thomas Orley and from Wm. Jolling of Cherry Point her now husband...search the Register Church Booke of the Parish of St. Mary White Chapel did find that the above declared Mary Orley, dau. of Thomas and Anne Orley was bapt. on the 25th day of April 1622, dated London September 29, 1664.

(?Rsh.130) Mr. Nicholas Hale requests satisfaction of Walter Price for entertaining his runaway servant, January 11, 1668, Northampton Co.

(Rsh.71) Northumberland Co., Thomas Orley, appointed Constable, June 22, 1669

?Jurors, November 9, 1675, recorded November 21, 1677, Charles Hoyle, Rice Hoe, Wm. Langford, Northumberland Co.

(Rsh.85) January 1677, Henry Hayly, aged 34 years, (b.c. 1644), Northumberland Co.

(Rsh.113) Petition of Jane Holly, widow and relicit of Thomas Holly, dec'd. Adm. to her, Court March 17, 1707/08, Northumberland Co

Thomas Hally, presented for swearing 21 oaths, January 21, 1713, Northampton Co.

VSL, Rappahannock Co., Va.

April 25, 1674, Thomas Beale, Jr., Rappahannock Co., appoint Major Isaack Allerton, my attorney, to acknowledge unto (Rsh.82) Edward Hawley my right of land which Hawley bought of Randolph Kirle

VSL: Shenandoah Co., Va.

Records, 1787-1814, year 1787, witness John Hawley, for Sarah Edmonds, widow, she is 75 years old

<u>VSL, Stafford Co., Va.</u>

(?Rsh.119) Court Orders, August 23, 1667, Capt. Giles Brent against John Jayle, Hale

(?Rsh.119) Court Orders, year 1689, pg.6, John Haley humbly complaining that sometime in October of last year your Orator upon coming to the house of Joseph Eyros in this Country, Eyros did offer to employ him and to Maul Rayles did make many fine promises...Haley did work..and did not receive the plantation offered him...Eyros intended wholly to deceive your Orator having not really any such plantation, he took Orators mare from him which he now withholds...and did use your Orator very unworthy threatening to have him wisp out of the Parish not allowing him one thing for his work and also retains the said mare, referred to Chancery, March 10, 1689

(?Rsh.119) Court Orders, pg.14, July 20, 1689, Robert Brent, Apprentice or Indenture, John Hall, Halle

(Rsh.107) November 1704, Stafford Co., Va., Henry Halley, Jr., age 25 or thereabouts, (b.c. 1679) with Joseph Carr, aged 45, declare that Christopher Woolcock, came to the house of Henry Hally, Sr., about April 1, 1704 and sickened and d.

(Rsh.119) Grantors, January 9, 1706, Elizabeth Halley, Hayley, gift to Catherine Saven, with husband's consent, 1 heifer, 3 years old, witness, James Ree, Judith Ree, Book Z. pg.360

<u>VSL, Westmoreland Co., Va.</u>

(Rsh.83) March 11, 1662, Juror, James Hawly, Nicholas Lansdowne, Westmoreland Co.

(Rsh.83) March 11, 1662, James Hawly doe acknowledge, Westmoreland Co.

(?Rsh.126) April 27, 1664, April 20, 1660 verdict of Jury, against Fran: Hales, title of land, Hales pleads the Statute of 5 Edward III, Hales alleged that he hath had the land in possession ever since April 20, 1660, land confirmed unto Francis Hales August 28, 1661, Westmoreland Co.

(Rsh.83) April 7, 1664, names Maggregger hath served Mr. James Hawly with a scire facias, Westmoreland Co.

(Rsh.83) August 31, 1664, Juror, James Hawly, Westmoreland Co.

(Rsh.81) January 3, 1667, acknowledged by John Samewaies, attorney of James Hawlye, Westmoreland Co.

(Rsh.82) February 25, 1668, Articles of Incorporation

between Henry Hawlye and Samll. Mumms...All things, lands, goods, chattels, profits, or commodities that either hath remain for the future in the corporation until either of them shall be minded to part and when either of them shall think fit all land goods, cattle, and hogs be equally divided between them. It may be lawful for either party at his death to dispose of his part, signed Henry Hawly, Henry (X) Mumms, Westmoreland Co.

(Rsh.81) February 2, 1669, articles of agreement, to William Bishopp and Mary Lansdon, Langsdoun, daughter in law of Patrick Spence, witness James (X) Hawlye, Samll. Bonam, Westmoreland Co.

(Rsh.82) February 28, 1670, Nicholas Jenkings of Copely Parish, Westmoreland, appoint wife Amie Jenkings, my attorney, witness Edward (X) Hawlye, Westmoreland Co.

(Rsh.81) Mary Lucas, the wife of Jacob Lucas, make my father James Hawlye my attorney to acknowledge my third of 200 acres which he liveth upon in Nomeni unto Lewis Markam, signed Mary (X) Lucas, Westmoreland Co.

(Rsh.81) March 15, 1670, Jacob Lucas of Copely Parish, Westmoreland Co., Planter unto Lewis Markeham, 200 acres, head of Valley falling into Nominie River, to Capt. John Lee's land, granted to Jacob Lucas by Mr. James Hawley, by Deed January 3, 1667, witness James Hawley, March 15, 1670, James Hawly, attorney of Mary Lucas

(Rsh.81) March 15, 1670, Bond of Jacob Lucas and James Hawly, of Copely Parish, Westmoreland Co., unto Lewis Markam for 18,000 lbs. tobacco, signed Jacob Lucas, James Hawlye

(Rsh.81, Rsh.82, Rsh.85) May 30, 1671, Henry Hawlye unto Elizabeth Lucas, dau. to Jacob Lucas, one brown heifer cropt and underkeeled of the left ear with a staple in right ear, Henry (X) Hawly, witness, Michael Willington, Joan Webb, Westmoreland Co.

(Rsh.82) August 30, 1671, deposition of Edward Hawlye, aged 26 years or thereabouts, (b. 1645), regarding George Richmond and Mr. Barrett, Westmoreland Co.

(Rsh.82) September 1, 1671, sworn Court statement regarding Mr. Nurse, signed Edward (X) Hawlye, Westmoreland Co.

November 19, 1673, Anne Rust, and Bridgett Earle, appoint loving friend George Hales my attorney..., Westmoreland

Co.

(Rsh.81) 1674, Jacob Lucas, aged 33 or thereabout, (b.c.1641) being at Capt. Hull's with Mr. Hawley, heard Col. Hull declare the same as above expressed, Westmoreland Co.

(Rsh.81), pg.189, June 25, 1674, James Hawly, aged 46 or thereabout, (b.1628), saith that your deponent went to Capt. Hull's last March, was seven years having a tract of land at the head of Nominy which Capt. Hull pretended a title to.... Westmoreland Co.

November 27, 1675, Daniell Holly ordain my friend George Southen my attorney in all cases betwixt myself and the estate of Mrs. Washington, Westmoreland Co.

(Rsh.83) November 21, 1677, Enis Whit, and Morgan Jones of Westmoreland Co., make agreement, witnessed: James Hawley, Christopher Colwill

Jacob Lucas is named as a tutor of Ann Hawley in 1682, Westmoreland Co., complains that John Manly and Patrick Spence are bound to indenture made to Edward Hawley which they deny to perform. Order Book

(Rsh.83) deposition of James Hawley and his son Edward Hawley in Westmoreland Co., by Peter Knight

(Rsh.85) April 8, 1691, Henry Hawley acknowledged sale of land to Arthur King, Mary Hawley wife of the said Henry relinquished her dower, Westmoreland Co.

July 26, 1693, Andrew Munrow presented a man servant named Dann Hayle and prayed judgment of his age. The Court do adjudge him eighteen years of age, Westmoreland Co.

(Rsh.85) November 1, 1694, Judgment granted to (Rsh.81) Jacob Lucas attorney of Henry Hawley against John Bolton, Clerk, and Frances his wife, for 900 lbs. tobacco due for housing by him (Henry Hawley) built on the plantation late of Mr. Thomas Kirton, dec'd, Westmoreland Co.

October 25, 1699, John Hailes confessed judgment to Samll. Nockles for 667 lbs. tobacco, Westmoreland Co.

April 1699, Juror, John Hailes, Westmoreland Co.

Mr. Anthony Jones his receipt of Bills due Mr. Fawknor, a list of Bills due to be paid as followeth... for Mr. Hawley for plantation, 0600 and Ca, Westmoreland Co.

February 26, 1707, Cornelius Harlee gives for his mark of cattle.., Westmoreland Co.

English
Coldham, Records, VSL, MdHR
Barbados
1635
Robert Haxley, April 3, 1635, Passengers on the Falcon of London, bound to Barbados: Robert Haxley, age 21

1636
Capt. Henry Hawley, September 10, 1636, Barbados is inhabited by 6,000 English but the Governor, Capt. Henry Hawley, would not provide arms.

Indentured
1659
Frances Hales, 1659, of Salisburg, (Wilts), to Edward Thornebury, 5 years Barbados
1660
James Hallie, May 25, 1660, seaman to Martha, wife of Thomas Braine, grocer, 4 years Barbados by Ship Dolphin
1664
Anthoney Holley, January 26, 1664, to John Webb, 3 years Barbados
1678
January 18, 1678, James Hallings to Owen, 5 years Barbados in the Ship Arthur and Mary

Prisoners
1664
Christopher Hawley, year 1664, February 19, and May 21, Norfolk Circuit prisoner reprieved to be transported to Barbados and America: Christopher Hawley of Exning reprieved for Barbados February 1664
1677
Mary Hawley, March 3, 1677, Newgate prisoners to be transported to Barbados, London, Mary Hawley, spinster, alias wife of Richard Hawley.
Mary Hawley, reprieved, for Barbados, March 1677

1679

Oliver Hawley, July 19, 1679, home circuit prisoners
reprieved to be transported to Barbados or
Jamaica...Kent: Oliver Hawley of Charlton.

1686

Joseph Hoyle, February 23, 1686, Oxford Circuit prisoners
reprieved to be transported to Jamaica, Barbados
or Bermuda, Staffordshire, Joseph Hoyle of
Uttoxeter

Edward Hawley, February 24, 1686, Newgate prisoners
reprieved to be transported to Barbados or
Jamaica, ...Mary Fisher alias wife of William
Fisher, Edward Hawley, Robert Brookes, Richard
Osborne...

No port listed

Joseph Hawley of Great Gaddesden, chimney sweep,
sentenced, October 1765

note: Penalties for very minor crimes were severely harsh and
the jails were cruel places to be. In the English records of
complaints from prisoners one citation, from the Virginia Colonial
Records Project, dated May 20, 1636 of Francis Potts in Fleet
Prison to the Privy Council, heard at the Star Chamber, Mr. Potts
states that he "has neither means nor friends. Requests to be set
at liberty to prevent him from famine and infection." Often
prisoners were sent to the Colonies rather than remain in jail.
One could be jailed for losing one's entire family and being alone,
not having money for food, etc.

Indentured
No Port Listed

William Halling, July 5, 1661, to William Jelfe, 4 years,
Nevis

Jamaica

Thomas Haley, 1746, February 4, apprenticed from
Christ's Hospital to his mother Elizabeth Garry to
serve Mr. Richard Bateman of Jamaica, Merchant.

note: Servants were often hard working individuals, and were
frequently educated and had trades, but they lacked the money

for passage to the Colonies. In October of 1640 the Maryland Legislature passed an order stipulating that the servant was entitled to "one good Cloth Suite of Jersey or Broadcloth, a Shift of white linen, one pair of Stocking and Shoes, two hoes, one axe, 3 barrels of Corn and fifty acres of land, five whereof at least to be plantable, for his time of service."

MdHR   Colonies

Maryland
1633

(Rsh.90) Jerome Hawley, 1633, Ship Ark, St. Mary's Co.
(Rsh.89) Gabriel Hawley, 1633, Ship Dove, St. Mary's Co.
1640

Thomas Hales, Isle of Kent, by Wm. Clayborne, Liber 1,
        Warrants, pg. 85
(Rsh.92) William Hawley, as early as 1640, see land
        records
1649

Wm. Hawley, February 25, 1649, see land records
Nicholas Hawley, see land records
1650

Robert Hawley, Cecil Co., Robert Hawley, September 1,
        1650, self, on condition 1636, see land records
1652

William Haile, Calvert Co., see land records
1658

Bernard Hawley, Liber 6, folio 95, transported 1658
1665

Hercules Hayle, Provencial Ct. Liber FF, pg. 115, declares
        for England
1668

John Hayles, Hailes, Co. of St. Mary's does declare his
        mark of cattle, Provincial Court, Liber FF, pg. 740
1671

James Harle, Dorchester Co., 50 acres, July 12, 1672,
        Warrants and Assignments, Vol. 18, pg. 127
(Rsh.79) Clement Helley of St. Mary's Co., on 4th day of
        May 1675, Clement Helley, of St. Mary's Co.,
        Planter, due 50 acres of land for time of service
        performed to Mark Blumfield, Bramfield,

Bacarnfield, Warrants and Assignments, Vol. 18, pgs. 310, 311

1673
Jasper Howley, proved right to 100 acres, Warrants and Assignments, Liber 15, folio

James Harle, July 12, 1673, Dorchester Co., Warrants and Assignments

1674
Spencer Hales, Will, Calvert Co., Liber 7, pg. 369, St. Marys, March 20, 1674

1676
Oliver Haile, Baltimore Co.

1678
Jasper Howley, December 16, 1678, transported himself and Ann Paritis, see land records

1679
Giles Hawley, Liber WC2 folio 50, 57, transported

1688
Nicholas Hailes, Maryland Rent Rolls, Baltimore and Anne Arundal, pgs. 93, 96, 97, June 29, 1688, 105 Acres, Patapsco Hundred

1693
Thomas Haley, Vestryman, St. John's Parish, alias Copely Parish, Dr. Allen's minutes, First Parishes of the Province of Md.

1694
Nicholas Haile, Hale, Hailes, see land records

Wm. Haley, Cecil Co., see land records

Darbey Haley, in Dorchester Co., TP18A, pg. 62, TP15C, pg. 139

1697
Darby Haly, Cecil Co., see land records

1719
Martha Hawley, sentenced February 1719, of Worcester, to Annapolis, Maryland, June 1719

Virginia

VSL and LC   ### 1624
John Haule, defendant in trial regarding hog killing on sabbath at John Johneson's house. Minutes

Christopher Hawle, deposition regarding sow of Capt.

Powells which Dr. Potts killed. Minutes
1625
Christopher Haule, Land joining Thomas Passmoure,
James City Island. Minutes
1626
John Haule, and wife Bridgett Haule, entered into real
estate mortgage with John Passmoure, Minutes
Thomas Haule and John Tyus. Minutes
1630
Public Records Office, London, Delegates Examination, Vol. 2,
Baltimore vs. Leonards
(Rsh.90) Gabriel Hawley, of London, Gent., under oath, in
the year 1635, states that he is 34 years old, and
that he has lived in London 5 years and before
that in Virginia 10 months, and before that in
London 5 or more years. This would place the
date of his arrival in Virginia c. 1630.
VSL and Coldman   1635
John Hales, July 24, 1635, Persons to be transported
from London to Virginia by the Ship Assurance,
John Hales, age 21, Henrie Haler, age 22,
Richard Lucas, age 16, William Coleman, age 16,
John Roberts, age 46
Merciful, Mournful, Halley, June 24, 1635, transported by
Capt. Adam Thoroughwood, in Ship Africa. note:
this name is found among women's names.
Richard Halley, October 3, 1635 Shippers in Ship
Paradise, bound from London for Virginia; Henry
Lucas, James Carey, Richard Halley, proceedings
190/115/1
Henry Hawley, age 34, August 21, 1635, transported to
Virginia, in the Ship Globe of London, b. 1601;
George Hawley, age 17, b. 1618
George Hawley, John Hale, August 7, 1635, Persons to
be transported from London to Virginia on the
Ship Globe, Edward Lewes, age 21, William
Talbott age 14, George Hawley, age 17, Edward
Hodgskynns age 21, William Saunders age 19,
John Hale, age 14, William Lewes, age 25
Henry Hawley, August 21, 1635, Persons to be
transported from London to Virginia by the Ship

George, Henry Hawley, age 34

Henry Hawley, age 34, Ship Safety, year 1635, b. 1602

Robert Hely, year 1635, transported by Mr. Willis Heyly
Accomac Co., Va.

Eleanor Heyly, year 1635, transported by Mr. Willis Heyly

Wm. Heyly, year 1635, transported by David Mansell,
James City Co., Va.

1636

Henry Hawley, Trader, in Virginia, from Isle of Kent, Md.

Jo: Halley trans. by Wm. Justice, Charles City Co., Va.

Joseph Hally, July 20, 1636, transported by James Berry,
along with wife Elizabeth Berry and Henry Lee,
Mary Nelson, Mary Nablett, Robert Man, Accomac
Co.

Lewis Hale, year 1636, transported by John Gater,
Elizabeth Co., Va.

1637

Susan Halle, year 1637, transported by Capt. Thomas
Panlett, Charles City Co., Va.

John Hely, year 1637, transported by Wm. Farrar, Henrico
Co., Va.

Willi Hely, year 1637, transported by David Mansell,
James City Co., Va.

1638

Jer. Hayles, year 1638, transported by Edward Sparshott,
Charles City Co., Va.

George Hayle, year 1638, transported by John Poteet,
Charles River Co., Va.

Barbary Hole, year 1638, transported by Edward Hill,
Charles City Co., Va.

1641

Ann Hale, year 1641, transported by Thomas Morrey, Isle
of Wight Co., Va.

James Hawley, (Rsh.83) 300 ac., Isle of Wight Co., Va.,
April 22, 1641, his wife Ann, and children, Francis,
Ann, Alice, and John Foster and Richard Darliman

1642

(?grandson of Rsh.89) year 1642, Gabriel Hawley,
apprentice pavier to William Hawley in Virginia.
Draper's Company +266, Quarterage Book,
Draper's Hall, London, E.C. 2, Emigrants to

Virginia, Survey Report 994
Lyonell Holley, Hawley, year 1642, by John Robins
1643
James Hawley, from England, 1643, Isle of Wight
Co., Va.
Erwin Heily, year 1643, transported by John Freeme,
Charles Co., Va.
John Hely, year 1643, transported by Benjamin Harryson,
Gentleman, James City Co., Va.
Nathan Haies, year 1643, transported by Robert Haies,
Lower Norfolk Co., Va.
Alex Haies, year 1643, transported by Robert Haies,
Lower Norfolk Co., Va.
Isabel Haies, year 1643, transported by Thomas Frye,
James City Co., Va.
Leonard Hawly, Hawley, April 17, 1643 by Richard Kemp,
Esq. James City Co., Va.
1645
Nico. Hayle, year 1645, transported by Mark Johnson,
Elizabeth City, Co., Va.
1648
James Hawley, Richard Hawley, transported April 9, 1648,
by John Landman, Nansemond Co., Va.
1650
John Holley transported 1650 by Capt. Moore Fautleroy
1651
James Hale, year 1651, by Capt. Stephen Gill,
Northumberland Co., Va.
Barbara Hayles, year 1651, transported by John
Rookwood, Gent, Northumberland Co., Va.
John Haies, Hailes, transported, September 16, 1651,
Northampton Co., Va., by (?Rsh.118) Thomas
Hales and Thomas Shepphard, others transported
were William James, John Elcock, Fra. Barnes,
Henry Grey, Thomas Morecock
1652
Tho Hale, year 1652, transported by Richard Longe
Tho. Hale, year 1652, transported by Richard Hill,
Northampton Co., Va.
Tyomll, Tyomell, Holly, Holley transported 1652 by Mr.
George Foster, Northumberland Co., Va.

1653

Edw. Hale, year 1653, transported by Col. Wm. Clayborne
Eliza Haies, year 1653, transported by Capt. Robert Abrall
(?grandson of Rsh.89) year 1653, Gabriel Hawley,
> apprentice pavier to William Hawley, in Virginia.
> Draper's Company +267 Quarterage Book,
> Draper's Hall, London, E.C. 2, Emigrants to
> Virginia, Survey Report No. 995

John Hawley transported by John Barten, March 1653,
> Elizabeth City Co., Va.

Nicholas Hale, (?Rsh.130) year 1653, transported by John
> Maddison, Gloucester Co.. Va.

Nathan Hale, year 1653, transported by James Turner
Thomas Orley, (Rsh.118) there is a note that he was
> transported twice, (this is possibly father and son)
> October 13, 1653, by Thomas Keene, land upon
> Cherry Point, in Northumberland Co., Va.

1654

William Hallyson, year 1654, transported by John Wyre,
> John Gillet, Andrew Gibson and John Phillipps

Jno. Haling, year 1654, transported by Randall Chamblett
James Haly, (Rsh.83) year 1654, Anne his wife, Fra., Ann,
> and Alice his children by Peter Knight,
> Northumberland Co., Va.

Barbara Hayles, year 1654, Barbara Hayles, transported
> by Lt. Col. Giles Brent, Westmoreland Co., Va.

1655

James Hawley, (Rsh.83) James Hawley, 1655,
> Northumberland Co., Va.

Elizabeth Haies, year 1655, transported by John Dorman,
> Northampton Co., Va.

Ann Haies, year 1655, transported by John Dorman,
> Northampton Co., Va.

1656

James Hawly, (Rsh.83) Ann his wife and 3 children,
> transported by Mr. Peeter Knight, October 1656,
> Elizabeth City Co., Va.

John Holly, Halley, 1656, transported by Major Wm. Lewis

1657

Susan Orly and Rebecca Orly, (?Rsh.118) March 13, 1657
> trans. by James Hawley, Northumberland Co., Va.

Margaret Hally, October 10, 1657, transported by Maurice
    Rose of Charles City Co., Va.
1661
James Hawley, 1661, Northumberland Co., Va.
1662
Thomas Holly, (?Rsh.128) transported by Henry Corbyn,
    September 10, 1662, by Henry Corbyn, Lancaster
    Co., Va.
Arthur Holly, transported by William Dudley, November
    12, 1662, Lancaster Co., Va.
Andrewe Hagley, March 11, 1662, persons transported
    into Country, Westmoreland Co., Va.
1663
Joyce Hales, Fra. Hailes, James Hailes, transported by
    Francis Heale and William Heabert, February 9,
    1663
James Hawley, 1663, Rappahannock Co., Va.
Joyce Hales, Fra. Hailes, James Hailes, transported
    February 9, 1663, by Francis Heale and William
    Heale, land between Potomac and Rappahannock
    Rivers.
Edward Hawley and Thomas Hawley, September 25,
    1663, transported by Mary Fortson, land on w.
    side of Paspentanke River, others transported are
    Edward Moulson, Sarah Samwayes
1664
John Harle, October 13, 1664, to Ann Butcher, 7 years,
    Virginia
James Hawley, 1664, Northumberland Co., Va.
Robert Halley transported by Howell Pryse, Charles City
    Co., Va.
1665
John Holly, 1665, transported, Isle of Wight Co., Va.
Thomas Holly, 1665, transported
1666
William Orly, transported, by John Davis, April 5, 1666,
    land in Accomac Co., Va., s. side Potomac River
James Hawley, 1666, Northumberland Co., Va.
James Hawley, 1666, Lancaster Co., Va.
1667
Edward Halley transported by Thomas Dyas and Richard

Granger, April 15, 1667, land between Potomac
and Rappahannock Rivers, also William Bayle was
transported

1668

Henry Hawlley transported September 26, 1668, by Col.
Wm. Kendall, land at Magette Bay, also
transported were Wm. Benefield, Ann Man,
Thomas Lucas, John Simpson and Mordecay
Evens

Obediah Hollys, Court, September 9, 1668, Certification to
John Pine for transportation

1669

John Holly, transported May 12, 1669, by Mr. George
Moore, land in Isle of Wight Co., Va.

1670

Richard Hally, September 12, 1670, to William Gorst, 4
years in Virginia by Ship Unicorn, apprenticed in
Bristol: others to William Gorst, Thomas Wootten,
John Wootten

Henry Howle, Hawley, transported by Col. Wm. Kendall,
Accomac Co., October 6, 1670, along with
Mordica Evens, Ann Man, Thomas Lucas, John
Simpson

1671

Mr. Robert Hawley, June 23, 1671, in the Ship James of
York; for Hull, carrying Virginia Tobacco

1673

Henry Hawley, trans. December 15, 1673, by John
Dorwood, New Kent Co., Va., with Mathew Price

1674

William Hawley transported, February 18, 1674, New Kent
Co., Va., by William Hernden

John Halley, transported by Mr. Richard Whitehead, April
8, 1674, New Kent Co., Va., with Thomas Amy

Henry Hawley, transported October 27, 1674, along with
Wm. and Mary Kendall, son and dau. to Wm.
Kendall, and John Simpson, Thomas Lucas,
Mordica Evens, Accomac Co., Va.

1677

Thomas Harly, July 5, 1677, to Jasper Jenkins, 4 years
Virginia, by Ship Susanna

1679

Thos. Holley, (Rsh.113) Court, February 18, 1679/80,
  Certification to Thos. Matthew for transportation of
  Thos. Holley from England

Anthony Hawley, transported, July 15, 1679, by Mr. John
  Pate and Mr. Robert Beverly, land on n. side
  Mappapony run

William Holly, transported by Richard Robinson,
  Middlesex Co., Va.

1680

John Hailes, transported by Richard Clarke, July 10,
  1680, New Kent Co., Va.

1682

William Hawly, transported September 22, 1682, by
  Thomas Bowry, James City Co., Va.

1683

Rac. Hailes, transported, April 16, 1683, by William Byrd,
  Nansemond Co., Va.

1686

Elizabeth Holly, transported April 27, 1686, by Samuell
  Bridgewater, Henrico Co., Va., Varina Parish,
  along with John Darby

1693

Richard Hailes, transported, April 29, 1693, by Capt.
  Joshua Storey

William Holly, transported April 29, 1693 by Mr. Robert
  Thompson, Henrico Co. near Falling Creek

1696

Thomas Harley, headright of Capt. Jno Haynie, July 15,
  1696

1699

Morris Haley, October 26, 1699, transported by John
  Higeson, Higgeston, New Kent Co., Va., St.
  Peter's Parish

1701

Joshua Haley, April 25, 1701, transported by William
  Winstone, Winston, King and Queen Co., Va.

1703

Antho. Haley, April 24, 1703, transported by William
  Temple, Charles City Co., Va.

Richard Halle, October 23, 1703, transported by

Honorable Edmund Jenings, Esq. King William
Co., Va.

Edward Hayles, October 23, 1703, transported by Thomas
Perring, Perrin, King William Co., Va.

1705

William Holly, May 2, 1705, transported by David Bray,
Richard Wharton, Henry Lightfoot and Robert
Ambrose, Essex and King and Queen Cos., Va.

1714

Daniel Hayley, June 16, 1714, transported by Andrew
Ross, Nansemond Co., Va.

John Haley, December 16, 1714, transported by Thomas
Standley, New Kent Co., Va., St. Paul's Parish

1716

Morris Haley, October 31, 1716, transported by John
Higginson, New Kent Co., Va.

1717

John Hales, July 15, 1717, transported by Richard Smith,
Sr., Prince George Co., Va.

(?Rsh.136) John Hally, July 15, 1717, and John Scott,
transported by Joseph Cutchins, of Nansemond
Co., Va.

no date

(?Rsh.118) Thomas Orly, transported by Col. William
Clayborne, land on Pamunkey on n. side of York
River

K.   LAND RECORDS

Land Grants, Patents, Deeds
with no County noted
Maryland

MdHR

(Rsh.92) Section 8, February 25, 1649, Capt. Wm. Hawley, 50 ac. to Henry Spink, as servant bought by him of (Rsh.130) Nicholas Hawley

(Rsh.40) Section 11, Robert Hawley for transporting himself in 1648 land near South River, Smith Branch: Robert Hawley, witness, September 1, 1650

(Rsh.92) William Hawley, land in St. Nicholas Hundred

(Rsh.83) James Hawley, Liber 7, folio 471, of Virginia acquired land in Maryland in 1664

Counties

MdHR, Baltimore Co., Md.

(Rsh.130) Nicholas Haile, Hale, Haile's Adventure, 56 acres, November 10, 1695, Book 40, pg.512

(Rsh.130) Nicholas Haile, Hale, Hale's Fellowship, 200 acres, November 10, 1695, Book 39, pg.51

(Rsh.130) Nicholas Hale, Haile, Hale's Folly, 100 acres, 1704, Book C.D.4, pg.167

(Rsh.130) Nicholas Hale, Haile, Mount Pleasant, 150 acres, January 10, 1706, Book DD5, pg.201, Book PL2, pg.136

(Rsh.130) Nicholas Hale, Haile, Haile's Forest, 100 acres, November 19, 1730, Book PL7, pg.569, Book ILB, pg.276

(Rsh.130) Nicholas Haile, Mishack's Garden, 200 acres, January 8, 1745, Book PT2, pg.159

Neal Haile, Forest, 278 acres, May 30, 1746. Book LGC, pg.561

(Rsh.130) Nicholas Haile, Jr., Haile's Adventure, 100 acres, May 22, 1747, Book LGC, pg.704, Book BT, pg.251

MdHR, Calvert Co., Md.

(?Rsh.92) William Haile, Calvert, Haile's Adventure, 150 acres, March 8, 1652, Book 24, pg.398, Book 29, pg.398

(?Rsh.92) William Haile, Calvert, Haile's Rest, 200 acres, February 8, 1682, Book 24, pg.362, Book 31, pg.494

MdHR, Cecil Co., Md.

(Rsh.40) Section 27, March 1650, 300 acres, North side of Potomac River near Hampton Creek, assigned to Robert Robins, Robert Hawley, Sgt., Richard Nevell, Cecil Co., Md.

(Rsh.92) May 1676. WRC#1, 1676-1699, Hawley, deposition, folio 632, 633; pg.7, Wm. Haley to George Warner, Cecil Co., sells land south side St. Cleers Creek, being part of a Manor laid out for Capt. Wm. Haly, Wm. Haley to John Deurllen, May 1676

Darby Haly, Cecil Co., Chance, 200 acres, December 7, 1697, Book 37, pg.528

(?Rsh.40 descendant or ?Rsh.90 or ?92 descendant) Robert Holly Holly's Expedition, 100 acres, June 10, 1727, PL6/536;OLA/696, PL7= patents 640 pgs. microfilm sr7466.ILB =certificates 508 pgs. microfilm sr7471 7471

(?Rsh.40) Robert Holly (Holy), Cecil Co., Confusion 220 acres, January 12, 1731, Patents 18, 205

(?Rsh.40) Robert Holly, Cecil Co., Md., Holy's Chance 68 acres March 18, 1747 by 2/535 by 2=patents 1747-1751 sr7489

Robert Holly, Holy, Confusion 220 acres, 1728, Book ILB, pg.470

(?Rsh.40) Robert Holly, Holy, Confusion, 220 acres, January 12, 1731, Book PL8, pg.205

(?Rsh.40) Robert Holly, Holy, Holy's Chance, 68 acres, March 18, 1747, Book BY2, pg.535

MdHR, Charles Co., Md.

(Rsh.1) John Holly, Charles Co., Md., Costly's Addition 25 acres, July 25, 1732, pl8/584;am1/127 P1=parents 1743-1747 sr7482

(Rsh.1) Liber M. Book 2, folio 354 August 14, 1733, Charles Co., Md., John Holly, Prince Georges, Co., Md., Planter, purchased from William Smallwood and James Smallwood a small parcel of land in Charles Co., Md., containing 2 acres. John Holly shall have free privilege of getting wood for firing during his life...

(Rsh.1) December 8, 1735, John Holly requested a Certificate of Survey #261 for 10 acres of land to be surveyed between Hopewell and Sharp, held of Zachia Manor and called "Costly" on the south side of Mattawoman Fresh adjoining a tract of land called "Smallwoods Hazzard," belonging to James Smallwood. Improvements on land, a small watermill.

(Rsh.1) On May 6,1748, Survey #262 "Costly Addition" patented to John Holly for 25 acres. Patent, TI#1 folio 383, Charles Co., Md., to be held of Zachia Mannor, T.I. # 3, pg.108, 14 acres granted, paid 14 shillings, 6 pence for additional land.

(Rsh.3) May 20, 1766, Costly patented to Nathaniel Holley to be held of Zachia Manor, Charles Co., Md., Certificate of Survey # 261.

(Rsh.3) November 20, 1766, Nathaniel Hawley received a grant for Charles Co., Md., land.

(Rsh.4) February 18, 1794, John Halley, Jr., leased "Exeter" to Thomas H. Marshall, P.G. Co., Md., JRM #2, pg.508

MdHR, Charles Co., Md.

(Rsh.1) John Holly, August 14, 1733, Liber M. Book 2, Folio 354, from William Smallwood and James Smallwood, John Holly, Prince George Co., Md., Planter, land in Charles Co., Md., containing 2 acres, John Holly shall have free privilege of getting wood for firing during his life, Wm. Smallwoods's wife named Mary.

(Rsh.1) May 6, 1748, TI#1, Folio 383, Patent 25 acres, between Hopewell and Sharpe, to be held of Zachia Manor, paid 14 shillings 6 pence for additional land, TI#, pg.108, year 1748, on May 6, 1748 Survey #262 "Costly Addition" patented to John Holly for 25 acres. Patent, TI#1 folio 383, Charles Co., Md., held of Zachia Mannor, T.I. # 3, pg.108. 14 acres granted, paid 14 shillings, 6 pence for additional land.

(Rsh.3) Nathaniel Holly, son of John Holly dec'd., Costly, 10 acres, May 20, 1766, Book C.30, pg.387, Book C 31, pg.345

MdHR, Dorchester Co., Md.

John Harle, Harle's Fortune, 40 acres, May 2, 1682, Book 24, pg.429, Book 31, pg.383

James Harles, Harles' Chance, 26 acres, September 19, 1684, Book 25, pg.203, Book 33, pg.247

James Haile, Haile's Chance, 93 acres, October 22, 1747, Book T14, pg.137, Book Y1, pg.394

James Haile, Haile's Choice, 50 acres, March 18, 1747, Book T., pg.161, Book T11, pg.242

MdHr, Frederick Co., Md.

(Rsh.1) May 12, 1752, John Holly of Charles Co., Md., Planter, purchased from William Diggs for 6,000 lbs tobacco, land in Frederick Co., Md. Land Book G., folio 204, "Fellowship," which consisted of 172 acres together with houses, edifices, dwellings, orchard garden, pasture, woods, underwoods....

(Rsh.9) October 6, 1761, Book G., pgs. 204, 205, 206, John Holly, Planter, of Prince George Co., Md., sells "Fellowship" in Frederick Co., Md., containing dwelling houses, tobacco houses, buildings and other improvements, to John Boone of the Providence of Pennsylvania, County of Berks, and also came Mary Ann Holly, wife of the said John Holly, who being by us privately examined out of the hearing of her husband did freely and willingly acknowledge the written Deed and gave the right of dower, without being induced by threats by fear or threats of ill usage of her husband or fear of his displeasure, Land Record G., Folio 204

(Rsh. 9) November 17, 1768 John Holly and Zachaiah Downs of P.G.County, Md., Planters, purchase "Deer Park" and Bear Garden", from Jermiah Prather of Hampshire County, Colony of Va., Farmer, Frederick Co., Md., 297 acres., Liber L. folio 575, 576

MdHR, Kent Co., Md.

Mr. Crouch servant to Richard Hawlyn of Kent, Co., April 9, 1650

Wm. Harris to Robert Hales, Lib. J.S. pg.77, year 1709

John Haly from Gideon Pearce, Lib. J.G.#16, year 1721, pg.262, Gideon Pearce of Kent Co., and Anne Pearce, his wife and John Haly of said Co., Planter 12,000 lbs. tobacco, land called SamlAndrews, 200 acres, to be held by the Manor of Baltimore, witness, George Wilson, George Kirven

Wm. Halys, years 1755, 1756, 1765

MdHr, Montgomery Co., Md.

(Rsh.9) October 25, 1783, John Hawley of Loudoun Co., State of Virginia, Planter and Zacariah Downs, Montgomery, State of Md., Planter. (Zacariah Downs is John Hawley's wife's brother), concerning 310 acres called "Deer Park" and Bear Garden", lying and being in Montgomery Co., Md., John Holly and J. Downs did purchase from Jermiah Prather of Hampshire

Co., Va., Montgomery Co., Md., Liber B, pgs. 170, 199

(Rsh.9) March 20, 1784, John Holly, Loudoun Co., State
of Va., Planter and Zachariah Downs of Montgomery Co., State of
Md., Planter of the other part and Absalom Beddow of
Montgomery County, State of Md., Planter, Deed for the sale of
Deer Park, Beer Garden 310 acres is recorded, Liber B., pg.199

(Rsh.9) October 25, 1797, John Hawley of Loudoun
County, State of Virginia and Zacharia Downs of Montgomery
County, Md., sell "Deer Park" and "Bear Garden" in Montgomery
County. Deeds

(Rsh.9) January 25, 1798, John Hawley and Zachariah
Downs the former of Loudoun Co., State of Va., and the latter of
Montgomery Co., State of Md., did sell and convey to Absalom
Beddo on October 25, 1797, tract of land called resurvey of Deer
Park and Bear Garden enlarged...part lays foul of an earlier
survey called Snowdens Mill land...made settlement. Liber H.
pg.44, Montgomery Co., Md.

MdHR, Prince George Co., Md.

(Rsh.1), Liber I.L. #B, folio 126, Land Office, Liber P.L.
#7, folio 96, January 22, 1722, John Halley, Prince George's
County, 173 acres Exeter, surveyed by virtue of a warrant granted
18th January 1722, unto John Halley of Prince George's County
for 170 acres, begin at bounded red oak standing on a point of
Anyukicke Branch, to be held of Calverton Manor. Patented
September 7, 1728.

(Rsh.1) July 9, 1728, John Hally, P.G.Co., Md., IL#B,
pg.126, PL#7, pg.96, 173 acres called "Exeter" patented to be
held of Calverton Mannoure.

(Rsh.1) John Hally, Prince George Co., Md., Exeter, 173
acres July 9, 1728, PL7/96

(Rsh.1), John Halley, P.G. Co., Md., Patent, IL#B, pg.126,
PL#7, pg.96, 173 acres, July 9, 1728, "Exetor" patented to be
held of Calverton Mannoure.

(Rsh.1) August 14, 1733, Charles Co., Md., John Holly,
Prince Georges, Co., Md., Planter, Liber M. Book 2, Folio 354,
purchased from William Smallwood and James Smallwood a
small parcel of land in Charles Co., Md., containing 2 acres.
John Holly shall have free privilege of getting wood for firing
during his life...

Melcor Haley, Prince George Co., Md., tract Masswander

30 acres, April 26, 1746, T1.4 pg.357, BY1 pg. 627, certificates 1743-1748

Melchor Haley, Prince George Co., tract Masswander, 30 acres, April 26, 1746, Book LGC, pg.539

(Rsh.2) Book BB, pg.499, August 27, 1758, Thomas Hally, Planter, of Prince George Co., from George Parker, Gentleman, lease for tract called "Carrick" lying on Potomac River in Pomonkey Neck, formerly leased by William Pile, said Thomas Holly now living on. Thomas Holley may get timber from Hickory Hills.

(?Rsh.4, ?Rsh.9) Book RR, pg.243, Indenture August 31, 1762, George Gordon, lst part, and John Hawley of Prince George Co., Md., 2nd part. John Hawley from George Gorden, Bargain and Sale.

(?Rsh.4) CC#2, pg.508, October 4, 1778, John Hawley presents certificate of stray iron grey mare which he says breaks into his enclosed grounds and her owner is unknown.

(Rsh.2) August 27, 1785, Thomas Hally, Planter, P.G. Co., Md., leased tract of land "Carrick" lying on the Potomac River in Pomonkey Neck. Thomas Holley may get timber from Hickory Hills. Book B pg.499, Prince George Co., Md., Waldolf, Md. Note: Robert Gordon purchased Hickory Hills at the head of the Pomonky Creek, October 31, 1765.

(Rsh.4) February 18, 1794, John Halley, Jr., P.G. Co., Md., leased "Exetor" to Thomas H. Marshall, P.G. County, Md., JRM #2, pg.508.

(Rsh.2) 1796, J.R.M. 3, pg.168, Indenture between James Burch Halley (Jr.) of Hardy Co., Va., and John Halley of Prince Georges Co., Md. Thomas Holly did by his last Will and Testament executed on the 21st day of February 1769 did give and devise the land on which he then lived or after the marriage or death of his widow to his sons, John, Samuel and James Burch Halley...in case either of his sons d. without lawful heirs then the said land to be equally divided between the survivors. James Burch Halley d. first leaving the aforesaid James Burch Hailey his son and heir at law and afterward the said Samuel d. without issue and the land became equally the property and estate of the said James Burch Hailey and John Hailey and their heirs. James Burch Halley now conveys property to said John Holly. 173 acres on a point of a fork of Aquakeek Branch known by the by the name of Exeter.

(Rsh.4) 1800, 1802, J.R.M. No.9, pgs. 168-173, indenture John Spalding of Prince George Co., Md., 1st part and Elizabeth Halley and Thomas Holley of said Co., and State and John Halley of Charles Co., Md., on the other part...John Halley late of Prince George Co., dec'd, lived on Exeter, Elizabeth Hally, Thomas Holley and John Halley, widow and sons of the said John Halley, dec'd, to sell to John Spalding.

(children of Rsh.4), August 28, 1811, IB#A, pg.20, Thomas and John Hawley, ordered a resurvey of "Little Troy" and were granted vacant land of 18 acres to the boundary of Piscataway Manor to the "Ridge."

MdHR, St. Mary's Co., Md.

(Rsh.92) Capt. Wm. Hawley assigned 2,000 acres for transporting January 8, 1648, land on south side of Patuxent River, Section 4 and 6, January 15, 1648

(Rsh.92) Capt. Hawley, Section 31, 1651, land adjoining Capt. Hawley and land of Nicholas Gwither in St. Nicholas Hundred

(Rsh.92) Section 29, Capt. Wm. Hawley, Esq., freehold 5700 acres by title derived from Jerome Hawley, dec'd from Provincial Court, March 24, 1652, St. Mary's Co., Md., Liber B, pg.429, Union motion made by Mr. Henry Coursey on behalf of Capt. Wm. Hawley of the Titles of Mr. Jerome Hawley, dec'd and upon perusal of the Deeds upon record of Mr. James Hawley, whereupon the said Capt. Hawley claims the Court conceiving that Mr. Jerome Hawley had right to 6000 acres and upward which is not taken up. It is thought fit with the Governors appropriation that for the present a Warrant be granted to the said Capt. Hawley for 6000 acres of Land only where he now liveth, not formerly taken up and that upon survey thereof a grant be passed to him or his assigns for the same towards satisfaction of the debt assigned to him the said Capt. Hawley by the said Mr. James Hawley. Court held St. Maries., March 24, 1652

(Rsh.92) year 1653, land on west side Chesapeake Bay formerly held by Wm. Hawley, dec'd. by patent dated September 12, 1653, and by Wm. Hawley's last Will and Testament, devised to the said Wm. Guither of St. Maries Co., tract containing 5,700 acres, Wm. Guither's wife Barbara Christine, and now being sold to John Lonellin, witness John Rousby, Thomas Grunnin

(Rsh.92) John Jarbo in 1653 assigns to John Pile

adjoining land of Wm. Astille, Wm. Hawley, St. Mary's Co., Md.

(Rsh.92) Vol. L1, Liber Pc, pgs. 110, 111, 112, Proceedings of Court of Chancery, year 1677, Capt. Wm. Hawley, late of St. Maryes County, Esq., having right to 6000 acres by title derived from Jerome Hawley, Esq., late of said province, dec'd, on May 24, 1652...Lord on 6th of August, 1636, recorded in the Secretary's Office in this province by letters Patent bearing date December 12, 1653, did grant unto said Capt. William Hawley all that tract of land on the west side of the Chesapeake Bay near unto a Creek called St. Jerome's Creek beginning on east side of said Creek at a chestnut tree near a marsh called St. David's Swamp and running west for 80 perches to an oak, thence H. 855 perches unto the land of Stanhope Roberts, called "Draper's Neck," thence to St. Jerome's Creek on S., containing 5700 acres more or less, the said land belonging to William Hawley, his heirs and assigns in the Manor of West St. Maryes...then said William Hawley did in about year 1654 make his last Will and Testament, in writing and did give devise and bequeath said lands and premises to the complainant, his godson, and his heirs and assigns, and shortly after d. leaving the complainant an infant about 2 years old, after whose (William Hawley's) death the complainant by virtue of said Will became legally entitled to said lands and premises. This was held for the complainant, Wm. Guyther, during his minority and he was lately attained the age of 21, but several persons have got possession of the original Will of William Hawley and did suppress same and refused to deliver up possession of land. Held in Chancery Court, St. Maryes City, Md., February 25, 1678

(Rsh.92) Deeds WRC#1, pg.653, October 5, 1693, deposition of Henry Coursey: Wm. Lucas bought 400 acres of Capt. Wm. Hawley; Henry Coursey came into this Providence in November of 1649 and took his habitation at the house of George Mee at St. Jeromes Creek in St. Mary's Co., and then Capt. Wm. Hawley lived there, and this desponants two brothers William Coursey and John Coursey and Henry lived together about 6 months: William Hawley sold land to Wm. Lucas and some to Wm. Cols.

MdHR, Somerset Co., Md.

(Rsh.133) Jeremiah Hales, Somerset, Tevey Neck 300 acres, October 1, 1729, Book PL7, pg.456, Book ILA, pg.837

MdHR, Talbot Co., Md.
Thomas Harlings, Hallings, Adventure, 100 acres, November 30, 1676, Book 24, pg.252
Thomas Harlings, Hallings, Talbot, Bachelor's Hope, 150 acres, November 30, 1676, Book 29, pg.250

North Carolina
Chowan and Bertie Cos., N.C.
(Rsh.136) November 16, 1717, Deed Book F1, pg. 23, Richard Church of Albermarle Co., and Jane Church, his wife, to John Holly of the same county, for love and affection I bear my son-in-law John Holly and my daughter-in-law Sarah Holly, his wife, 60 acres adjoining Francis Macklendon
(Rsh.135) Patents, Nathaniel Holly, March 1, 1719, Book 3, pg. 173, 615 Acres on the south side of Morattock River, adjoining Wm. Maule, William Brown
(Rsh.137) Patents, John Holly, March 1, 1719, Book 8, pg. 195, 615 acres in Chowan, south side Morattock River (Roanoke River) adjoining William Brown and (Rsh.135) Nathaniel Holly. Sold November 25, 1733, Edgecomb Book 1, pg. 51, by John Holly and wife Elizabeth.
(Rsh.136) November 21, 1720, Deed Book F1, pg. 534, John Smith of Chowan and his wife Judith Smith to John Holly of Chowan, 100 acres, adjoins John Smith, witness William Williamson and Mary Williamson
(Rsh.136) Deed Book D., pg. 262, indicates that Sarah Holly had m. John Gilbert before 1735

Duplin Co., N.C.
(Rsh.136) Land Grant 722, 300 acres, March 31, 1750, John Holly, sold on June 20, 1754 to John Gilbert, witness by Richard Holly and James Holly.
(Rsh.136) Land Grant, Richard Holly, Book 10, pg. 434, year 1754, 600 acres.
(Rsh.136) Land Grant, James Holly, October 10, 1755,
(Rsh.136) Deed Book 2, pg. 242, January 14, 1764, John Holly and wife Rebecca Holly, sold land to William Ball

Johnston Co., N.C.
(Rsh.136) Deed Book 1, pg. 41, year 1747, John Holly purchased land from Joseph Howell.

140

New Hanover Co., N.C.
(Rsh.136) Jacob Holly, year 1747, Book G., pg. 153, November 30, 1747, to Benjamin Clemons 200 acres.

Sampson Co., N.C.
(Rsh.136) Edward Holley, Deed Book 1, pg. 130, Edward Holley to John Holley, April 11, 1768, the property Edward Holley is selling, "fell by heirship" from John Holly to his son Edward Holly.

Virginia
VSL, Accomac Co., Va.
(?Rsh.71) February 23, 1663, Thomas Orily, transfers 300 acres, adj. Roger Ternon and John Lewis, October 30, 1669, 1/2 of his patent

VSL, Albermarle Co., Va.
(Rsh.13) February 28, 1821, Book 22, pg.334, Thomas Jefferson to Abraham Holly, 4 acres, limestone land, Mr. Jefferson retained by Deed lifetime interest for himself and the house at Monticello and it inhabitants the right to obtain as much limestone "as they think proper for their own use but not to dispose of to others" from the quarry. The present Highway 250 runs through a part of the quarry which is the present day site of Limestone Farm south of Charlottesville, Va., conveyance to Thomas Jefferson from Robert Sharpe, October 5, 1773, Deed Book 6, pg.286
(Rsh.13) June 2, 1821, Abram Holly purchased 24 acres from George Gilmer beginning at a point on the road leading from the Three Notched Road to the Fredericksburg Rd., and running south southwest to the Three Notched Road on Stage Road, Book 27, pg.158.
(Rsh.13) May 19, 1828, Abraham, Hawley purchased 21 1/4 acres for $84. from Nathan Hall, Sr. on both sides of Three Notched Road bounded at Charles Hucksteps line., Deeds Book 27, pg.153.
(Rsh.13) September 4, 1834, Abram Holly, Lime Kiln Tract on "which Abraham now resides and additional 45 3/4 acres" to enter into trust with John Rogers to cover bond to Martin Dawson for $89.33, Book 32, pg.81.
(Rsh.13) 1834, Albermarle Co., Va., names son Washington as living on property.

(Rsh.54) Book 33, pg.206. 1834, William Hawley, Trust Book 31, pg.479, to G.C. Omohundor crops in field, furniture and personal property until note is paid.

(Rsh.13) February 17, 1836, Book 33, pg.206, Abraham Holly indebted to Fontaine Wells of Fluvannah Co., Va., mortgages 3 tracts of land consisting of 4 acres on Stage Road containing valuable Limestone occupied by son Washington, one other tract lying just below the proceeding one on both sides of Stage Road and occupied by William Hawley, containing 21 1/4 acres and one other purchased of George Gilmer containing 24 acres and also the said Holly's interest in a stallion purchased of James McCall, and all household furniture belonging to said Holly, including kitchen furniture, two feather beds and furniture, one table, six windsor chairs, one dining table, one cupboard, six plates, 12 cups and saucers, one block, one pot, two ovens, sundry other articles. Said Abraham Hawley will pay to Fontaine Wells $396. before 1st June 1836 with interest. note: (year 2000 Elizabeth Anderson's house, Keswick, Va.)

Note: (Rsh.13) Abraham Hawley d. shortly after February 1836. The records indicate that it might have been an unexpected demise. He final mortgage transaction states, "the lime kiln tract on the Stage Road (now 250) was occupied by his son (Rsh.55) Washington and another tract below that on both sides of the Stage Road was occupied by (Rsh.54) William Hawley." Because the mortgage document above covers the property on which two of his sons are presently residing, and mentions personal items, I Believe, this indicats his intention to quickly repay this mortgage.

(Rsh.54) May 6, 1836, William Hawley, indebted to Fontaine Wells hereby sells his interest, consisting of 1/6, in dec'd father's estate, called Limestone Tract, containing 4 acres now occupied by said William., Albermarle Co., Va., Records, Charlottesville, Va.

(Rsh.13) July 1838, to Mary Ann Hawley 1/3 part of lands the of Abraham Hawley dec'd at Limestone, a lot including dwelling house

(Rsh.13) Mary Elizabeth Hawley, wife of Henry Harlow deeded to Fontaine Wells, Deed Book 68, pg.27 and Book 36, pg.508 share of Three Notch Road Property

(?Rsh.53) July 1, 1872, James O. Hawley, Deeds 21, pg.59, Homestead for 50 acres Co., of Fluvanna, Va., on which he now resides

(Rsh.7) March 5, 1792, William Halley, Town of Alexandria, Commonwealth of Va., 450 lbs. for Lott # 114, Town of Alexandria, Va., from Patrick Allison of the Town of Baltimore, State of Maryland and Mary his wife. Book U, pg.57, rec. Fairfax Co., Va.

(Rsh.7) January 8, 1802, Deed Book A., 173,31, Ind., William Holly and Henry Walker of Frederick Co., and David Henderson and Phineas Janey + William Gore. Henry Walker indebted to William Holly transfer land by Ind. 10/l/1798.

(Rsh.7) April 29, 1802, Deed Book D. 456, Ind., between Thomas White and wife Elizabeth and Edmund Jennings Lee. witness William Halley, Archibald Taylor, Presley Sanford, Rec. 7/5/03, pg.458, Alexandria Co.

(Rsh.7) 1805, William Halley to Adam Lynn, Lot #10, conveyed by Patrick Allison to William Halley in 1792.

(Rsh.7) October 26, 1805, Deed Book L, 1219, Ind., between William Halley and wife Esther and John Wise. Land orig. leased by indenture 11/21/1798 by William T. Alexander and wife Lucy to Halley. Witness, Jacob Hoffman, Peter Wise, Jr., Robert Halley, Nathaniel Seton Wise. Rec. 12/21/05 pg.271

(Rsh.7) October 4, 1809, 2133, Indenture, Deed Book R., Between Esther Halley + Edward Stabler, execs of last Will and Testament of William Halley, and Adam Lynn. Land sale, by Patrick Murray bought from John Alexander by Deed 12/1774. Witness Adam L. Webster, William Dodson, William L. Webster, John Stewart, Richard H. Litle, John Johnston. Rec. 12/19/09, pg.477. Alexandria

(Rsh.4) Deed Book T., 2399, Ind. December 8, 1810, between Henry Stanton Earle and wife Phoebe and Joseph Smith and James Keith and Rebecca Lawrence. Land conveyed by indenture 12/2/02 by Absalom Wroe to Earles, in trust by indenture 1810 to Smith and Keith to protect note endorser Benjamin Baden, with permission of Bank of Potomac to Lawrence. Witnesses R. Withers, Christopher Neale, Hillary Hally, A. Faw. Rec. December 19, 1810, pg.329.

year 1831 (Rsh.7) William Hawley moved to Marietta, Ohio, Washington, Co., Ester d. 1831, gave personal belongings to poor and baptist church in Alexandria, Va. He bought land

and slaves between 1779 and 1796 in Alexandria, Va., Book E., pg.7, Book H. pg.337, Book S, pg.493, Alexandria, Va. He lived in area where in 2000 the Alexandria Courthouse stands.

VSL, Caroline Co., Va.
September 1728, John Cheadle and Thomas Hakitt, 400 acres, Caroline Co., adj. David Murry, Joseph Hayle, John Hammon and Robert Holmes

VSL, Charles Co., Va.
John Howle, John Howle, Jr., Rent Roll, year 1704

VSL, Culpeper Co., Va.
(Rsh.78) Deed, Henry S. Hawley, Jr. 1818
(Rsh.52) April 8, 1823, Thomas Hawley purchased land town of Fairfax, County of Culpeper, Va.
(Rsh.78) Deed, Henry S. Halley and wife, March 21, 1825
(Rsh.52) Thomas Hawley and wife Deed transactions 1838 1845
(Rsh.52) December 24, 1844, a negro was sold at public auction by trustee belonging to Thomas Hawley
(Rsh.56) April 22, 1856, sale made by James Barbour, Trustee, for Charles M. Hawley
Deed, Lillie Co., Trustee for John D. Hawley 1902

VSL, Elizabeth City Co., Va.
Henry Hawley, 50 acres, Elizabeth City Co., October 20, 1643, for trans. of Thomas Hatchway.
July 24, 1669, William Morris, 50 acres, Elizabeth City Co., originally granted to Henry Hawley, who is now dec'd and by inquisition dated March 5, 1667

VSL, Fairfax Co., Va.
(Rsh.108) year 1760, Tenant of George Mason, Benoni Halley, 100 acres, 4 slaves; Ownership, James Halley, Jr., 230 acres; James Halley, Sr., 459 acres; William Halley 230 acres.
note: Thomas Hanson Marshall, of Prince George Co., Md., was among those Maryland residents who owned land in Fairfax.
(Rsh.76) June 15, 1773, Liber L & K. Fairfax Co., pg.107, William Hawley, wife Catherine land known as Ravensworth.
(Rsh.5) September 23, 1773, Samuel Hawley, Barbary

Hawley his wife and James Burch Hawley, his nephew, appear on Deed of Lease for 200 acres which was part of the Ravensworth Tract in Fairfax Co., Va. In 1991 this area is known as Annandale, Va., Deed of Lease Wm. Fitzhugh, Jr. to Samuel Hawley, rec. October 18, 1773, Liber L. #1, pg.20, Fairfax Co., Va., Land Records. "200 acres (except all mines, minerals and quarries whatsoever) in Parish of Truro County of Fairfax and being a part of a tract of land of 21,996 acres called Ravensworth Tract, the bounds as followeth...for and during the life or lives of Samuel Hawley, Barbary Hawley, his wife and James Burch Hawley, his nephew, and for the natural life or lives of the longest liver of them. Yielding and paying yearly 1000 pounds crop tobacco beginning December 25, 1773, provisions for planting fruit trees and fencing and warehouse for tobacco. Provisions for repair."

June Court 1799, Deed from Nathan, Matthew, William Halley to Alex. Smith, proved by James Keith, David Henderson, John Dundas and ordered certified to the County of Fauquier to be recorded. June, Fairfax County Court Orders 1799 - 1800.

(Rsh.13) November 16, 1807, <u>Abraham Halley, co-def. vs. Samuel Adams</u>, Fairfax Co., Court Records, pg.197

(Rsh.9, Rsh.14) April 16, 1810, Book KK, John Hawley from Turner to Barton D. Hawley, Fairfax County (book missing)

(Rsh.14) LL#2, pg.306, June 12, 1811, Barton D. Hawley and Catherine his wife of Fairfax Co., Va., and Sandford Lyne, Co., of Loudoun, Va., land in Fairfax 100 acres sold for $900, on Carter line, witness Robert Lyne, Jeremiah Hutchison, Jr., James Turner, Zachariah Hussey

(Rsh.14), November 9, 1816, Barton D. Hawley and Hannah his wife, sell to Dean James land and negroes, estate derived from William James and his widow, for $450. Witness Charles Lewis, Aris Buckner.

(Rsh.11) William Hawley, Sr., to Joshua Hutchison, each of Co. of Fairfax, $1,450. March 4, 1819, Book RR pg.133, 181 acres, test Anthony Thonton, Robert Newman, Lewis Hutcheson, Wm. Henbley, Thomas Hutchison, Jeremiah Hawley, proved by Wm. Ambler, Thomas Hutchison and Jeremiah Hawley

(Rsh.14), October 18, 1816, Barton D. Hawley, of the County of Fairfax, Va., purchases 111 acres for $1,100, from Hopwoods exrs. Test. William Hawley, Jeremiah Hawley, William Hawley, Jr., Book OO, pg.397

(Rsh.11) March 4, 1819, William Hawley, Sr., of Fairfax

Co., Va., sells to Joshua Hutchinson, Fairfax, Co., 181 acres for
$1,450., being a part of Grimes Patent beginning at the line of
Andrew Hutchisons patent to Turner's Corner. Witnesses:
Anthony Thonton, Robert Newman, Lewis Hutchison, William
Henbley, Thomas Hutchison Jeremiah Hawley, William Ambler
RR, pg.133

    (Rsh.27) January 18, 1830, William Hawley, Jr., 1829
pg.162. recorded Deed from William and Margaret Lyne for 100
acres land certificate in Fauquier Co., rec. 12/22/1824.

    (Rsh.28) February 15, 1830, Jeremiah Hawley, William
Hawley, Jr., Elizabeth Hawley (also in 1829, pg.170) with others
Deed to Mary Ann Hutchison.

    (Rsh.14), Barton D. Hawley purchased 130 acres, for
$800, Fairfax Co., Va., Book MM., pg.402, land on border of
Loudoun Co., Witness, Thomas Davis, James Turner, William
Hutchison, not dated.

Fairfax Co., Va., Index to Deeds, C.H. Archives
    B. pg.480, William Harle
    C. pgs. 481, 482, Harle and others; pg.558, Halley, June
21, 1753, George Mason of Parish of Truro, Fairfax and Bononi
Halley, same Parish
    D. pg.203, June 5, 1753, Wm. Harle; pg.529, James Harle
to Wm. Harle; pg.598, Wm. Harle
    E & F. pg.16, Halley
    G & H., pgs. 148-150, Halley, book missing
    (Rsh.77) L & K., pg.107, June 25, 1773, Wm. Hawley, wife
Catherine, land known as Ravensworth, mentions Henry Hawley,
name spelled Holly; pgs. 396, 397 Richard Halley to Wm. Halley
    S. pg.17, Robert Hally to wife
    (Rsh.7) TT & U, F & A, 1790-1792, pg.57, William Halley,
Wm. Halley, Town of Alexandria; (Rsh.76) pg.101, Halley and
Peake, Marriage Contract; (Rsh.7) pg.362, William Halley, of
Alexandria set free two slaves, January 21, 1793; (Rsh.110)
pg.460, Francis Halley, and his wife, September 20, 1792
    (Rsh.7) HH to 1806, book missing, pg.389, Wm. Hawley
from Charles J. Love
    (Rsh.77) GG to 1807, pg.380, Catherine Halley renounces
husband's Will, June 17, 1806, she is dissatisfied
    (Rsh.14) JJ to 1808, John Hawley to Barton D. Hawley
    (Rsh.14) KK to 1808, pgs. 10, 12, 255, Book Missing, to

Turner from Halley

(Rsh.14) MM, pg.402, John Turner to Barton D. Hawley
(Rsh.78) LL, pg.112, Henry S. Halley and Ratcliff, appraisal, Halley and Ellzeys, div; pg.175, George Halley; pg.306, (Rsh.14) Barton D. Hawley and wife Catherine, June 12, 1811; (Rsh.9) pg.332, John Hawley, Lewis Turner, April 14, 1810
(Rsh.14) MM, pg.402, Barton D. Hawley
(Rsh.78) NN, pg.132, James Halley to Henry S. Halley; pg.194, William Halley and wife to George Halley
(Rsh.14) OO, pg.397, Barton D. Hawley from Hopwoods exrs, October 18, 1816, Charles Lewis of Co., of Loudoun and Barton D. Hawley of the County of Fairfax, test. William Hawley, Jermiah Hawley and William Hawley, Jr.
(Rsh.14) PP, pg.1 to 62, missing, pg.1, Barton Hawley and wife to Stephen Daniel, pg.328, Wm. Hardy, consto; pg.391, Wm. Halley to Geo Halley
(Rsh.78) QQ, pg.103, John H. Halley from James Hampton and wife
(Rsh.76, Rsh.78) RR, pg.67, Wm. Halley to Henry S. Halley; pg.133, March 14, 1819, William Hawley and Joshua Hutchison, witness Lewis Hutchison and Jeremiah Hawley, signature, William Hawley; pg.134, Hawleys exrs. to Wm. Hawley, February 24, 1819, James McKim of Loudoun Co., and Robert Latham of Prince William Co., exrs. of John Hawley, dec'd and William Hawley of Fairfax, witness Wm. H. McKim, Wm. Ambler, Jr., Lewis Hutchison, Thomas Hutchison, Jeremiah Hawley; pg.29 contains Will, of John Hawley; pg.15, Will of Henry Simpson Halley
(Rsh.78) SS, pg.256, John H. Halley; pg.385, Henry Simpson Halley, heirs

VSL, Fauquier Co., Va.

(Rsh.84) Raleigh Halley, sold land, Book 15, pg.276, September 23, 1772, he lived in Stafford Co., Va.; February 28, 1803 Deed, lists, Charles Colvin, William Colvin, Elizabeth Colvin, Raleigh Colvin, Aggetha Colvin, John Colvin, Charles Colvin, Nancy Colvin, Rolly Halley and Mary Holly
(Rsh.55) May 20, 1840, Washington Hawley purchased land in Fauquier County, Virginia.

VSL, Fluvanna Co., Va.

(Rsh.13) year 1804, Jeremiah Hutchison and wife Mary Ann living in Fluvanna Co., Va., on 200 acres convey same to Major Parish of Louisa Co., Va., adjoining lands of Charles Thompkins, Davis Ross, Abner A. Strange for $1,000 consideration. Witness Peter Ross, John Johnson, John R. Perkins, Bartleyh Ford, Richard Bragg, Rowland Jones, Richard Allen, Abraham Hawley, John Bartley. Book 4, pgs. 299, 402.

James O. Hawley, Trust 1868, Book 20, pg.125

Grantor Judith H. Hawley, Grantee, Thomas Walker, Book 11, pg.548, lives in Ganard, State of Kentucky, dau. of Henry Martin, dec'd, 1938

VSL, Frederick Co., Va.

February 4, 1800, Peter Halley, Release Book 26, pg.259

Peter Hawley, September 2, 1800, from Denny Fairfax of Great Britian, Lease 27, pg.4

VSL, Goochland Co., Va.

September 13, 1723, Matthew Ligon, 1000 acres, Goochland Co., adj. his own, Capt. John Woodson, Col. William Randolph and land of John Haile, at head of a bridge of Fiting Creek on William Allen's line.

VSL, Hanover Co., Va.

Book 17, pg.403, John Haley, August 15, 1737, 400 acres, by the road in Statham's line, in Nuckoll's line.

VSL, Isle of Wight Co., Va.

(Rsh.83) James Hawley, 300 acres, Isle of Wight Co., April 22, 1641, due for the per-adv. of himself, Ann his wife and trans. of 4 persons, Francis, Ann and Alice his children, September 27, 1643, patented April 10, 1647

(Rsh.117) October 8, 1688, Paroah Cob, of Isle of Wight Co., to John Hole of Devon, Gent. for 11000 lbs. tobacco, 130 acres, bounded by Col. Smith and Col. Arthur Smith

Mallachi Hawley was living at his plantation, Red Point, Isle of Wight, in 1689

April 24, 1689, Thomas Green gives all the land Mallarke Howly lived on to his father-in-law (stepfather) Phillip Codin and his mother Mary, now the wife of Phillip Codin

January 9, 1693, Richard Hutchins and wife, reference

130 acres sold by Cobb to John Hole

September 17, 1731, John Parson, 800 acres, Isle of Wight Co., s. side Maherin River, adj. William Hill, Robert Hill, Robert Hill, Jr., and land of James Haley consisting of 185 acres

VSL, James City Co., Va.

Daniel Halles, granted 150 acres, James City Co., January 27, 1663, for trans of 3 persons

VSL, King William Co., Va.

October 23, 1703, Joseph Hayle, 200 acres, King William Co., on Herring Creek, for transport of 4 persons.

July 11, 1719, Joseph Hayle and John Hammon, 400 acres, s. fork Polecat Creek, border Wm. Terrill, Robert Chanler, Phillimon Hawkins line.

July 9, 1724, David Murry, 400 acres, King William Co., St. John's Parish, adj. Robert Holmes, Hayle and Hammond line.

June 4, 1725, Thomas Clarke of Middlesex Co., 350 acres in King William Co., in St. John's Parish, beg. at a corner of Joseph Hayle, John Hamon and Robert Holmes and by Robert Chandler's line to Mr. William Terrill's line.

August 17, 1725, Thomas Hackett of Middlesex Co., 400 acres, in King William Co., in St. John's Parish, border of North Anna River, adj. corner of Hayle and Hammond and Robert Holmes and Robert Chandler's line

VSL, Lancaster Co., Va.

(Rsh.128) Richard Lawrence, Gent, of James City Co., Va., sold to John Fflower of Lancaster Co., 450 acres, December 17, 1669, witness Thomas Hawley and Elizabeth, Sr., Elizabeth Lawrence, wife of Richard

no date: Mr. George Haile, 1950 acres, Lancaster Co., Va., near bridge of Corotoman River, formerly taken up and sold to Nick Haile

VSL, Loudoun Co., Va.

(Rsh.9) October 21, 1781, John Hawley of Prince George Co., Md., and William Smalley of Loudoun Co., Va., assign to Lewis Ellzey indenture lease dated November 10, 1767, 350 acres, Richard Major, on September 11, 1769, sold to Isaac Smally, who d. and left Wm. Smalley to assign, John Hawley to pay annual rent, during the natural lives of Richard Major, Elijah Major and James Major his sons land transaction, S.E. section Loudoun Co., on border of Fairfax Co., in what was in 1781, Cameron Parish, Witness, James Lewis, John Debell, James Lewis, Nat. Gist. William Gist. Lam's Adam, William B. Sears, acknowledged April 8, 1782 Asst. L. Book N. pgs.252-254

(Rsh.9) April 8, 1782, Loudoun Co., Va., Minute Book, Assignment of Lease from Wm. Smalley to John Hally acknowledged and ordered recorded.

(Rsh.11) September 8, 1783, William Hawley, of the County of Fairfax, lease indenture, with Bryan Fairfax, of the County of Fairfax, for 152 acres south side of Little Difficult Run, Western Part of Fairfax, Co., Va., in the year 2000, houses, etc. for 21 years for the payment of one ear of indian corn. William Halley to build houses, fences, plant trees. Witnesses, John, James and Henry Gunnell, Jr., Book N. #2, pg.513.

(Rsh.3) April 9, 1790, Loudoun Co., Va., Nathaniel Hawley and Wife Mary purchase two parcels of land totaling 356 acres for 1,000 lbs. tobacco containing houses, buildings, fencing, orchards, gardens and ... Book S., pg.7

(Rsh.10) March 30, 1791, Alsalom Holly purchased 198 1/2 acres for 30 lbs in Cameron Parish (in 2000 considered Washington Metropolitan Area, bedroom community of Washington,D.C.) from Michael Howdershall of Shenandoah Co., Va., Asst. L. Book T., pg.134, note: if this land record is traced forward it might show the wife of Absalom if she gives dower rights in this land transfer.

(Rsh.9) November 1, 1796, John Hawley of Loudoun Co., Va., paid 212 lbs current money of Virginia for 385 acres, lying and being in the County of Loudoun on Elk Licking Run, was granted to the late proprietor to George Statler (Stabr),to Thomp. and Marmaduke Beck with surviving heirs of Lewis Ellsley dec'd. late of FFX., Witness, Barton Hawley, Joshua Hutchison, Ezekiel Smally, Tom Ellsey, M. Beckwick, Deeds, Book X, pg.307

(Rsh.13) Deed Book 2C, pg.438, February 20, 1802, Abraham and Mary Ann Hawley, of Fluvannah Co., Va., 1st part and Aris Buckner of Loudoun, Va., 2nd Part. For the sum of 5 shillings, all that tract of land in Cameron Parish which descended to Abraham Hawley and Mary Ann his wife from Thomas Oden dec'd who was the father of Mary Hawley, 41 acres. Bargain and Sale. Witness, George Hutchison, Jermiah Hutchinson, John

Davis and Thomas Oden., Deeds 2C, 438, note: heirs of Thomas Oden can be found in Loudoun Deed B. 22, pg.334. Mary Ann Oden Hawley is referred to in one of the estate documents as "Polly."

(Rsh.14, 1808), Liber JJ to 1808, Barton D. Hawley, Liber KK. to 1808, John Hawley

(Rsh.13) 1820, Abraham Holly and Mary Ann, his wife, formerly Mary Ann Oden, a dau. and heir of Thomas Oden dec'd and Martha Oden, also now dec'd. Total Acreage 192 1/2 acres, their share 19 1/4 they are selling., Loudoun Co., Va., Bargain and Sale Deed Book #G (30 or 39) pg.176.

(Rsh.13) Book 39, pg.176, Indenture 1820, Abraham Hawley and Mary Ann his wife, formerly, Mary Ann Oden of 1st part, a dau. and heir of Thomas Oden dec. and Martha Oden, 192 1/2 acres, their share 1/10 or 19 1/4 acres sold to Jacob Summers.(Rsh.13) Abraham and Mary Ann Oden Hawley, B.& S. Book 36 (39) pg.176 show her as being Thomas and Martha Oden's daughter

VSL, Middlesex Co., Va.

Alice Holley received a mare from Sarah Varey, Widow, August 1, 1698, Deed Book 2, pg. 259

VSL, Nansemond Co., Va.

October 30, 1686, John Hundnell, in right of his wife Mary, Nansemond Co., part of patent granted to Anthony Wells which after several sales and c. descended in fee to said Mary and Elizabeth, daus. of Robert Haile

VSL, New Kent Co., Va.

Charles Hawley, April 7, 1674, 250 acres, New Kent Co., for transport of 7 persons

May 30, 1679, Col. Robert Abrahall, 250 acres, granted to Charles Hawley on April 7, 1674, and deserted

July 10, 1680, Richard Clarke, 736 acres, New Kent Co., for transport of 15 persons...John Hailes

March 26, 1680, Mr. James Tayler, 950 acres, New Kent Co., which he lives upon, 100 acres purchased of Joseph Haile on March 26, 1680

September 20, 1683, Mr. John Lewis, Jr., 250 Acres, New Kent Co., originally granted to Charles Hawley on April 7, 1674 and which he died seized of, escheat, July 25, 1681

October 30, 1686, Mr. Joseph Haile, 1000 acres, New Kent Co., for transport of 20 persons

VSL, Norfolk Co., Va.

October 28, 1672, Malachy Thruston, 100 acres, lower Norfolk Co., escheat land of William Holley, Halley, and escheat by inquisition under William Alford, Deputy

VSL, Northampton Co., Va.

George Hailes, sells 300 acres to Tho Mallett, February 21, 1651, Northampton Co.

(Rsh.83) Mr. James Hauley, adm. of Raphy Horsley, tailor, gives Deed for property, September 20, 1658, Northampton Co.

VSL, Northumberland Co., Va.

(Rsh.118) April 1, 1651, Thomas Orley, 100 acres, n.e. abutting Potomac River, s.e. upon land of William Medcalf, trans of 2 persons, John Hawkrs and Henry Wickers

(?Rsh.118) September 16, 1651, to Thomas Hales and Thomas Shepphard, 300 acres, Northumberland Co., s. side of Potomac River near Herring Creek, for transport of 6 persons, John Haies, William James, John Elcock, Fra. Barnes, Henry Grey, Thomas Morecock

(?Rsh.118) September 18, 1651, Tho. Hayles, grant of Sir William Berkeley to Tho. Hayles in Northumberland on south side of Potomac River, adj. land of George Knott, Edward Walker and John Powell, 300 acres, for trans of 6 persons into Colony, signed William Haylles, Northumberland Co.

(Rsh.118) May 20, 1653, Northumberland Co., Thomas Orlye, his cert for land "According to sufficient proofs made before this court there is due to Thomas Orlye one hundred acres for his own transportation twice into this colony."

(?Rsh.118) James Hawley, 1000 acres, Northumberland Co., October 13, 1653, land on s. side of Potomac, trans of Susan Orly and Rebecca Orly

(?Rsh.118) September 20, 1653, sale of land by John Hull to Thomas Hailes, witness John Davis

(?Rsh.118) November 22, 1653, I Thomas Hailes sell patent to John Tingey, test. Tho. Kedby and Thomas Hawkins, Thomas Hailes, his mark, on margin of Hulls patent made over.

note: his mark was that of a T and H together.

(?Rsh.118) July 21, 1654, Thomas Hayles, assignments to Robert Lord, patent signed, Tho Hayles, his mark, Northumberland Co.

(?Rsh.118) January 1656, Thomas Hayles, age 50 or thereabouts, says upwards of 7 years ago he had 100 acres surveyed by Wm. Cook...the land where Mr. Nicho Jernew now liveth.

(Rsh.118) June 12, 1658, Mr. Charles Ashton, 100 acres, Northumberland Co., in Cherry Point Neck, adj. his own and upon land of Thomas Orly and Wm. Medcalfe

(Rsh.71) Deed that is referenced in year 1661, Richard Holden, 100 acres, Northumberland, upon Potomac River and upon a creek dividing this from land of Thomas Hailes, sold to Robert Lord and Nly, upon Yoacomacoe River, upon Deed dividing this from 14000 acres in Charles City Co. note: when this tract of land is referenced on July 10, 1661, and September 16, 1661, the names are referenced as John Hailes and Thomas Shepherd. Note: Property had most likely transferred to John, a son, upon his father's death.

(Rsh.83) September 12, 1662, grant to James Hawley, 700 acres near head Nominy River, point called Herring Point, adj. land of Hawkins, Northumberland Co.

(Rsh.83) John Paine, sells 406 acres, Northumberland Co., June 1, 1664, 300 acres pur. of James Hawley and 100 acres for trans. 2 persons.

(Rsh.83) James Hawley 700 acres, June 26, 1666, Northumberland Co., s. side Potomac and head of Machoatick River, for trans of 14 persons.

(Rsh.83) September 26, 1668, Col. Peter Ashton 485 Acres, Northumberland Co., on n. side of great Wiccomic River between Mr. James Hawley and Wm. Betts and c. (?company)

(Rsh.118) March 23, 1672/3, Charles Scarbvurgh Devorax Brown and Capt. John West, 4500 acres, Northampton Co., near Hunting Creek, adj. Tho. Orly and John Lewis

(Rsh.83) January 4, 1679, Wm. Tignor, 550 acres, Northumberland, land granted to James Hawley, June 2, 1657, assigned to Wm. Leech who sold said to Tignor

(Rsh.85) April 1670, Robert Edwards, Mary his wife, upon Nomini River, bounding upon land of Thomas Ewell and Henery Halley, Northumberland Co.

(Rsh.52) September 17, 1850, Thomas Hawley, Loan 41, Deed, mentions John W. Hawley, Orange Co., Va., Property sold in Orange Co., 1844, 1848, and later

Deeds Index:
1738 James, Mary Haley
1739 Edward Hawley
1741 James Hawely
(Rsh.72) 1742 Ambrose Hawley
(Rsh.73) Deed Book 12, pg.429, year 1757, John Haley of
    St. Margaret Parish, Caroline Co., Va., and wife
    Mary, execute Deed for land in Orange Co., Va.,
    adjoining William Haley; year 1760 Benjamin for
    Catherine Haley, for Thomas Haley
(Rsh.72) 1760, Thomas Haley to (Rsh.74) Benjamin for
    Catherine
1765 William Haley to Catherine
(?Rsh.72) 1771, Katy Hawley for Thomas Hawley
1786, 1791, 1793, 1798, 1800 to 1848, Benjamin Hawley
1794 William Haley to John Brown
December 26, 1844, 1848, 1850, Thomas Hawley
September 17, 1850, Thomas Hawley, Loan 41, John W.
    Hawley

Prince William Co., Va., C.H.
(Rsh.107) April 20, 1733, Deed Book B, pgs. 37,38, Thomas Halley purchased a grist mill from John Brutt.
(?Rsh.110) Francis Hawley and Sarah Hawley, his wife, year 1800, to John Taylor, Jr., property on Broad Run, Town of Buckland, Deed Book 1, pgs. 154, 159
John Love and Elizabeth, his wife, to (Rsh.110) Francis Hawley, December 13, 1805, Town of Buckland, Madison and Elizabeth Streets
Craven J. Halley, year 1827, from Richard Glade, Deed Book 11, pg.372
Eleanor Halley to John Arrington, year 1846, Deed Book 20, pgs. 159, 160, from Jane Peake, sister to Eleanor Hawley
A.B.D. Hawley, from Francis A. Hearth, year 1858, Trust

<u>VSL, Rappahannock Co., Va.</u>
Tho. Hobson, Rapp. Co., 500 acres, June 1663, trans. of John Hawley and 9 others.
Mr. Francis Haile, 1865 acres, Rappahannock Co., April 17, 1668, on east side of Pye Cr. adj. to land he now lives upon, same as granted to said Haile and Mr. William Heabert, February 9, 1663, this land in freshes on n. side of river.

<u>Shenandoah Co., Va., C.H.</u>
Peter Halley in 1788 helped lay off Frederick Co., Va. Note: In the year 2000 this is Front Royal, Va.

<u>VSL, Spottsylvania Co., Va.</u>
Edward Hayley, of King William Co., October 13, 1727, purchased 980 acres, Spottsylvania Co., St. George's Parish, s. side Rappidan River.
September 28, 1728, James Hayle and Edward Hayle, Jr. 840 acres, Spottsylvania Co., St. George's Parish, adj. Rev. Hugh Jones, Edward Hayle and Mr. Bledsoe's line.
September 28, 1728, Henry Berry 720 acres, in St. George's Parish, adj. Edward Hayley, Jr., on sw side of Purvice's Run.
September 28, 1732, granted George Purvice, September 28, 1728, William Johnson, Gent, 1000 acres, Spottsylvania Co., in St. George's Parish, on border of Terry's Run, Black Walnut Run and Mine Run adj: Edward Hayles, William Bledsoe; Edward Hayles, Jr., and John Purvice.

<u>VSL, Stafford Co., Va.</u>
(Rsh.76) Book P., pgs. 29, 30, Grantee, James Halley, lease, release, Grantor John Simpson, date not recorded
William Halley and Henry Lucas, patent 520 acres, on south side of Occoquan main run, year 1710, note: in 1723, William Hawley listed on Quit Rent Roll, Overwharton Parish for 520 acres.

<u>Warren Co., Va., C.H.</u>
Thomas Hawley purchased land in 1858 and conveyed same to Susan Hawley, it appears she was his daughter-in-law and wife of his son Cornelius, land record appears again in 1860

(Rsh.83) March 27, 1663, parent to Stephen Warman, 750 acres...south side of the Eastern branch of the creek which divideth this land from the land of Mr. Hawly, Westmoreland Co.

(Rsh.83) November 30, 1664, Mr. Isaac Allerton, agt. Mr. Hawly, Westmoreland Co.

(?Rsh.128) John Lord and Wm. Horton 2500 acres, Westmoreland Co., February 9, 1663, trans. Thomas Hawley

(?Rsh.82, ?Rsh.128) Mrs. Mary Fortson, 2000 acres, trans. 2 persons, Ed. Hawley and Thomas Hawley, Westmoreland Co.

(Rsh.82) March 22, 1665, Wm. Basely and Edward Hawley, 1000 acres in Westmoreland Co., between two rivers of Potomack and Rappahannock upon branches of Nomony, partly along back line of Mr. Whiston, for transportation of 20 persons into Colony, Governor Wm. Berkley, pg.327, March 1665, land surveyed for William Baseley and Edward Hawley, patented by Wm. Berkley, to William Overett and George Browne 400 acres.

(Rsh.81) March 22, 1665, patent of Sir Wm. Berkeley, unto Randolph Kirke, 1,000 acres, Westmoreland Co., between rivers of Potomack and Rappahannock, on branches of Nominy, line of Edward Hawlye, due for trans. of twenty persons into Colony

(Rsh.82) February 12, 1666, Wm. Basely and Edward Hawley assign our interest in the above patent unto (Rsh.81) Jacob Lucas and Samuel Munns, signed William Basely, Edward Hawley, Westmoreland Co.

(Rsh.83) June 26, 1666, James Hawley, 700 acres, Westmoreland Co., near head of Nomine River, beginning at Herring Point, and adj. to his own land for transfer of 14 persons

(Rsh.81, Rsh.82) January 3, 1667, 1668, James Hawley of Nomony in Westmoreland, Co., unto Jacob Lucas, 200 acres, signed James Hawley, witness John Samways, Edward Hawley

(Rsh.82) October 31, 1667, Edward Hawley of Nomony unto Martin Cole, one half money of my part of this patent, Edward Hawley, William Beasely of Westmoreland Co., to Jacob Lucas, Samuel Munns, one equal half of patent to myself and Edward Hawley, Westmoreland Co.

(Rs.82) November 28, 1667, Edward Hawley of Westmoreland Co., to Samuel Bradley, 250 acres, adjoining Edward Witherington and William Web, part of 500 acres which Martin Cole is in possession of, signed Edward Hawley

(Rsh.81, Rsh.82) January 3, 1667, James Hawly unto Wm. Clayton, signed James Hawlye, witness, Edward (X) Hawlye, Westmoreland Co.

(Rsh.82) April 15, 1667, patent on line of William Bayle and Edward Hawlye, Westmoreland Co.

(Rsh.82) March 9, 1669, George Browne of Nomenie unto Andrew Reade 200 acres, on line of William Beasly and Edward Hally, Westmoreland Co.

(Rsh.85) April 6, 1669, Robert Edwards and Mary wife of Robert, to Henry Hawly and Saml. Mumms...300 acres, land sold on April 10, 1671 to Michael Willington, pg.386. Westmoreland Co.

(Rsh.82) November 17, 1669, Randolph, Randall Kirke and wife Amie of Nominie, unto Edward Hawley, Westmoreland Co.

(Rsh.82) November 17, 1669, Wm. Beaseley and Edward Hawley do remain contented with the division we have made, if any part of the land should be taken away by and elder patent, both to bear the loss, signed William (X) Beaseley, Edmond (X) Halley, Westmoreland Co.

(Rsh.82) April 16, 1670, Thomas Ludwell, Esq., 1432 acres, Westmoreland Co., adj. Col. Thomas Beale and Randall Kirk, Mr. Wm. Bazeley and Edward Hally and c., for transport

November 9, 1670, Robert Nurse and wife Elizabeth unto George Hailes, all my interest in patent of 189 acres, Westmoreland Co.

(?Rsh.71) Robert Edwards and Mary Edwards of Westmoreland Co.,...180 acres upon the land of Thomas Youle, Youell and (Rsh.85) Henry Hawlye

(Rsh.81) January 10, 1671, Wm. Cleyton of Nominie unto John Sansome, Sansun, Sansum, Samewaies, witness James Hawley, Westmoreland Co.

(Rsh.81) February 29, 1671, James Hawlye of Westmoreland Co., to Henry Hawlye of same, parcel of land, for 6000 lbs. tobacco, Jacob Lucas his corner, Walter English his line, upon John Payne, his line, then to line of Lewis Markham, along James Clarkes, and upon land formerly John Wilsons, signed James Hawlye, February 29, 1671, acknowledged James Hawlye; pgs. 92a, 93, same land: James Hawlye, Gent., of Westmoreland Co., unto Jacob Lucas, 100 acres upon maine branch of Nomenie, part of 700 acres, line of Walter English, signed James Hawlye

(Rsh.81) October 25, 1671, acknowledged by Jacob
Lucas and John How, attorney of Mary Lucas, wife of Jacob
Lucas, acknowledge unto Nicholas Jenkings my right of 400
acres, Mary (X) Lucas, witness James Hawlye, John (X) Heyres,
recorded October 25, 1672, Westmoreland Co.

(?Rsh.126) November 29, 1671, Anthony Bridges of
Washington Parish, Westmoreland Co., Merchant, as also the
reversion of that Plantation formerly belonging unto Francis
Hayles in the possession of Mr. William Stroke...

February 26, 1672, Lewis Markam unto Capt. John Lee,
all my interest to the bond, Westmoreland Co.

(Rsh.81) November 9, 1672, Nora Sillivant unto Walter
English, witness James Hawley, Westmoreland Co.

(Rsh.85) December 14, 1673, Henry Hawley of
Westmoreland Co., to Saml. Mumms, 100 acres, to Jacob Lucas
his corner tree, Walter English his line, upon the swamp, north
side of an Indian field, corner tree of Lewis Markam, James
Clerke, his line, signed with mark, Henry (X) Hawley, witness
Jacob Lucas, Peeter (X) Dunkin, February 25, 1673,
Westmoreland Co.

(Rsh.81) September 25, 1673, land formerly belonging to
Mr. James Hawley of Nominy, Planter, down the swamp and
bounding on Capt. Lee's line, Westmoreland Co.

(Rsh.81) Deeds and Patent Records, James Hawley, of
Westmoreland Co., Va., in deposition given June 25, 1674, says
that he was b. c. 1628.

Susan Adington, widow of Benjamin Adington,
Westmoreland Co., land formerly surveyed for George Hayles and
Thomas Territt, June 8, 1661, who assigned their right to John
Arrington, who conveyed same to Benjamin Adington, land to
escheat to proprietors office because Benjamin Adington dec'd
without any heir apparent in this Country or elsewhere

(Rsh.85) Henry Hawley and wife Mary Hawley sold land to
Arthur King, April 8, 1691, Order Book

year 1703, Francis Wright, Gent, petitions for land due for
importation of Ann Price, Danll Hayly into this Colony,
Westmoreland Co.

December 30, 1703, George Weedon, Gent, made oath
for land due him for transportation of Wm. Holly, Westmoreland
Co.

(Rsh.81) September 23, 1709, Copley Parish, Nominy River, part of 700 acres, patented by James Hawley June 21, 1666, by Hawley sold to James Lucas by James Lucas sold to James Brechin, Westmoreland Co.

VSL, Land Patents 4;156, 170, 171, 172, 174, 177, 228, 229, 258, 259, 281, 303, 307, 309, 363, 571
Land in the area of the Freshes of the Potomac, south of Alexandria, Va., Little Hunting Creek, was taken up by John Hayles, John Ayres and William Davis, William Knott and others note: this area is across the Potomac River from Accokeek, Maryland where (Rsh.1) John Holly m. Hester Burch

Military Records
Pertaining to Land

NA

(Rsh.52) March 4, 1852, # 46266 bounty land for service in War of 1812 issued to Thomas Hawley and located at the Chicago, Ill. land office upon the E 1/2 NW 1/4 Sec. 17, T.32, R.12, Illinois, by Sheldon W. Peck, Assignee.

(Rsh.52) July 14, 1857, # 39992 bounty land for service in War of 1812 issued to Lucy Ann Hawley, widow of Thomas Hawley. Located at the land office at Warsaw, Mo., upon the N 1/2 lots 1 & 2 of NW 1/4, Sec.30, T.46, R.30, Missouri, by Charles Hodges, Assignee.

L. MARRIAGE RECORDS

England
VSL: Chapel of Westminister, 1556-1699, London, year 1886
June 1, 1664, John Hawley and Margaret Boylton, at St. Magts., Westminister

(?Rsh.126) February 3, 1696, Lord Francis Hawley, of Buckland Co., Somerset, Bachelor; and Lady Elizabeth Ramsay, spinster, 18, of St. Giles in the Fields, Middlesex, her father is dead, consent of her mother and grandmother. Attested by Henry Hawley, Esq., of St. James, Westminister, at Christ Church, London

Washington D.C.
Washington, D.C. Marriage Licenses 1811-1830 Family Line Publications, Silver Spring, Md., 1988
Elizabeth Holley to Samuel Robertson, May 29, 1813
Catherine Holley to Elias Grimsley, August 7, 1813
Mary Holley to Elias Cole, May 9, 1818
(Rsh.78) Margaret P. Halley to Allen N. Elkins, March 18, 1828
Leannah Holley to Charles Johnson, August 2, 1830

Maryland
MdHR Early Marriage, Maryland, date, name, parish
1705, Elizabeth Haly, St. Annes Church Records
1705, Elizabeth Haly, St. Annes Parish, Anne Arundel Co.
(Rsh.1) 1712, John Holly, King Georges Parish, St. Johns, P.G.Co.
1714, Mary Haley, St. James Parish, Anne Arundel Co.
1733, Martha Holly, St. Peters Parish, Charles Co.
1735, Geo. Haile, St. Pauls Parish, Baltimore Co.
1735, Ann Haile, St. Pauls Parish, Baltimore Co.
1741, Margaret Holly, Talbot Co.
(Rsh.130) 1745, Susannah Haile, dau. of Nicholas Haile, Jr., Baltimore Co.

Ann Arundel Co., Md., Gentry, Harry Wright Newman
(?son of 4) Samuel Worthington b. 1734 d. 1815, b. St. Anns Parish, child, Anne b. November 29, 1763 m. Wm. Ridgely, he d. and then she m. Thomas Hawley

Prince George Co., Md., C.H.
(Rsh.1) March 4, 1712, King George Parish I, St. John's Parish, John Holly m. Hester Burch

Montgomery Co., Md., C.H.
(Rsh.4) June 28, 1792, Penellopy Hawley m. William Peacock

MdHR: Index to Marriage License, Prince George Co., Md., compiled by Helen W. Brown (Rsh.4) January 29, 1800, Thomas Hawley m. Amy Downes

MdHR: Marriages and Deaths in St. Mary's Co., Md., Fesco, Margaret K.
Nancy Holly m. in 1798 Jeremiah Rhyman
Harriett Holly m. in 1816 to Benjamin Mason
Sarah Holly m. in 1802 to Joseph Mason
Thomas Holly m. March 1816, brides name not known
Joseph Holly m. July 20, 1816 to Prescilla Mason

MdHR: Marriage Reference Index, date is Record in which marriage is found not date of Marriage:
Halley (Hully) m. Layfield Collier, son of John and Tabitha Collier, Chancery Papers #4170, Worchester Co., Md.
Elizabeth Haly m. John Cary, St. Annes Church Records, 1705
Margaret Holly m. Joseph Redish, marriage date September 21, 1741, Talbot Co., Md.
Susannah Haile m. Green 1745, dau. of Nicholas Haile, Jr., Baltimore, Co., Md., Deeds Lib. T.B. #E, folio 10, Baltimore City Ct.
(Rsh.2) Sarah Holley m. Robert Gordon 1769, dau. Thomas and Elizabeth Holly, Prince George Co., Md., Wills, Liber #1, folio 617, T#1, folio 48 and 95, Prince George Co., Md.
(Rsh.2) Thomas Holly m. Elizabeth Emmerson, 1769, dau. John Emerson, Prince George Co., Md., Wills, Liber #1, folio 716, T#1, folio 48 and 95, Prince George Co., Md.
Mathew Haile m. Rebecca Robinson, 1792, dau. of Charles Robinson, Chancery Papers #551, Baltimore Co., Md.
Neil Haile m. Sarah Robinson, 1792, dau. of Charles Robinson, Chanc. Papers #551, Baltimore Co., Md.

_____, Holly m. Mary Ann Melton, widow of John Melton, Prince George Co., Md., Test, Book 27, pg.359, November 9, 1726

Maryland Marriages, Robert Barnes 1634 - 1777, Gene. Pub., Baltimore, Md., 1975
Elizabeth Haly m. John Cary, December 30, 1705, St. Anns Parish, Anne Arundel, Co., Md.
(Rsh.1) John Holly m. Hester Birch, March 4, 1712, St. Johns (King George or Piscataway) Parish, Prince George Co., Md.
Mary Haley m. Alexander Carvill, March 1, 1714, St. James Parish, Anne Arundel, Co., Md.
Martha Holley, m. John Anderson, August 13, 1733, St. Peter's Parish, Talbot Co., Md.
George Haile m. Elizabeth Crawfinch, January 17, 1735, St. Paul's Parish, Baltimore, Md.
Ann Haile m. Wm. Carter, September 18, 1735, St. Paul's Parish, Baltimore Co., Md.
Mary Haley m. Richard Moffitt, January 7, 1744, Shrewsbury Parish, Kent Co., Md.
Mary Haley, of Philadelphia m. John Thompson, son of John, May 4, 1765, St. Stephen's Parish, Cecil Co., Md.

Montgomery Co., Md., C.H.
Coly Brown M. Elizabeth Holly, August 20, 1779
James Haley m. Mary Robinette, October 12, 1789
(Rsh.4) William Peacock m. Penelope Holly June 28, 1792
(Rsh.4) Thomas Holly m. Amy Downes, January 29, 1800
Joseph Mason m. Sarah Holly, October 28, 1802
Thomas Holly m. Ann Bean, March 15, 1816
Benjamin Mason m. Harriet Holly, November 5, 1816

Maryland Historical Marriage Register, Montgomery County, Md., Marriages 1798-1876 (Loudoun Co., Va., Library)
Catherine Halley m. Thomas Parkins 24 April 1798
Lawrence O. Holly m. Sarah Oden, Jan 12, 1802

Virginia
Albermarle Co., Va., C.H.
Benjamin Hailey m. Ann Sisk, April 26, 1805

Susan Hawley m. Thomas Kindred, September 4, 1806
Eliz. Hawley m. John Cave, September 26, 1806
(Rsh.54) William Hawley m. Mary Ann Gillium, August 18,
1829
(Rsh.53) James O. Hawley m. Mary M. Jones, December
6, 1842

Amelia Co., Va., C.H.
Perdue Holly m. Elizabeth Diston, June 1798

Berkley Co., Va., C.H., Martinsburg, W.Va.
Mary Holly m. Jacob Curtis, September 28, 1820, sur.
Jacob Skimp
December 27, 1813, William Haley and Salley Moore, m.,
Fauquier Co., Va.

Marriage Records of Berkley Co., Va., 1781-1854 Compiled and
edited by Guy L. Keesecker, Baltimore Geo. Publ, Baltimore 1983
Thomas Haley m. Mary Whealand, March 7, 1789
pg.105 Mary Holly m. Jacob Curtis, September 28, 1820
pg.90   John Haley m. Mary Bartley, Nov. 12, 1839

Culpeper Co., Va., C.H.
John Haleys m. Rachell Fleshman, June 3, 1787
(Rsh.78) Henry S. Halley, Jr., m. Elizabeth Reed,
September 26, 1816
(Rsh.13) Amanda Hawley m. William H. Bridwell,
September 1, 1841
James D. Reese m. Mary V. Hawley, December 23, 1844
(Rsh.52) John W. Hawley m. Marietta Beasley, February
26, 1850
(Rsh.56 Lucy Ellen Colvin m. Charles M. Hawley, October
10, 1854
(Rsh.52) Mariah Alice Hawley m. James W. Rush, July 12,
1855
(Rsh.52) Savilla Benton Hawley m. Thomas Sherman,
September 2, 1857
(Rsh.52) Lucy Hawley m. Simon Wise on October 13,
1864

note: date given is that of record in which proof of marriage is found, not date of marriage:

(Rsh.108) Benone Halley m. Mary Ellzey, exr. of Thomas Ellzey dec., Minute Book 1749

John Hally m. Sythe Summer, January 15, 1795, Minute Book 1855, pages 6 and 7

(Rsh.11) William Halley m. Bathsheba Hutcheson, Loudoun Deeds Book Y pg.343 and Loudoun Chancery M. 717

(Rsh.5) Barbary Halley, widow of Samuel Halley m. Ratcliffe, Will Book, Deed Book T, pg.540

(Rsh.78) Catherine T. Halley m. Edmund Payne, Chancery Suit FF 43

(Rsh.78) Elizabeth Halley, heir at law of John H. Halley m. Newman Burke, Chancery FF 43, Minute Book 1847, pg.55

(Rsh.78) Fanny Hally m. John Debell, dec. by 1846, Chancery 43, then Rezin Wilcoxon

Julia Ann Haley of Schuyler Co., Mo., dau. of Sarah Halley m. Thomas W. Martin, Deed Book U3, pg.119, Minute Book 1852, pg.110

Lucinda Halley of Warren Co., Mo. dau. of Sarah Halley m. Joshia Chappell, Deed Book U3, pg.119, Minute Book 1852, pg.110

(Rsh.78) Margaret P. Halley m. Allen N. Elkin, Chancery Suit 43

(Rsh.85) Sarah Halley m. Capt. Wm. Harrison, Family Bible of William West 1739-91, Maryland Historical Society

Sarah Enfield Halley, dau. of Sarah and George Halley m. Mermes Reeves, Deed Book R3, pg.385; E3, pg.41; U3, pg.119

(Rsh.76) Susannah Halley dau. of James Halley, Sr., m. William Said, Will Book F1, pg.134, moved to Delaware Co., Ohio

(Rsh.76) Sybil Halley, dau. of James Halley, Sr., m. Jesse Wm. Peake, Will Book F1, pg.134, Deed Book L., pg.101

VSL: Fauquier Co., Va.

John Robert m. Sally Holly, June 22, 1789

Fauquier Co, Va., C.H.
Book 1:

(Rsh.84) Liddy George Halley, dau. of Rawley Halley, m. Richard Colvin, no date given

John Hailey m. Peggy Jett, September 1785
William Hailey m. Nancy Jett, December 25, 1786
(Rsh.84) Rolly Holly m. Mary Colvin, December 26, 1788
James Garrett m. Phebe Hailey, January 28, 1789
Anthony Hailey m. Martha Wigfield, September 23, 1793
Richard Hawley m. Nancy McBee, December 1794
Angus Camron m. Anna Haley (widow) October 30, 1794
Joseph Halley m. Sally Hummins, October 26, 1798
Elzey Courtney m. Sarah Haley, September 23, 1806

Book 2:
Joseph Halley m. Sally Hummins, October 26, 1797
Abner Haley m. Polly Jett, December 5, 1803

Book 3:
Elzy Courtney m. Sarah Haley, John Haley's dau.,
September 20, 1806
James Moore m. Ruthy Haley, December 17, 1807, John
Haley's dau.
Daniel Halley m. Nancy Coblin, December 24, 1807

Book 4:
Thomas Harley m. Jane Kirkland, November 24, 1830
Alexander Haley m. Lucinda Skinner, July 27, 1830
Abner Hawley m. Jane Fletcher, February 10, 1845
Martha N. Haley, age 21, m. Erasmus Taylor, her father
Thomas Haley, January 4, 1847

Book 5:
Alexander Haley m. Lucinda Skinner May 1831
James Mills and Tacy Haley, dau. of William Haley, m.
November 12, 1834
James Washington Haley and Wm. Haley gave bond for
Washington Haley to m. Mary Mills, June 21, 1835
James Haley m. Mary Bolton, August 24, 1841

Fluvanna Co., Va., C.H.
(Rsh.54) Book 2, pg.5, John A. Hawley, May 10, 1862 m.
Margaret Shipp, husb. 23, wife 18, both b. Albermarle, husbands
parents Wm. and Mary Hawley, wife Lewis and Martha Shipp.
(Rsh.54) Schyler Hawley to Sarah Sprouse, November 26,
1877, husb.34 wife 18, husb. widower, wife widow, parents Wm.
and Mary Hawley, wife Shelton and Eliza Sprouse; Henry Hawley
to Jackeleemen Sprouse, husb.23, wife 22, both b. Fluvanna,
parents husband Henry and Mary E. Hawley, wife Shelia and

Eliza Sprouse, September 7, 1878

George W. Haley to Perla L. Profitt, January 8, 1895, husb.21, wife 21, parents husband James N. and Cynthia E. Haley, wife Jas. and Sarah J. Profitt

Frederick Co., Va., C.H.

William Hawley m. Ann Debell, February 20, 1827

Giles Co., Va., C.H.

John H. Hawley m. Charlotte Burton, February 13, 1840

Goochland Co., Va., C.H.

(Rsh.73) Bartlett Haley m. Jean Streatum, August 16, 1770

Isabella Halley m. William Clements, December 2, 1783

Greene Co., Va., C.H.

(Rsh.57) November 15, 1885, Edwin Barbour Hawley m. Laura Elmore Dickerson at Cedar Grove Church, Greene County, Virginia. Witnesses, Charles Gilbert, James Mitsel, Minister, Rev. E. Hartman. Greene County, Virginia Marriage Records, Book I, pg.43

Greenville Co., Va., C.H.

Ezekiel Holly m. Anna Jones, March 15, 1801, Robert Watkins, sec.

Henry Co., Va., C.H.

William Haley m. Nancy Jackson, December 20, 1792
Frances Northcut m. Lucy Haley, May 26, 1794

VSL, Isle of Wight Co., Va.

William Pope m. Mary Haille, February 11, 1708, both of Nansemond Co., Va.

Loudoun Co., Va., C.H.
Date given is date of record in which proof of marriage is found, not marriage date:

(Rsh.14), Catherine Heath was the dau. of Andrew Heath and proof of this along with her heirs can be found in Chancery M721

(Rsh.11) William Halley m. Bathsheba Hutcheson, Loudoun Deeds Y 343 and Loudoun Chancery M. 717.

Marriage Records

(Rsh.14) Barton Hawley m. Catherine Heath of Cameron Parish, April 8, 1799, sec. Joshua Hutchison

(Rsh.11) Jacob Zinn m. Elizabeth Halley of Cameron Parish, May 6, 1833, sec. William Ambler

John Haley m. Emily Hunt, February 23, 1839, sec. John Hunt

note: unpublished notes Mrs. Jewell, Marriage Contract 6th May, 1833, Jacob Zinn of Preston Co., State of Va., and Elizabeth Holey of Fairfax Co., recorded October 14, 1833

Louisa Co., Va., C.H.

(Rsh.73) James Dyches m. Tabitha Haley November 8, 1773
(Rsh.73) Wm. Dyches m. Sarah Haley, September 28, 1778
(Rsh.73) Henry Dyches m. Delany Haley, January 10, 1779
(Rsh.74) Benjamin Haley m. Judith Dyches February 18, 1779

Lundenburg Co., Va., C.H.

William Haley m. Olive Winn, April 2, 1795
Henry Slaughter m. Lillie Haley, August 18, 1799
Obedia Henrick m. Polly Haley, December 18, 1800
William Crafton m. Wealthy Haley, June 18, 1819
Ambrose Haley m. Nancy P. Smithson, December 8, 1823
Henry B. Haley m. Casandra Smithson, November 30, 1830

Madison Co, Va., C.H.

(Rsh.55) John Abram Hawley m. Susan Ann Pope, September 15, 1870, husb. 26, wife 24, husband b. Fauquier Co., Va., wife Madison Co., Va., husband's parents George W. Hawley and Mary E. nee Waldridge, wife's parents Sanford Pope and his wife nee Wilks, husband's occupation, Farmer

VSL, Middlesex Co., Va.

(Rsh.114) William Holley m. Sarah Chaseman, January 9, 1683, at Christ Church in Middlesex Co., Virginia

widow Sarah Holley m. Samuell Smitheman by April 1689, Deed Book 2, pg. 359, 367

Richard Moor, More m. Alice Holly, Holley, October 26, 1704, Christ Church, Middlesex Co., Va.

Orange Co., Va., C.H.
Benjamin Hawley m. Francis Edwards, dau. of Joseph
Edwards, September 14, 1803
(Rsh.52) William F. Colvin m. Lucy M. Hawley, husb.20,
wife 22, parents husband John D. and Francis Colvin, wife's
parents Thomas and L.A. Hawley, February 15, 1855
(Rsh.55) George W. Hawley m. Elvira S. Crooks, husb.
44, wife 40, he widower, b. Albermarle Co., Va., she b. Orange
Co., Va., parents husb. Abram and Mary A. Hawley, wife 's
parents Joseph Bond and Catherine Crooks, May 28, 1857

Rappahannock Co., Va., C.H.
John Haley m. Mary Wood, he was 60 years old and b. in
Fauquier Co., Va., he was a widower, and son of Joseph and
Salley Halley, she was 30 and a widower, she was b. in Page Co.,
Va.

Shenandoah Co., Va., C.H.
John Holly, son of Peter, m. Nancy Edwards, October 3,
1792

Warren Co., Va., C.H.
John Hawley m. Jane Robinson, widow, April 11, 1838
Susan Hawley m. Alfred Garrett, in 1854, she was the
        widow of Cornelius Hawley

West Virginia
Book of Marriages by John Anderson, Jr., Pastor Linville Creek
Baptist, Rockingham Co., Va., and Greenbriar Baptist Church at
Alderson, Greenbriar Co., Va., now Monroe Co., W.Va., as
recorded by Virginia Baptist Historical Society, University of
Richmond, Va.
William Holly m. Prudence Castile, March 2, 1786
John Lowance m. Sarah Holly, March 8, 1791
Mary Holly m. Moses Shepherd, January 22, 1795

Family Search International Genealogical Index, IGI Record
John Holly m. Sarah Bush, about 1701, Isle of Wight, Va.

M. MERCANTILE CLAIMS

British

<u>VSL, Virginia Genealogist</u>

British Mercantile Claims, John Harley, of Fairfax, due July 3, 1774, removed to Carolina about 27 years ago

<u>VSL, British Mercantile Claims 1775-1803</u>

(Rsh.73) Bartlett Hailey of Louisa Co., Va., resides in Albermarle Co., Va., to which he has removed since the peace. His property has been sufficient to pay his debts but he has incumbered it with conveyances to his children. He will endeavor to pay from the ensuing crop.

N.   **MERCHANT'S RECORDS**

Maryland
Scottish Merchants
John Glassford & Company, Piscataway Store

<u>LC:</u>

(Rsh.3) August 13, 1766, Nathaniel Hawley, charges for self, a Prayer Book, 3 pence. September 12, 1766, he pays for prayer book. Manuscript Division, Madison Building

O.   MILITARY RECORDS

Colonial Militia

MdHR

(Rsh.1) 1747, Colonial Militia Payroll, Private, John Holey, Haley, Capt. Samuel Magruder, Box 1, Folder 8.

(Rsh.1) 1749, Maryland Colonial Militia, Capt. Samuel Magruder, John Haley, Box 1, Folder 8, Colonial Wars, P.G. Co., Md.

French and Indian

VSL: French and Indian War Bounty Certificate #828
Pvt. William Holley of Botetourt, Va.

Revolutionary War

VSL: Lincoln Militia under Capt. Nathaniel Hart, to build fort at the fols of Ohio under command of Col. Benjamin Logen, C.L.
(Rsh.9) John Holly, Virginia
(Rsh.13) Thomas Oden, Virginia

NA: Grants for Revolutionary War Service
(Rsh.84) Raleigh Hawley, Book 1, pg.363, Certificate No. 1827, 200 acres, October 6, 1783
Daniel Hawley, Mississippi
Francis S. Hawley, Tennessee
Peter Hawley
#1091, Thomas Haley, 200 acres, Private, Va. Cont. Line, term war, June 24, 1783
#1571, William Haly, 233 1/3 acres, Private, Cont. Line, term war, August 14, 1783
#1885, William Haley 233 1/3 acres, Private, Va. Cont. Line, term 7 years, 1783

DAR Patriot Index
Ambrose Haley b. c. 1763, d. between March 25, 1846 and August 2, 1847, he m. Mary Woodward, Pvt., Va.
Anthony Haley b. 1759 d. August 6, 1842, Anthony Haley m. Mary Dennison, Pvt., pension, certificate #150463, Mary Dennison, Warrenton, Fauquier Co., Va., 1785, children, Nancy

Haley

Benjamin Haley d. 1801 m. Agatha Hawkins and then Elizabeth, PS, Va.

(Rsh.110) Francis Haley, Halley, b. 1739 d. August 23, 1813, m. Ann, P.S. Va.

Henry Haley, b. c. 1748, d. June 7, 1801, m. Lettisha Hyde, P.S. Va.

(Rsh.76) James Holly, Sr., b. June 14, 1707 d. July 7, 1792 m. Elizabeth Simpson, P.S., Va.

James Haley b. c. 1720 d. 1795, P.S. Va.

(Rsh.100) James Haley b. May 4, 1732 m. Frances, d. August 25, 1827, Sgt., Va.

James Haley, b. 1743, m. Mary Jane, d. 1794, Sgt., Va.

(Rsh.112) John Holley, b. c. 1735 d. December 27, 1802, m. Judith, Judah, Goad, Soldier, P.S. Va.

(Rsh.99) # 490812, John Holley b. Prince William Co., Va., November 17, 1760, d. Bedford Co., Va., 1846 m. Anne Gaddy lst then Nancy Douglas, Children, Elijah, Percilla, Ruth, Jermiah, John, Trudy, Henry.

Lewis Haley b. 1748, d. 1833, m. Nancy Loveless, Sgt., Va.

Richard Haley, b. 1750, d. 1816, m. Lydia, Sol., Va.

William Haley, Sr., b. 1720 d. 1796, m. Mary, Pvt., Va.

(Rsh.125) William Haley, Jr., b. January 1750, d. 1818 m. Bathshiba Dulin, Pvt., Va., dau. Mary m. John Moore

William Haley b. 1755, d. November 28, 1811, m. Margaret Conner, Pvt., Va.

Wm. Halley, wife Harriet Forrester, children Nancy Haley b. 1763, Wm. Haley b. 1737, d. 1818 in Virginia m. 1759, enlisted 1777, Kent Co., Md., and served under Wm. Henry, moved to Botetourt Co., Va., dau. Nancy m. Edward Mitchell

#103806, Wm. Haley, b. 1737 d. 1818, m. Harriet Terester of Cecil Co., Md., Pvt., Md., children Wm. Jr., d. Army 23 years old and Elizabeth

(Rsh.125) #141884, #119059, William Haley, Sr., b. Stafford Co., Va., 1720, d. Fairfax Co., Va., 1796 and wife Anna: children: James Haley, b. 1743 m. Mary Jane; John Haley; William Haley, Jr. b. 1750 d. 1818 in Fairfax, Va., m. Bathsheba Dulin who was b. 1752 m. 1771, Children: William Hally, Jr. b. 1798 m. (?) children: Anna, Abram, Samuel, Robert, Thompson, Mary

Peter Hawley, alive in 1835, pension #2173
(Rsh.84) Raleigh Hawley

NA: Revolutionary Archives
Ambrose Haley S 8680, Pension App.
(Rsh 2, or Rsh.9) John Haley, Maryland S 10213
John Haley, Pvt. Rolls of Pa., Pension rec from Pa., Rank
Corporal, Reg., 3rd Md., Capt. W. Smith, disability wounded by
musket balls and right arm and left thigh disabled July 1779,
Stoney Point, Residence Philadelphia, entitled to 3/4 pension.
Enlisted October 1777 for 3 years on rolls in 1780. Allowed
pension from Sept. 4, 1794 at which time he was residing in Pa.
and still there in 1819, d. July 22, 1823, age not given or place of
death and buriel shown, #397
(?Rsh.3 or Rsh.4) Thomas Haley, Maryland S 41625
Thomas Haley, Pvt. Rev. War, 18 March 1800, #41625,
appears to have gone to Ohio to live.
Peter Hawley, Virginia S13328
Peter Hawley, S13328 - Montgomery Co., State of
Virginia, Pvt., in 1833 he states he is 80 years old, about March
1777, he enlisted in the County of Frederick, State of Va.,
(Winchester, Va., area) There is an inquiry in file from Lucy
Hawley of Logan, W.Va., in 1931.

NA: Hoyts Pension Index
Thomas Holley, Md., S41625
John Holley, Va., S9588
John Hailey, 4676

MdHR, Revolutionary Papers, Index 349
(Rsh.4 or Rsh.9)) John Halley on payroll of Capt. Hezekia
Wheeler's Company 11th Battalion of Militia, April 1781, Box 6,
Folder 21, 1782, June 8, 7 items, P.G. Co., Md., others on payroll
were Edelen, Boarman, James Emmerson, Athey, Clagett.

MdHR, Rev. Patriots of Prince Georges Co., Md., Henry Peden
(Rsh.4 or Rsh.9) pg.132, John Halley private, Capt.
Hezekiah Wheeler Co 11th Militia Battalion, April 1781, reb. r58,
ll19970, Box 6, Folder 21, private select militia, Capt. Hezekiah
Wheelers Com., July 14, 1781, rev. s6636, Box 31, Folder 5.

(Rsh.9) pg.143, Absalom Hawley, John Hawley, William Hawley, Oath of Allegiance given to Christopher Lowndes 1778

MdHR:
    (Rsh.4 or Rsh.9) January 1778, Oaths of Fidelity, P.G. Co., Md., John Holley, Jr., William Diggs, William Diggs, Jr., William Diggs 3rd, William Peacock, John Emerson, Box 4, Folder 31

    (Rsh.9) February 23, 1778, Oath of Fidelity, John Hawley, Prince George Co., Md., and again on March 1778, (Rsh.10) Absalom Hawley, Town of Bladensburg, Md., P.G. Co., Md., Oath of Fidelity to Maryland along with Henry Downs, (Rsh.11) William Hawley, Henry Piles, George Knight, Morris William Lucas and John Hawley.

    (Rsh.3) March 4, 1778, Oath of Fidelity to State of Maryland, Charles County, Md., Nathaniel Hawley, Blue Book 5 # 38, pg.4 taken by John Dent

note: Before March 1, 1778 every male inhabitant of the State of Maryland over 18 had to subscribe to an Oath of Fidelity to the State or pay a fine equal to 'treble' of his normal tax besides forfeiting all civil rights and being disbarred from any learned profession or trade.

    Caleb Haley, Hayle, Hazel, dec'd, soldier in 2nd Md. Reg. Anne Arundel Co., Orphans Ct. Proceedings, 1777-1779, pgs. 4, 8, 16; 1782-1784, pgs. 11, 13, 18, Anne Arundel Co., Certificate of Discharge, Folder 14

note: notation says see Hailey, Healy, Haily, Haly, Healley, Haulin, Holly, Holley

Muster Rolls of Maryland Troops in the American Revolution 1775-1783, Archives of Maryland, Vol. 18, Genealogical Publishing, Baltimore, Md., 1972

    Thomas Haley, enlisted Baltimore July 1776

    Wm. Halley, Haley

    Caleb Hailey

    Daniel Hailey, Haly

    John Hailey, Hayley

    Michael Hailey, enlisted 6th Regt. April 20, 1777, d. April 1779

    Thomas Hailey, Haley, was prisoner

    Wm. Hawley, 6th Reg., spent time in hospital

Muster Rolls, Vol. 1

(Rsh.4 or Rsh.9) John Hayley, Sgt., enlisted May 20, 1777, disc. April 16, 1780, June '79, Corp. enlisted October 1778, Smallwoods Regt.

(Rsh.4 or Rsh.9) Roll of Capt. Wm. Wilmots Com. 3rd Regt., Dec. 1779, 6th Com., Oct. '79, John Halley, enlisted May 3, 1777, 3 years, remarks sick, present

<u>VSL, Pension Index S9588</u>

(Rsh.112) John Holly from Bedford, Va., imprisoned by Indians. Served under Col. Boone, then James Davis. Signed up at John Mills, Dan River, Boutet. Co., N.C. Honorable discharge at Old Iron Works, N.C. Drafted Marched to Norfolk then Campbell Co., Va. He was b. in Prince William and resided in Bedford Co., from 1765, except for one year in Boute. Co., in Kentucky 1777-78, not in Ill. 1782

<u>Draper Manuscripts, Vol. 32</u> - letter from George Rogers Clark pg.6, printed in Richmond Paper December 28,___, an Intelligence report called General Clark, the Rebel.

Spring of 1782, in the month of May, one soldier who volunteered for General Clarks at 1782 Camp in Big Miami, says he was there at Big Licks battle site, General Clark was Commander, with Benjamin Logan 2nd in Command. There were 110 men, (volunteers).

There are newspapers accounts of this battle Kent 1782, Royal Gazette, Wed, May 29, 1782, Gazette of S.C. 1779, April 15, 1812, Charles S.C. Times; Charleston Morning Post, Jul. 13, 1787, Richmond, September 28, 1782, November 30, 1782...

<u>Guide to Draper Manuscripts by Josephine L. Harper, State Hist. Soc of Wisconsin, Madison 1983</u>

11J George Rogers Clark spent 1809 -1818 with his sister in Louisville. Ruddles Station Attack occurred 1763-1774.

Maryland Journal 1786-1787 has "transcr info pts" on GRC as well as Kentucky Gazette 1793 - Pa. Packet 1786-87, June/July 1782, November 5 - 24 1782.

<u>Historical Register of Virginia in the Revolution, Soldiers, Sailors and Marines 1775-1783, John H. Gwathmey 1938 The Dietz Press, Publ., Richmond, Va.</u>

(Rsh.9) John Holley, Illinois Papers, Richard Holley, Illinois Papers, Thomas Holley E=index Rev. Records in Virginia State Archives, (Rsh.13) Thomas Oden Illinois Papers

VSL

(Rsh.9) June 27 to July 15, 1782, a pay roll of Lincoln Militia under Capt. Nathaniel Hart ordered on a Tower of duty to Build a fort at the fols of Ohio under the Command of Colo. Benjamin Logen, C.L.. Paid for 18 days service, John Holley and Thomas Oden; Thomas Oden 20 days November 5, to November 24, 1782, Lincoln Militia under George Rogers Clark Brig. General.

(Rsh.9) April 15, 1783 John Holly, a payroll with Lincoln Militia under Capt. Nathaniel Hart to build fort at the falls of the Ohio under the command of Col. Benjamin Logen, C.L. Payroll Note: (Rsh.9) John Hawley is not found in the Loudoun County records from 1778-1781.

VSL: Names of Captains and Privates, Col. Nathaniel Grists, Va., Regt. in 1777, 7th Co., Frances Muir Capt. and Paymaster of Reg.

Pvt. William Haley

War of 1812

VSL

(Rsh.13) War 1812, Abram Hawley, Albermarle Co., Va., Pvt., 8th Regt. (Walls) Virginia Militia, Capt. Triplett T. Estes, stationed Camp Carter, Virginia for term of war. Distance travelled 100 miles. Archives, Washington, D.C.

(Rsh.13 and Rsh.52), War 1812, Payroll Goochland Co., Va., Camp Carter, August 1814 to February 1815, Abram Holly Private 6 months; Thos. Holly 5 months 28 days.

(Rsh.52) August 28, 1814, Thomas Hawley volunteered at Charlottesville, Va., for six months as a Private in the Company of Capt. Triplett T. Estes, 8th Virginia Militia, commanded by General John H. Cocke, and was stationed at Camp Carter's near Richmond and honorably discharged at Richmond, Virginia on or near the last day of February 1815. Application for bounty land given by Thomas Hawley at Culpeper Co., Va., August 1852, and his widow on August 10, 1855, War Records, 1812, National Archives, Washington, D.C.

Civil War

(Rsh.55) March 1862, John A. Hawley, enlisted, Culpeper Co., Va., Roll of 1898, Company B., 13th Virginia Infantry, Frys Artillery, Jackson's Corp.

(Rsh.56) January 5, 1864, Charles McKee Hawley, Sr., enrolled in the Army of the Confederate States at Lynchburg, Virginia to serve the War; May 28, 1864, assigned to Conscript (Light Duty) Medical Department, Camp Lee, near Richmond, Virginia. Records of the Confederate States, Virginia Archives, Richmond, Virginia; July 4, 1864, report to General Surgeon Owen, Lynchburg, Va., for Assignment to duty, Medical Director's Office, Richmond, Va.; July 26, 1864, Discharge, Medically, requested. 37 years old, five feet seven inches high, light complexion, blue eyes, brown hair and by occupation, when enlisted, a farmer. Unfit for duty the past sixty days, on account of deafness and scrotal hernia, and is unfit for duty in any Department of the Government; October 5, 1865, Discharge date.

VSL, Civil War Service

A.B.D. Hawley, C.F. Hawley, Erastus Terry Hawley, H.A. Hawley, J. Hawley, J.E.M. Hawley, Capt. J.J. Hawley, J.L. (Holly) d. in service, James Hawley, James H.S. Hawley, Jeremy Hawley, John Hawley, John Hawley, (Rsh.54) John A. Hawley, Jno. A. Hawley, John A. Hawley, Capt. L.J. Hawley, Lorenzo D. Hawley, Newton E.A. Hawley, R.T. Hawley, Rufus Hawley, Thomas Jefferson Hawley, William E. Hawley

Virginia Militia

Loudoun Co., Va., Militia Records 1793-1829, transcribed from the originals by Don Blincoe, Sr. Iberian Pub. Co., Athens, Georgia. 1993

Roster of the Company of Grenadiers, 1st batt., 57th Regiment Virginia Militia, Class No 9, (Rsh.13) Abraham Hawley, Benjamin Hutchison, George Robinson, December 22, 1792, Capt. Charles Lewis 57th Regiment, Virginia Militia, class no. 7 (Rsh.10) Absolum Hawley; year 1824, List of Delinquents, Capt. Summers, (Rsh.94) Samuel Hawley, 2 fines, year 1825, delinquent, Samuel Hawley, 2 fines, John Hawley, 1 fine, Bat'n., .75, Capt. Summers 1827 year, (Rsh.78) John H. Hawley, 1 fine.

VSL: Roll of 1898, Culpeper Co., Va.

Minute men in the 3rd Va., Regt., Privates Joseph O. Hawley and A. B. Hawley

(Rsh.52) M.R. Hawley enlisted April 1, 1862, 6th Va., Cal. Payne's Brig., Fitz Lee's Div.

P. RENT ROLLS

Virginia
Fairfax Co., Va., C.H., Rent Rolls

year 1761:
    (Rsh.76) James Halley, (Rsh.100) James Halley, Jr., (Rsh.76) Will Halley
year 1764:
    (Rsh.76) James Halley, (Rsh.100) James Halley, Jr., (Rsh.76) Wm. Halley

Maryland
MdHR, Maryland Rent Rolls, Baltimore and Anne Arundal
    (Rsh.130 pgs. 93, 96, 97, Nicholas Hailes, Hale, Baltimore Co., Patapsco Hundred. Nicholas Hailes, for the Orphans of John Arding, May 2, 1689; also, Hailes Adventure, 56 acres, north side Patpasco River possessed by Nicholas Hailes

Q.   **TAX RECORDS**

Maryland

Harford Co., Md., C.H.
> (?Rsh.4 or ?Rsh.9) 1783 Tax list Harford County, Maryland, Deer Creek Middle Hundred. John Haley, number of whites 6, John Haley, Jr. number of whites 3.

MdHR: Prince George's Co., list of Taxables in Piscattaway Hundred, taken by John Middleton, year 1719
> (Rsh.1) John Hawley

Lower part of Piscattaway Hundred, taken by Thomas Stonestreet, 1733
> (Rsh.1) John Haly

Ohio

1806 Tax List, Caleb Hawley, Resident Proprietor, Columbiana Co., Ohio

North Carolina

Chowan Co., N.C. 1721
> (Rsh.135) Nathaniel Holly, 1 poll
> (Rsh.136) John Holly, 1 poll

Virginia

VSL
Albermarle Co., Va., 1800 Tax List
> St. Anne's Parish, (Rsh.73) Bartlett Haley, Silas Haley, Charles Haley, (Rsh.74) Benjamin Haley

Bedford Co., Va., 1800 Tax List
> (Rsh.110) Joshua Holley, (Rsh.110) Sanford Holley, (Rsh.110) William Holley, (Rsh.110) Francis Holley, (Rsh.99) John Holley, Sr., John Holly, Jr., Joseph, son of John, John Holley

Berkley Co., Va., 1800 Tax List
> Larkin Haley, Thomas Haley, Elias Oden, John Halley

Campbell Co., Va., 1800 Tax List
> James Halley, Charles Halley

Caroline Co., Va., 1800 Tax List
    Malry Haley, Meriday Haley

Culpeper Co., Va., Tax Report
    (Rsh.55) John A. Hawley, No Inher. Tax Report, Culpeper
Co., Va. Book 9, pg.375, January 24, 1928

Fairfax Co., Va., C.H. Personal Property Tax
NAME, WHITE 21+, BLACK

1782
Richard Hally   1   1
James Hally   1   4
Francis Hally   1
Nathaniel Hally 1   10 (Rsh.3)
William Hally   1   14 (Rsh.7 or Rsh.11)
James Hally   1   0

1783
Francis Hally   1   0
James Hally   1   1
William Hally   1   0

1784
Richard Hally   1
Nathaniel Hally 2 (Rsh.3)
William Hally   1 (Rsh.7 or Rsh.11)
James Hally   1
James Hally   2 (2nd James)
Francis Hally   1
William Hally   1 (2nd William)

1785
James Hally   1 white 21+/16+ = 2
Simpson Hally   1
Richard Hally   1
William Hally   1 (Rsh.7 or Rsh.11)

1786
John Hallys   0
Simpson Hally   1

181

James Hally   2 white 21+/16+ =2
William Hally   2

1787
very bad copy
James Hally,Jr.
Richard Hally
James Hally
Simpson Hally
William Hally (4/16)

1788
William Hally (4/21)	1
James Hally (4/30)	3
Richard Hally	1
Henry S. Hally	1

1789
Thomas Holley (6/19)	1	2
James Hally 2	5	
Simpson Hally 1	1	
William Hally (3/16	1	4
James Hally 2		

1790
William Hally (7/21)	1	0
Thomas Hally (6/8)	1	2
James Hally(4/19)	3	1
Henry Simpson Hally	1	1
William Hally	1	5

1791
James Hally, Jr. 2	2
Thomas Hally 2	1
William Hally 1	2

1792
James Hally, Jr. 2	2
James Holly 1	3
Simpson Holly 1	3
Thomas Hally 2	1

182

1793

Henry S. Hally 1   1
James Hally   1   2
George Halley (of James)   3   2
James Hally, Jr. 1   1

1794

Henry S. Hally 2   1
James Hally, Jr.   2
John Hally   1
John Hally, Jr. 1
James Hally   1
George Hally   1

1795

John Hally, Jr. 1
Henry S. Hally 1
James Hally   3

1796

Henry S. Hally 1
Jeremiah Hutchison 1
James Hally, Jr. 1
James Halley   3

1797

Henry Simpson Hally   1   1
James Hally   4
James Hally, Jr.   1
William Halley 1 (on diff.list than those above)

1798

James Hally, Jr.   1
Henry Simpson Hally   1   1
James Hally   4
William Hally   1   2 (diff.list)
William Hally   1   12 (Rsh.11)
Joshua Hutchison   2   4
Benjamin Hutchison   2   3

1799

James Hally, Jr.   1
Henry Simpson Hally 1   2
William Hawley 1   2
Joshua Hutchison   1   3
William Hally   1   12 (Rsh.11)

1800
George Hally 1   1
James Hally   2   1
Henry S. Hally 1   3
Vincent Hutchison   2   3
Moses Hopwood   2   2
William Hawley 1   2

1801
Henry S. Halley   1   2
Benjamin Hutchison   1   1
William Hally   1   14 (Rsh.11)
William Hally, Jr.   1   2 (Rsh.27)
George Hally 1   2
James Hally   2   1

1802
Henry S. Halley   1   3
James Hally   3   2
George Hally 1   2
William Hally   1   3
William Hally   1   15 (Rsh.11)

1803
George Hally 3
William Halley 1   16 (Rsh.11)
James Hally   2   1
Henry S. Hally 2   2
John Hally (Est. F. Turner decd)=0   1
George Hally (a free Negro)   1

1804
James Hally   2   1
George Hally 2   0
Henry S. Hally 1   2

William Hally   1   16 (Rsh.11)
Vincent Hutchison   1
George Hally (a free Negro)   1

1805
William Halley, Jr.,1   3 (Rsh.27)
George Hally   1
James Hally   2
Benjamin Hutchison   1
William Hally   1   15 (Rsh.11)
Henry S. Hally 1   3

1806
William Hally   1   15 (Rsh.11)
James Hally   2
George Hally   1
Henry S. Halley 3   3
William Hally, Jr. 1   3 (Rsh.27)

1807
George Halley 1   0
Barton Hally   1   (Rsh.14)
William Hally   1   4
James Hally   2   3
William Hally   all blank
Henry S. Halley 3   9
Catherine Halley 4

1808
James Halley   2   4
Barton D. Hawley   1   0 (Rsh.14)
William Hawley 1   4
Henry S. Halley   4   8
George Halley 1   1
note: 1809 - 1839 available, but not recorded here.

Loudoun Co., Va., C.H.,Personal Property Tax List
NAME, WHITES 21+, 16+, NEGROES, HORSES, CATTLE

1783

NAME	WHITES 21+	16+	NEGROES	HORSES	CATTLE
John Hally	2	1	3	16	
Thomas Oden	1	3	3	11	

William Holly   3

<u>1784</u>
William Halley   0   1

<u>1785</u>

Name	White			
William Halley	0	4		
William Halley	2		2	2
Nathaniel Halley	2	5	10	4
Thomas Oden	1	3	5	8

<u>May 8,1786 by Sam Love</u>

Name				
John Hawley	1	0	3	16
William Hawley	1	0	3	4
Thomas Oden	1	3	10	5

<u>1786 different list than Sam Loves</u>
William Halley   0   4   2   13

<u>1787</u>

Name				
Nathaniel Hally (3/15)	0	4	5	15
Thomas Hally (3/24/1787)	0	0	0	3
John Hawley (4/1787)	0	1	0	4
William Hawley	0	0	0	4
Absolom Hawley	0	0	0	1
William Hally (5/1787)	0	5	2	2
Over 21, George William, Jr.				
Thomas Oden	1	3	5	8

<u>Name, White 16+, Black 16+, Blacks 12+, Horses</u>
<u>1788</u>

Name	White 16+	Black 16+	Blacks 12+	Horses	
Nathaniel Hawley (3/20)		0	6	1	5
Thomas Hally (3/20)	0	0	0	3	
Absolum Hally (5/12/87)	0	0	0	1	
William Hally (6/28)	1	5	2	4	
John Hally (8/14)	0	1	0	5	
William Hally (8/14)	0	0	1	4	

<u>Name, White 16+, Black 16+, Blacks 12+, Horses</u>
<u>1789</u>

Name	White 16+	Black 16+	Blacks 12+	Horses
Nathaniel Holley (4/1)	1	6	1	4

186

Absolom Holley	1	0	0	1
John Holly (8/1)	1	1	0	7
Amos Holly	1			
William Holly	1	0	1	3
Thomas Oden (8/1)	3	3	1	6

Tho Oden Thomas
Rut Oden Richard
Jon Oden John

1790

William Hally,Sr.(8/20)	1	0	2	6

over 16 - William Green

Absalom Holley (8/23)	1	0	0	1
John Holly (8/27)	3	1	0	0

Tithable - John, Amos, Abm Holly

William Holly	1	0	1	3

tithable - Wm. Holly

Nathaniel Holly	1	6	1	7

1791

William Holley	1	0	0	3

John Holley
over 16 - Abm. Holly, A. Holly

Richard Oden	2	0	0	2

over 16 - Richard Oden, Thomas Oden

1792A

John Holly	2	1	0	7

over 16 - John, Abm

William Holly	1	1	0	3

over 16 - William

Absalom Holly	1	0	0	1
William Halley	2	12	1	11

over 16 - William Kelly, N. Money

Mary Holly(Nathaniels Widow)	5		0	3
Thomas Oden	2	2	0	5

over 16 - Thomas Oden, John

1793

very bad copy
John Holly

John Holly, Abm

Name, White 16+, Black 16+, Blacks 12+, Horses
1794B
William Hally (5/21)   2   13   0   13
  over 16 - Wm. Hally, Henry Jones
Mary Hally (5/21)   0   4   0   6
  over 16 - none
John Hally (5/29)   1   2   0   5
  over 16 - John, Abm., Barton
William Hally (6/2)   1   1   0   4
  over 16 - William Halley
Absolom Hally (6/6)   0   0   3
  over 16 - Absolom
Thomas Oden (5/12)   1   3   0   5
  over 16 - Thomas Oden

1795
Absalum Hally (4/7)   2   0   0   4
  over 21 Absolom Hally, Lewis Harrow
John Hally (6/20)   2   2   0   4
  over 21 - John Hally, Barton Hally
William Hally   1   1   0   4
  over 21 - William Hally
William Hally (7/16)   2   13   0   14
  over 21 - William Hally, Lewis Sudduth
Amos Hally   1   0   0   1
  over 21 - Amos Hally
John Oden   1   0   0   1
Thomas Oden   2   3   1   5
  over 21 - Thomas Oden, John Oden

1796
Absolom Hally (3/12)   1   0   0   3
William Hally(9/19)   2   10   1   14
John Hally (9/24)   3   2   0   5
William Hally   1   1   0   3
Mary Hally (10/12)   0   4   0   6
John Oden (4/16)   2   0   0   1
Thomas Oden   1   3   0   5
Hezekia Oden   1   0   0   1

1797

William Hally	1	1	0	4
John Hally	2	3	0	4
Absalom Holly (7/10)	1	0	0	4
William Holly (11/8)	1	13	2	14
John Oden (8/16)	2	0	0	1
Thomas Oden	1	2	1	7

1798

Absalom Halley	1	0	0	3
John Halley	2	2	0	5

1799

Bad copy - if need see at VSL in Richmond, Va.

1800

Absalom Halley	1	1	0	3
Jno Halley	1	2	0	2
Barton Halley	1	0	0	1
Martha Oden	1	1	0	2
Hezekiah Oden	1	0	1	2
Thomas Oden	1	0	0	1

1801

John Halley (4/8)	1	3	0	4
Barton Halley (4/25)	1	0	0	2
Absalom Halley (5/19)	1	0	0	4
Thomas Oden (4/13)	1	1	1	4
Hezikah Oden	1	1	0	2
Richard Oden	1	1	0	0

1803

Barton D. Halley (3/26)	1	0	0	2
John Halley (3/31)	1	2	0	4
Absalom Hally (6/1)	1	0	0	7
Thomas Oden (3/26)	1	1	0	1
Hezekiah Oden (5/27)	1	0	0	2
Alexander Oden	1	0	0	1
Martha Oden	1	0	1	3

1804

Absalom Halley (3/9)	1	0	0	5
John Halley (3/16)	1	2	1	4
Cambridge Halley (4/19)				
Free Negro	1		2	1
Martha Oden (3/10)	0	1	0	3
Elias Oden	1	1	2	1
Thomas Oden	1	1	2	1
Hezikah Oden	1	1	1	3
Charles Oden, Alexander Oden				

1805

name, whites 16+,	blacks 16+,	black 12-16,	Horses
John Halley(3/18)	1	2	1	4
Absalom Halley	1	1	0	6

1806

Absalom Halley (3/11)	1	1	0	5
Cambridge Halley (3/29) free negro				
	1	1	0	3
Jeremiah Hutchison (3/29)	1	2	1	3
John Halley (4/17)	1	2	1	5
Thomas Oden (3/10)	1	2	1	3
Elias Oden	1	2	1	3
Hezekia Oden	1	0	2	4

1807

Jeremiah Hutchison(3/28)	2	2	1	4
Cambridge Halley (4/10)	free negro			
	1	1	1	1
John Halley	1	1	1	5

1809

John Halley (4/5)	1	3	0	6

1810

John Halley (5/7)	1	3	0	6

Loudoun Co., Va., C.H., Loudoun Tithable List

This is a list of tithable found at the C.H. It is only a partial list,
but it is believed other records exist at the VSL in Richmond, Va.

1783

August 1783, (Rsh.9) John Holly, (Rsh.10) Absolom Holly, (Rsh.11) William Holly, Negro, Dark 4

1784

Cameron Parish, taken by Charles Eskridge
(Rsh.9) John Hawley
(Rsh.10) Absolom Hawley
   Dayes or Daveas 3
taker Charles Love
   September 15, 1784, Titables of Cameron Parish,
Loudoun Co., Va., (Rsh.9) John Holly, (Rsh.10) Absolum Holly

1785

taken by Has Lane
   William Hawleys - tiths Gerrard
   George, Jean, Mill 4

1810

   (Rsh.9) John Hawley, 1 male 45 and up, 1 female 45 and up,2 females 16-26, 5 slaves
   note: Andrew Heath next house to John Hawley, pg.4
   Martha Oden on pg.4 she was surrounded by Hutchisons, Ruben Suttle lived 8 houses away and William Ambler 5 houses away.
   John Hawley, 2 males under 10, 1 male 26 to 45, pg.25, 2 females under 10, 2 females 10 to 16, 1 female 26 to 451 female 45 and up.

SLAVE RECORDS

Note: These are included with the hope they will enable
Americans of African descent to trace their heritage.

Prince George Md., C.H.
(Rsh.2), Liber I.L.#B, folio, pgs.617, 618, 1769 Probate,
written February 21, 1769, Thomas Hawley, Will, Prince George
Co., Md., negroes, Frank, Harry, Will, Lanord, Jane

Amherst Co., Va., C.H.
Gilbert, Will written February 23, 1778, proved May 1,
1778. wife Mary to have use of 450 acres of land where I know
live, ten negroes, and land to be sold after death of wife...

Alexandria Va., C.H.
(Rsh.7) January 21, 1793, William Halley of Alexandria,
Va., frees 2 negro men. Witnesses William Summers, John
Butcher, Fairfax Co., Va., Book U., pg.362
(Rsh.7) November 4, 1805, Deed Book M. 1307,
Emancipation by William Halley of slave Robert Bell. Witn.
Nathaniel McAlister, George Drinker. Rec. 3/3l/06, pg.89,
Alexandria City and County
(Rsh.3) November 23, 1816, Deed Book C 2, Oath, by
Penelope Stone and sister Alevia Stone that they moved from
Fairfax Co., to Alexandria with slaves (yet undivided), Dennis 27,
Bil Halley 9, and Dennis 4 wo evasion of import laws. Witness A
Faw. Rec. November 26, 1816, pg.270

Fairfax Va., C.H.
(Rsh. 5), May 17, 1779, presented, written April 4, 1777,
Will, Lib. D #1, pg.117, Samuel Hawley of Fairfax Co., Colony of
Va., beloved wife Barbery, all estate, except three negroes
Cambridge, young Jerry and Jacob, she to enjoy them during her
natural life and at her death my will is that my brother-in- law,
William Halley shall receive and enjoy the three negroes as his
right and property...if William Halley dies before my wife then the
whole of my estate to be at the disposal of my wife...
(Rsh.5) February 16, 1790, I Barbara Ratcliff, late Barbara
Hally, of Fairfax Co., Va., and I William Hally of Alexandria, Va.,
free and emancipate negro Cambridge, age 36, said negro

Cambridge was devised to Barbara Ratcliff then Barbary Hally by Samuel Halley during her lifetime and then to William Hally. Witnesses John Bowen, George Fielder, Rebekah Killgore, Anna Halley, Book T. pg.540, Fairfax Co., Va., note: see 1804 Loudoun Co., Va., Tax List

(Rsh.3) August 29, 1791, Nathaniel Hawley, Estate account L #1, pg.291, Fairfax Co., Va., 6 slaves to be delivered to legatees, estate settled September 19, 1818.

June 8, 1803, Deed Book G., pg.688, Emancipation by John Campton, Fairfax Co., of slave George, late property of John's father, and slave Clary wife of George, late property of Charles Hagon, and slaves Jonathan and Thomas, both children of George and Clary. Witness, Robert Brockett, (Rsh.7) William Halley, Robert Halley. Rec. December 8, 1803, pg.191

(Rsh.11) September 30, 1827, proved October 20, 1829, William Hawley, negro woman named Caroline, 2 children, negro man named Nelson, negro girl Eleanor, esteemed friend Joshua Hutchison. P #1, 330, Fairfax Co., C.H., Archives, Fairfax, Va.

October 17, 1842, Joshua Hutchison, Book U pg.38, Fairfax Co., C.H., Va., Will written January 1, 1839. "salves if hired out for two years can go to Liberia or any free state of this Union.

Sarah Halley, W#1, pgs. 3, 49, X1, pgs. 7, 26, 1853, negro woman age 46 named Wireney, negro Mary Ellen age 24, negro Dinah Ann age 14, negro Emeline age 12, negro John age 9, negro Israel age 13 mos, negro Alcindy age 20

Loudoun Co., Va., C.H.

(Rsh.9) August 18, 1791, Chancery Suit, M 2484, Loudoun Co., Va., Hawley vs. Sears, female slave Tamor dec'd left two children

(Rsh.9) John Hawley mentions the following slaves in his Loudoun Co., Va., Will Book L pg.105, Book O pg.488, dated March 13, 1815, Rachel, Anne, Westley, Malinda

(Rsh.14), November 9, 1816, Barton D. Hawley and Hannah his wife, sell to Dean James land and negroes, estate derived from William James and his widow, for $450. Witness Charles Lewis, Aris Buckner. Loudoun Co., Deeds, Leesburg, Va., note: Cambridge Halley, see 1804 Loudoun Co., Va., Tax List

(Rsh.11) September 30, 1827, proved October 20, 1829, William Hawley, negro woman named Caroline, 2 children, negro man named Nelson, negro girl Eleanor, P #1, 330, Fairfax Co.,

Archives

1782 - Loudoun Co., Va., Titables - taker Charles Love
    Jeremiah Hutchison, Jr. 1
        (next door - Samuel Adams
        negroes = Sam and Sarah 3)

1785 Loudoun Co., Va., Titables - taker George Summers
    William D'Bell, Schoolmaster
        negroes - Stephen, Dark, Arthur 4

Abstracts of the Newspapers of Georgetown and the Federal City
1789-1799 compiled by F. Edward Wright, Family Line Pub. 1986
    (Rsh.9) August 20, 1799 - The Centennial of Liberty -
Zachariah Downs, Montgomery County, near the Paint Chapel
offers reward for negro woman Kate Harbert, about 19, 5'6" to
5'7", marked with small pox and curses much when angry.

Loudoun Co., Va., Titables, August 1783, C.H. Leesburg, Va.
Charles Love taker
(Rsh.13) Thomas Oden, negroes - Peter, James, Rick, 4

Barbados, West Indies

(Rsh.91) January 24, 1676, Henry Hawley, son Henry

(Rsh.91) June 6, 1679, Will, Capt. Henry Hawley, left two daughters, Susanna and Mary, son Henry

(Rsh.93) Valentine Hawley, July 20, 1651, wife Mary, brother Thomas Hawley

Patrick Haly, witness Will, 1681

English

(Rsh.89) James Hawley of Brainford Co., Middlesex, Esquire, Will, September 2, 1622, proved May 1624, to my son William Hawley, to my daus. Katherine and Susan, to my 3 children which I had by my last wife, Henry, Valentine and Thomas to be paid at their ages of 14 years, residue to my son Jerome Hawley, sole exr.

(Rsh.90) Jerome Hawley, last Will and Testament, October 20, 1633, William Hawley of Grossmont, Moumouthshire, Arthur Dodington, Lewis Hele, exrs., probation also at Provincial Court of Maryland granted, adm. to Capt. Thomas Cornwallis, (Rsh.89) with complaint from one James Hawley, Mincing Lane, London and New Brantford County Middlesex, on July 18, 1649

(Rsh.91) February 1668, James White of Barbados, merchant, who d. in Boston, New England, probate to William White with similar powers reserved to Henry Hawley, Edward Pye, James Beake, William Bate and Jeremy Edington

(Rsh.126) Francis Halley of All Hallows Staining, London, Gent, who d. in Va., dated June 28, 1698. My two messuage in Mincing Lane, Fenchurch Street, London, to my son Francis Halley with remainder to my sister Mary Ward, wife of John Ward, and Nicholas Wright of St. Giles Cripplegate, London, L5, to my brother Thomas Waller, a guinea for a mourning ring, to my cousin Edmond Halley, Mary, his wife, and their daughters Margaret and Katherine, my father and mother, Richard and Eleanor Pyke, my brothers Thomas and William Pyke and Edward Day, my sisters Jone Day and Susan Pyke, residue to my said son Francis, exrs. my cousin Edmond Halley and my father Richard Pyke, wits David Griel, Thomas Carr, William Dean and Lancelot Kerby, clerk to Mr. Carr. pr 28 Sept. 1702 by the exrs. named. prob 11/466/1449

October 1698, Will of Hobbs, Elizabeth was wife of Francis Weekes in Middlesex Co., Va., probate to Sir John Hawles, John Lilly and the relict, Catherine Hobbs with similar powers reserved to Sir John Somers.

(Rsh.90) 1651, January, reference that adm. of Jeremiah Hawley of Maryland, was granted to the principal creditor, Thomas Cornwallis

Thomas Paper, Rapier, City of London, December 4, 1658, (?Rsh.81) Susannah Rapier gave Maryland land to a Hawley who lived in Virginia.

Lewis Phillips of Huntingdon, whose cousin, John Throckmorton, was in Va., probate to William Hally, March 1670

Sir John Colleton, of Withycombe Raleigh, Devon, dated April 22, 1751, had Barony of Fairlawns, other bequests to my unhappy daughter Elizabeth, late wife of Edward Hawley Esq., proved November 13, 1754

Philip Delegal, January 22, 1762, dwelling in the Parish of St. Peters Port, Guernsey, Capt. of a Company in Lt. Parsons Regt of invalids now quartered in Guernsey, witness, Andre Migault, George Hawley and Edward Knight.

December 1817, Will of Blagborne, surviving exrs. Rowles Scudamore and Thomas Holy, renouncing.

Kentucky

Lexington Ky, Wills

(Rsh.74) Benjamin Haley, July 27, 1895, prob. 1857, wife Judith, one son James, son of wife, balance of estate to son John Haley

Maryland

MdHR, Baltimore Co., Md.

Book 15, pg.291, act. of Frances Haile, exr. of Richard Haile late of Baltimore Co., dec'd, date not recorded.

MdHR, Calvert Co., Md.

(Rsh.131) year 1674, Lib.2, folio 409, 410, Spencer Hales, Gent, sister Ann Hales to have lands, tenements and real estate, including England, Wales and America, signed Spencer Hales, March 20, 1674, proved November 14, 1675, test. Christopher Rousby, Gent, Jane Halfhead, Spinster

year 1675, Will, Wm. Edwn, upon the Cliffs, probate

February 15, 1675, appraisers, John Halles and James Veitch, before Philip Calvert, friend Rich. Ladd, Jno Edmund

year 1684, Will of Thomas Banks, wife Anne, Lib. I4, folio 126, 127, (her Will Lib.X6, folio 43 - states tract on which now lives Merine Ripp) to John Hales, a house and 800 lbs. tobacco, signed Thomas Banks, made November 10, 1684, proved July 23, 1685, test Richard Keene, Edward Molins, Wm. King, before Henry Darnell

year 1685, Lib.4, folio 86, 87, Will, Joseph Dawkins, wife Mary and her brother Thomas Hale, now living in Poakamock, test, John Steward, Thos. Owens, before Henry Darnell, proved May 9, 1685

MdHR, Cecil Co., Md.

Probate, May 10, 1740, Cecil Co., Md., Vol. 27, Folio 47, Robert Holy, wife Ann, Lot 17 Charleston and 100 acres on east side of Elk River called Holys Expedition, plantation to Stephen Smallwood when he comes of age if he does not make it, reverts to wife, gave current money of Pennsylvania, probate June 26, 1749.

Ann Holy, Probate Cecil Co., Md., August 24 1761, Vol. 31, pg.430, beloved dau. Ann Rodolph, grandson Thos. Taylor, grand daus. Elizabeth Kerr, Anne Bristoe, Rachael Bristoe, Rebecca Bristoe, Elizabeth Bristoe, Milligent Bristoe, Isabella Clark, Hannah Alexander, Maery Veazyore, grandson John Bristow, Grand dau. Ann Consitheisone, cousin Ann Cowther, Jr., son Wm. Bristoe.

MdHR, Charles Co., Md.

(Rsh.79) Will, John Long, November 19, 1697, proved January 10, 1697, Book 7, pg.335, wife Eleanor to care for Mary and Elizabeth Haley daus. of Clement dec'd who were left in care of Test. by father, when Mary and Elizabeth Haly are educated and come of age, their estate property belongs to them. Should wife die in minority of aforesaid children, their grandfather Edward Turner to have charge of them and their estate, test Jno Scott, James Williams, Abednego, Jen Kinson, Wm. Howell. Probate, Vol. 15, pg.299, December 30, 1697.

(Rsh.127) John Haley witnessed, (he made mark +) along with Richard Morris, and Matthew Murphy, Will of Benjamin Warren in Charles Co., Md., on February 11, 1705.

(Rsh.127) John Haley, late of Charles Co., Md., adm.
Elizabeth Haley, May 18, 1718, Inv. in Will Books
    (Rsh.127) Elizabeth Haley, adm. of John Halley, late of
Charles Co., Md., dec'd., probate May 6, 1719, final act. Orphan,
Inv., Lib. 4, folio 238
    (Rsh.127) 1718, Elizabeth Haley, 1718-1719, adm. of John
Haley, late of Charles Co., intestate, pd. Wm. Em Hinter,
plantation whereon intestate lived.
    (Rsh.127) Accounts, Charles Co., Md., 1718/1719, #. 1,
folio 299, Adm. Elizabeth Haley of John Haley, knowth a crop of
tobacco by weight 2541 lbs., Wm. Hunter rent of plantation
whereon intestate lived, tobacco due Patrick Connelly, final
account Elizabeth Haley adm. Act. #7. Stephen Manakin and
John Butts, adm. of Elizabeth Haley late of Charles Co., dec'd.,
paid John King, Corner, for an inquisition on the body, paid
Thomas Haley a minor one of the children of the dec'd.
    (Rsh.127) Goods and Chattels of Elizabeth Haly, late of
Charles Co., Md., dec., appraised August 19, 1720, L.B5
    (Rsh.127) 1720, Elizabeth Haley, Book 4, pg.134, act. of
John Butts and Stephen Manakin, adm. of Elizabeth Haley, late of
Charles Co., Md., balance to be paid to 3 minor children of dec.
    (Rsh.127) 1722, Elizabeth Hally, Accounts 1722, Vol.5,
folio 78.
    March 1748, Patrick Halley, Inv., Charles Co., Md., pg.11,
#3299, pt14
    (Rsh.1),Will, John Holly, July 16, 1755, September 20,
1755, Probate, (John Holly signed name) Charles Co., Md., Book
30 #1, pg.41, Book A.D. #5, pg.49, #2, BT #2, pgs. 41, 42, June
16, 1755, Test. Pro #36, pg.227, January 16, 1756, left three
tracts of land to his three sons. Thomas received tract called
Exetor in P.G.Co., Md., Nathaniel received two tracts where John
Sr. now resided, Costly and Costly Addition, also 3 sows and pigs
and the cattle that belong to this Plantation, and son John
received tract called Fellowship in Frederick Co., Md. Executor
wife Easter. Witnesses June Summers, John Burch and James
Greene. June Summers in proof of Will said that she thought
"John Holly was out of his head."
    (Rsh.1), Inventories #63, August 4, 1757, Charles Co.,
Md., pg.495, August 4, 1757, John Halley, Charles Co., Md., 39 -
16 -0 Creditors, John Sample, Samuel Hanson. Kin, Nathaniel
Hoslley and Esther Halley; by Samuel Middleton.

(Rsh.1) August 4, 1757, John Halley, Charles Co., Md., 39 - 16 -0 Creditors, John Sample, Samuel Hanson. Kin, Nathaniel Hoslley and Esther Halley, Samuel Middleton. Inventories #63, August 4, 1757, Charles Co., Md., pg.495.

(Rsh.1) Book 63, pg.494, August 4, 1757, goods and chattels, John Holly, Charles Co., Md., 1 bible, 4 flag chairs, 4 elm bottom chairs, 2 small looking glasses, 6 lbs. old pewter, 1 cupboard, parcel lumber, 1 sq. table, 1 oval table

(Rsh.2) Thomas Marshall of Charles Co., wife Sabina Truman Marshall, tract of land called Canick, Canick Mistake, son Thomas Hanson Marshall, nephew Thomas Marshall, Richard Marshall, father of Thomas, Sarah Stoddert? (relationship not stated) McCubbin, Thomas, grandson, McCubbin, Zach?, bro. of Thomas McCubbin, exrs. Sabina Truman Marshall, wife, Thomas Hanson Marshall, son, witnesses, Alison Ford, Thomas Holley, and John Ford, probate June 4, 1759

(Rsh.1) September 22, 1761, Hester Burch Hawley's estate Inv. in Charles Co., Md., Book 76, pg.301-303; Box 19, Folder 34, Hall of Records, Annapolis, Md., to contain a small old looking glass, 3 old chairs, 1 washing tub, 1 lanton and tin kinnell, 1 old small book, 1 teapot, cups, saucers and hop bason, 8 earthern plates, 6 3/4 lb of perter, 5 1/2 lbs old perter, 1 old fiddle, nearest of kin Nathaniel Hawley, nearest next of kin John Hally, Thomas Hally, Adm. Creditors - John Baynes for Robert, Robert Wade for Christopher Loundes and Com.

MdHR, Dorchester Co., Md.
    December 1688, Joseph Halles, Will, Test, Dorchester Co.

MdHR, Kent Co., Md.
    John Haleys, Book 2, folio 76, Book 1, folio 99, folio 299, Book 62, accounts 1708, pgs. 222, 226, 162, 178
    Probate, Kent Co., Md., Box 14, Folder 31, 1748, Patrick Holley, Inv., note: in poor condition, difficult to read.
    (Rsh.134) William Haleys, Book 31, pg.171, land of William Haleys boundary "The Gift," probate February 1762.
    (Rsh.134) Elizabeth Smithers, widow, give to god dau. Mary Elizabeth Haley, dau. of Wm. Haley, my white silk damask gown...other half to be divided between Elizabeth Hanna Haley and ...Wm. Haley, exrs. along with brother W. Comogys, probate February 10, 1762

Acct. Ann Haley, 1769, Box 17, folder 40, balance, Liber 5, folio 229

(Rsh.134) William Haley, Haly, signed April 24, 1770, Book 37, pg.525, Will, William Haley, son William under 21 years of age, wife Elizabeth Hennretta, pregnant, all my daus. under age 21, witness Samuel Thompson, James McClure, Mary McClure, #635, 1775

MdHR, Montgomery Co., Md.

(Rsh.9) October 7, 1813 probate date, Mary Downs, Montgomery Co., Md., names children: (Rsh.9) Mary Holly, Zachariah Downs, Henry Downs, Lucy Hallsal. Will written October 11, 1804, Montgomery Co., Md., Wills X LH F 315/L2, pg.355

MdHR, Prince George Co., Md.

(Rsh.1) TB#5, 1720-21, pgs. 220, 221, Box 2, Folder 62, John Burch, Planter, Prince George Co., Md., Will written April 12, 1720, proved November 12, 1720, wife Elizabeth, witnesses, Thomas Edelin and James Green, to wife Elizabeth 1/2 of estate, to son Francis Burch and dau. Easter Haly, the other 1/2, to Mary Panty, one cow and calf, two sows, pigs, son Francis, personality bought of Stephen Cawley, kin Francis Burch and John Holly, John Holly signed his name, note: by July 24, 1721, the widow Elizabeth Burch had m. James Reid, and James Reid d. shortly thereafter leaving legacy to heirs in Scotland

(Rsh.1) John Burch, Inv. #4, 1720, P.G.Co., Md., pgs. 329, 331, December 23, 1720. Box 2, Folder 62. Thomas Edelin and James Green (+) Creditor James Stoddert

Test, November 9, 1726, Book 27, pg.359. This day came Mary Ann Holly the relicit of John Melton, dec'd and declared that she would not be anyway concerned with her former husband's estate, given under her hand and seal this day and year, Mary Ann Holly, her mark+

(Rsh.1) 1729 Test P.G.Co., Md., November 12, 1729, Vol. 28, pg.428, Richard Shophard his adm. bond in common for by Elizabeth Shophard his adm. with James Roodz, John Holly, her sureties post 30 lbs.

(Rsh.1) December 1743, Will Test George Gentle by John Holly, Prince George Co., Md.

(Rsh.1) P.G. Co., Bonds, Box 13, Folder 6, April 9, 1745,

Humphry Deverson, late of P.G. Co., John Holly, Thomas Holly and John Emerson of P.G. Co., Planters, post bond of 50 lbs. sterling money, exhibit unto the Prerogative Court at Annapolis before the 9th day of July, Inv. of goods, chattels and credits of dec'd., by John Holly, adm.; Box 14, folder 42, Humphry Deaverson, John Holly adm., horse, saddle, silver buckles, parcel of old tools, small chest, tankard, 2 razors, old gun, table, handsaw, skillet, year old heffer, 10 lbs. feathers, 5 lbs. deerskins, total 8-17-10 1/2; Book 23, pg.91, Book 32, pg.45.

(Rsh.2) Joseph Williams, his Will and Test. bond in common form by Catherine Williams, his adm. with Thomas Holley and Thomas Athey of P.G. Co., Planters her sureties, 100 lbs, February 16, 1746

(Rsh.1) November 24, 1746, John Hally, adm. of Humphrey Deverson, dec'd, Accounts #23, 1747-1747 P.G. Co., Md., pgs.91, 92, 24 Nov. 1746.

(Rsh.2) Richard Edelin, Will, dated July 16, 1760, grandson Philip Edelin of Thomas bequeathed 200 acres of Calverton Manor, where Thomas Hally and Joseph Crown live.

(Rsh.1) June 23, 1761, Bonds, P.G., Co., Thomas Halley, Thomas Marshall and James Wood, Bond of L 50 Sterling on estate of Ester Halley, witnesses, Benjamin Brookes, G. Scott, Bonds, P.G. Co., Md., Box 14, Folder 60.

(Rsh.2), Liber I.L.#B, folio, pgs.617, 618, 1769 Probate, June 16, 1769, written February 21, 1769, Thomas Hawley, Will, Prince George Co., Md., leaves dwelling plantation during widowhood to wife, then to my sons John, Samuel and James Burch Hawley equally. To my son John my negro Frank; to my son Samuel my negro Harry; to son James Burch my negro Will; to my dau. Bathsheba Halley my negro Lanord and personality; to my dau. Elizabeth Halley my negro Jane; residue equally to my children John, Samuel, John, James Burch Hally, Bathsheba and Elizabeth at remarriage of my wife. I have already given to my dau. Sarah Gordon her part of my estate; Wife Elizabeth and son Samuel exrs. Witness: John Emerson, John Lovejoy.

(Rsh.2), May 19, 1769, Bond, 1769, Box 17, Folder 35, P.G. Co., Md., L 400, England, Elizabeth Hally and (Rsh.5) Samuel Hally, exrs. Sureties, John Wynn & Francis Green, witness G. Scott(Rsh.2) June 16, 1769, Thomas Holly, Inv. L 390 - 3 - 10, including 8 negroes. Appraisers; Jno. Hawkins and Ignat Wheeler, Kin Nathl Hally and John Halley, Jr., Creditors, Rob

Ferguson for John Glassford, George Oswald for David Dalyell and Thomas Clagett.

(Rsh.2) August 8, 1769, Elizabeth and Samuel Halley, Exrs. made Oath.

(Rsh.2), Inv. L 390, pgs. 3 to 10, June 16, 1769, Thomas Holly, including 8 negroes. Appraisers; Jno. Hawkins and Ignat Wheeler, Kin (Rsh.3) Nathl Hally and (Rsh.9) John Halley, Jr., Creditors, Rob Ferguson for John Glassford, George Oswald for David Dalyell and Thomas Clagett. August 8, 1769, Elizabeth and (Rsh.5) Samuel Halley, exrs. made Oath.

(Rsh.2), June 20, 1769, # 37, folio, 276, 341, Elizabeth Hally renounces husband's Will and takes her lawful part of her dec'd husband, Thomas Hally's real and personal estate. Witnessed by James Brown and Robert Ferguson

(Rsh.2), Accounts #66, 1771-1772, P.G. Co., Md., pg.272, July 15, 1770, Thomas Holly, dec'd, additional account filed with Court by Elizabeth Holly and Samuel Holly exrs. of Thomas Holly dec'd.

(Rsh.2), Box 22, Folder 32, December 20, 1771, Elizabeth Holly swore to Original Inv., P.G. Co., Md.

(Rsh.2) Elizabeth E. Hawley, Book T., #1, Lib. 49, Prince George Co., Md., August 24, 1773, probate written January 26th 1773, Elizabeth E. Hawley, Will, being low but of sound and disposing mind and memory, gives to dau. Elizabeth Holly negroes Nell, Nan and Tom. Appoints Robert Gordon, exr. of Will and guardian of Elizabeth until she reaches 16 years of age. Witnesses John Emerson, Richard Emerson.

(Rsh.4 or Rsh.9) CC#2, pg.152, June 7, 1775, Bill of Sale, between John Halley, Jr., Planter of P.G.Co., Md., and John and Richard Emerson and John Dyer

(Rsh.2) Liber #11, folio 6l7, T #1, folio 48 and 95, John Emmerson, Will, September 12, 1777 names his children Elizabeth Holly, Lucy Emmerson, George Emmerson and dau. Eleder Shing. He left his children 190 acres called "Little Troy."

(Rsh.4) John Edelen, 1786 bequeathed negroes to his son John. But if John Edelen m. either of the daus. of John Halley then the slaves were to revert to his grandson Robert P. Edelen."

(Rsh.4) John Halley, February 22, 1800, T#1, folio 439, Prince George Co., Md., wife Elizabeth, two eldest sons, Thomas Halley and John Halley to have tract of land Exeter after death of mother, bequests to Hillery Hanson Wade, alias Halley, and Elizabeth Meeks Emerson, 50 lbs., after death of Elizabeth property to be equally divided between remaining children, Samuel Halley, Nathaniel Halley, Penellopy Peacock, Mildred Emerson, Mary Athey, Ama Pyle, Elizabeth Price Pumphery, witness, John Harris

<u>MdHR, St. Mary's Co., Md.</u>

(Rsh.92) Wm. Hawley's, Will, reference is made to, March 24, 1652, Capt. William Hawley declared before Provincial Court that Jerome Hawley had right to 6,000 acres of land that were not taken up at the time of his death, a survey was authorized of the 6,000 acres for Capt. Hawley in satisfaction of a Deed from James Hawley, land on west side of the Chesapeake Bay on St. Jerome's Creek, surveyed September 12, 1653. Capt. William Hawley d. at his seat on St. Jerome's Creek in 1654 testate, last Will and Testament lost during the Puritan Rebellion. Most of landed estate of William Hawley descended to his godson William Gwyther.

(Rsh.79) Book 2, folio 51, John Roberts, May 4, 1671, proved April 9, 1675, to John Roberts son of Peter...at 16 years of age and in case of mortality before said to be equally divided between Wm. Sommerhill and Clement Haly, give all the rest of my estate to Clement Haley, his heirs, that is to say my Plantation during the term of the lease, Clement Haley to be my executor in the presence of Ed. Connerie, Joshua Gilbert, Gurbert, folio 51, Will proved by Edward Comerie, May 4, 1675, William Rosewell send to swear in warrants to Edward Connerie and Thomas Carville to appraise.

(Rsh.79) John Barecroft, June 4, 1693, proved July 20, 1693, Book 6, pg.43, godsons viz, John son of Col. Nehemiah Blackiston...Madam Susan Blackiston, wife of Col. Blackiston, the children of John and Rebecca Newman to be brought up as protestants...brother Stephan personal property in England, St. Eleanor in Worchester City England, exrs. John and Rebecca Newman, overseers Clement Haly, John Rose, Wm. Escott, Chris. Knight, George Perry, Wm. Heather

(Rsh.79) Edward Turner, December 28, 1693, proved July 27, 1709, Book 12, folio 158A, Edward Turner, ...it is my will that if it shall to fall out my two grandchildren Mary Hly, Hey, or Elizabeth Hly, Hey, two daus. of Clement Hly, Hey, shall come to

want and poverty then I do hereby order and charge 1st eldest
son Thomas Turner to care for them, second son Samuel Turner,
and third daughter Elizabeth Turner to care for my two
grandchildren to allow grandchildren a convenient maintenance
until they shall grow up to years of discretion to be able to
maintain themselves or shall be m., beloved wife Mary Turner, in
accordance with anti-nuptial...want to be bur. between the graves
of my two former wives...witness, Wm. Hodgson, Mary Hodgson,
Wm. Heather, Robert Foster, Lofler, Phillip Briscoe, endorsed,
July 27, 1709

(Rsh.79) Clement Haley, Book 7, pg.335, January 4, 1694,
to Tacy Price, Abraham Price 400 lbs. tobacco, to Anne Taylor,
property to daus., John Long to care for daus., Clement Haley
signed his name, exr. John Long, test. James Harris, Thomas
Harris, Cleborne Lomax

MdHR, Queen Anne Co., Md.

November 1738, Patrick Halley, Will, Test, Queen Anne's
Co.

North Carolina
Chrowan and Bertie Cos., N.C.

(Rsh.135) August 22, 1726, Isaac Ricks adm. of the estate
of dec'd. Nathaniel Holley, Deed Book B., pg. 175

(Rsh.136) John Holly, Will dated December 23, 1728, two
sons, John and Richard, wife Sarah.

(Rsh.136) James Holly, Will dated December 19, 1761,
names children, John, James, Tamor, and wife Sarah and states
that wife is pregnant.

Virginia
VSL, Accomac Co., Va.

(?Rsh.90) Will of Francis Wharton, October 6, 1695, prob.
June 4, 1700, Accomac Co., witness Robert Hawley

(Rsh.86) Will of Peter Watson, February 24, 1776, probate
March 26, 1776, Accomac Co., witness Abel Hawley

(Rsh.86) Abel Hawley, Will, written October 1, 1795,
proved, January 26, 1796, wife Sarah, gave tool chest and silver
smiths tools son Henry, proved by Ephraim Watson and Levi
Hutchinson, sureties Wm. Read and Samuel Trader

(Rsh.80) William Haley, Will, November 24, 1799, found in

Haley's Lessee, vs. Ejectment Proceedings, That William Haley, the elder, late of the County of Accomac, was in his lifetime...made and published his last Will and Testament on November 24, 1799, to son James Haley, all my land and for want of heirs, if no heirs land to my son William Halley, (wife and Jesse Kellan, exrs.) said William Halley departed this life November 1813, that at the date of making the said Will the said William Halley, the elder, had four children, James, William, Leah and Benjamin, and after the date of said Will and before the death of said William, he had additional children b. to wit, George Halley, b. September 1800, Jesse Halley, b. March 11, 1805, John Halley, b. November 9, 1809... the son James Halley departed this life before his father without having m., May 26, 1818, Court Records, Accomac Co., Va.

Albermarle, Co., Va., C.H.

(Rsh.13) May 7, 1838, County Court ordered Inv. of Abraham Hawley's estate, Book 13, pgs. 132, 224, Albermarle Co., Va.

(Rsh.13) May 7, 1838, Court Order, Inv. of Abraham Hawleys estate, "one crobar, 1 rock auger, hand saw and mataxe, rock hammer, ox joke, lot of old iron, old plough, waggon breechen (old) lot of hatters tools, lime sive and frame, bedstead, set of plough gear, cutting knife and fox, grindstone, wheel barrow, one day clock, old waggon, but saw, cotten wheel, log chain, pair stulyard, walnut table, 5 old windsor chairs, 1 dish, 2 plates, 3 forks, hocte, lot of old books, one feather bedstead, underbead, furniture, one feather bedstead, one small bed, 4 butter pots, cullender, axe and snuffers, oven pot, 2 pairs hooks a small pail, 1 cotton wheel, 1 flax wheel."

(Rsh.13) July 1838, Mary Ann Hawley receives her 1/3 part of land of Abraham Holly dec'd, including a lot with dwelling house, kitchen and smokehouse, together with the privilege of using water from the Spring near the Branch and an additional 12 acres of woodland to be taken off north corner of tract purchased of Gilmer. Book___, pg.135, Albermarle Co., Va.

(Rsh.13) 1839 adm., Mary Holly, Abraham Holly, Albermarle Co., Va., Inv., Book 13, pg.l32, adm., Book 13, pg.224

(Rsh.13) July 24, 1843, between James Fitz of the one part, and Mary A. Hawley of the other part, both of the County of

Albermarle, Mary A. Hawley for the sum of $85.34 which has been paid to Richard N. Anderson and the balance $51. secured by bond this day given and due the 24th of July 1844, hath granted bargained and sold to the said Fitz all my dower interest in the estate of Abraham Hawley dec'd my late husband called Limestone. Adjoining the lands of David Hancocke, Charles Huckstep and Dr. Blatterman and the woodland adjoining the land of David Hancock, Charles Huckstep and Martha I. Minor...signed Mary Ann Hawley, James Fitz, witness Lyman Bromham, James Dolue, William E. Blomson.
note: Dr. Blatterman, was reportedly a very colorful figure. He was brought from Germany by Mr. Thomas Jefferson to teach German at the University of Virginia in Charlottesville.

VSL, Alexandria, Va.
William G. Halley, Jr., Will Book 4, pg.227
(Rsh.7) December 5, 1808, William Hawley, Will Book C., pg.l52, Alexandria, Va., names wife Ester.
(Rsh.7) Esther Hawley d. September 1831, gave personal belongings to poor, gave to Baptist Church in Alexandria, Va., and bequeathed to Nancy Bridwell

VSL, Amherst Co., Va.
William Cabell, Will, January 3, 1769, proved June 6, 1774, witnesses, John Savage, Samuel Banks, John Hawley, Book 1, pg.262
Daniel Perrow, Will, June 15, 1801, John Harley, adm.

VSL, Caroline Co., Va.
year 1771, Thomas and Mary Haley, exr. John Haley

VSL, Charles City, Co., Va.
John Hally, chirurgeon, (sp?) paid 350 lbs. tobacco from Maj. Jo. Westhorpe, dec'd estate in 1656

VSL, Essex Co., Va.
Will of Hailes, August 17, 1744, names Francis Hailes, John Hailes, Thomas Hailes, Benjamin Hailes, Mary Hailes, Susanna Hailes

Fairfax Co., Va., C.H.

John Harle, wife Elizabeth, son John Harle, dau. Frances Harle, September 27, 1749, July 13, 1749, exr. Benjamin Sebastian, Wm. Elzey, wit. Jacob Laswell, Benjamin Shreve, Moses Pinnett, Wm. Groome

Wm. Harle, Harley, 1750, of Truro Parish, probate March 27, 1750, daus. Ann, Betty, Sarah and Jermima, sister and brother-in-law Mary and Daniel James

(Rsh.76) Richard Simpson, September 19, 1761, proved December 21, 1762, Wife Sary (Sara), sons George, Moses, Richard, dau. Elizabeth Halley, Sary Windsor, Mary Canterbury, grand dau. Caron Happack, grandson George Windsor

(Rsh.76) Sarah Simpson, August 10, 1766, sons Moses, George, Richard, Wm., 3 daus. one named Elizabeth Halley, granddau. Sarah Simpson, dau. of George and grand dau. Sarah Halley, grand dau. Sarah Windsor, Sarah Simpson, dau. of Richard

(Rsh.5) Will Book C., Will of John Sheridin, written September 6, 1767, proved May 16, 1768, legatees, Barberry Sheridin, wife, John Sheridin, father, witness Samuel Johnson and Samuel Fielder

(Rsh.5) July 8, 1771, Samuel Halley, Barbara Halley and Stephen Donaldson, witness Will of Hannah Johnson, Fairfax, Co., Va., presented September 17, 1771, son John , daus. Tamor Simpson, Frances Cleveland, Ann Thompson, Susannah Johnson, Hannah Johnson, witness Samuel Halley, Barbara Halley, Stephen Donaldson; Hannah Johnson's husband's Will, Book C., Samuel Johnson, presented June 19, 1769, May 1, 1769,written, wife Hannah, sons Samuel and John, daus. Susannah, Hannah, Frances Cleveland, husband James Cleveland, Tamer Simpson and Ann Thompson. Grandchildren, Hannah Johnson, dau. of son Samuel, Samuel Simpson, exrs. wife and son Samuel. Witness, John Orr, Joseph Thompson, Thomas Triplett

(Rsh. 5), May 17, 1779, presented; written April 4, 1777, Will, Lib. D #1, pg.117, Samuel Hawley of Fairfax Co., Colony of Va., beloved wife Barbery, all estate, except three negroes Cambridge, young Jerry and Jacob, she to enjoy them during her natural life and at her death my will is that my brother-in- law, William Halley shall receive and enjoy the three negroes as his right and property...if William Halley dies before my wife then the whole of my estate to be at the disposal of my wife. Witness

John Ratcliff, Zachariah Morris, George Bozwell.

(Rsh.5) Samuel Hawley, Inv. 1780

(Rsh.3) August 29, 1791, Nathaniel Hawley, Estate account L #1, pg.291, Fairfax Co., Va., Mary Halley, widow, cash paid to Thomas Halley, a witness and order of court, cash paid to John Halley, 6 slaves to be delivered to legatees...John Moore acting for William Halley's exr., William Haleys now dec'd. Estate settled November 19, 1818.

(Rsh.76) James Hawley, proved July 6, 1792, children, William, James, Jr., John, Richard, Frances, Henry Simpson, Sarah Hanigane (Haney) Sybill Peak, Mary Crump, Susannah Said

(Rsh.4) September 19,1796, Will Book G, DI 118, DBT 540, Will Barbara Ratcliff, left to nephew George Fielder, and legatee Baptist Church at Backlick. Witness William Halley, Edward Potter.

(Rsh.77) Book I., pg.460, Wm. Hawley, dated January 17, 1798, presented 1806, wife Catherine, brothers Henry Simpson, James, son of James (Wm.) brother Richard, sons of Henry Simpson, Henry and James, sister Tuckery Laid, her son Elkanah Laid, sister Mary, sister Tibble Peake, brother John, sisters Sarah Haynie, sons Richard and Henry Haynie, sisters Mary Crump, Suckey Said, Witness Gust. H. Scott and Robert Marshall

(Rsh.3), August 17, 1799, William Hawley adm. of Nathaniel, dec'd against Francis Stone and Daniel Lewis for 297.12.10

(Rsh.77) June 17, 1806, Liber GG to 1807, Catherine Halley, wife of William Halley, renounces Will. another reference on pg.380

(Rsh.14) Liber K. pg.169, November 15, 1813, Barton D. Hawley and Coleman Lewis appointed guardian to James Turner, Orphan

(Rsh.77) May 25, 1819, William Halley, Superior Court Will Book, William Halley, County of Fairfax, nieces, Catherine Halley, Sarah Ann Halley, Mary Maria Halley, nephews James H. Halley, Henry S. Halley and William F. Halley children of brother Henry H. Halley, tract of land in Fairfax County willed to me by Uncle William Halley 130 acres. Silas Burke, exr.

(Rsh.77) August 16, 1819, William Halley dec'd, Inv. of estate recorded.

(Rsh.75) George W. Halley, Book N. pg.168, September

15, 1823, wife Sally, mentions children but not named, witness James M. Halley, Caleb Simpson, Peyton Simpson

(Rsh.11) October 10, 1829, William Hawley, Will, presented to Fairfax Co., Court. Written September 30, 1827, Left farm to be equally divided between sons Jeremiah and William. Names grandson William Hutchison, grandchildren Barthsheba Hutchison, Joshua Hutchison, John Hutchison. Negro woman named Caroline with 2 children, negro man named Nelson, negro girl Eleanor, esteemed friend Joshua Hutchison, witness Gustaves H., Scott, Jr., Robert Marshall.

(Rsh.11) October 21, 1829, William Hawley, dec'd, Will again presented further proved by Richard J. Daniel, exr. Joshua Hutchison and exr. Elizabeth Hawley refused to act. Elijah Hutchison to adm. estate. Appraisers, George Hancick, Andrew Heath, Thomas B. Mersheons, Thomas W. Lee or Andrew Hutchison, William Hawley, 1829, pg.135, October 20, 1829, Will presented by Joshua Hutchison, exr. proved by Gustaous H. Scott

(Rsh.78) Henry Simpson Hawley, February 18, 1835, presented December 5, 1838, children, Hampton, Henry, James, Samuel, Killey, Tammy, Elizabeth, Margaret, appoints 3 sons adms. John H. Hawley, Henry S. Hawley and James M. Hawley

Sarah Halley, W#1, pgs. 3, 49, X1, pgs. 7, 26, 1853, 3 dau. m. Isaiah Chappell, dau. m. Hermes Reeves, dau. m. Thomas W. Martin, negro woman age 46 named Wireney, negro Mary Ellen age 24, negro Dinah Ann age 14, negro Emeline age 12, negro John age 9, negro Israel age 13 mos, negro Alcindy age 20, Thomas Martin, adm.

(Rsh.4) other husband for Barbara Hawley, Radcliff, proved by Fairfax Co., Va., Will Book D I, pg.118, Deed Book T., pg.540

VSL, Frederick Co., Va.

Jacob Hawley, 1758, Inv.

VSL, Isle of White Co.

(Rsh.116) Thomas Poole, age about 60 years, leg. grandchild Poole Hawle; 100 acres, where John Hawle lives, to my grandchild John Hawle, dau. Christian Hawle, wife Christian, exrs. September 12, 1681, rec. June 9, 1682

(Rsh.117) John Hole, Book 1, pg.70, dying intestate, adm.

requested by relict Mary, August 9, 1688

<u>VSL, Loudoun Co., Va.</u>
(Rsh.9) Fielding Turner, March 10, 1793, proved 1794, sons Lewis, Major, Fielding, John Turner and unborn child, wife Winnifred, exrs. Jere. Hutchison, John Hawley, Charles Lewis, witnesses, John Berkley, John Davis, James Dutton, John Hutchison
note: Fielding Turner was a Justice of the Fairfax County Virginia Court 1752 to 1757. The Justices were land owners appointed to the Court by the Governor.
Elizabeth Harley, Book E., pg.212, February 26, 1796, proved October 10, 1796, legatees John Gunnell and William Shreve of Maryland, suit of adm. of John Harle, Elizabeth Harle, to be renewed by her executors.
(Rsh.11) Benjamin Hutchison, November 15, 1796, appraisers (Rsh.9) John Hawley, Andrew Heath and Timothy Pagit.
(Rsh.10) 1804, Estate of Benjamin Jorden, June 9, 1804, Ann Jordan, Adm., witness Absalom Hawley, Sinous Lucas, Peter A. Abyer
(Rsh.77) January 17, 1798, presented April 22, 1806. Book I, folio 460, William Hawley of Loudoun County, Va., wife Catherine, brothers Henry Simpson, James, son of James, William, Richard, brother Elkanah Laid, sister Mary, sister Tiibble Peake, brother John, sisters Sarah Haynie, Mary Crump, Tuckey Laid, Book L #1, pg.372, appraisers, James Langster, Richard Windsor, John Lee, sworn by Henry H. Halley
(Rsh.9) March 13, 1815, Will, proved, John Hawley, February 20, 1815, written, Wills, Loudoun Co., Va., Book L. pg.105, and Book O. pg.488. Leave all land whereon I now live to my dau. Mary during her life provided she remains single but if she should marry it shall be sold together with my other property not named herein and an equal division among my children shall be made, except to my son Barton to whom I have heretofore given what my judgement dictated to me was right. I give to Mary D. Hawely, two negroes named Rachel and Anne and likewise a bed and furniture and a cow and calf, bequest to grandson Thomas Davis, a negro boy named Westley, likewise a bed and furniture and a cow and calf, grandau. Mary Davis, a negro girl named Malinda, likewise a bed and furniture and a cow and calf. I

nominate James McKim and Robert Latham my executors to this my last Will and Testament and do hereby revoke all other wills made by me. Signed, sealed and delivered in the presence of Lewis Hutcheson, Lewis Ambler, William James, Sanford Lyne note: later exhibits in Chancery Records prove Mary D. Hawley to be wife, not dau.

(Rsh.14) year 1819, Chanc. M6575, Orator and Oratrix, Barton D. Holley and Hannah his wife, late Hannah James, Nancy James, William James, Enoch Hutchison and Abigail his wife late Abigail James....William James d. intestate, October 1813...300 acres, 8 negroes, estate...Dean James Adm. guardian to John James infant., Loudoun Co., C.H. Leesburg, Va.

(Rsh.14), November 8, 1819, Will of Andrew Heath, names son Isaac to have land in Prince William Co., Va.,+ $5.00 and no more, dau. Rhuhannah McKim, m. James McKim, and then Thomas Beck, Sarah James, m. Abel James, Lindia Heath and 7 grandchildren of Catherine Hawley. Catherine is dec'd - give and bequeath to Barton D. Hawley $5.00, and no more - share to 7 children of Catherine Hawley. Grandchildren are named as Andrew H. Hawley, Louisa Hawley m. E.P. Church, Sarah Hawley, Lucinda Hawley m. Chapin H.Harris, Lamech Hawley, Malinda Hawley m. John Shoff, and d. witness to Will Thomas Davis, William James, Timothy Paget. Loudoun Chancery Records M21, M721, Loudoun Co., C.H., Leesburg, Va., Andrew Heath's estate $5,195.89

VSL, Louisa Co., Va.

Francis Clark, Will, January 8, 1770, Book 2, pg.75, land to Isham Haley, 100 acres, bequests to daug. Agnes Haley, Elizabeth Haley and granddau. Cordelia Haley

(Rsh.73) John Haley Sr., wife Mary, his Will Louisa Co., Va., 1777, Book 2, pg.327, children: Tabitha m. James Dyches, Ursuly m. Crews, Sarah m. Will Dyches, William m. Elizabeth Clark, Benjamin m. Judith Dyches a widow, Randolph m. Agnes Clark, John Randolph Jr., m. Martha Fulcher, Bartlett m. Jane Statnam, Delia m. Henry Dyches

VSL, Northumberland Co., Va.

(?Rsh.118) George Higgins, Northumberland Co., proved September 20, 1651, give to Thomas Halles, half my shallop with half of all that doth belong to her with one yearling bull that is black. Give to Samuel Lening and (Rsh.71) John Hayles, son of Thomas Hayles, a cow and calf, witness John Pitts, Hugh Lee, exr. John Trussell

(?Rsh.118) November 25, 1652, Account of Thomas Hailes, adm. of Robert Honnebourne, late of Yeacomocoe, in the Co. of Northumberland dec'd.

Thomas Hales, Will, September 3, 1658, proved November 23, 1658, estate left to wife Anne. Small estate.

(Rsh.118) Northumberland Co., Thomas Orley, Will written August 11, 1662, probate October 8, 1662, names wife, sister and her family. Wm. Jollard, Jollins m. widow of Thomas Orley, Rebecca Orley, estate of Thomas Orley, Cherry Point. Large estate, L31.998

(Rsh.82) November 21, 1677, Major Pierce, Will, Joh. Neale to receive...white and colored linen at Edward Halleyes...father John Sinckler, Merchant, in Colleraine Ballamony...witness, Samll: Sinkler, Northumberland Co., note; reference in Will Book dated November 27, 1709, Wm. Calvert, Esq., father to Charles Calvert of Stafford, Gent, part of 3000 acres on Piscataway in Charles Co., which was granted to Wm. Calvert, Esq., father to Charles, said 600 acres was given or intended to be given in marriage with Elizabeth, daughter of Wm. Calvert, to James Neale

Peter Knight, Will, November 1702, proved July 18, 1705, of Wicomico, sons Leonard Knight, James Knight, daus. Elizabeth Knight and Mary Knight; Eliz. Knight to have gift from Grandfather James Hawley

(Rsh.113 or ?Rsh.71 descendant) Jane Holley, widow and relict of Thomas Holley, dec'd, March 17, 1707, Book 4, pg.507

pgs. 350, 351, October 29, 1677, Grace Ashton, widow of Capt. John Ashton, witness John Hallek, Robert Readman, Northumberland Co.

VSL, Orange Co., Va.

(Rsh.74) Will Ben Haley, Book 3, pg.549

(Rsh.72) Edward Haley, Sr., Will, proved 1753, Book 2, pg.186, wife Catherine, December 29, 1752, St. Thomas's Parish, very sick and weak in body, children: Edward Jr., m. Mary, he d. before 1728, children, Sarah, Mary; James m. Susanna; (Rsh.74) Benjamin; William; Thomas; David; Elizabeth m. Christopher; (Rsh.73) John m. Mary; Ambrose; Sarah m. Oakes; Valentine m.

James Herndon, wife Catherine adm. with Thomas and Benjamin Haley, witness Lancelott Rea, Hampton Haley, Volentine (her mark) Haley, Benjamin Cave, William Haley, presented September 27, 1753, by Catherine Haley and Thomas Haley, proved by Benjamin Cave, Gent, and Humphrey Haley, securities, Benjamin Cave and James Herndon

VSL, Prince William Co., Va.
       year 1792, Elizabeth Hawley, dec., Inv. Book H, pg.28
       year 1838, Sarah M. Hawley, Will, Book O, pg.389
       year 1850, Eleanor Hawley, Inv., Book P., pg.465, sale pg.466

VSL, Shenandoah Co., Va.
       Peter Arter Burn, wife Sarah, sons and daughters not named. Will Book F., pg.146, witness - Bradford Taylor, John Hawley, Nancy Hawley, dated May 23, 1796 and proved July 11, 1803

VSL, Stafford Co., Va.
       (?Rsh.126) Court Orders, pg.4, April 7, 1664, Francis Hales presents himself as security for widow Ann Porter, adm. of estate of dec'd husband Jacob Porter,
       (?Rsh.126) Court Orders, pg.38, February 15, 1665, Francis Hales, adm. estate of John Giles, Hiles
       (Rsh.119) Book Z, pg.448, January 12, 1708, John Halley, Inv., Estate of John Hayley, total Inv. 650, signed Elizabeth Hayley, Joel Stribling, James Halls

VSL, Westmoreland Co., Va.
       Henry Hawly, and Jacob Lucas, adm. for estate of Edward Hawley vs. Edward Waite's exr., September 29, 1680
       (?Rsh.118) Thomas Haile, witness Will of Nathan Hickman, March 26, 1655, Westmoreland Co.
       (Rsh.81) December 20, 1668, Will of Teage Olathman, witness James Hawley, Joseph Bell, Westmoreland Co.
       (Rsh.82) April 1669, Mr. Hull, dec'd. debts due estate, from, Edward Coney, John Wilson, Edward Haley, Westmoreland Co.
       (Rsh.82) August 9, 1670, Mrs. Ann Wheston, widow of John Wheston, Inv., debts due estate, from Edward Hawly, Jacob

Lucas, Westmoreland Co.

(Rsh.81) May 31, 1671, Will of John Wilson, witness Thomas (X) Moore, James Hawley, Westmoreland Co.

John Hale wit. to Robert Francis, Will, October 22, 1671, Westmoreland Co.

(Rsh.81) Will of Suzannah Rapier, being sick in body, dated March 22, 1673, one cow unto Jacob Lucas, 2 cows unto James Lucas the son of Jacob Lucas, All of land in Maryland unto Elizabeth Lucas the daughter of Jacob Lucas. Susannah Rapier, Witness, James Hawley, Hugh Downing, April 29, 1674, proved by Mr. Edward Hawley, 1674, Westmoreland Co.

(Rsh.85) February 25, 1674, adm. Wm. Overritt, Henry (X) Hallige, Edward (X) Wirrington, Westmoreland Co.

(Rsh.82) August 11, 1675, Inv. of Nicholas Jenkins, John How, Edward Hawley, James Courtney, Westmoreland Co.

(Rsh.85) September 28, 1692, last Will and Testament of John Awbry, proved by Henry Hawley, Thomas Chandler and Capt. Willoughby Allerton, probate granted to Jane Awbry, adm. of husband John, Westmoreland Co.

(Rsh.85) September 27, 1693, Mr. Henry Hawley, appraise the estate of Wm. Gibbs and widow Elizabeth Gibbs, Westmoreland Co.

(Rsh.81) August 29, 1695, Will, Anne Spencer, being very sick and weak in body, unto my daughter Elizabeth Haley, one iron pot and one hog, and all my wearing clothes except my best gown and petticoat, unto Ann Lucas my best gown and petticoat, unto sons William and Richard Anckram..former husband Richard Chapman, signed Anne Spencer, proved by Richard Wall and Samuel Lucas, Westmoreland Co.

(Rsh.82) June 29, 1698, petition of Ann ?Redman, widow of Solomon Redman, Charles Lucas and Edwd. Hawley, her securities, Westmoreland Co.

(Rsh.82) Will, Edward Haley, dated November 5, 1702, proved November 25, 1702, son John Haly is a year old December 19, 1702, dau. Elizabeth Haly is four years old August 11, 1703, wife executrix of my whole estate, signed Edward Haly, witness Thomas Simmonds, John Moren, William Smoot, probate Sarah Haley, executrix.

(Rsh.82) November 25, 1702, Last Will and Testament of Edward Hawley was proved, probate granted Sarah Hawley, Executrix therein named... appraisal by John Mohun, James

Tayler, Thomas Simmons and Wm. Smoot ordered, Westmoreland Co.

(Rsh.82) Edward Haley, Inv., December 19, 1702, value. 7104 lbs. tobacco, signed Sarah Hawley, December 30, 1702, (Rsh.85) Henry Hawley, adm. and "next of kindred" to Edward Hawley, Jacob Lucas, adm. "next of kindred," to Edward Hawley.

February 25, 1707, Rosger, Roger Moss, Inv., signed Elizabeth Moss, witness John Harley, Westmoreland Co.

(?Rsh.119) John Moon, June 26, 1717, mentions wife Elizabeth's granddaughter, Elizabeth Hawley

Richard Hailey, September 20, 1774, names sons John and Anthony Gerrard and Anthony Gerrard's grandson, Richard Gerrard

DESCENDANTS OF FEMALE HAWLEYS

(Rsh.38)

1. Fannie J. Hawley (dau. of Rsh. 38) b. January 2, 1880, d. June 9, 1933, bur., East Oak Grove, Morgantown, W.Va., m. George Bart Spangler, who was b. 1879 and d. 1908 in a mine accident, then John Milton Johnson, children

1.1 James Edward Spangler b. January 28, 1901, d. July 20, 1991, m. Mable Everly b. March 9, 1903 d. 1989, children:

1.1.1 Jane S. Spangler m. Tom Wade in Texas
1.1.2 Robert K. Spangler b. August 8, 1923 (U.S. Marine, Employed by American Red Cross), lived at McCormick, S.C., m. Ruth Ann McGinnis who was b. December 20, 1926, children, Robert Everly Spangler b. January 9, 1955 at Elkins W.Va., m. May 24, 1986, Kathy Tuschl McAlister, children Andrea Adele Spangler and Sarah Ann Spangler, Anne Elizabeth Spangler b.October 11, 1959, Columbus, Ohio, Thomas Edward Spangler b. August 10, 1961 in Columbus, Ohio, m. March 12, 1988, Kimberly Pierce, Gregory Mark Spangler b. October 23, 1962 in Canton, Ohio, m. Wendy Lee on August 1 1987, child Allison Lee

1.2 Ray Fillmore Spangler b. February 17, 1904 d. 1992, m. Latrice Naola Calvert on June 2, 1925 she was b. February 18, 1906 and d. March 26, 1986, children,

1.2.1 Donna Spangler b. March 31, 1932 Masontown, W.Va., m. Harold Joseph Rehe on December 6, 1950, he was b. October 19, 1927 at Bretz, W.Va., and was a self-employed Coal Operator, their children, 1.2.1.1. Pamela Rehe b. August 4,1951 Masontown, W.Va., m. James Leroy Friend who was b. January 14, 1953; 1.2.1.2 Harold Joseph Rehe b.August 6, 1952 in Morgantown, W.Va., m. Dottie Thomas, their children, Ann Rehe, b. December 27, 1978, Terrie Rehe b. January 20, 1974; Brandon Rehe b. December 25, 1985; Sharon Rehe b. December 28, 1953 m. Van Born, children, Jason Van Born, b. August 18, 1976, Eric Van Born, b. February

1977, Derek Van Born, b. October 1984, Kendra Van Born, b. November 23, 1986 and Tiffany Van Born, b. September 1990 1.2.1.3 Deborah Rehe b. September 9, 1957 in Elkins, W.Va., m. James Robert Haney who was b. June 6, 1956, their children Mathew Haney b. January 25, 1982, Kistra Haney b. May 1, 1984, Nathanel Robert Haney b. January 24, 1992 1.2.1.4 Karen Rehe b. February, 23, 1960, Morgantown, W.Va., m. Jack Bremer who was b. January 30, 1960, their children Andrew Bremer b. September 16, 1989, Kayla Bremer b. October 15, 1990 and Rebecca Rehe Bremer, b. December 13, 1982, 1.2.1.5. Diana Louise Rehe b. October 20, 1963: 1.2.2. Erma Spangler b. July 28, 1939 m. Dick Summers on September 14, 1962, he was b. April 20, 1938, children, 1.2.2.1 Naola M. Summers b. August 3, 1963 m. Gregory Clark b. October 16, 1957, their children, Megan E. Clark b. January 8, 1984 and Tyler P. Clark b. January 12, 1987 1.2.2.2 Randall A. Summers b. March 9, 1968 m. Donna Bremer b. January 25, 1970 1.2.3 Clara Spangler b. March 29, 1928 d. March 1937 1.2.4 Frank B. Spangler b. February 10, 1927, Masontown, W.Va., Member Coast Guard and U.S. Navy, m. Virginia A. Faulkner b. January 17, 1932 in Baltimore, Md., their children, Donna Spangler b. May 21, 1949 m. Steven Shouman, children, Frank Spangler b. July 28, 1952 in Baltimore, Md., m. Stephanie Spangler then April Spangler: George Spangler b. October 7, 1955 in Baltimore, Md., m. Heather Spangler then Amanda Spangler: Kathy Spangler b. January 6, 1957 in Baltimore, Md., m. Livengood, children Shawn and Shelly: Walter Spangler b. March 27, 1954 in Baltimore, Md.: Joe Spangler b. September 10, 1959 in Baltimore, Md., and Ray Spangler b. September 21, 1961 in Baltimore, Md.: Second husband of Fannie J. Hawley (dau. of Rsh.38) John Milton Johnson, b. August 15, 1876 d. November 5, 1936, children, Frank Johnson m. Gladys, child

Billy Johnson lived in Florida; Glenn Johnson m. May____, lived Morgantown, W.Va.

2. Lattie L. Hawley, (dau.of Rsh.38) b. October 3, 1887 d. February 23, 1977 m. Clarence Shaffer who was b. December 22, 1885 and d. December 22, 1935, children:

2.1 Charles Denzel Shaffer b. September 10, 1911 m.
Pearl Johnson on September 11, 1938, she was b. December 24, 1916, they lived at Manown, W.Va., he retired from the State of W.Va., child Charles Shaffer b. June 25, 1939 m. Judy Whisler b. July 6, 1942, he owns a Printing Shop, children, Michael Shaffer b. June 13, 1969 and Tammy Shaffer b. February 4, 1974

2.2. Neva Shaffer b. October 18, 1913 d. February 4, 1994, bur. Kingwood, W.Va., m. Virgil (Spud) Menear who was b. September 26, 1916, children, Theo Menear, b. December 4, 1939, d. March 4, 1940; Drema Menear b. January 19, 1949 m. 1st Gary Castell who was b. March 13, 1946, children David Castell b. December 11, 1969 (serving in U.S. Army), Jenny Castell, b. March 21, 1979 and Lorie Castell b. September 3, 1974, m.2nd Harold Brown who was b. April 29, 1958, child Rebecca Joy Brown b. April 28, 1987 d. May 3, 1987

2.3 Thelma Agnus Shaffer b. February 24, 1909, Florist, b. Irona W.Va., lives Ethel, Washington, m. Kermit Church b. July 9, 1905 d. February 23, 1982, children Okay Roland (Sonny) Church b. August 15, 1928 m. Phyllis Jean Parker who was b. February 19, 1955, children Michell Lynn Church b. August 16, 1960, Kathy Elieen Church b. November 21, 1956, Jeffery L. Church b. February 21, 1979 and James Michael Church b. April 24, 1980; Nancy Ellen Church b. May 25, 1933 m. Calvin Dee Core on July 11, 1952, he was b. July 21, 1933, children, Susie Core b. February 15, 1959 (Nurse in Olympia, Washington) m. Don Seely, who was b. September 19, 1951, he is a Pharmacist; Kevin Core b. March 25, 1956, Advertising Manager for Logger's World

Magazine, m. Nancy M. Bowden who was b. October 1, 1955, children Wanda Carolyn Core b. July 2, 1978, Dudley Jayson Core b. June 2, 1980: Beverly Core b. March 21, 1968, Driver, m. Bradley Singer who was b. August 27, 1988, Computer Draftsman, child Magan Ellen Singer b. January 30, 1989

3. Lula M. Hawley (child of Rsh.38) b. April 25, 1884 d. 1924, m. Samuel Voss Inskeep. he was b. 1875 and d. 1960, children,

    3.1 Katie Inskeep m. Otis Bruce Moran, child, Kathy Ellen Moran b. November 4, 1956, Attorney in Richmond, Va., m. Woody Ascher Beach of Bristol, CT. (his Grandmother was a Hawley)

    3.2 Paul Wallace Inskeep b. April 29, 1906 d. May 21, 1976, Foreman, Dupont Chemical Co., m. Margaret Florence on August 7, 1936, she lives at Niagara Falls, children, Paul Wallace Inskeep, Jr., b. May 23, 1938, m. Patricia Ann Sobczak on June 13, 1959, she was b. May 1, 1938, they live in Youngstown, NY, he is a Design Engineer, children, Paul Michael Inskeep, III, b. April 6, 1960, Truck Driver, m. Gay Patterson on December 21, 1984, she is an attorney, children, Curtis McKenzie b. May 6, 1978 (foster child) and Alex Michael Inskeep b. April 14, 1990; Dawn Patricia Inskeep b. May 19, 1961, Physician, Buffalo, N.Y., m. Kevin Stephen Hrab, on September 13, 1961 (divorced); Michael Eric Inskeep b. July 9, 1962, Purchase Agent, m. Tracey Ann Kozar in 1989, she was b. April 8, 1964 and is a free lance Designer, Minneapolis, Minn.

    3.3 Robert Bruce Inskeep b. June 15, 1945, m. Joanne Haley b. September 1, 1985, they live outside Detroit, Mich, Personnel Manager with Stroah's Brewing, Joanne is an ultrasound technician, child Matthew Robert Inskeep b. July 26, 1987

(Rsh.13)

1. Amanda F. Hawley, (dau. of Rsh. 13) b. 1826 m. William Holmes Bridwell on September 1, 1841 in Culpeper Co., Va., known children:

<u>1.1</u> Martha Ann Bridwell b. August 3, 1842, d. September
    1, 1842
<u>1.2</u> Mary F. Bridwell, twin to Martha Ann, b. August 3,
    1842, d. August 30, 1842
<u>1.3</u> Oswald Holmes Bridwell, b. October 9, 1843 at
    Raccoon Ford, Culpeper Co., Va., m. May 21,
    1872 in Orange Co., Va., to Sallie E. Thompson,
    dau. of Reuben L. Thompson and Mariana
    (Quisenberry) Thompson. He served in the
    Confederate Army and fought at Chancelorsville,
    The Wilderness, Cold Harbor, Petersburg and
    other battles around Richmond. He was captured
    at Spotsylvania Court House, taken to prison in
    Washington, D.C. and then to Fort Delaware
    where he was released. He was transported to
    Richmond, rode a train to Gordonsville and from
    there walked the twelve miles to his home at
    Orange Va.
<u>1.4</u> William Theopolis Bridwell, b. October 10, 1845,
    Raccoon Ford, Culpeper Co., Va., m. 1st Barbara
    Cox
<u>1.5</u> Ella Gray Bridwell b. December 26, 1848, Raccoon
    Ford, Va., m. November 25, 1870 in Orange Co.,
    Va., to John G. Thompson, son of Reuben L.
    Thompson and Marianna, nee Quisenberry,
    Thompson.

(Rsh.102)

1. Susan Laura Halley, (dau. of Rsh.102) b. February 16,
1834, d. June 6, 1930 m. James Reeves Collins, October 23,
1856, children,
    <u>1.1.</u> William Reeves Collins, b. July 28, 1857
    <u>1.2</u> Presley Halley Collins b. September 20, 1859
    <u>1.3</u> Elizabeth Hays Collins, b. June 19, 1861, m. David
    Caples Walker, b. July 31, 1859, children, Charles Fisher
    Walker, b. April 3, 1884, Glen Collins Walker, b.
    September 9, 1886, Horace Melton Walker, b. October 8,
    1888, Mary Elizabeth Walker, b. November 14, 1894, m.
    Malcolm Everett Brnhiss, November 23, 1921
    1.4 James Henry Collins, b. February 22, 1863, m. Ada
    Wood on December 24, 1909, child Pressley Halley

Collins, b. December 27, 1902

1.4 Charles Thomas Collins, b. December 13, 1867, m. Mary Catherine Geers, May 10, 1893, children: Hazel Elizabeth Collins, b. February 22, 1894, Walker Francis Collins, b. August 6, 1895, James Henry Collins, Jr., b. August 23, 1897, Ruth Desdemonia Collins, b. August 29, 1900, Laura Katherine Collins, b. February 23, 1904, John Geers Collins, b. February 22, 1906, Charles Paul Collins, b. March 1, 1910

Research on Families
                   who Married Hawleys

Bridwell Family (Rsh.56)
<u>1790 Census, Maryland</u>
        Benjamin Bridwell, Worchester Co., Md., one male over
16, one male under 16, three females, no free persons, no blacks.

<u>1810 , Census, Culpeper Co., Va.</u>
        Amamian Bridwell (possible father of Frances Bridwell
who was b. 1804).

<u>1850 Census</u>
        Amamian Bridwell, Males under 10 = I, 10-16=1, 26-45 =
1 <u>Females 1 under 10</u>, 10-16 = 2, 26-45 = 1

<u>Culpeper Co., Va., Marriages</u>
        Guthbert Bridwell m. Mary Hilton, March 7, 1796
        Patterson Heaton m. Polly Bridwell, January 17, 1813
        Source: E.W. Wise, The Bridwell Family in America, P.O.
        Box 99, Sulphur, LA 70663

<u>Overwarten Parish Register, Stafford Co., Va., Compiler/Pub.</u>
<u>George H.S. King</u>
        Births: January 13, 1743 - Sarah daughter to John
Bridwell
        May 23, 1743 - Sarah daughter, to Isaac and Abigail
Bridwell
        July 25, 1747 - Sarah daughter to Abraham and Mary
Bridwell

Burch Family (Rsh.1)
<u>Index of Church Registers 1686-1885, 2 Vols., compiler Helen W.</u>
<u>Brown, pub. P.G. Co. Hist. Soc. 1979, King Georges Parish I (St.</u>
<u>Johns) Queen Anne Parish, pg.248.</u>
(Rsh.1) John Burch, son of John Burch, m. and had children:
        Francis Burch m. Alee (Allec) Owin, July 20, 1720
                children: John Burch, b. October 18, 1721
        Hesther Burch m. John Hawley, March 4, 1712.

<u>MdHR</u> (Rsh.1) November 12, 1720, Will probate for John Burch,

Planter, P.G.Co., Md., written April 12, 1720, to wife Elizabeth exr. 1/2 estate absolutely. To son Francis and Daughter Easter Holly remaining 1/2 equally. To Mary Panty and son Francis personality bought of Stephen Crawley. Witness Thomas Edelin, James Green, Box 2, Folder 62, T.B. #5, 1720-21, pgs. 220, 221., P.G.Co., Md., Bonds P.G.Co., Md., Box 5, Folder 18, Inv., Box 5, Folder 27, Test Proceed #24, pg.290.

(Rsh.1) Box 5, Folder 27, P.G.Co., Md., Inv....certain items including one woman servant with 2 years to serve, 8 pieces of old turnery and pigens, plates, 5 beds, 11 pieces of old tinware, 1 lanthron, total value 57-5-7.

(Rsh.1) July 21, 1721, Elizabeth Burch (who might have been the second wife of John and not the mother of Hester and Francis Burch) requested P.G.Co., Court to pay their account as James Reid, Et Ux, indicating that Elizabeth Burch had m. James Reid. Expenses include the funeral and heirs as listed as son and daughter. Test. Proceedings, 1721-22, pg.15, pg.59.,

Accounts #4, 1721-24, P.G. Co., Md., pg.42, October 1721, James Reid & Elizabeth his wife, exr. of John Burch late of P.G. Co., Md., dec'd. Inv. 57-5-7, expenses 25-0-10, balance 32-4-9. Expenses included L 2 for funeral, heirs, widow, son and daughter.

(Rsh.1) March 3, 1735/36 an Inv. of James Read is found in P.G.Co., Md., Probate Records. This does not mention Elizabeth which implies she had predeceased him. Disbursements included funeral expense and heirs if any in Scotland. Inv. #21, 1735-36, P.G.Co., Md., pgs.267, 268.

note: John Burch d. November 12, 1720, his widow m. James Read, Reid, by November 21, 1720

Colvin Family (Rsh.56)

NA: Three brothers are found in pension abstracts of War of 1812: John Colvin, Mason Colvin, Harry Colvin

NA: March 6, 1837, Mason Colvin of Rappahannock County, Virginia made the following declaration. That along with his brother John Colvin he served a tour of service lasting three months or upwards about Williamsburg, Norfolk and Petersburg, Virginia. He recollects, perfectly well, that the said tour of service was performed after the marriage of his brother John Colvin to his wife Sarah Colvin (the precise time of their marriage he cannot recollect). He further declares that his brother John Colvin was called out to serve a tour in the south and hired his brother Harry Colvin to perform it for him the length of the tour was 18 months, as well as he recollects, and after his marriage to the said Sarah Colvin.

Sarah Dillard Colvin states that she was m. to John Colvin on the 7th day of October 1778, in the County of Culpeper, and State of Virginia by Parson Jones, a clergyman of the Episcopal Church, who many years ago removed from said County and is presumed dead. She further declares that her husband John Colvin d. on the 29th day of May 1832, and that the date of his death was recorded in his family bible, and that she had remained a widow since that period. Note: the clerk inspected the family registry to confirm death date. File indicates that John Colvin was b. on March 16, 1758, Sarah Dillard was b. on January 11, 1762, W18951

On October 7, 1778, in Culpeper Co., Va., John Colvin m. Miss Sarah Dillard, their children were: Priscilla, b. July 16, 1780, (James) Robert, b. June 14, 1784, John D. b. September 29, 1800; on September 22, 1775, John Colvin enlisted for one year as a private under Capt.John Green, lst Regiment, Virginia Line. August 1, 1777 - March 1778, John Colvin served in the Militia of Culpeper County, Va., May 1, 1779, John Colvin enlisted for six months - no details of this service. On May 29, 1832, John Colvin d., W18951

On December 14, 1836, Sarah Colvin of Culpeper County, Virginia, age 75 years on the 11th day of January, b. 1762, made the following declaration to obtain the benefit of the provision of the Act of Congress dated July 4, 1836. She is the widow of John Colvin, late of Culpeper, a soldier in the Minute Service and Militia of Virginia, in the War of The Revolution from the County of Culpeper, Va. She often heard her husband say that he performed two tours of military service before their marriage, the first of which was for 12 months, performed about Williamsburg in Virginia two years before their marriage. She thinks she had heard him speak of Capt. John Mdaugh from within Culpeper or Orange being in the same service also of Churchile Gibbs. She has heard her husband say that he was under the command of Capt.John Green from Culpeper Co., during that tour of duty. His second tour of service was as a drafted militia man from same county and went to the north under General Washington and was in sight of Philadelphia when captured. "According to the best information I recollect this tour commenced August 1, 1777 and ended 1 March." She believes he acted as Sergeant but on what tour she cannot say. After her marriage with said John Colvin he was called into service several times. His first tour after marriage commenced 1 May "in planting time in 1779" and was then out in service about Williamsburg, or Norfolk or Petersburg, she doesn't remember which, for about 6 months. His second tour after marriage occurred when he was drafted for 18 months for the South and his brother Harry Colvin was employed to serve.

On March 21, 1838, Sarah Colvin of Culpeper County, Virginia age 76, b. 1762, made a declaration for a pension under the Act of Congress of July 4, 1836, for the service of her late husband John Colvin during the Revolutionary War. She omitted to state the one tour of duty and now desires to amend the same. John Colvin employed his brother to serve an 18 month tour for him the year that Cornwallis was in Virginia. She often heard her late husband speak of a battle near Petersburg and thinks he stayed until the siege at York., W18951, Extract from Pension Bureau

MdHR: Baltimore Records List of Levels and Establishments City Commissioners Supplement, 1729-1813, Wilber F. Coyle, City Librarian, Baltimore 1909

pg.35, Samuel Colvin owned Stone Tavern close to Jones Falls. Richard Colvin and Samuel Colvin are cited in these records. May 1812

MdHR: Baltimore Town and Fells Point Dir. 1796, from original by Thompson and Walker, supp. contains Baltimore Naturalization 1796-1803 by Robert Barnes.

pg.10, Richard Colvin, Store Keeper, Old Town, 16 Bridge St.

1850 Culpeper Co., Va., Census # 259
  John D. Colvin 49, white, farmer
  value real estate 2,664, b. Virginia

Francis Colvin	46	white	female
Sarah A. Colvin	17	white	female
Lucy E. Colvin	15	white	female
school within year			
Franklin Colvin	16	white	male

farmer
Daniel F.S. Colvin 17   white   male
        school within year
Robert Colvin   10   white   male
        school within year
Columbus Colvin 8   white   male
Mary V. Colvin   4   white   female

<u>VSL: Marriage Records</u>
        February 15, 1855, Orange Co., Va., Circuit Ct. Marriage
Record, William F. Colvin m. Lucy M. Hawley, husband 20, wife
22, places of birth Culpeper Co., Va., place of residence husband
Culpeper Co., Va., wife Orange Co., Va., Parents John D. and
Francis Colvin husband, Thomas and L.A. Hawley wife's parents.

<u>Notes of Elva Hawley Saunders,</u> in possession of author: Dillard
Colvin b. in 1800 in Culpeper Co., had one sister who m. Hume
and one brother James. Elva Hawley Saunders was a
granddaughter of John Dillard Colvin and Frances Bridwell. Elva
Hawley was b. to Lucy Ellen Colvin and her husband Charles
McKee Hawley on October 6, 1874 she m. William O. Saunders
and had one daughter Frankie R. Saunders. Elva Hawley
Saunders d. September 5, 1961 in Richmond, Va.
        John Dillard Colvin b. in 1800 m. Frankie Bridwell of
Culpeper, of this union there was b.:
        Sarah Colvin m. Meredith and had four daughters.
        Fanny Colvin m. Carpenter
        Nellie Colvin m. Wiggleworth
        Sally Bell Colvin m. Miller
        Carrie Colvin who moved to Arkansas
        James Colvin, who went west and family lost trace of
        Daniel Colvin who d. in war
        Robert Colvin, who d. in war
        Mollie Colvin, who d. young
        (Rsh.52) William Francis Colvin who first m. Lucy Mildred
Hawley, left four daughters and next m. Bettie Hudson, d. about
1920. Bettie Colvin left 3 boys and 3 girls.
        Lucy Ellen Colvin b. Feb. 28, 1839, d. December 1, 1921,
m. October 11, 1854 to (Rsh.56) Charles McKee Hawley of
Culpeper,Co., Va., 3 sons, 9 daughters.
        Columbus Colvin m. Miranda Shipley had two boys,

Earnest and Eddie.

Historic Roads of Virginia, Albermarle County Road Orders 1783-1816, Charlottesville, by Nathaniel Mason Pawlett, Faculty Research Historian, Virginia Highway and Transportation Research Council, Charlottesville, Va., December 1975.
pg.163, February 6, 1809, Order Book 1808-1810, Male Tithable to work on road from Carr's Brook to Charlottesville, James Madison, John Colvin.

Davis Family (Rsh.11) and (Rsh.85)
Sarah Hawley b. c. 1686, m. William Harrison, and after his death she m. Thomas Lewis of Difficult Plantation.

John Lewis b. c. 1683, d. Stafford Co., Va., m. and had children, Thomas Lewis, b. 1720, and John Lewis

Samuel Lewis b. P.G. Co., Md., m. Winefred Thomas. b. April 4, 1714, at Piscataway, Md., the dau. of Daniel Thomas and Anne Thomas. Deed between Samuel Lewis of P.G. Co., Md., and Thomas Lewis of Prince William Co., Va., for sale of 262 acres, formerly in Stafford but now in Prince William, in 1734. Known children, Thomas Lewis; Stephen Lewis; Daniel Lewis; John Lewis.

Thomas Davis m. Jane Lewis, b. c. 1685, Thomas Davis d. in Loudoun Co., Va. John Davis and Margaret Davis, his wife adm. of Thomas Davis the elder, dec'd, agent vs. Elizabeth Davis, adm. of Thomas Davis the Younger. Also, Elizabeth Lewis, as agent, complaint vs. John Davis and Margaret his wife, late Margaret Davis widow and relict and adm. of Thomas Davis, Sr., late of Loudoun Co., Va., Chancery Court.

son John Davis named in Will of Grandfather, John Lewis. Will Book A., pg. 117, September 12, 1761, Loudoun Co., Va. Elizabeth Lewis, late Elizabeth Davis, adm. of estate of Thomas Davis, Jr. (Rsh.11), Mary (Molly) Hawley, m. Thomas Davis in Loudoun Co., Va.

Dickerson Family (Rsh.57)
1st Census of U.S. Albermarle Co., Va., 1790
Thomas Dickerson - 10 white souls, I dwelling, 12 other buildings
John Dickerson - 9 white souls, 2 dwellings, 9 other buildings
William Dickerson - 6 white souls - 0 dwellings - 5 other buildings
(Rsh.57) William Dickerson, father of Barnett Simms

Dickerson, who was b. in 1829, was b. 1779. William was 11 years old in 1790.

<u>1850 Census, Reel 947, Greene Co., Va., No. 762, October 2, 1850, pg.709</u>
William Dickerson   71   white   male
Farmer, value of real estate owned: 1300 - everyone
in family b. in Virginia
Mary Dickerson   56   white   female
Lucy A. Dickerson   27   white   female
Barnett S. Dickerson   26   white   male
Martha A. Dickerson   23   white   female
Mary E. Dickerson   19   white   female
James B. Dickerson   14   white   male
note: Gilberts are found on next pg.

<u>pg.710, Greene Co., Va., 1850 Census as above</u>
Edward Gilbert 57   white   male
Farmer, value of real estate owned 4000.
All family members b. Virginia
Susan Gilbert   48   white   female
Sarah A.Gilbert 23   white   female
Nancy Gilbert   22   white   female
William Gilbert 21   white   male
John Gilbert   16   white   male
Andrew Gilbert 14   white   male
Cornelia Gilbert 12   white   female
Elizabeth Gilbert 11   white   female
Henry Gilbert   9   white   male
Susan Gilbert   6   white   female

<u>1880 Census, Greene Co., Va., Ruckersville Dist.</u>
B.S. Dickerson, white male, 54, m., farmer
Cornelia Dickerson, white, female, 39, wife keeping home
John T. Dickerson, white, male, 14, son at school
Laura Dickerson, white, female, 9, dau.
Mary Dickerson, white, female, 7, dau.
Eugene Dickerson, white, male, 6, son
Barnett Dickerson, white, male, 4, son
Tinsley Dickerson, white, male, 6/12, b., September, son

Robert Dickerson and Ruth Parish, February 10, 1787, witness J. Williamson and John ?Jones, Bondsman, William Robinson, she was the dau. of Joseph Parrish

William Dickerson m. Ann P. Madison, daughter of Ambrose Madison, Louisa Co., Va., January 24, 1809

Albermarle Co., Va., William Dickerson and Ellen Lane, m. January 25, 1831

License December 1, 1855, marriage December 6, 1855, Marriage Barnet S. Dickerson, Esquire and Miss Cornelia A. Gilbert, husband 26, wife 18, both single, husband b. Orange Co., Va., now Greene, wife b. Albermarle Co., Va., residence both Green, wife's parents Edward and Susan Gilbert, husband's parents William and Polly Dickerson, husband's occupation Farmer. Minister P.M. Carpenter.

VSL: Wills

Will Book E., pg.157, Nathaniel Dickerson of St. George Parish, Spotsylvania Co., Va., d. October 21, 1775, probate May 16, 1776, wife Elizabeth, sons William, Nathaniel, Richard, Elijah and Betty Pulliam, Fanny Garton. Book E., pg.524, Nathaniel and William were sergeants to whom Richard Dickerson is heir.

(Rsh.57) January 29, 1897, Cornelia A. Dickerson, Wills, Greene Co., Va.,...it is my will that my beloved husband Barnett S. Dickerson shall hold, control and manage all my estate both real and personal during his natural life. It is my will that after the death of my husband Barnett S. Dickerson the whole remaining estate be equally divided between my living children or their heirs as follows: Mattie E. May, Eugene T. Dickerson, Barnett S. Dickerson, Tinsley G. Dickerson, Russell G. Dickerson and the children of (Rsh.57) Laura E. Hawley dec'd. It is my will that the share of Laura E. Hawley's children be placed in the hands of my nephew Charles E. Gilbert to hold in trust for them until they arrive at a legal age to receive the same.

January 20, 1901, Will, Barnett S. Dickerson, Greene Co., Va., Book 2, pg.184

Aunt Elva Hawley Saunders notes, in the possession of Laura Hawley

Barnett Simms Dickerson, b. 1829, d. c. 1901, m. Cornelia A. Gilbert on December 6, 1855, children, Martha Elizabeth

Dickerson, known as Mattie May; Eugene T. Dickerson; Barnett S. Dickerson, Jr.,; Tinsley G. Dickerson; Russel G. Dickerson, Laura Elmore Dickerson m. Edwin Barber Hawley; John T. Dickerson

Orange County Virginia Families, Author, William Everett Brockman Vol. 1, pg.68 - Richard Simms Brockman of Albermarle and Amherst Co., Va., m. Martha (Patsy) Dickerson, daughter of Wiley Dickerson December 22, 1812.
        Vol. 1 pg.69 - John Dickerson settled in the northern part of Albermarle Co., while yet a part of Louisa, Va. He lived in the north fork of the Rivanna, not far from Piney Mountain. He d. in 1778. He and his wife, Mary, had three sons, John Dickerson, William Dickerson and Thomas Dickerson. Thomas d. in 1897, his wife's name was Mildred and his children were Frances, the wife of Rev. John Goodman, who m. 2nd Wm. Thurman, and third John Crossthwait, Thomas Wiley Dickerson m. Nancy the daughter of Rev. Jacob Watts, Griffith Dickerson and Lucy Dickerson. Another brother - Wiley Dickerson in 1789 m. Mary the daughter of John Carr. Wiley Dickerson d. in 1847. His children were William Dickerson, Malinda Dickerson the wife of George W. Turpin, Martha Dickerson the wife if Richard Simms Brockman and then the wife of B.C. Johnson; Mary Dickerson the wife of Elisha Thurman and Sarah Dickerson the wife of Archibald Duke.

Military Records
        DAR #506113, Wm. Dickerson, b. Caroline Co., Va., 1760, d. September 18, 1823, m. Anne Hoomes, Virginia, children Nancy, Sally, Harriet, Charlotte

NA, and Pearl May Hill, of Brandy Station, Virginia, granddaughter of Barnett Simms Dickerson October 1861 through June 1862, Barnett S. Dickerson, Private Company H., of the 57 Reg't of Va., Stewarts Brigade, Rivanna Guards, Albermarle Co., Va., Commanded by Capt. John B. Magruder, Confederate Army. The 57th Regiment Virginia Infantry was organized September 25, 1861 by the addition of five independent companies to the five companies of Keen's Battalion Virginia Volunteers. Company A had prior service as Company F. 20th Regiment Virginia Infantry. The Regiment was reorganized May 7, 1862. note: Richmond State Library records have not been checked, only those at the NA.

230

Dillard Family (Rsh.58)

<u>DAR</u>: #472456, In 1725, George Dillard was b. at Culpeper Co., Va., the son of James Stephen Dillard, Jr. and Lucy Wise of James City Co., Va., For further research see:

<u>The Striblings of Walnut Hill, Ray Carter Author, CS71.E47 1960</u>

#47256, George Dillard m. Priscilla Major who was b.in New Kent County, Va., and she is named in Mother's, November 26, 1764, Will. George Dillard, Patriot, furnished beef for army as shown by original public claims, Culpeper Co., Va., Book 1, pg.13, November 19, 1781, and September 26, 1781. Register of Virginians, pg.225; Letter Adjut.Genl. War Department, Washington, D.C.

George Dillard on February 18, 1777, enlisted in Capt. Anthony Singleton's Company, 1st Artillery, Continental Troops, Commanded by Col. Charles Harrison. Name on Muster Roll October 21, 1777.

George Dillard, March 2, 1790, at Culpeper County, Va., Will probate September 20, 1790. Will Book A., pg.396, Culpeper County, Va.

<u>The Stribings of Walnut Hill and Related Families, Ray Carter, CS 71S9155 1979</u>

Source 14 <u>The Dillard Family of Uvalde County, Texas</u>" author Gelzdaner, George Belle, Chedwato Service, W. Hartford, Conn. 1956

Source 15, McHall, Mrs. Howard H.

"The Dillard Name was of French origin, having been abridged from "Carbonne d'Iliard, used to designate a family living in the Carbonne area along the Rhine River in Northern France.

According to tradition, John Carbonne d'Illard, to escape religious oppression in France, came to England with William the Conquerer and settled in Wilshire. John Carbonne d'illard, his son, changed his name to John Dillard.

George Dillard, b. in Wilshire, England c. 1634, was sent by the British Government to Jamestown, Va., as an attorney for King George, III, and became the common ancestor of the Dilliards in America.

James Stephen Dillard, b. in Wilshire in 1658 came to America, m. Louise (Laura) Page, and lived and d. in James City

County, Va. His monument there bears the inscription: James Stephen Dilliard, son of George Dillard of Jamestown, Va., and great grandson of John Carbonne d'illiard of Wilshire, England.

James Stephen Dillard, (Jr.) was b. in James City Co., Va., in 1698. He m. Lucy Wise and shared with her father, Capt. Wise, the 25,000 acre Williamsburg Plantation.

George Dillard b. 1725, d. 1790, Rev. War Soldier, m. Priscilla Major b. in New Kent Co., Va., and dau. of Samuel and Constance Major, George Dillard was a landed proprietor of Culpeper Co., Va., a member of the Colonial Militia, and was a "Patriot" in the Revolutionary War, known children: Major Dillard b. 1747, d. 1764, John Dillard d. 1797, Samuel Dillard b. 1749, d. 1805 m. Ann Hutchins, Capt. James Dillard b. 1755 d. 1836 m. lst. Mary Ramage and 2nd Mary Puckett; Ann Dillard m. Robert Freeman, Elizabeth Dillard m. Charles Duncan, Sarah Dillard m. John Colvin, Jr., they were the parents of (Rsh.56) John Dillard Colvin, note: see also, "Mumford-Peeples and Allied Families" 1944, Mary Mumford Memorial Library, Cartersville, Ga.

Downs Family (Rsh.9)

Abstracts of the Newspapers of Georgetown and the Federal City 1789-1799 compiled by F. Edward Wright, Family Line Publications 1986

January 8, 1796, Columbian Chronicle, Zachariah Downs to petition Montgomery County Court for commission to mark and bound tracts Bear Garden and Deer Park.

August 20, 1799, The Centennial of Liberty, Zachariah Downs, Montgomery County, near the Paint Chapel, offers reward for negro woman Kate Harbert, about 19, 5'6" to 5'7", marked with small pox and curses much when angry.

MdHR, Maryland Church Records

> April 25, 1751, James Gordon Downs, bapt. , son of William and Ann Downs
>
> March 1, 1752, Catherine Downs, bapt. dau. of John and Elizabeth
>
> May 24, 1752 Lucy Downs bapt., dau. of Benjamin and Mary Downs
>
> July 20, 1755, P.G. County Md., St. Johns, Ann b. dau. of

Benjamin and Mary Downs

July 24, 1763, Doyal Downs, bapt., son of John and
Amealia Downs

December 14, 1771, Josias Downes b., son of William
and Elizabeth Downes

February 7, 1773, Katharine b., dau. of William and
Heneritta Downs

July 27, 1774, Theophilus Downes b., son of William
and Elizabeth Downes

February 12, 1775, Daniel Downs b., son of William and
Heneritta Downs

April 1, 1776, Latitia Downs b. dau. of Eleanor

February 15, 1779, Lucy Downs m. John Halsal, Prince
George Co., Md.

April 12, 1798, George b., son of Josias and Mary Downs

John Downs m. Sarah Underwood, December 11, 1789

December 13, 1789, John Downs m. Elisabeth
Underwood

Lucy Ann Downs confirmed November 23, 1793

Eliza. Downs m. Benjamin Bacon, December 23, 1797

February 1768, Charles Co., Md., Manor of Zachaiah, Rent Rolls,
Benjamin Downs age 54, b. 1714, Mary Downs age 52 b.
1716.

Brumbaugh Maryland Records, Vol. II, State of his Lordships
Manor, Rent Rolls Partial Census, Manor of Zachaiah, Charles
Co., Md., Feb. 1768, pgs. 30-31. Date of lease - August 20, 1745
to Benjamin Downs, Mary Downs.

1776, Census, Montgomery Co., Md.
Benjamin Downs, age 62, b. 1714, one other male 30.
Mary age 59, b. 1717, females 24, 20, 17, 2, 1 and 9 negroes.
Henry Downs, age 26, 3 males, Winfred, age 24, 1
female, 2 negroes.

Montgomery Co., Md., C.H.
March 26, 1783 probate, written November 27, 1777, Will,
Benjamin Downs, Montgomery Co., Md., to wife Mary Downs and
after her death to children. Liber T l, folio 163.
Liber H., folio 315, Liber 2, folio 355, October 11, 1804,

proved October 7, 1813, Dau. Lucy Hallsal, son in law Leonard
Hurdle, negroes named Linny and Teresa, grandchildren,
children, Mary Holly, Zachariah Downs, Henry Downs, Lucy
Hallsal, witness, Wm. Culver, John Needham

1783 Tax Record Montgomery Co., Md.
       Zachariah Downs, Bear Garden and Deer Park, log
dwelling house, frame tobacco house, old log house, 75 acres,
cleared, sapling land and thin soil.

1790, 1st.Census of Md.
       Zachariah Downs, Montg.Co., 1=16+, 4=16-, 4 females,
2 free persons.

The Maryland Militia in the Rev. War, S. Eugene Clements and F.
Edward Wright, Family Line Publications, 13405 Collingwood
Terrace, Silver Spring, Md., 20904, 1987
       Mont Co., Md., Lower Battalion, Zach Downs 29th -
source Maryland Hist Soc. pg.198, Militia Lists of Daughters of
Founders and Patriots

Montgomery Co., Md., C.H.
       October 7, 1813 Mary Downs, probate, written October
11, 1804, Mary Downs, Montgomery Co., Md., names children
Mary Holly, Zachariah Downs, Henry Downs, Lucy Hallsal. Wills X
LH F 315/L2, pg.355.
       1831, Wills, Montgomery Co., Md., Zachariah Downs, 7
children, Benjamin, Ann M., John, Richard M. Elizabeth Wheeler,
William, Leanah Jones, Book S., pg.137, Montgomery Co., Md.

Rev. Patriots of Mont. Co., Md., 1776-1783, Henry Peden. pg.98,
Zachariah Downs, Downes, c 1784-1826, Private 1st Com. Lower
Bn. Militia, Sept. 1777, m-198, t5:44 references. Took Oath of All.
before Edward Burgess, February 28, 1778, Private Lower 7th
Com. lived in lower part of Newfoundland Hundred, one taxable
in 1777, he m. Elizabeth Ann Mason, r. 31:5, dar I:201
r=Maryland

Genealogical Society Bulletin, obits of Rev. Soldiers, by Robert W.
Barnes vol. 6, no. 1, pp 6-7, no 2, pp 14-15, no. 3 pp 52-53, no 4,
pp 996-98, vol. 10 #2 pg.57, dar=dar patriot index

DAR Patriot Index, Zachariah Downs, b. c. 1748, Md., d. February 15, 1837, Md.

<u>State of his Lordships Manor, Rent Rolls, Partial Census, Manor of Zachaiah, Charles Co., Md., February 1768</u>
pgs.30, 31, date of lease, August 20, 1745, to Benjamin Downs, 94 acres, tenant in possession, John Nally Roby, lease term lives of Benjamin Downs age 54 and Mary Downs age 52, term lease Benjamin age 54, and Mary age 52 and John Griffin age 30

<u>MHS, Bible Records</u>
Downs Family, Stuart, Sarah E. and Frances E., Bible Record, typed and bound.

Emerson Family (Rsh.2)
John Emerson, Prince George Co., Md., Liber T.#1, Liber 95, dated September 12, 1777, children, Elizabeth Holly, son John Emerson, dau. Lucy Emerson, son George Emerson, dau. Elender Shing, gave them tracts of land called "Little Troy."

Gilbert Family (Rsh.57)
<u>Amherst Co., Va., C.H.</u>
(Rsh.57) A Gilbert, Will, written on February 23, 1778, proved May 1, 1778, wife Mary to have use of 450 acres of land where I know live, ten negroes, and land to be sold after death of wife and divided between sons Thomas and Richard Gilbert, sons, Henry, George, John Wiatt Gilbert, Ezekiel Gilbert, Josias, Maurice, Richard, daus. Ann Gilbert and Mary Gaines, exr. Gabriel Pinn, Daniel Gaines, codicil "I forgot to dispose of my sword and case of razors these to my son Henry Gilbert, witness John Stewart, Sr., Mary Brown, David Shopherd and Joel Franklin

<u>VSL: Orange County Virginia Marriages 1747-1850</u>
(Rsh.57) Thomas Jefferson Gilbert m. Anne Fearneaugh, May 11, 1778, license bondsman James Taylor, Jr., witness Wm. Farnyho and John Terrill, daughter of Thomas Fearneaugh
Joseph Gilbert and Agness Fearneyhough, December 29, 1817, bondsman John Fearnough, m. December 30, 1817
Note: See Louisa Co., Va., Marriages 1790 - 1800 for the following Sandridge marriages: Charles, Richard, Joseph.

1850 Virginia Census
        pg.710, Greene Co., Va.
(Rsh.57) Edward Gilbert 57, white, male, farmer, value of real,
estate owned 4000. All family members b. Virginia

Susan Gilbert	48	white	female
Sarah A.Gilbert	23	white	female
Nancy Gilbert	22	white	female
William Gilbert	21	white	male
John Gilbert	16	white	male
Andrew Gilbert	14	white	male
Cornelia Gilbert	12	white	female
Elizabeth Gilbert	11	white	female
Henry Gilbert	9	white	male
Susan Gilbert	6	white	female

Greene Co., Va., C.H.
(Rsh.57) License December 1, 1855, marriage December 6, 1855,
Barnet S. Dickerson, Esquire and Miss Cornelia A. Gilbert,
husband 26, wife 18, both single, husband b. Orange Co., now
Greene, wife b. Albermarle Co., residence both Greene, wife's
parents Edward and Susan Gilbert, husband's parents William
and Polly Dickerson, husband's occupation, Farmer. Minister
P.M. Carpenter

Information from Gerald H. Burnett, Rt. 2, Box 156, Ruckersville,
Va. 22968
        (Rsh.57) Edward Gilbert, father of Cornelia Gilbert, b.
1792 Albermarle Co., Va., m. January 5, 1821, Albermarle Co.,
Va., d. 1871 Greene Co., bur. Gilbert Cemetery at home
"Hollywood," Greene Co., Va., m. Susan S. Sandridge whose
mother was Sarah, b. 1802, d. before 1871, Greene Co., Va., bur.
"Hollywood," (family burial plot on farm) her mother m. c. 1779,
d.c. 1860, Louisa Co., Va.
        Edward Gilbert's father was:
        Thomas Jefferson Gilbert - Rev. War Capt. in Wm.
                Tucker's Com., Amherst, Va.
        b. c. 1730, Orange Co., Va.
        m. May 11, 1778, Orange Co., Va.
        d. Aug-Sept. 1819, Albermarle Co.
        m. Ann Nancy Ferneyhough who was b. possibly in
                England

d. Sept.-Oct. 1844, Albermarle Co., Va. She was dau. of
Edward Ferneyhough, Sr.

Frederick Co., Md., Marriage Licenses 1778-1800,
Thomas Gilbert M. Hannah Burton, July 13, 1779 - DAR Magazine

Baltimore Co., Md., Families 1659-1759 Robert W. Barnes, Geno.
Pub. Co., Inc. Baltimore
Many Thomas Gilberts, are found in this resource book.
One Thomas was b. 1705, and another Thomas was b. 1732,

Baltimore Town and Fells Point Dir. 1796, from original by
Thompson and Walker, supp. contains Baltimore Naturalization
1796-1803 by Robert Barnes
pg.20. Gilbert and Brown, Couriers 2, Cheapside
Thomas Gilbert, dwelling, Old Town 19 So. High St.
Augustine Gilbert of St. Domingo, Old Town, South Green
St.

DAR
(Rsh.57) # 657781, Bettye Gilbert Dickerson, contains marriage
certificate of Edward Gilbert b. c. 1793, d. c. 1850, at Greene Co.,
Va., and Susan Sandridge b. c. 1802, at Orange Co., Va., d. c.
1850 at Greene Co., Va., m. January 5, 1821, and Will of Anne
Gilbert

(Rsh.57) #645262, Barbara Dozier Spuregin
Thomas Gilbert b. c. 1735, Orange Co., Va., m. Anne
Fearneyhough b. c. 1760, on May 11, 1778, known children:
Susannah Gilbert, b. c. 1760 m. Edward
Fearneyhough
Thomas Gilbert, Jr., b. 1779 m. Dorothy
Fearneyhough
Edward Gilbert, m. Susan Sandridge
Joseph Gilbert, m. Agnes Fearneyhough
Weston Gilbert, m. ?

#714967, Myrtle Adele Smith Carter
(Rsh.57) Thomas Gilbert, Sr., resided at Orange Co., Va.,
served From January 14, 1781 until March 26, 1781, a total of 72
days. His name is on the payroll of Capt. William Tucker's
Company of Militia from Amherst Co., Va., Burgess Virginia

Soldiers of 1776
(Rsh.57) Thomas Gilbert, Sr. m. c. 1760 probably in England, he m. 2nd. Anne Fearneyhough, at Orange Co., Va., on May 11, 1788, he d. September 6, 1819 at Albermarle Co., Va., known children:
Susannah b. c. 1760 m. Edward Fearneyhough
Thomas Gilbert, Mr., b. c. 1779 m. Dorothy Fearneyhough
(Rsh.57) Edward Gilbert b. c. 1781 m. Susan Sandridge
Joseph Gilbert m. Agnes Fearyneyhough
Weston Gilbert m. Matilda Pritchett
James Gilbert, unmarried
Robert Gilbert
William Gilbert m. Frances Harlow
John Gilbert
Nancy Gilbert m. Thomas Waters
Polly Gilbert m. Paul Wyate
Frances Gilbert m. John Fearneyhough

Military Records
DAR #350078, Capt. John Webster Gilbert, b. December 27, 1738 d. 1809 m. Sallie Rebecca then Mary Craig.

Hutchison Family (Rsh.11) and (Rsh.13)
Hutchison Family Bible, Furnished by Miss Hutchison, Loudoun Co., C.H., Leesburg, Va.
Andrew Hutchison b. March 13, 1687 d. 1760, m. 1710 Jane Browning dau. of Thomas Browning
Issue:
Thomas Hutchison b. July 21, 1711
John Hutchison b. March 8, 1712, d. Sept. 1800, m.
    Rosamond
William Hutchison b. August 2, 1715...unknown
Richard Hutchison b. Oct. 26, 1717...known
Daniel Hutchison b. May 13, 1719 d. after
    1757...known
Benjamin Hutchison b. April 10, 1722 d. October 1, 1796
    m. Elizabeth ...#2 Mary (Polly)
Joseph Hutchison b. March 14, 1723 d. 1805 m. Elizabeth
    Gray, about 1750
Hannah Hutchison b. February 19, 1726/27 m. December
    25, 1753 to Joseph Clark

Mary Hutchison b. December 22, 1732
Jeremiah Hutchison b. October 20, 1729, d. October 25,
    1797, m._____
    one daughter Jermima m. William
    Ambler m. 2nd Keziah Settle b. August 9, 1726,
    dau. of Henry and Anne Settle, children:
    Benjamin Settle b. April 3, 1757 d. November
    1823 m. Elizabeth Ashford who d. 1833
    George Settle b. 1763 d. November 17, 1823 m.
    #1, Elizabeth Berkley #2 Esther Barbour, Edward
    Vincent Settle b. 1767 d. before 1823 - no issue
    Joshus Settle b. 1769 d. Sept.23, 1842 never m.
    Keziah Settle b. 1760 d. 1852 m. Lewis
    Hutchison 1775 (son of Uncle Benjamin 1722)
    Jeremiah Hutchison d. Feb. 25, 1829 m. Mary
    Anne Lewis, widow, Bathsheba Hutchison d.
    before 1815 m. William Hawley d. 1829

Fairfax and Loudoun Va., Cos., C.H.

October 20, 1823, Benjamin Hutchison, Will N. pg.174,
Fairfax Co., Va., C.H.

February 20, 1834, Jermiah Hutchison, Will, Estate act.
R.pg.l03, R. pg.351, Fairfax Co., C.H., Va.

October 17, 1842, Joshua Hutchison, U 38, Fairfax Co.,
C.H., Va., Will written January 1, 1839. "slaves if hired out for two
years can go to Liberia or any free state of this Union."

William Halley m. Bathsheba Hutchison, Loudoun Deeds
Y 343 and Loudoun Chancery M. 717

(Rsh.11) October 20, 1823, Benjamin Hutchison, Will N.
pg.174.

(Rsh.11) February 20, 1834, Jermiah Hutchison, Will,
Estate act. R. pg.l03, R. pg.351

1782 - Loudoun Titables - taker Charles Love

Jeremiah Hutchison, Jr. 1
        (next door - Samuel Adams
        negro = Sam and Sarah 3)

VSL: Land Records

September 6, 1798, Jeremiah Hutchinson, of Loudoun
Co., Va., purchase 216 1/2 acres of land in Fluvannah Co., Va.,

from John England and Wife Ann of Fluvanna for $397.09. Property on branches of Adrons and Burkes Creeks, adjoining George Thompson, now called Bakers Land. Witnesses Richard Bragg, Abner A. Strange, David Ross, Deed Book 3, pg.400, Fluvannah Co., Va., C.H., Palmyra, Va.

August 1804, Mary Hutchison of Pittsylvania Co., Va., purchased land in Fluvanna Co., Va., witness William Ambler, Book 4, pg.244, Fluvannah Co., C.H.

Fluvannah Co., Va., C.H., August 1804, Book 4, pg.244, Mary Hutchison of Pittsylvania Co., Va., purchased land Fluvannah, witness, Wm. Ambler

(Rsh.13)_____,1804, Jeremiah Hutchison and wife Mary Ann living in Fluvannah on 200 acres convey same to Major Parish of Louisa Co., Va., adjoining lands of Charles Thompkins, Davis Ross, Abner A. Strange for $1,000 consideration. Witness Peter Ross, John Johnson, John R. Perkins, Bartley Ford, Richard Bragg, Rowland Jones, Richard Allen, Abraham Hawley, John Bartley. Book 4, pgs. 299, 402. witness Abraham Hawley NOTE: Fluvannah next County south of Albermarle Co., Va.

December 14, 1804, Mary Ann Hutchison, could not conveniently travel to Fluvannah Court so relinquished dower at Loudoun Co., Va., Fluvannah Co., C.H., Records, Palmyra, Va.

February 20, 1834, Jermiah Hutchison, Wife Mary Ann Hutchison, Estate Account R 103, R 351, proved. Loudoun Co., Va.

NOTE: In a Fairfax Co., Va., Court Record, dated October 1841 a Mary Ann Hutchinson names nephew Thomas M. Sherman. In August of 1804 a Mary Hutchinson of Pittsylvania Co., Va., purchased land in Fluvanna Co., Va. Witnessed by William Ambler. Two William Amblers in records, one m. Jermia Hutchinson sister of this Jeremiah Hutchinson and one m. Susan Hawley daughter of William and Bathsheba Hawley Hutchinson, possibly father and son.

VSL: Richmond Co., Va.

(Rsh.11) Will Book 7, pg.117, Richmond Co., Va., Henry Settle's Will, dated October 16, 1770, "The Settle-Suttle Family"

Oden Family (Rsh.13)

Census, MdHR, 1775-1778, Maryland Census, Benedict Hundred
Thomas Oden, Vincent Oden, James Green

<u>Census, Maryland, 1st Census - 1790</u>
<u>name, white 16+, white 16-, females, black</u>

David J. Oden- P.G.Co.	3, 1, 3, 0
Elias Oden - Charles	1, 0, 1, 5
Elle Oden pg.88	2, 0, 2, 6
Isaac Oden - Charles	
John Oden - Charles	2, 0, 0, 0

<u>Census, 1810 Loudoun Co., Va., Leesburg, Va., pg.4</u>
Martha Oden (surrounded by Hutchinsons, and on same
pg. as John Hawley).
1 male under 10, 2 males 16 to 45
1 female 16 to 26, 1 female 26 to 45

<u>Cemetery Records, Leesburg, Va.</u>
Alexandria Oden, April 15, 1830 - 1905
Henry Oden 1863-1904

<u>Church Records, MdHR: King George Parish, Md.</u> Also known as
Piscataway or St. Johns at Broad Creek, Francis Ann Oden,
bapt., dau. of Thomas & Sarah Oden, May 12, 1751

<u>Court Records, 1774-1778, Charles County Court Record Book</u>
<u>x#3, every name Index,</u>
Oden, Elias 639, Thomas 631, 645, 763, Vincent 439, 522,
524, 631, 645, 657, 724

<u>Court Records, Every Name Index 1791-1803, Charles Co., Md.,</u>
<u>Orphans Court Proceedings</u>
Vincent Oden/Odon a266, 213, 285, 313, 331

<u>Court Records, M1478, Loudoun Co., Chancery Records, Va.</u>
March 5, 1775, Thomas Oden of Charles Co., Md., and
Richard Major, James Major of Loudoun Co., Va., involved in land
transaction. Book M 16, pg.118/5.

<u>Court Records, Chancery M. 2497, Separate Maintenance,</u>
<u>Loudoun County, Va., C.H. Leesburg, Va.</u>
November 15, 1793, Martha Oden stated that they had
been m. 26 years, had 10 children, 4 sons grown and laboring for
themselves, one daughter 16 years (living with friends) and

remainder living with Thomas except young suckling at mother's breast. She stated that Thomas "was cruel and taken to drink so she must fly him." Thomas was ordered to pay Martha Oden 15 lbs per annum to be paid in quarterly payments. She was staying with friend Samuel Adams who was later administrator of accounts for estate of Thomas Oden and guardian of his orphan children Alexander, Elias, Lewis and Elizabeth.

Court Records, Fairfax County, pg. 246
Samuel Adams, Fairfax County, Va., on June 19, 1786 is shown in court records to have a mill on Pimmitt Run, had road recommended from mill through his plantation to Alexandier Road, Benjamin Lebantians former house and from mill to Little Falls/Alexander Road, 1783

Court Records, Vol II, pg.208, Unpublished Notes - Law Suits and Misc. Records of Loudoun Co., Va., Mrs. Walter Towner Jewell, 1958-59
        April 15, 1800 - Samuel Adams was named guardian of Alexander, Elias, Lewis and Elizabeth Oden - orphans of Thomas Oden., sec. Reuben Settle and Joseph Lewis
        (Rsh.13) February 20, 1802 Thomas Oden dec'd. Abraham Hawley and Mary Ann his wife, sell their share. Book 2C, pg.438, Loudoun Co., C.H.

Immigration, A list of Servants Transported by Samuell Gibbons of Bristoll in Ship Bachelor of Bristoll year 1674, Internet
        Richard Odean to St. Mary's Co., Md., along with 89 other persons, Charles Calvert gave Samuell Gibbons 4,500 acres, in year 1674

Immigration, Settlers of Md., 1766-1783, Coldham
        Vincent Oden, St. Mary's Co., Md., Oden's Fortune, 16 acres 12 June 1770, bc41/409;bc43/399, bc41=cert.1769-1771 sr 7538 bc43 pat 1770-1773 sr 7540
        John Oden on Grand Jury in Prince George Co., Md., June 1698, with Wm. Eldin, Jo Peake, et al.

Immigration, Baltimore Co., Families, 1659 to 1759, Robert W. Barnes, Geno. Pub.Co., Inc., Baltimore
        pgs. 189, 191 - Elioner Odan m. John Durbins in

Baltimore Co., Nov. 13, 1743. She was his second wife, they had a son Ralph.

<u>Immigration, Charles Co., Maryland Historical Society, Early Settlers Charles Co., Md.</u>
John Caine and wife Elizabeth give gift of Deed October 5, 1713 to his daughter Elizabeth and her husband Francis Oden and Deed of gift to his son Thomas Caine October 5, 1713.
Thomas Cave, next of kin, Elizabeth Oden his sister, adm. Mary Cave. April 18, 1730
May 20, 1725, Elizabeth Oden adm. for Francis Oden, mentions Thomas Oden, Thomas Caus

<u>Land Records, Charles Co., Md., C.H.</u>
Lib. S/3, pg.3, pg.629, Elias Oden, August 12, 1772, of James Co., Va., purchased land in Charles Co., Md., 116 acres, wife Catherine, Deed Recorded October 12, 1774 Deed Book Lib. RS/3 pg.284, recorded October 12, 1774, 2 parts of tracts or parcels of land in Charles Co., Md., 113 acres.
Deed, February 8, 1793, Catherine Oden and Elias Oden of Montgomery Co., Md., and William Waters of Charles Co., Md., property Water's Risque, 55 acres.

<u>Marriage, MdHR: Maryland Historical Marriage Register</u>
Montgomery County Marriages 1798-1876
Lawrence O. Holly m. Sarah Oden, January 12, 1802

<u>VSL: Marriage Records of Berkley Co., Va.</u> 1781-1854
Alex Oden m. Martha Porterfield, August 8, 1831
Elias Oden m. Ann Shearer, June 6, 1799
Martha Oden m. William Cunningham, October 15, 1840

<u>Marriage License, Frederick Co., Va., 1778-1810 Margaret Meyers, 2nd Ed., Family Line Pub. 1986</u>
Thomas Oden to Elizabeth Lloyd, June 1, 1805

<u>Tax 1775-1778 Charles Co., Md</u>
Thomas Oden

<u>Tax Records, VSL: Virginia Taxpayers 1782-87 Augusta B. Fothergill and John Marknaugle 1940</u>

Jessee Oden 2   -   Prince Wm.
Thomas Oden 1   6   Loudoun

Loudoun Co., Va., Tithables, August 1783, C.H. Leesburg, Va.
Charles Love taker
Thomas Oden
negroes - Peter, James, Rick 4
NOTE: Thomas Oden is next to John Hawley in sequence,
indicating next door neighbor, same taker, Charles Love, took
Census of Jeremiah Hutchison, Jr., in 1782

Military:
NA   Thomas Oden, French and Indian War, Illinois Papers
Bounty Land

VSL   (Rsh.13) Thomas Oden - War against Shawnee Indians
under command of George Rogers Clark, Brig. General -
November 1782 shows Thomas Oden

        June 1782, July 1782, April 15, 1783 - Thomas Oden and
John Holly, Lincoln Militia under Capt. Nathaniel Hart to build fort
at falls of the Ohio, under command of Col.Benjamin Logen C.L.
Payroll.

DAR: #46790, #660113 shows Hezekiah Oden, Sr. b. 1735 at
Maryland to be the child of Thomas Oden and Sarah Sussanah.

        #728022 shows Thomas Bussey Oden to be the child of
Alexander Oden. Alexander Oden was b. c 1752 at Fredericks
City, Md, d. at Autauga Co., Alabama on 26 May 1834, and can
be found in application #714846. Alexander Oden's wife was
Letitia Bussey. Thomas Bussey Oden was b. before 1777 at
South Carolina.

        #714846 shows Elias Oden to be a child of Thomas
Bussey Oden b. 1774-77 at South Carolina and d. before May 16,
1832. Elias Oden m. Nancy Howle who was b. 1784-90 at South
Carolina.

        #693799 shows Eleanor Nellie Oden to be a child of
Alexander Oden. Alexander Oden was b. 1752 at Fredericks City,

Md., and his wife was Letitie Bussey.

#514930 shows Alexander Oden also.

#693799 shows Alexander Oden and Letitie Bussey's children to be:
Elias Oden b. 1780 m. Elizabeth Howle
Sarah Oden b. 1780 m. James Minor
Eleanor Oden b. 7/6/1783 m. Alexander Oden, cousin
Alexander Oden b. April 9, 1788 m. Mary Francis Pope
John Oden b. 1790 m. Beda Ward
Joshua Oden b. 22/1/1796 m. Charlotte Funderburg
Dempsy Oden b. Dec.6 1798 m. Rebecca Cabiness
When Letitie d. he remarried: of the second marriage:
Bartley Oden b. 1802 m. Elizabeth Wyche

#713797 shows Thomas H. Oden. Thomas H. Oden is also shown in #467980 to be the child of Hezekia Oden. It shows Thomas H. Odens wife to be Luraney. Thomas H. Oden was b. in Edgefield Co., S.C. after 3/8/1797.
Children:
Andrew Oden b. c. 1765 m. Elizabeth Howle
Peter Oden b. c. 1768 m. Sarah
Thomas H. Oden b. between 1760 and 1770 m. Millie
    (Emily) Terrell
Hezekiah Oden b. c. 1777 m. Mary Terrell
Dorcus Oden
John Oden b. 1770-1774

#660113 shows Hezikiah Oden Sr. was b. 1735 at Maryland. His wife was Luraner. He d. Edgefield Dist. S.C., Will Book A, pgs. 133-34, Edgefield Co., S.C.

Alexander Oden b. 1752 d. 1834 m. Leteria Bussey first then Elizabeth Boyd, Pussey S.C. Private

Hezekiah Oden d. August 3, 1797 m. Lurcney P.S. S.C.

#467980 shows Hezekiah Oden Sr. who was b. 1735 at Maryland to be the child of Thomas Oden and Sarah Sussanah.

<u>Military, Draper Manuscripts, Mass. Hist. Soc.</u>
Vol. 17 - a list of carriers of Col. John Bowman, collection for 1782 that has not yet been paid, Thomas Oden, 17 J -pg.56

<u>Rev. Patriots of Charles Co., Maryland Historical Society</u>
(Rsh.13) Thomas Oden Corporal, Militia 12th battalion, Capt. Peter Woods Com., 1777, name listed as Odan, took Oath of Allegiance of all 1778, resident of Benedict Hundred 1778
Elias Oden, Corporal, Militia 12th Battalin, Capt. Alex. McPherson's Com., 1777, resident of Bryan Town Hundred 1778
Isaac Oden, Private Militia 12th battalion, Capt. Peter Wood's Com., 1777
Sara Biggs Oden, notation see Edward Lloyd Wales
Vincent Oden, Corporal 12th batt. Capt. Peter Wood's Com., 1777, Odan, took oath 1778, name Odin, resident of Benedict Hundred 1778.
Edward Lloyd Wales, resident Benedict Hundred 1778, he was b. Sept. 25, 1758, m. Sarah Biggs Oden, migrated to Georgia where he d. Jan 27, 1809

<u>Military, Loudoun Co., Va., Militia Records 1793-1829, transcribed from the originals by Don Blincoe, Sr. Iberian Pub. Co., Athens, Georgia. 1993</u>
Capt. Skinner 1st bat. 57 regm. class no. 7, James Neale, Jeremiah Hutchison, Thomas Oden, Richard Hutchison, James Hutchison (son of Andrew) Henry Settle, David Lewis, James Lewis, Jr. 57th regs., Nov. 1816, Thomas Oden, fined.

<u>Military, VSL: War Against Shawnee Indians, Command George Rogers Clark</u>   November 1782, Thomas Oden

<u>Wills and Probate, Estate Settlement of Thomas Oden, Loudoun Co., Va., C.H.</u>
May 10, 1796 - Dr. Elias Lacy was paid for medicine and visit.
June 11, 1798, Dr. Elias Lacey was paid for medicine and visit.
August 17, 1798 - Dr. Elias Lacey was paid for medicine and visit.
September 1798, Joseph Bears was paid $7.00 for coffin with ridged top.

September 10, 1798, Martha Oden, adm., Thomas Oden dec'd bond $4,000, sec. Samuel Adams and Reuben Settle.

<u>Wills and Probate, Loudoun Co., Va., C.H.</u>
(Rsh.13) year 1820, Martha Oden's estate distributed. Abraham Holly and Mary Ann his wife, daughter of Thomas and Martha Oden, sell share of estate. Deed Book # G (30 or 39) pg.176.
Martha Oden property disbursement. Book 2E, pg.257, and 2 K, pg.357.

<u>Military, Historical Register of Virginia in the Revolution, Soldiers, Sailors and Marines 1775-1783, John H. Gwathmey 1938 The Dietz Press, Publishers, Richmond, Va.</u>
John Holley, Illinois Papers, Richard Holley, Illinois Papers, Thomas Holley E=Index Rev. Records in Virginia State Archives, Thomas Oden Illinois Papers

<u>Wills and Probate, Charles Co., Md., Estate Inventories,</u>
Francis Oden, August 11, 1725, Elizabeth Oden, adm.
Michael Oden, November 1766, Elias Oden and Vinson Oden, nearest of kin, Elizabeth Oden adm.
Michael Oden additional Inv., May 3, 1768

<u>Wills and Probate, Charles Co., Md.</u>
Elias Oden of Charles Co., Md., infirm of body, wife Catherine, son Elias, daughter Vilinda, land Water's Risque, son Elias, signed Jan 16, 1787, proved August 1787

<u>Wills and Probate, VSL:</u> Loudoun Co., Va., records show disbursement of Thomas and Martha Odens property after her death, which followed his, in Book 2E pg.257 and 2 K pg.357. Heirs Alexander Oden, Hezikiah, John and Thomas Oden.

<u>Will Records, from Loudoun Co., Va., show:</u>
Thomas Oden m. Martha in 1767, known children:
Mary Ann Oden m. Abraham Hawley (Rsh.13)
Hezekiah Oden m. Elizabeth
Thomas Oden m. Lydia
John Oden m. Margaret, removed to Fauquier
Alexander Oden (he was a minor in 1800)

Elias Oden m. Sarah of Fauquier Co., Va., (he was a
    minor in 1800)
Fannie Oden m. Charles J. Love, purchased
    land of Wm. Halley, Fairfax Co., 1806
Richard A. Oden
Elizabeth Oden m. William Cooksey, living in Muskingum
    Co., Ohio, January 8, 1814. (she was a minor in
    1800)
Lewis Oden

Perkins Family (Rsh.58)

Cemetery Records
    Oakwood Cemetery, Richmond, Va., Section D., Lot 71,
Part of Lot 2, Book No. 5, Cert No. 98, J.E. Perkins
    Riverview Cemetery, Richmond, Va., Plat B., Div. 3, Sect.
37, Emma Ruth Seay, wife of E.A. Perkins, d. January 1, 1899,
age 50 years; Egbert A. Perkins, b. August 17, 1853, d. October
23, 1927; Mary Baughn Perkins, June 4, 1879 - July 18, 1956

1790 U.S. Census, 1782-1785
    Fluvannah Co., Va., Stephen Perkins 2 white souls, 3
blacks; Michael Perkins 6 white souls, no blacks

1810 Census Index - Va.
Archelaus Perkins, #710, Goochland no twp
George Perkins, #706, Goochland no twp
Greif Perkins #710, Goochland no twp
Nat. Perkins #709, Goochland no twp
William Perkins #710, Goochland no twp

1820 Census Index - Va.
Archelaus M. Perkins, 14A, Goochland
Archelaus Perkins 15A, Goochland

1830 Census Index - Va.
Robert Perkins, Goochland #150 no twp

1840 Census Index - Va.
Thomas J. Perkins, #391, Goochland no twp
A.M. Perkins, #396, Goochland no twp
G. Perkins, Jr., #391, Goochland no twp

G. Perkins, Sr., #391, Goochland no twp

1850 Census Index - Va
Joseph Perkins, #113, Goochland no twp
Joseph Perkins, #135, Goochland no twp

1860 Census Index - Va
Joseph H. Perkins, #660, Fluvannah
Joseph H. Perkins, #658, Fluvannah

1870 Virginia Census
Roll 1649, pg.85, M593, Goochland, Dover Township, Post Office
Dover, September 15, 1870
Joseph E. Perkins, age 50, b. 1820, male white, farm
        laborer, Value RE 60, value PP 10, b. Va.
Pauline Perkins, age 42, b.1828, F. white, keeping house b. Va.
Egbereth Perkins, age 17, b. 1853, male, white, coal miner, b. Va.
William Perkins, age 11, b. 1859, male, white,at home, b. Va.
Benjamin Perkins, age 9, b. 1861, male, white, at home, b. Va.
Inoriannah Perkins, age 5, b. 1865, female, white, at home, b. Va.
Emma Perkins, age 1, b. 1869, at home, b. Va.
Samella Perkins, age 27 b. 1843, F. white, housekeeping, b. Va.

1880 Virginia Census
Reel # 1367, Vol. 14, ED 55, Sheet 26, Line 25., Goochland
County, Dover Dist.
        Egbert Perkins, Farmer, white male, age 25, b. 1854
        Emma Perkins, Wife, keeping house, age 26, b. Va.
        Eddie L. Perkins, son, age 6, b. 1884 Va.
        Lotty M. Perkins, daughter, age 4, b. 1876 Va.
        Maude Perkins, daughter, age 1, b. 1879 Va.
        Inda Perkins, sister, age 14, b. 1866 b. Va.
        husband and wife's parents both b. Virginia

1900 Virginia Census
Henrico, Tuckahoe Dist.,Ed.34, vol. 26, sheet 21, line 98, Roll
1713
Edward A. Perkins, white, male, b. 1853, age 47, b. Virginia, m. 5
        years, m. in 1885. Occupation Carpenter, 1729 Jacqueline
        (Street Address)
Mary V. Perkins wife, b. 6/4/1879, age 22, b. Virginia, m. 5

years, m. in 1885, Occupation Paper Box Maker.
Gertrude F. Perkins, daug. b. November 1884, age 15, b.
Va., Occupation - Cigarette maker
William L. Perkins, son, b. November 1886, age 13, b. Va., at
school
Ernest N. Perkins, son, b. October 1888, age 11, b. Va.,
at school
Maggie R.Perkins, dau., b. November 1890, age 9, b., Va.,
at school
Thomas Baughan, brother-in-law, b. November 1876, age,
23 b. Virginia
Blanch V. Brown, Boarder, b. June 1884, age 15, Virginia
Note: Parents of both Edward A. and Mary V. Perkins b.
in Virginia, Because of children's names and birth dates,
this has to be Egbert A. whose name was written on
Census as Edward.

Edward Perkins, white, male, age 40, b. Va., Henrico,
Fairfield Dist.
Mary Perkins, wife, age 37, b. Va.
Mary Perkins, dau., age 14
William A. Perkins, son, age 9
Bernard Perkins, son, age 7
Susan Perkins, dau. age 4
Lenard Perkins, son age 1

1910 Virginia Census
pg.625, 039-0038-0175, #1631
Edward A. Perkins, Carpenter, husband white 56 yrs. old,
number of years present marriage 10 years, m. 2
times, Pepper Ave., Tuckahoe Dist.
Mary V. Perkins, wife age 20, b. Va., m. 10 years, mother
of four children
Joseph Perkins son, 7 1/2, b. Va.
Roy H. Perkins son, 6 3/12, b. Va.
Ralph B. Perkins son, 3 2/12, b. Va.
Irene Perkins dau., 2 1/2, b. Va.
Luther Perkins son, 26, b. Va., stone cutter
Nettie Perkins dau.in law, 23, b. Va. m. 1 time
Evelyn Perkins grand dau. 2/12, b. Va.
Servant, Lelia Evans, black, cook, m. 1 time

General Information from Margaret Perkins and Delores Noel Weeks, with additions from Federal Census, City of Richmond, Henrico County, Commonwealth of Virginia Records, and Law and Equity Court, City of Richmond, Va.

Joseph E. Perkins m. Pauline T. Lloyd, (6 children), the Census shows him as a Coal Miner

Child: Egbert A. Perkins, b. August 17, 1853, d. October 23, 1927, m. Emma Ruth Seay Bessnard, a widow, daughter of W. and E.R. Seay. (9 children), Emma Ruth Perkins d. January 1, 1899, of these children:

1. Edward L. Perkins m. Lily (5 children) founded Edward L. Perkins Monumental Works. He was a Mason and his picture is in the Masonic Lodge, known children:
   1. Bernard L. Perkins m. Nettie, 4 children, Lewis L. Perkins, Richard Perkins, Clarence Perkins, Betty Jean Perkins
   2. Percy L. Perkins m. Pearl, 7 children, played Mandolin in band
   3. George Perkins m. Hilda, 2 children
   4. Ruth Perkins m. Ernest Walsh, 3 children
   5. Earl Perkins m. Laura, 1 child, played Banjo and singer in band named Pocomo Ramblers, played on WMBG Radio station weekly in Richmond, Va.

2. Luther Perkins, b. June 13, 1883, d. September 29, 1938, Stonecutter, m. Nell, owned Ash Cake Inn on Washington Hwy., Richmond, Va., child Evelyn Perkins m. a Woodfin.

3. William Lawrence Perkins m. Lena, 7 children. He was a Stonecutter, known children:
   1. Estelle Perkins m. Blount, 1 child
   2. Lorraine Perkins m. Otto, 1 child
   3. Louise Perkins m. Smith, 1 child
   4. Thelma Perkins m. McVeigh
   5. William Perkins m. Wollsever, he had his own band, played at night clubs.
   6. Ray Perkins

4. Ernest Norman Perkins m. Ruth E. Clarke, Stonecutter,

known children:
1. Helen Mae Perkins m. Hopkins, no children
2. Vernille Virginia Perkins m. Martin, 2 children
3. Myrtle Eleanor Perkins m. Arbough no children
4. Ernest N. Perkins, Jr., m. Henley, 2 children
5. Margaret A. Perkins
6. Marian Elizabeth Perkins m. Horton, 3 children
7. Roger Martin Perkins m. Eubank, 2 children then
   m. a Woodfin, no children
8. Barbara Anne Perkins m. Kirby, 2 children

5. Gertrude Perkins m. Howard Traylor, known children:
   1. Marie Traylor m. L. Snieder, 2 children
   2. Raymond Traylor m. Thelma Day, designed
      window displays for Miller and Rhoads
      Department Store, Richmond, Va.
   3. Philys Traylor m. Arnold, 1 child, then m. a
      Smith, 1 child
   4. Corrine Traylor m. Lowman Snisler, no
      children
   5. Lillian Traylor m. Lowman Snider, 1
      child
   6. Margaret Gertrude Traylor, d. as an infant
   7. Aubrey Traylor
   8. Alvin Traylor

6. Daisy Perkins m. Edward Walton, known children:
7.
   1. Kathryn Walton m. Hopkins and Corville,
      no children, worked at Dupont Chemical,
      Richmond, Va.
   2. Willie Earl Walton
   3. Edward Walton
   4. Herbert Walton
   5. Nellie May Walton
   6. Elsworth Walton
   7. Irene Walton m. Moore

8. (Rsh.58) Margaret Ruth Perkins m. John Edward Hawley,
   she was an active leader in the Eastern Star, in LaMesa,
   California, where they lived, and he was active in the
   Masonic Lodge, they had no children. She had child by

previous marriage to a Granger, his name was Lewis Granger, and he lived in LaMesa, California. He owned his own plumbing company, and was active in the Masonic Lodge in LaMesa, no children by John Edward Hawley.

9.   Maude Perkins m. George R. Crowder who was a Justice of The Peace in Clay Ward, Richmond, Va., 2 children, dau. (Margaret) Madeline Crowder m. a Napier, had one child; and dau. Blanche Fagan Crowder

10. Lottie May Perkins m. James Washington Trexler, on February 17, 1895, she was b. April 22, 1876 in Richmond, Va., and d. there September 4, 1924, she is bur. in Riverview Cemetery. James Washington Trexler was b. February 22, 1878, he was a Shop Foreman for Richmond, Fredericksburg, and Potomac Railroad, known children:
   1. John Joseph Trexler m. Margaret (Mary) Virginia Talley, children, Herbert Julius Trexler, John Joseph Trexler, Jr., Robert Earl Trexler, George Herndon Trexler, Margaret Trexler, Joyce Ann Trexler, Lottie May Trexler, Mable Lorraine Trexler
   2. Grace Bell Trexler m. Carlyle Noel, children, William Carlisle Noel, James Leslie Noel, Charles Jefferson Noel, Marian Coleman Noel, Alvin Douglas Noel, Grace Laverne Noel and Delores Ann Noel
   3. Mable Lorraine Trexler m. Percy Linwood Butler, children, Edith May Butler, and James Linwood Butler
   4. James Herman Trexler m. Helen Gertrude Fines, children, Charlotte Ann Trexler and Rose Edith Trexler
   5. Ruth Virginia Pastora Trexler d.in her early 20's she never m.
   6. Walter Ignatius (Edward) Trexler m. Nettie M. Blair, children, Walter Warren Trexler, Nancy Lorraine Trexler
   7. Edward Coleman Trexler m. Mary Ida Hicks, children, Edward Coleman Trexler, Jr., Mary Diane Trexler,

Peter Lynn Trexler, Jeremiah Trexler
8. Gladys May Trexler m. Earl Kessler Auld, d. childless
9. Daisy Adelaide Trexler b. June 15, 1915 m. John
Edward Hawley (widower of her Aunt Margaret
Ruth Perkins Hawley) and had the following
children, Laura Mae Hawley, b. July 23, 1941 and
Betty Sue Hawley b. March 21, 1947. Daisy
Adelaide Trexler Hawley m. 2nd Horace Beverly
Childress, Sr., and had no children.
10. Herbert Leslie Trexler, d. as a baby

Following the death of his first wife, Egbert Perkins m. second
Mary Virginia Baughan, who was b. June 4, 1879, d. July 18,
1956, her nickname was Molly, they had 4 children + 1 adopted
1. Joseph Perkins m. Magaline, 2 children
2. Roy Hillsman Perkins b. February 20,
1904, d. May 10, 1967, m. Kathleen, 3
children
3. Benjamin Ralph Perkins, b. July 12, 1906,
d. November 29, 1942, no children
4. Mary Irene Perkins, b. August 4, 1908, d. January
14, 1915
5. Emma Lou Perkins m. a Townsend, Emma Lou
adopted child

VSL, Marriage Records.
January 25, 1872, Egbert A. Perkins m. Emma Ruth
Bessnard, Benard, widow. He was b. in Henrico, She was b. in
Goochland. Groom 19 years old, Bride 22 years old. Parents
husband, J.S. and P.T. Perkins, wife W. and E.R. Seay. His
occupation, Lock Keeper. Marriage performed by B.B. Reynolds.

Military Records, Revolutionary War
DAR
John Perkins b. 1754 d. December 9, 1799, m. Mary
Anthony P.S. Va.
William Perkins, Sr., b. c. 1722, da. c. 1800, m. Lucy
Watkins, P.S. Va.

NA: War of 1812
Benjamin Perkins, widow, Elizabeth A., Pvt. Capt.

Nathaniel Perkins and Wm. M. Thompson Cos., Va. Militia, wo 16992, wc 10109

    Edward Perkins, Capt. Walter Oley's Com., Va. Militia, so 16511, sc 11528

    Elijah Perkins, widow, Frances, Capt. James Watsons Com., Va. Militia, so 4513, sc 3290, wo 29412, wc 20199

    John H. Perkins, Lucy Perkins, widow, Capt. A. Nicholls Com., Va. Militia, Capt. Geo. Boders', wo 2680

    Jonathan Perkins, widow, Martha A. Newell, Capt. Comer and Raines, Va. Militia, 35, 321

    Peter Perkins, widow, Nancy Perkins, wo 4422, wc. 21919, Pvt., Capt. Francis Movres', and Wm. Bailey's Com., Virginia Militia

    Robert Perkins, widow, Elizabeth C. Perkins, Pvt., Capt. John L. Jennings, Va, Militia, so 5193, sc 7451, wo 27017, wc, 25962

    Thomas Perkins, widow, Margaret Perkins, Capt. Given's, Com., Va. Militia, wo 10129

    Whitney Perkins, widow, Rosie M., Pvt., Capt. Henry Digg's Com., Va. Militia, wo 5168, wc 1796

Trexler Family (Rsh.58)

    Ignatius Trexler, b.c. 1787, by Trade a Cooper, m. Anna (Nancy) Murray on November 8, 1812, at St. Johns German Catholic Church, Baltimore, Md. They moved to Richmond, Va., in 1817 from Baltimore, Md. At the rank of Corporal, he served in the Battles of North Point and Ft. McHenry in Baltimore, Md., War of 1812. He is bur., in an unmarked grave, at Shockoe Hill Cemetery, Richmond, Va., known children:

1.   John Joseph Trexler b. October, 1813, a Cooper by Trade, lived Franklin Co., Va., and Richmond, Va., never m., bur. Mt. Calvery Cemetery, Richmond, Va.

2.   William Trexler b. August 11, 1815, d. February 8, 1855, a Cooper by Trade, m. Nancy Ann Ellis, daughter of Jeremiah and Virginia Ellis, 5 children

3.   Appolonia Julia (Abby Gail) Trexler b. May 2, 1817, bapt. St. Johns German Catholic Church, Baltimore, Md., m. William Miller July 6, 1839. She d. May 9, 1850, Richmond, Va.

4.   Mary Ann Trexler b. July 7, 1821, m. Christian S. Allbrecht

February 16, 1842, children Joseph Allbrecht,
Eutaw Allbrecht, Christian Allbrecht
Rosetta Trexler b. October 8, 1825, m. Gottlieb Allbrecht
(Allbright), June 22, 1843, children: Mary Louise
Allbright, Nonnie Allbright m. Wm. Kuhn, Margaret
Allbright m. Christian Schneider, Virginia Allbright
m. Robert Shilling

William Trexler, Sr., (#2 above), b. August 11, 1815, bapt.
St. John's German Catholic Church, Baltimore, Md., by Trade a
Cooper, m. Nancy Ann Ellis on May 29, 1843, (she was the
widow of James Hughes), he d. February 8, 1855, Richmond, Va.,
Funeral Mass said at St. Peters Catholic Church, Richmond, Va.,
he is bur. at Shockhoe Hill Cemetery, Richmond, Va., in an
unmarked grave, known children:
1.   John Ignatius Trexler b. September 2, 1844 d. April 26,
            1905 m. Mary A. Elizabeth Simpson, 6 children
2.   Rosetta Trexler b. March 17, 1847 d. May 13, 1857
3.   Isabella Trexler b. October 15, 1849 d. October 12, 1851
4.   Joseph Trexler b. September 23, 1852 d. May 21, 1857
5.   William Trexler b. May 8, 1855 d. June 3, 1931 m. Mary
            Margaret Poh (Poe), 6 children

note: after her husbands death in 1855 Nancy Ann Ellis
(Hughes) Trexler m. Albert Liggon, a Policeman with the
City of Richmond, Va., known children: Reuben Henry
Liggon b. February 3, 1858 m. Sarah_____, children,
Edgar and Nellie; and Alonzo Columbus Liggon b. April 5,
1864, m. Willie Ann Wright, children, Ivy E. Liggon, Annie
Alease Liggon, Lottie Dell Liggon, Alonzo Liggon, Jr.,
Willie Pleasant Liggon, Ruby May Liggon, Irvine Edgar
Liggon. The Liggon family plot is in Riverview Cemetery,
Richmond, Va.

John Ignatius Trexler, (son of William Trexler, # 1 above),
b. September 2, 1844, in Richmond, Va., m. Mary A. Elizabeth
Simpson, daughter of James M. and Sarah Simpson of
Buckingham Co., Va., on September 6, 1865. He served in both
the Confederate States Army and Navy. It is believed that his
employment at Tredegar Iron Works, which made armaments for
the Confederacy, had influence on his dual military service. He d.

on April 26, 1905 and is bur. in an unmarked grave in Riverview Cemetery, Richmond, Va., known children:

1.   Isabella Trexler b. April 29, 1866, m. Charles Dance, m.second Powhatan J. Dance who was nicknamed "Pop" and had no children, known children by Charles Dance:
   Mrs. J.A. Carter
   Mrs. Albert Haas
   Mrs. William Wright
   Mrs. H.D. Pettis
   Ella Dance m. Cole
   Loretta R. Dance
   Annie Phippen Dance
   Lawson H. Dance

2.   John Joseph Trexler b. April 2, 1876, a Commercial Painter, m. Lena Madeline Bennett Totty, widow with two children, Estelle Totty and Hazel Totty, by her 1st marriage, known children:
   Joseph Edward Trexler, Sr., m. Helen Leary, children, Joseph Edward Trexler, Jr., Francia L. Trexler, and Madelyn Trexler
   Frank James Trexler (noted Richmond, Va., Baseball Player), m. Ruth S. Bowles, children Donald Lee Trexler, Frank James Trexler, Jr.
   Violet Trexler m. Dewey W. Blanton
   Mary Trexler m. Lee Tyler
   Eunice Trexler m. Robert Winfrey Shepherd

3.   James Washington Trexler, b. February 22, 1878, Shop Foreman at Richmond, Fredericksburg, and Potomac Railroad, m. Lottie May Perkins, daughter of Egbert A. Perkins and his wife Emma Ruth Seay, dau. of W. and E.R. Seay. Emma was a widow, without children, at the time of her marriage to Egbert Perkins. See Perkins Family information, pg.253, for their descendants.

4.   Charles Herndon Trexler, Sr., b. March 20, 1881, a Machinist, m. Etta May Johns daughter of Dr. and Mrs. John Alexander Johns, nee Elizabeth F. Roach, children: Lucille Herndon Trexler m. John Schluter and then John Basala; Minor Davidson Trexler m. John Letcher Stone;

Marian May Trexler m. Newell Hamilton Houchens; Evelyn
Edward Trexler m. Silas Westly Craps; Carlton Urban
Trexler m. Grace; Charles Herndon Trexler, Jr., nickname
"Doc" m. Pearl Estelle Gerhardt, child Donn Gregory
Trexler

5.   Nancy McCarthy Trexler, b. May 8, 1885, m. Arthur T.
       Ford, d. January 1930, Richmond, Va., children:
       Georgie Ford m. a Trainum then James H. Burns
       Mrs. H. B. Tucker
       Doris Ford
       Margaret Ford
       Harden Gartney Ford
       Ashley F. Ford
       Mowray A. Ford
       Clyde J. Ford

6.   Bertha McCarthy Trexler b. June 1, 1888, m. Clyde H.
       Childress, d. May 20, 1964, no children.

       William Trexler, Jr., (son of William Trexler, Sr.), was b. on
May 8, 1855 in Richmond, Va. He was by Trade a Builder. He
m. Mary Margarett Poh (Poe), dau. of Jacob and Eva Poh, who
were both b. in Germany. He built the old Henrico County
Courthouse and much of his work is seen today in the Fan
District of Richmond. He d. June 3, 1931. known children:
       William, Trexler, III, m. Addie Webb, and had Marie Trexler
              who m. a Heath; George Nelson Trexler, Robert
              G. Trexler, stepchildren: William E. Trexler, Mrs.
              Charles Burnner, Mrs. Leo Kudig
       Charles Augustus Trexler b. April 6, 1876, Richmond, m.
              Susie B. Davis, children Sara B. Trexler and
              Charles William Trexler.
       Rosa Alice Trexler b. September 5, 1882 d. July 12, 1918
       Eva Trexler b. June 15, 1884, d. February 2, 1920
       Jacob Eddie Trexler b. March 8, 1878 d. May 30, 1895
       Minnie Trexler m. M. Wardell then Bernard Morgan she d.
              October 8, 1928.

Woolridge, Waldridge Family (Rsh.52)
<u>1810 Culpeper Co., Va., Census</u> Jeter Woldige, Jr., Jeremiah and

John Wooledge, Peter Worldridge

<u>1850 Culpeper Co., Va., Census</u> pg.233, Dwelling 262,
John Wooledge, b. 1780, male, farmer, value R.E. 1400, b. Va.
Mildred W. Wooledge, b. 1785, female, b. Va.
Agnes Wooledge b. 1810, female, b. Va.
Elizabeth Wooledge , b. 1816, female, b. Va.
Mildred Ann Wooledge, b. 1823, female, b. Va.
Caroline Wooledge, b. 1827, female, b. Va.
William Wooledge, b. 1830, male, b. Va.
Webster Wooledge, b. 1832, male, b. Va.
Sarah Wooledge, b. 1836, female, b. Va.

<u>Death Records, Culpeper County</u>
A.G. Woldridge, November 9, 1886, age 68, b. 1818,
Culpeper Co., parents John and Mildred Woldridge.
Mildred Webster Walridge, January 2, 1866, b. 1782, age
84, b. in King George Co., Va.

<u>Emigrants from England 1773-1776 Fothergill</u>
Peter Woillidge age 24,painter and glazier of Suffolk in
Ship Planter to Virginia as servant January 30, and 7 February
1774
Peter Woillidge, Port of arrival Alexandria, Va.; John
Woolridge, b.c. 1680, d. 1757, appears in records first in 1699 as
Blacksmith of Henrico and Chesterfield Co., Va.

<u>Marriage Records, Culpeper Co., Va.</u>
Peter Waldridge m. March 12, 1802 to Fanny Blackwell
John Waldridge m. Milly Hendrick December 26, 1805
Lucy Ann Waldridge, m. lst Thomas Hawley and had 14
children, m. second on October 17, 1864 to Simon Wise. There
is a prenuptial agreement at the Culpepper Co., Va., C.H. for the
marriage of Lucy Hawley to Simon Wise. The record of her
second marriage gives her parents as John Waldridge and
Mildred Webster Waldridge.

<u>Marriages from LDS Church, Utah, Bonds through 1850</u>
Peter C. Worlladge m. Mary D. Rees, December 23, 1844
John A. Shackleford m. Charlotte A. Worllidge, December
21, 1848

Coleman Shackleford m. Drucilla Worledge January 10, 1833

Notes on Culpeper Co., Va., Dr. Philip Slaughters, Gene. and His.
Albert B. Woolridge m. Maria S. Hasbrough October 28, 1863 in Orange Co., Va.

1783 Culpeper Tax list - Peter Wollage

1800 Culpeper Co., Tax list - Peter Wallage

Orange County Virginia Families, Author, William Everett Brockman, Vol. 4, pg.83:
Samuel Brockman and wife, Ann (Anestar) Simms of Albermarle: seven children, Richard Simms m. Martha Patsy Dickerson in 1812; Julia A. Simms m. James Waldridge and had son James Waldridge.

V.   ADDITIONAL INFORMATION

Colonial Records Project   **English**
        April 25, 1622, Letter from John Carter at Southward to
his uncle Ralph Hawtrey, at Ruislip, Middlesex, telling him of his
arrival in Va., and his business at James Town, VSL.
        year 1624, on a list of those living in Virginia, at The Rest
at West and Sherlow Hundred Island, Thomas Haile, a boy, VSL
        (Rsh.90) June 27, 1636, letter of Jerome Hawley to Sir
Francis Windebank, sends him a memorial which is most
important for the regulating of tobacco and the trade in foreign
plantations. VSL
        (Rsh.90) November 11, 1636, letter from William
Steventon to Edward Nicholas, Portsmouth, complaints on Ship
Black George, the Ship has proved leaky and a small leak has
been found and repaired. She should have been examined
completely, but with all the goods on board this is impossible.
One Mr. Hawley, especially who has many goods in the Ship, has
prevented examination, though people complain "because their
humors are not in all points observed." VSL
        (Rsh.90) February 26, 1637/8, George Reade, James City,
Va., to Robert Reade, his brother. Does not think much of Mr.
Hawley. Thanks to the support of the Governor and Mr. Kemp,
the writer has survived. Mr. Menephe has brought many
servants. Mr. Hawley has promised the writer that the next lot of
servants coming to Virginia would be for him but he does not
believe it as Hawley is in Maryland. VSL
        (Rsh.90) March 20, 1637/8, Jerome Hawley to Sir Francis
Windebank. The Assembly has passed Act concerning tobacco
which should meet the abuses. Many in Virginia fear that they
will be reduced to the same difficult position as the Bermuda
Islands. VSL
        (Rsh.90) May 8, 1638. Jerome Hawley to Sir Francis
Windebank, commission from the Queen of Sweden wishing for
free trade in tobacco and desiring to plant tobacco at Delaware
Bay. The King must prevent this. Proposes to use only English
Ships for trade. The revenue of the Colony will defray the
pension for the Governor. VSL
        (Rsh.90) May 16, 1638, Jerome Hawley to Robert Read,
Reed's brother and the writer have referred their differences about
accounts to Mr. Kemp, who has postponed a decision but the

writer promises that nobody will have reason to blame him. VSL (Rsh.90) May 17, 1638. Jerome Hawley to Robert Read. Gives details about his account with Read's brother. Mr. Kemp is not a friend of the writer and he would advise Read's brother not to follow his advice in everything. Gives him reasons for difficulties with Mr. Kemp. VSL
(Rsh.91) July 11, 1639, Capt. Hawley, Hawley is about to go to Florida he is now of Barbados VSL
(Rsh.91) August 1, 1660, Capt. Henry Hawley seized Governor John Powell who was taken forcibly to England VSL Harry Wright Newman (Rsh.90) "Third in importance of the Adventurers connected with the Settlement of Maryland was Jerome Hawley, Esq., Joint Commissioner with Captain Thomas Cornwalys, and certainly the most colorful and most unpredictable councilor of the group. He was the son of (Rsh.89) James Hawley, Esq., and b. in the year 1590, he was brother to (Rsh.91) Henry Hawley, Governor of the Barbados and to (Rsh.92) William Hawley, one time Deputy Governor of the same isles, later of Carolina and Maryland. Jerome was one of the heaviest investors in the enterprise and was likewise the heaviest loser. Jerome Hawley and brother Gabriel, Roman Catholic investors in the establishment of Maryland, were of an excellent family of Middlesex England. Negotiations began in September of 1633 for a voyage to Maryland aboard the Dove. (Rsh.89) Gabriel Hawley, in or about the year 1630, spent 10 months in Virginia. (Rsh.90) Jerome Hawley was in Jamestown, Virginia in November of 1634, in June 1635 and April 1636 Jerome Hawley was in London. Jerome Hawley carried on trade with the Indians. On April 25, 1638, Leonard Calvert wrote his brother that Jerome Hawley intended to move his wife and family to Virginia. Jerome was named Royal Treasurer of Virginia and in August of 1637 he arrived in Virginia in the Ship Friendship. Prior to his sailing on the Ark there is evidence that Lord Baltimore granted Jerome Hawley at least two manorial holdings, "St. Jerome", of 6000 acres, and "St. Helen," of unknown acreage. His consort, who was his second wife, came to Maryland, but there is no evidence of her accompanying him on the Ark in 1633. He lived on his townland in St. Mary's Hundred which he gave the name of "St. Peter, " this was undoubtedly the most pretentious house in the Providence. There were at least three white servants at his Maryland Plantation, St. Peters, at the time of his death in 1638.

He worked with John Lewger, Esq. in the preparation of "A Relation of Maryland; "Together With a Map of the Countrey, The Conditions of Plantation, His Majesties Charter to the Lord Baltimore, translated into English, September 8, 1635", with the objective of selling Maryland to prospective British settlers. Jerome Hawley made his last Will and Testament shortly before sailing on the Ark and the Dove on October 20, 1633, naming William Hawley, of Grossmont, Mommouthshire, Arthur Dodington, and Lewis Hele, his executors, his widow, and second wife, Eleanor was the widow of Thomas Courtney, Esq. She returned to England after Jerome's death. Captain William Hawley, Esq., removed from the Barbados to Maryland and settled on his brother's Manor of St. Jerome sometime before 1650"

General
Notes of Henry I. Hutton, Warrenton, Va., c. 1927
　　　Among some of the Halleys, in Virginia, there is a tradition, that, from England, came "three brothers," one of whom settled in Massachusetts, one in Maryland and the other in Virginia or further south. Information from a Diary, in the possession of Mr. Hutton, is furnished in the Halley Family in England and America. This was privately published, in pamphlet form, in 1933.

The Halley Family in England and America, edited by Eugene Fairfield MacPike, Member of the Society of Genealogists of London, Chicago 1933
　　　...Surnames Halley and Hawley were often interchangeable, and, sometimes, pronounced alike. The spelling of surnames even so late as the 17th and 18th century was far from uniform.
　　　(Rsh.90) Jerome Hawley, of Maryland, was one of the gentleman in attendance upon Queen Henrietta Maria, and was a Councillor of Maryland, c. 1630-1637. He was a brother of Henry Hawley, who, for many years, was Governor of Barbados and of William Hawley, a squire, in 1650 of the Protestant Declaration of Maryland. He was also a brother of James Hawley of Brainford, county Middlesex, England...we must, therefore, commence our formal tabulation of the genealogy of the Halleys in Virginia, with:
　　　Thomas Halley, who was b. in England c. 1662, and was

the progenitor of a large and representative branch of that family in Virginia. In the Diary of Henry Simpson Halley (1789-1872) a great-grandson of Thomas Halley, it is recorded that the latter was b. in Wales, but we have no other authority for this statement.

Thomas Halley emigrated from England c. 1679, or before, for his name appears in the Parish Register, in 1679 of the place now known as Truro Parish.

He settled on Dogue Run, a small stream which empties into the Potomac River, just below Mount Vernon, then in Westmoreland Co. Here he built a long cabin wherein he and his good wife reared their family. At that time, c. 1679, Alexandria was an Indian Village. While Thomas Halley was living on Dogue Run, he was captured by some of the neighboring Indians, tied, and carried up the Potomac River to Harper's Ferry. One night after he had been securely tied and placed for the night, between two Indians, they all fell asleep. As the Indians slept, he picked up a mussel shell, cut the rope with which he was bound, slipped from between the two Indians, and taking the trail homeward arrived in safety before he was overtaken. The Indians reached his log cabin a few hours after his arrival. They looked in and said: "Tom, is that you?" Strange to relate, they did not try to harm him, but each and all filed away quietly to their own haunts.

Thomas Halley m. but the name of his wife is not known. It is believed that (Rsh.76) James Hally, b. June 14, 1707, is the son of Thomas Halley.
note: To date this lineage has not been proved.

Halley Family Bible, copied by Rev. J.G. Moreton, Baptist Minister, Bible in the possession of Mr. Samuel Halley, Macon, Georgia c. 1915, house later burned with bible. Copy was made for Mrs. J. Stanford Halley, Corsicana, Texas, descendant of Rsh.3
Item 1. Thms Halley...Ludburgh...15 to...
Item 2. Jeromie Hawley...life ye 17 (or 19th) day...16...
Item 3. Wm. and Thomas Hawley declared of...protesting
         faiths...and signers...thereof...ye...16
Item 4. Thms Haley and clerk Francis Walford Staffordshire
         with...cousin Sara Hawley with/wife...to the
         number of twenty souls...with familys and

indentured servants...in province of
Maryland...Enterprise

Item 5. J...Haley to E. Bunch, Burche (Rsh.1)

Item 6. Thomas Halley to Elizabeth Burche, Bunche, wid w/2
1728 (or 23) with...children, underneath this is the
name of John Halley and another not distinct
enough to read.

There were a number of other names without dates, at
the end of the book is a notation that the "Holy Evangels"
was consumed in the flames." The indistinctive names
are 1 & 2 Jerry and Omy, twins 3. James Hawley, 4.
Jeromy Hally, 5. Gabriel Hally, 6. Clemmie Hally, 7.
Jerimy Halley, 8. Daniel Holly, 9. John S. Hally, 10. Henry
L (or S) Hally, 11. William Hally, 12. William Hally, 13.
Edward Hally

Item 7. John Halley to Elizabeth Price, wid. with two children,
January 31, 177_, England (Rsh.4)

Hawley Family, Cleo Goff Bartels, Hawley Family Historian,
February 16, 1977

1. Thomas Hawley, b. England c. 1662, d. Virginia c.
1750, by 1733, he and his family were in Prince William Co., Va.
(Rsh.76) 1.1 James Halley, a prosperous planter, b. June 14,
1707, England, d. July 6, 1792 in Fairfax Co., Va., m. Elizabeth
Simpson, b. November 8, 1717, d. July 22, 1785, issue: William,
James, II, John, Richard, Francis, Sr., Henry Simpson, Sarah,
Sybil, Mary and Susan
(Rsh.76) 1.1.1 William Halley, 1721-1806 m. Catherine, issue:
Henry Simpson Halley, only child, lost at sea
1.1.2 James Halley, II, was living December 5, 1831 in
Prince William Co., Va., m. Eleanor, Deed book B., pg.37, Deed
Book 12, pgs. 151, 497
(Rsh.76) 1.1.3 John Halley, settled in Boonsboro, Ky, Est. Ist
store, planted Ist orchard and was Ist man in Kentucky to ship
tobacco to New Orleans via the Kentucky, Ohio and Mississippi
River, date 1785, m. Susan Anne Hart, marriage bonds of Bedford
Co., Va.
1.1.4 Richard Halley, d. Winchester, Ky, age c. 66 years
(Rsh.110)1.1.5 Francis Halley, Sr., came from Prince William Co.,
to Bedford Co., Va., in 1761, Will dated June 28, 1808, proved
August 23, 1813, recorded Bedford Co., Va., he d. Richmond Ky.,

Issue: Francis, Jr., Sabina (Sebia), Prudence, Chloe and others
      1.1.5.1 Sabina Halley m. John Goff, May 19, 1800,
Bedford Co., Va., family lived Lincoln Coi., Ky, Issue: James
Urish, Mary, Alexander, Almira, Lucinda, Caroline, John, Nancy,
Malinda, Creed Pascal and Hansford Goff
      1.1.6 Henry Simpson Halley, May 18, 1762 to November
28, 1838
      1.1.7 Sarah Halley, d. about 80 years old m. Haney
      1.1.8 Sybil Halley, m. Jesse Peake, lived Prince William
Co., Va., 1831
      1.1.9 Mary Halley m. Crump
      1.1.10, Susan Halley m. William Said
notes of Cleo Goff Bartels: in England, the two families of Goff
and Halley lived in adjoining parishes in Salisbury, Wiltshire Co.,
England, the Goffs lived in Broade Chalke Parish and the Halleys
in St. Thomas Parish

<u>Hawley Family, Contribution of Betty Painter of Pennsylvania,
Bedford Co., Va., from Liberty, Va., and Alexandria, Va., Records</u>
      William Halley, Holly, Haley, served in the French and
Indian War, Capt. Easoms, Dunmores War, Battle of Point
Pleasant, lived Bedford Co., Va., Territory in 1758, moved to
Botetourt Co., Va., purchased land, in 1785, 1786, 1789, 1790,
1799, 1802.
      dau. of William Halley, Charlotte m. Henry Ogburne,
Botetourt Co., Va., January 27, 1790
      Mary Haley, m. Thomas Crawford, December 26, 1845
      John B. Holly m. Elizabeth Blankenship, September 14,
1835
      (Rsh.3) June 19, 1799, William and Thomas Halley
witness to Nathaniel Halley's Will, Wm. Halley d. while settling the
estate of Nathaniel Halley
      Tax record: Wm. Halley, 1740-1783, William Halley, 5
horses, 12 cattle, at headwaters of the South Fork and Little
Rivers
      William Halley, Prince William Co., Va., 1782
      Bedford Co., Va., March 1758, Court Case, <u>William
Simpson and Elizabeth Campbell vs. Michael Wood and William
Halley</u> of Bedford Co., Va.
      William Holley, b. 1816, in Ohio, m. Susannah, children
Sarah, Mary, Carolina

William Halley of Alexandria, Va., Mill Wheel Maker

<u>Hawley Surname:</u>
English: habitation name from any of various places so called. One is in Kent, with old English halig holy + leah wood, clearing, and would therefore have once been the site of a sacred grove. One in Hants, has its first element Oeh(e)all hall, manor, or the homonymous h(e)all rock, stone. The surname is common mainly in South Yorkshire and Nottinghamshire and mainly derive from a lost place called Hawley, near Sheffield, which is from ON (Old Norse) haugr mount + OE leah clearing. note: Card Index file MdHR, says for Hawley see Hailey, Healy, Haily, Haly, Healley, Haulin, Holly, Holley

<u>Amos Hawley,</u> (Rsh.12), research of Arthur William Hawley of Morgantown, W.Va. Family legend says that Amos came to America with his sister, who m. a man by the name of Davis, from Wales, England. Amos Hawley is first seen on the Loudoun Co., Va., Census in 1789 as being over 16 and he is named in his father (Rsh.9) John Hawley's estate chancery suits in Loudoun Co., Va., M1155, as being a son. John Hawley had been in America for sometime and it is likely that Amos Hawley was b. in Maryland. Amos Hawley's first cousin Mary (Molly) Hawley, dau. of (Rsh.11) William and Bathsheba Hutchison Hawley, m. Thomas Davis. Further research will likely prove that additional Hutchisons were speculating in W.Va., see Hutchison Bible Records for family of Bathsheba Hutchison Hawley.

<u>Catherine Heath Hawley,</u> (Rsh.14), death date and the birthdate of Andrew H. Hawley can be found in the Heath Family Bible, file number 267, Loudoun Co., Library, Leesburg, Va.

<u>William Hawley,</u> b. 1785, Manchester, Vermont, d. January 23, 1845, bur. beneath chancel of St. John's Church, Washington, D.C. He m. Wilhelmina Douglas Potts, dau. of John and Eliza, nee Ramsey, Potts, at Christ Church, Alexandria, Va., on August 25, 1818. He was a minister in Culpeper Co., Va., and came to Washington, D.C., St. John's Church, in 1817. Bishop Moore ordained Mr. Hawley to the priesthood in Culpeper, Virginia, in 1815.

Historic Roads of Virginia,(Rsh.13) January 7, 1811, Abram
Hawley, a male tithable, and others, to keep the road in good
repair from Shifletts Old Place to Charlottesville. James H.
Craven appointed surveyor of road. Albermarle County Road
Orders 1783-1816, Charlottesville, by Nathaniel Mason Pawlett,
Faculty Research Historian, Virginia Highway and Transportation
Research Council, Charlottesville, Va., December 1975.

Library of Congress, Index to Thomas Jefferson's Papers,
Manuscript Division
        Nathan Haley to T.J. 1800, Oct. 6, s1, p3
        Nathan Haley Fr T.J. 1808, Jul.14, s1, p1
        Nathan Haley to T.J. 1808, Se.8, s1, p2
        Horace Holly Fr.T.J. 1825, Apr.5, s1, p1
        Jessee Hawley to T.J. 1803, Nov.2, s1, p3

Thomas Jefferson's Farm Papers, written in his hand, Alderman
Library, University of Virginia, Rare Manuscripts Division,
Charlottesville, Va.
    (Rsh.13) December 10, 1818, "gave ord. on James Leitch
for 12.D in favor of A. Hawley for himself and Monroe for lime."
    (Rsh.13) February 28, 1821, Abraham Holly. paid first
installment of $100. for a small limestone quarry
    (Rsh.13) March 5, 1821 "having sold my limestone quarry
(4 acres) to Abraham Hawley for 400.D. of which 100. payable
immediately and 300 D., January 1, 1822, Charles Vest being
security, I give him credit for Meek's order ante August 19, to wit
59.86, his own acct. 2.70., and I now receive the balance in cash
37.44D., making up the 100.D."
    (Rsh.13) July 31, 1821 "sent for lime .50 to Holly,
Abraham"
    (Rsh.13) September 23, 1821, "Abram Holly for lime,
I.D."
    (Rsh.13) February 7, 1822, "rec'd of Abraham Hawley in
part payment see March 4, 21.12, I am to credit him 5.D. more
on acct. lime."

Note: in year 2000, Limestone Farm, is on Rt. 250, Keswick, Va.,
which is south of Charlottesville, Va. Thomas Jefferson of
Monticello retained by the transfer Deed, for himself and the
house at Monticello and its inhabitants, the right to obtain as

much limestone "as they think proper for their own use but not to dispose of to others" from the quarry. Deed Book 22, pg.334, Albermarle Co., Va.

Thomas Jefferson's Papers, Alderman Library, University of Virginia, Charlottesville, Va.
William Hawley, Jr. of Winchester, Va., paid for hanging wall paper. University of Virginia, Charlottesville, Va.

Thomas Jefferson, VSL, Tyler's Quarterly: Petition, signed at Monticello, Charlottesville, Va., January 17, 1827, by (Rsh.13) Abram Hawley and (Rsh.11) William Hawley. The Petition urged the General Assembly of Virginia to buy the Cerrachi marble Bust of Thomas Jefferson which was included in the sale of furnishings at Monticello following Jefferson's death. The Petitioners felt the Bust should be placed in the University of Virginia Library and not be sold to the State of Louisiana.

Page Johnson, descendant of John Hawley, Personal Notes: An Aerial Photo, was located at the Library of Congress, of the original tract of land in Loudoun County, Virginia owned by (Rsh.9) John Hawley. The property is owned by a surgeon in Florida and is managed by Delbert Linton of Arcola, Va. The photo shows a grave yard on the property. The house is of post and beam construction, and it is obvious that the timbers were hand hewn. The former owners, named Synder, bought the property from Wilson who acquired title to it following John Hawley's death. The estate currently contains 190 acres. The house was built June 17, 1778-1779. This is a private residence and is, in the year 2000, adjoined by a horse farm and surrounded by new home subdivisions.

Limestone Farm, Richard B. Florence, Owner, October 1972
(Rsh.13) Present day "Limestone" is a part of the John Crawford grant of 1734 and the Charles Lewis grant of 1731. Subsequent owners of portions of the tract included James Monroe and Thomas Jefferson; the latter in 1773 having purchased 4 acres on Three Notched Road and Plum Tree Branch now called Limestone Branch. The lime used by Jefferson for the construction of Monticello was burned here. This vein of limestone gives the estate its name. The oldest

residential structure bears the date of 1794. James Monroe's brother Andrew is known to have been living here in 1817 when James was elected to the Presidency. In 1828, the farm was purchased by Dr. George L. Blaetterman, a German survivor of the Napoleonic Wars brought from England by Thomas Jefferson to be the first Professor of Modern Languages at the University of Virginia. It is thought that the manor house was completed by Dr. Blaetterman soon after arriving.

VSL: Ohio Co., Legislative Petitions, 1787
        James Halley petitioned for a ferry across the Ohio River on October 29, 1787

VSL: Scotts History of Orange Co., Va., 1907
Edward Haley appointed Constable and Surveyor of Highways

Peerage and Baronage, London, England
        John Hawley of Auber, in Somersetshire, m. Dorothy, sister of William Walmoit, and had two sons: William of Auder, and Jeremy.
        (Rsh.88) Jeremy Hawley, of Boston, near Brentford, Middlesex m. Kynburgh, dau. of Valentine Saunders, of Sutton Court, Middlesex, and d. June 1593, leaving, with other issue, James, his heir, b. 1558, of Brentford, m. twice, and had several children, some of whom settled in America and second son John m. Amy Studley, and had issue.
        Oldest surviving son of James Hawley was Richard Hawley, M.D. of London, b. 1592, m. Dorothy dau. of Henry Ashworth, M.D. of Oxford, and was survived by his son, Henry Hawley, of Brentford, b. 1629, d. 1706, m. Alice dau. and co-heir of Robert Curtis of Teoterden, had two daus. Curtis m. Thomas Collum, and Susanna m. Anthony Lybbe and one son.
        Surviving son James Hawley of Brentford, b. 1676 m. Dorothy 2nd dau. of Sir Christopher Musgrave, and by two sons, Henry b. 1703, d. 1756 and James Hawley
        James Hawley, M.D. of Leybourne Grange, Kent, b. March 2, 1705-06 m. November 1744, Elizabeth Banks, dau. of Joseph Banks of Revesby Abby in Lincolnshire. She d. November 12, 1766. He d. December 22, 1777, leaving Sir Henry Hawley, and Elizabeth Hawley who m. John Crawley, of Stockwood Co., Beds

Robert Thompson, Robert Thompson Smith, Maysville, Ky.,
descendant of (Rsh.3) Family legend says Robert Thompson,
father of Mary Thompson, was from Scotland and that he was a
Presbyterian Minister. He graduated from Edinborough University
in Scotland and he was a cousin to Ann Thompson who was the
first wife of George Mason of Gunston Hall, Va. Robert
Thompson was a tutor to George Mason.

George Mason Gentleman Revolutionary, Helen Hill Miller, UNC
Press, Chapel Hill,
(Rsh.3) In addition to Mason's assumption of economic
and political responsibilities in his immediate vicinity at the end of
the 1740s he became a partner in the Ohio Company, the vast
economic and political enterprise initiated by Thomas Lee of
Stratford in 1747. Lee had been a Virginia Commissioner at
Lancaster, Pa., during the making of the Treaty with the Iroquois
Indians. This Treaty opened the way to new English settlement
further west. Taking advice from Thomas Cresap, a well known
Marylander, an experienced trader of western Maryland, the
Company petitioned the Crown in 1748 for a grant of 500,000
acres west of the mountains and south of the Folks of the Ohio;
*200,000 acres to be conveyed at once, and the remaining
300,000 on the company's fulfillment of a pledge to build a Fort
near the Folks and establish one hundred families around it within
the space of seven years.

Barbados

Barbados Records, Vol.1, Vol.2, compiled by Sanders, Sanders Publishing Co., Houston, Texas

English and Welch

American Wills and Administrations in the Prerogative Court of Canterbury, 1610-1857, compiled by Peter Wilson Coldham, Genealogical Publishing Co., Inc. 1989

American Wills proved in London 1611-1775,, compiled by Peter Wilson Coldham, Genealogical Publishing, Inc.

The Bristol Registers of Servants Sent to Foreign Plantations, 1654-1686, Peter Wilson Coldham, Genealogical Publishing Co., Inc., Baltimore 1988

The Complete Book of Emigrants, 1607-1660, Peter Wilson Coldham, Genealogical Publishing Co., 1987; 1661-1699

English Estates of American Colonists, Vol, 1 by Peter Wilson Coldham, Baltimore Genealogical Pub. Co. 1980

The Complete Book of Emigrants, 1661 - 1699, Peter Wilson Coldham, Baltimore Genealogical 1988

The Complete Book of Emigrants, 1700 - 1750, Peter Wilson Coldham, Baltimore Genealogical Publishing

The Complete Book of Emigrants in Bondage 1614-1775, Peter Wilson Coldham, Genealogical Publishing Co., Inc., Baltimore 1988

England, Public Records Office, Ruskin Avenue, Kew, Richmond, Surrey England, TW9 4DU , www.pro.gov.uk/about/aboutsites.htm, www.sog.org.uk/leaflets/researcher.html

English Adventurers and Emigrants, 1609-1660, Peter Wilson Coldham, Genealogical Publishing Co., Inc., Baltimore 1984

272

English Convicts in Colonial America, Vol. II, London 1656-1775, compiled and edited by Peter Wilson Coldham, Polyanthos, New Orleans, 1976

English Estates of American Colonists, American Wills and Administrations in the Prerogative Court of Canterbury, 1610-1699, by Peter Wilson Coldham, Baltimore Genealogical Publishing Co., Inc. 1980

The Genealogist, new series, Vol. XXV, London, July 1908

London and Middlesex Published Records, A Handlist, compiled by J.M. Sims, London Record Society, 1970

Notes and Queries, London, 1902-1933, General Indices to the 9th, 10th, 11th, 12th, 13th, Series and following years

Original List of Persons of Quality, 1600 to 1700, ed. John Camden Hotten, 1832-1873, Baltimore Genealogical Publishing Co., Inc., 1974

Wales, Department of Manuscripts and Records, National Library of Wales, Ceredigion SY23 3BU, www.pro.gov.uk/leaflets/ri2272.htm

General
The Bridwell Family in America, Erbon W. Wise

CSP Calendars of State Papers, American and Colonial Series, 1574-1660, ed. W. Noel Sainsburg, Longman and Green, 1860

Colonial Families of the United States of America, George Norburg MacKenzie, Vol. II, Baltimore, 1911

Colonial Papers, Vol. 9, pg.33

Hawley Family, Mr. Charles W. Hawley, President Emeritus, The Hawley Family Society, Trumbull, Ct. (Rsh.1)

Hawley Data, Amos Hawley, (Rsh.12), Blenda Hawley Martin, Davidsonville, Md.

Hawley Data, Nathaniel Hawley, (Rsh.3, 87, 88, 89, 90), Robert Thompson Smith, Maysville, Ky.

Hawley Data, Henry Hawley, Halley, and General, Ann H. Mack, Salinas, California, (Rsh.76, 81, 85, 107, 112, 115)

Hawley Family, Cleo Goff Bartels, Hawley Family Historian, February 16, 1977

Hawley-Halley Family, Some unpublished Hawley-Halley Data by M.T. Corey, The Maryland Historical Magazine, June 1939, pg. 175

Hawley Data, Mable Christie Halley, Miscellaneous note collection, and Pedigree, Austin, Texas, early 1900 (Rsh.98)

Hawley Family Early History of the dating back to the year 1700, Arthur William Hawley, Preston, W.Va.(Rsh.12)

Mr. Clifton Harvey Hawley, Jr.
358 Cocran Drive, N.W.
Atlanta, Georgia, descendant of Absalom Hawley, Rsh.10

Halley Family, Sworn Statement of Mrs. Minnie Halley Smith, State of Louisiana, Parish of Lincoln, taken in 1954, dau. of (Rsh.95, 111)

Halley Family Bible, copied by Rev. J.G. Moreton, Baptist Minister, Bible in the possession of Mr. Samuel Halley, Macon, Georgia c. 1915, house later burned with bible. Copy was made for Mrs. J. Stanford Halley, Corsicana, Texas, descendant of Rsh.3 (Rsh.98)

Hawley Family, Contribution of Betty Painter of Pennsylvania, Bedford Co., Va., from Liberty, Va., and Alexandria, Va., Records

The Halley Family, London, England 1933, a pamphlet

Page Johnson, Vienna, Va., descendant, furnished information and aerial photo from the Library of Congress on (Rsh.9), John Hawley's house in Loudoun Co., Va.

Hawley, Limestone Farm, Charlottesville, Va., Richard B. Florence, Owner, October 1972 (Rsh.13)

The Tie That Binds, The Hawley-Holley Family, by Norva Hawley Jernigan, Gateway Press, Inc., Baltimore 1985

Unpublished notes: Elva Virginia Hawley Saunders, b. October 6, 1874, the Hawley family, currently in possession of the author of this publication.

Henry I. Hutton, Warrenton, Va., Misc. Note Collection (Rsh.76)

Library of Congress, Washington, D.C.

Eugene F. MacPike, Editor, Correspondence and Papers of Edmond Halley, Oxford, The Clarendon Press, 1932

Magazine of History, New York, 1908, Vol. III, 1906, Extracts from English Archives

National Archives, Washington, D.C.

Slave Trading in the Old South, Frederic Bancroft, Frederick Ungar Pub., Co., New York 1959

Mr. William C. Woolridge, family historian, Rt. 2, Box 374 R., Troutville, Va. 24175 has worked with Laurence B. Gardiner over the years studying John Woolridge

Kentucky
Kentucky Genealogies, VI, Some English Halleys and Hawleys who emigrated to America, Eugene F. McPike

Clay City, Ky, The Clay City Times

Maryland
Archives of Maryland, Maryland Hall of Records, Rowe Blvd., Annapolis, Maryland

Capt. George Athey of Galway and Maryland and his descendants. Second Ed. 1989, Lawrence F. Athey, Jr., 3834

Overbrook Lane, Houston, Texas 77027.

The Flowering of the Maryland Palatinate, Harry Wright Newman, Baltimore Gen. Pub.Co., Inc., 1985

Maryland, The Founders of Maryland, E.D. Neill, Munsell, Albany, N.Y., 1876

Maryland Genealogists, Vol.II, taken from Maryland Historical Magazine, pub. Genealogical Pub. Co., 1980, Some Unpublished Hawley-Halley Data, by H.T. Cory

Settlers of Maryland 1701-1730, Peter Wilson Coldham, Genealogical Publishing Co., Inc.; Settlers of Maryland 1731-1750; 1679-1700; 1766-1783

Maryland Early Settlers, Land Records, etc., Liber A.B.H. compiler, Annie Walker Burns, Annapolis, Md. 1936

The Early Settlers of Maryland, Bust. Skordas, Geo. Pub. Baltimore, Md. 1968, 1974

Early Maryland 1634 #9, Streeter, pgs.115,116,119,120,122,123

The Maryland Historical Magazine, pgs. 176, 177

Maryland Hall of Records, Rowe Blvd., Annapolis, Md. 21401

Maryland, Abstracts of Wills of Charles and St. Marys Counties, Md., Annie Walker Burns, Annapolis, Md.

Maryland Calendar of Wills 1738-1743, Vol. VIII Geo. Publ.Baltimore 1968.

Maryland, MdHR, Chancery Ct. Proceedings, Court Series 5, pgs. 496,503, 1669-1679

Maryland, MdHR, Provincial Court Records

Maryland, MdHR, Provincial Court Index to Deeds JG 1658

North Carolina
The Tie That Binds, The Hawley-Holley Family, by Norva Hawley
Jernigan, Gateway Press, Inc., Baltimore, 1985

Virginia
Accomack, Co., Va., Land Causes, 1727-1826, compiled by
Stratton Nottingham, Onancock, Va.

Alexandria City and County, Virginia Deed Book Extracts, Vol. 1,
1801-1818 compiled by Patrick G. Wardell, Lt. Col. U.S. Army,
Retired, Heritage Books, Bowie, Md., 1989

Cavaliers and Pioneers, Abstracts of Virginia Land Patents and
Grants, Nell Marion Nugent, Vol. 1, 1623-1666, Virginia State
Library and Archives, Richmond, 1992; Vol. 2, 1666-1695, Virginia
State Library, Richmond 1977; Vol.3, 1695-1732, Virginia State
Library, Richmond 1979; Supplement

County Court Records of Accomack-Northampton, Va., 1640-
1645, Edited by Susie M. Ames, Pub. The Virginia Historical
Society, The University Press of Virginia, Charlottesville

Early Virginia Immigrants, 1623-1666, George Cabell Greer, W.C.
Hill Printing Co., Richmond, Va., 1913, reprint Baltimore
Genealogical Pub. Co. 1960

Commonwealth of Virginia Death Certificates, Richmond, Va.

Commonwealth of Virginia, General Court Office, Virginia State
Library, Richmond, Va.

Fairfax County, Virginia in 1760, Beth Mitchell, Office of
Comprehensive Planning, Fairfax Co., Va., 1987

Hanover Co., Va., Land Patents and Grants of Hanover Co., Va.,
1721-1800, Compiled by Charles P. Blunt, IV

Isle of Wight Co., Marriage, Blanche Adams Chapman, Smithfield,
Va., 1933

17th Century Isle of Wight Co., Va., John Bennett Boddie 1938

Isle of Wight Co., Va., Deeds 1647-1695, and Guardian Accounts
William Lindsay Hopkins, 1993

Jamestown Minutes of Council and General Court, Library of
Congress.

Unpublished notes of Mrs. Jewell, Law Suits and Misc. Records of
Loudoun Co., Va., Vol. 1, pg.80, Vol. II, Mrs. Walter Towner Jewell
1958-59, originally held by Rev. Melvin Steadman, now deceased.
note: check VSL

Middlesex Co., Va., Parish Registers Christ Church, 1653-1812,
The National Society of the Colonial Dames of America and the
State of Virginia, Baltimore Genealogical Publishing Company
1964

Northumberland Co., Va., Deed and Will abstracts, of edited and
published by Ruth and Sam Sparacio, Antient Press, McLean, Va.
1992

Virginia Colonial Abstracts, Vol. II, Northumberland County
Records, 1652-1655, abstracts from Court Order Book No. 2,
September 1652 to October 1665, Record Book 14, 1652 to 1655,
abstracted by Beverly Fleet, Baltimore Gen. Pub., Co., 1961
Virginia Colonial Abstracts, Vo., XXIII, Westmoreland Co., 1653-
1657, abstracted by Beverly Fleet, Baltimore Gen. Pub., Co., 1961

Virginia Colonial Abstracts, Vols. XX, XIX, Northumbria
Collectanea, 1645 - 1720, abstracted by Beverly Fleet, Baltimore
Gen. Pub., Co., 1961

Virginia Colonial Abstracts, Vol. XIX, Northumbria Collectanea,
1645-1720, abstracted by Beverly Fleet, Baltimore Gen. Pub., Co.,
1961

Virginia Corolorum by Nellis, pgs. 131, 139, 141

The Virginia Genealogist, Hawley/Halley in 17th Century, Va., by
Ann H. Mack, 24265 Pheasant Ct., Salinas, CA 93908

Virginia Historical Magazine, Vol. 9, pg.43, Vol. 10, pg.424

Virginia Colonial Records Project, Archival and Information Services Division, (804) 692.3888, www.lva.lib.va.us

Virginia State Library, 800 E. Broad Street, Richmond, Va. 23219

Westmoreland Co., Va., Order Book 1690-1698, 1694-1698, abstracted and complied by John Frederick Dorman, Washington, D.C. 1962

Westmoreland Co., Va., Order Book 1698-1705, Parts 1 and 3, 1701-1703

VSL: Records, 1661-1664, Westmoreland Co., Va.

VSL: Deeds and Patents, Etc., Westmoreland Co., Va., 1665 - 1667

Westmoreland Co., Va., Deeds and Patents, etc. 1665-1677, Part and two, abstracted and compiled by John Frederick Dorman, Washington, D.C. 1973

West Virginia
A History of Preston County, W.Va., by Oren F. Morton, B. Lit., Kingwood, W.Va., The Journal Publishing Company 1914

RARE
The Hawley Record, Elias Sill Hawley, Buffalo, N.Y., Press of E.H. Hutchinson & Co., 1890

INDEX

INDEX

INDEX

BRENT, Family 34 George
34 Giles 117 127 Robert
117
BRENTFORD, Middlesex 34
35 270
BRIDGES, Anthony 158 Mary
Alice 42
BRIDGEWATER, Samuel 130
BRIDWELL, Abigail 222
Abraham 222 Amamiam
222 Benjamin 222 Ella
Gray 220 Family 222 273
Francis 22 23 222 226
Frandie 226 Guthbert 222
Isaac 222 John 222
Martha Ann 220 Mary
222 Mary F.220 Nancy 4
206 Oswell Holmes 220
Polly 222 Sarah 222
William H.163 William
Holmes 7 219 William
Theopolis 220
BRISTOE, Anne 197
Elizabeth 197 John 197
Milligent 197 Rachael 197
Rebecca 197 Wm.197
BRNHISS, Malcolm Everett
220
BROCKETT, Robert 193
BROCKMAN, Ann Anestar
260 Richard Simms 230
Samuel 260 William
Everett 230 260
BROOKES, Benjamin 201
Robert 121
BROWN, Coly 164 George
156 157 Gilbert and
Brown 246 Glenda
Carolyn 16 Harold 224

BROWN, cont.,
Helen W. 86 162 James
207 John 34 154 Mlary
245 Rebecca Joy 224
William 140
BROWNING, Jane 238
Thomas 238
BRUMLEY, Elizabeth 53 98
BRUTT, John 154
BUCKLEW, Delialah 7
BUCKNER, Aris 145 150 193
BUDA, Linda 18
BULLOCK, John 96 97
BUNTON, Harry Heryford
Terrill 47 Joshua Terrill
47 Margarithe Lynn 47
BURCH, Alee 222 E.265
Elizabeth 1 200 201 204
223 265 Family 222
Francis 200 201 204 222
223 Hester 1 159 161
199 200 201 203 222 223
James 201 John 1 198
200 201 204 222 223
BURGESS, Edward 234
Virginia Soldiers 237
BURKE, Anna 43 Catherine
43 Creek 240 James 43
Newman 31 164 Silas 43
208
BURNS, Annie Walker 276
James H.258 Peter Arter
213
BURNELL, Elizabeth 35
BURNER, Mrs. Charles 258
BURNETT, Gerald H.236
BURTON, Charlotte 166
Hannah 237 Middleton
Parish Register 87

INDEX

INDEX

INDEX

INDEX

INDEX

EDWARDS, cont.,
  Joseph 168 Mary 153
  157 Nancy 168 Robert
  153 157
EDWN, Wm.196
EISEMAN, Audie Elma
  Hawley 14 Charles 14
  Grace Edna 14
ELCOCK, John 126 152
ELDIN, Wm.242
ELGIN, Catherine 43
ELKIN, Allan 31 Allen N.160
  164 Margaret P.Halley
  160 164 Mariam 31 39
  Mary Fletcher 39 Martha
  44 Mary 39 Rev.Robert
  39 Zachariah 39
ELLIOTT, Louise 12 15
ELLIS, Nancy 255 Nancy
  Ann 255 256 Jeremiah
  255 Richard 94 Robert
  101 105 Virginia 255
ELLSLEY, Lewis 150 Thomas
  47
ELLYS, Robert 100
ELLZEY, Halley and Ellzeys
  147 Lewis 149 Mary 164
  Thomas, 47 164
EMMERSON, also Emerson,
  Elizabeth 1 161 Elizabeth
  Meeks 3 203 Family 235
  George 202 235 James
  173 174 John 1 161 174
  201 202 203 235 Lucy
  202 235 Mildred 203
  Mildred E. Hawley 3
  Richard 202
ENGLISH, Walter 157 158
ENNALS, Barthod 105

ERVIN, Jacob 13 Jennie 13
ESCOTT, Wm.203
ESKRIDGE, Charles 191
ESTES, Capt.Triplett E.176
EUBANK, Nancy 30 Thomas
  30
EULICH, Charity 5
EVANS, Lilia 250
EVELIN, Robert 35 92
  Thomas 91
EVENS, Mordecay 129
  Mordica 129
EWELL, Thomas 153
EXETER, place name 1 2
  134 136 137 138 202
EXON, Henry 97
EYROS, Joseph 117
FABER, Eva 14 19
FAIRFAX, Bryan 150 Denny
  148 Col. John 6
FARNYHO, Wm.235
FARRAR, Wm.125
FARTHING, Edmund 87
FAUTLEROY, Capt. Moore
  126
FAW, A.143
FAWKNOR Mr. 119
FEARNEAUGH, also
  Fearneyhough, Agnes
  235 237 Anne 235 237
  238 Dorothy 237 238
  Edward 237 238 John
  238 Thomas 235
FEARYNEYHOUGH, also
  Fearnough, Agens 238
  John 235
FELLOWSHIP, place name 1
  4 135 198 Hale's 53 132
FENWICK, Gulthb 104

INDEX

INDEX

INDEX

INDEX

INDEX

HALLEY, cont.,
Robert Burns 48
Robert Joseph 47 Robert
Pressley 44 47 Robert
Samuel 40 Rolly 33 147
Ruth 41 50 Sabina 48
266 Sally 168 Sanford 48
Samuel 3 31 39 40 49 50
56 111 164 193 202 203
207 264 Samuel
Hampton 45 Samuel
James 44 Samuel Leroy
48 Sarah 49 50 164 193
207 209 266 Sarah Ann
208 Sarah Ellen 43 Sarah
Enfield 164 Scott Winfred
42 Silas Burke 43
Smithson G.49 Suky 48
Surname 263 Susan 266
Susan Elizabeth 41 47
Susan Laura 44 220
Susan Victoria 47
Susanna 49 Susannah 29
164 Sybill 29 164 266
Tammy 31 Thms 264
Thomas 2 46 48 55 58 64
95 103 154 201 202 208
263 264 265 266 Mr.
Thomas 58 Thomas F.60
Thomas Heryford 45
Thomas Jefferson 31
Thomas Richard 58
Timothy 50 Uriah 42
Virgil Marshall 46 Virginia
Hampton 40 Washington
67 Wesley M.49 Will 179
William 3 28 29 32 43 44
47 48 56 61 62 63 87 94
106 107 108 143 144 145

HALLEY, William, cont.,
146 147 150 152 155 164
167 172 174 183 184 185
186 187 188 192 193 205
207 208 239 248 265 266
267 William Jr.185
William Benjamin 48
William F. 208 William
Francis 43 William G.206
William H. 42 William
M.49 William Nathaniel
41 William Thomas 41
William Woodward 41
Winifred 60 Wilson 67
Zella Eloise 42
HALLEYS, Family 58 108
263 266 275 location 108
HALLEYES, Family 212
HALLIE, James 120
HALLIGE Henry 214
HALLING, James 120
Thomas 53 99 140
William 121
HALLON, Thomas 98
HALLS, James 213 John 51
96 97 99
HALLSAL, Lucy 200 234
HALLY, Absalom 186 188
189 Amos 5 188 Barbara
192 193 Barton 185 188
Clemmie 265 Edward 32
157 265 Elizabeth 138
198 201 202 Fanny 164
Francis 181 Gabriel 265
George 65 183 184 185
George, a free negro,
184 185 George of
James 183 Henry 265
Henry Sr.117 Henry H.65

INDEX

INDEX

HAWLEY, cont.,
Mrs.Ann 115 Anna Mae
Crum 10 Anne 32 51
Annie 19 Anthony 130
Archibald 66 Arthur 128
Arthur William 14 15 267
Audie Elma 14 Augustine
66 B.83 Baby 84 Barbara
3 144 145 192 209
Barton 5 7 13 63 74 113
147 150 167 Barton D.5 7
110 111 145 146 147 151
185 193 208 210 211
Barton L.12 Barton
Luther 15 Barton R.6 11
Barnett C.77 Bathsheba
2 3 6 55 201 240 267
Benjamin 75 154 168
Benjamin Jacob 40 41
Benoni 46 Bergus 75
Bergus R.21 Bernard 122
Betsey 73 Betsy 5 Betty
Sue 24 254 Biem 54 74
Blenda Ray 17 273 Boyd
70 78 Brownie C.Hodges
9 Bruce P.15 Burgess R.
21 Burnett C.75 Burton
D.63 C.Bonnie 80 C.F.
177 C.W.56 Caleb 180
Caleb Fortney 11 13
Calvin 71 Capt.91 92 94
103 262 Caroline Sharps
12 Carolyn Fay 16
Catherine 10 144 145
146 147 208 210 211
Catherine Heath 7 110
111 211 267 Catherine
Jeffries 30 Caty 154
Charity Eulich 5

HAWLEY, cont.,
Charles 151 Charles
McKee 20 22 23 56 70
74 78 85 107 144 163
177 226 Charles Robert
17 19 Charles W.9 273
Charles Wesley 12 15
Charles William 9 Charles
Wirt 16 Chester C.77
Christie A.Barnhill 9
Christina 54 74 Christine
77 Christopher 120
Clement 38 Clifton
Harvey 10 274 Clifton
Harvey III 11 Connie Sue
19 Cora L.Rags 12 15
Cornelius 168 Crocket 75
78 Custer W.13 Cynthia
E.77 Daisy Adelaide
Trexler 24 254 Daniel 171
David 18 65 David B.78
Dawn Ann 19 Deliah 7 26
74 83 Donald Charles 19
Dorothy Walnot 35
Dorothy Olga Meyrowitz
16 E.56 Earl U.80 Ed.56
Edgar Bruce 41 Edith
Crum 10 Edmond 157
Edward 27 32 33 34 115
116 119 121 128 154 156
157 196 214 214 215
Edward E.85 Edward
Sheppard 10 Edwin
Barbour 22 23 166 230
Elbert 13 Eldridge 12 72
Eleanor 4 41 55 154 213
Elmer 13 Elinor Brereton
de Courtney 36 37 Elisha
11 13 74 83 Elizabeth 1 2

302

INDEX

INDEX

HAYLE, cont.,
James 155 John 51 65
174 Joseph 144 149
Nicholas 113 Nico.126
property line 149 Thomas
27 51 114
HAYLES, Barbara 126 127
Edward 131 155 Edward
Jr.155 Elizabeth 213
Francis 52 158 George
158 Hercules 98 Jer.125
John 27 96 98 122 159
212 213 Thomas 27 51
114 115 152 153 212
HAYLEY, Daniel 131 Edward
155 Elizabeth 117 213
Henry 34 John 51 174
175 213
HAYLIE, Edward 64
HAYLLES, Wm.51 William
152
HAYLMYS, Thomas 53 98
HAYLY, Danll 158 Henry 116
John 65
HAYNEI, Sarah 30
HAYNEY, John 114 Thomas
27
HAYNIE, Henry 30 208 John
130 Richard 208 Sarah
208 210 Sibel 29 William
29
HAZEL, Caleb 174
HEABERT, William 128 155
HEAD, Elizabeth 45 John
Calvin 45 Lillian Verline
Halley 45 Mary Elizabeth
45 William Ethel 45
HEALE, Francis 128
HEALY, John 77 Harrell 77

HEALY, cont.,
Martha 77 Mary 77
Surname 174 267
HEATH, Andrew 7 110 111
166 191 209 210 211
Andrew Shelton 111
Catherine 5 7 100 111
Catherine 166 167 267
exor 111 Isaac 211
Lynda 111 211 Marie
Trexler 258 Rhuhannah
111 211 Sarah 111 211
HEATHER, Wm.203 204
HEATON, Patterson 222
HEILY Erwin 126
HELE Lewis 195 263
HELEY, Clement 101 Darby
51 101 Elizabeth 101
HELLEY, Clement 105 122
Griffith D.76
HELLY, Clement 31 105
HELMS, Andrew 43 Caroline
32 Leah 43 Mary Halley
43 Nancy 43 Peter C.43
Thomas 43 Thomas J.43
Uriah 43
HELY, Clement 31 97 100
101 John 125 126 Willi
125 Robert 125
HENBLEY, Wm.145 146
HENDERSON, David 108
143 145 Winona M.12
HENLEY, Mrs.Ernest N.
Perkins 252
HENRICK, Obedia 167
HENRY IV, of France 36
HENSLEY, Hugh 42
HERANDEZ, David 19
HEREFORD, Frances 28 43

INDEX

HEREFORD, cont.,
Jane 43 John 43
HERNDON, James 28 213
HERRICKE, John 89
HERRINN, Patricia 19
HERYFORD, John 30 Sarah
47 William 44
HEY, Clement 31 203
Elizabeth 203 Mary 203
HEYLMYS, Thomas 53 98 99
HEYLY, Eleanor 125 William
125 Willis 125
HEYRES, John 158
HIBBARD, Mary E.12 15
HICKMAN Nathan 213
HIGDON, Janey 8 9
HIGESON, also Higgeston,
John 130
HIGGINS, George 211
Nancy 30
HIGGINSON, John 131
HILL, Clement 105 Edward
125 Hickory 137 Pearl
May 230 Richard 126
Robert 149 Robert Jr.149
Shockoe 255 256 Walnut
231 William 149
HILLES, Wm.96
HINTER, Wm.Em 198
HLY, Clement 31 203
Elizabeth 203 Mary 203
HOARD, John 96 97
HOBBS, Catherine 196 legal
Will 196
HOBSON, Tho.155
HODGES, Brownie C.9
Charles 159
HODGSKYNNS, Edward 124
HODGSON, Mary 204

HODGSON, cont.,
Wm.204
HOFFMAN, Jacob 143
HOGGNECK, place name 98
HOLE, Barbary 125 John 50
109 148 149 209 John of
Devon Gent 148 Mary 50
209
HOLEY, Clement 31 101
Elizabeth 56 167 John 1
2 56 171 Mary 55 56
Nathaniel 2 55 56
Susanna 55 Thomas 55
56 William 5
HOLLE, James 86 John 95
Francis M.75
HOLLEY, A.187 Abel 62
Abraham 66 187
Absalom 5 187 Addie 26
84 Alice 151 167 Amos 5
187 267 Anthoney 120
Bailey 67 Barton D.5 211
Benjamin 66 70 78
Catherine 59 160 Charles
27 84 Charles Henry 84
Charlotte 68 Clement 31
Crockett 70 David 59 64
Edmund 67 Edward 141
Edward H.70 Edwin H.78
Elener 76 Elizabeth 56 70
76 83 160 Elias 66 Elijah
66 78 Ellen 26 84 Family
275 277 Fannie 78
Frances 69 Francis 48
180 Hannah 26 84 Henry
50 62 64 66 82 Hester
103 Isaiah 59 J.69 Jacob
76 James 28 James H.78
Jane 212 Jefferson D.78

309

INDEX

HOLLY, cont.,
George W. 67 82 Grace
76 Greenville 70 82
Griffieth D.70 Harriet 59
71 161 162 Henry 50
146 Henry L.67 Hester 55
Horace 268 Hillary H.59
Hunt 66 67 Isabelle 82
Isam 27 83 J.82 J.C.27
83 J.L.177 Jacob 54 59
62 68 141 James 54 59
63 65 66 67 68 76 82 140
172 182 204 James A.68
Jane 73 109 116 Janey
73 Jeremiah 25 26 69 72
73 82 Jerry 71 Jesse 76
Jiles 62 Joel 66 69 82 84
John 1 4 25 27 54 60 65
69 72 73 76 82 83 86 102
103 105 127 128 129 133
134 135 136 137 140 141
159 160 161 162 168 171
175 176 180 187 188 191
198 199 200 201 204 244
John A.66 82 John B.
266 John C.27 83 John
H.82 John L.82 John P.
64 John W.25 72 Joseph
25 60 61 63 65 67 69 72
82 161 Joseph Jr.82
Julius 67 Katherine 76
Lawrence O.162 243
Leannah 160 Lefsse 25
72 Leonard 63 66 70 Lily
27 83 Lorenzo D.82
Louisa 25 Louisa W.72
Lucy 59 Malry 27
Mandania 27 83 Madison
71 76 Maretta 82

HOLLY, cont.,
Margaret 160 161 Maria
76 Marshall 82 Martha 25
27 72 76 83 160 Mary 25
59 71 72 73 81 83 147
163 168 187 200 205 234
Mary Ann 102 135 151
200 247 Mary Ann Melton
162 200 Mary A.26 Mary
C.26 73 Mary Colvin 33
Mary E.25 72 Mary M.26
73 Matelan 25 72 Matilda
61 69 71 Milton 71 76
Moses 82 Nancy 26 71
72 73 161 Nathaniel 2 54
134 140 180 187 Nealy
82 Obediah 129
Penelope 62 162 Percella
C.82 Perdue 163 Perry
82 Peter 63 168 Phillip 68
Raleigh 33 Rebecca 83
140 Richard 54 140 204
Richard N.76 Robert 133
Rolly 147 165 Rosa 27 83
Rosaline 76 Ruben 59
Sally 66 Samuel 3 26 63
70 73 202 Rufus 76
Sabra 59 Sally 164 Sarah
25 54 70 72 76 82 140
161 162 168 Shedrick 71
Simpson 182 Smithson
G.69 Stephen G.66
Sterling 63 Surname 174
267 Tamor 54 204
Thomas 1 26 27 55 63 64
67 70 73 76 82 83 103
109 116 128 137 161 162
176 201 202 Thomas H.
26 73 Thomas J.76

INDEX

LEE, cont.,
Fitz 178 Fitzhugh 20 178
Henry 125 Hugh 114 115
212 John 118 158 210
Philip 51 102 property
line 158 Surname 24
Thomas 271 Thomas
W.209 Wendy 216
LEECH, Wm.153
LEFTWICH, Littleberry 48
LEGG, Ailsy 73 Elijah 4 62
63 67 73 112 Eliza 77
Mary 73 Sarah 73
Tabitha Hawley 4 112
Willis 4 Zephania 4
LEITCH, James 268
LEONARDS, Baltimore vs.35
38 89 124 Leonard 89
LEWES, Edward 124 William
124
LEWGER, John 36 263
LEWIS, Charles 110 111 145
147 177 193 210 269
Coleman 108 112 208
Daniel 108 208 227 David
246 Elizabeth 227 James
150 James Jr.246 Jane
227 John 10 141 153 227
John Jr.151 Joseph 242
Keziah Settle 239 Mary
Ann 239 Mary Elizabeth
10 Samuel 227 Stephen
227 Thomas 34 102 227
Thomas Watson 16 Major
Wm.127
LEYBOURNE GRANGE, 270
LIGGON, Albert 256 Alonzo
Columbus 256 Alonzo Jr.
256 Annie Alease 256

LIGGON, cont.,
burial plot 256 Edgar 256
Irvine Edgar 256 Ivy E.
256 Lottie Dell 256 Nancy
Ann Ellis Trexler 256
Nellie 256 Reuben Henry
256 Ruby May 256 Sarah
256 Willie Ann Wright
256 Willie Pleasant 256
LIGON, Matthew 148
LILLIEN, Anne Elizabeth 24
Errol Hermann 24
LILLY, John 196
LIMESTONE TRACT 141 142
206 268 269 275
LINCOLN MILITIA 4 171 176
244
LINCOLNSHIRE, Revesby
Abby 270
LINDSAY, Jacob 29
LINTON, Anthony 115
Delbert 269
LISLE, Fannie 40 Hampton
40 Henry Edward 40
James 40 James Lee 40
Mariam 40 Mary Margaret
Halley 40 Nancy 40
Rufus 40 Rufus II 40
Lizzie 40 Samuel 40
Virginia Hampton 40
LITLE, Richard H.143
LITTLE, Difficult Run 150
Falls 242 Hunting Creek
159 Rivers 266 Troy 202
235
LLOYD, Elizabeth 243
Pauline T.251
LOCKERMAN, also
Lockaman, Dr.Jacob 105

316

INDEX

INDEX

INDEX

INDEX

INDEX

INDEX

SHREVE, Benjamin 207
William 210
SILLIVANT, Nora 158
SIMMONS, Edward 54
Elizabeth 54 Jane 54
Thomas 215
SIMMS, Ann Anestar 260
Julia A.260 Richard 260
SIMPSON, Caleb 209
Elizabeth 28 31 172 207
George 207 James
M.256 John 129 155
Mary A.Elizabeth 256
Mary Canterbury 207
Moses 207 Peggy 43
Peyton 209 Richard 207
Richard Withers 28
Samuel 207 Sarah 207
256 Sary Sara 207 Sary
Windsor 207 Tamer 207
Wm.207 266
SINCKLER, also Sinkler,
John 212 Samuel 212
SINGER, Beverly Core 219
Bradley 219 Magan
Ellen 219
SINGLETON Anthony 231
SISK Ann 162
SISSON, Anne Winona
Sisson 23 Maude
Covington Hawley 23
Mr.23
SKINNER, Ames 111
Capt.246 Lucinda 165
Nathan 111 Peter 111
trade 89
SKIPP, Margaret 21
SLANESBY, John 97
SLAUGHTER, Henry 167

SLAUGHTER, cont.,
John 98 Philip 260
SMALLEY, Wm.149 150
SMALLWOOD, James 133
134 136 Mary 134 Regt.
175 Stephen 197 William
133 134 136
SMALLWOODS HAZZARD,
134
SMALLY, Ezekiel 150 Isaac
149
SMITH, Alex 29 108 145 Ann
Elizabeth Duerson 2
Arthur 109 148 Branch
132 Col.148 Elinor Welch
42 Elizabeth 2 Elizabeth
Lyle 2 Elkanah 2 Eugenia
Halley 48 Eva Charity 15
Fannie Alice Kiser 2
Fanny Botts 2 George
C.42 Harry Rodes 2
Jefferson Wright 2
Joseph 143 Judith 140
Lewis 30 John 2 89 140
John Ransome 48 Lidia 2
Louise Perkins 251 Mr.92
Mary 2 Mary Eleanor
Hawley 2 Mary Ingels
Ranson 2 Minnie Halley
274 Nancy 2 Nell H.44
Phoebe 143 Philys
Traylor Arnold 252
Richard 131 Robert T.2
Robert Thompson 2 271
274 Sarah 2 29 Sarah
Green 2 Smith and Keith
143 trade 34 W.173
William 2 29 91 92
William Halley 2

INDEX

INDEX

TREXLER, cont.,
Gladys May 254 Grace
258 Grace Bell 253 Helen
Gertrude Fines 253
Helen Leary 257 Herbert
Julius 253 Herbert Leslie
254 Ignatius 255 Isabella
256 257 Jacob Eddie 258
James Herman 253
James Washington 24
253 257 Jeremiah 254
John Ignatius 256 John
Joseph 253 255 256 257
Joseph Edward 257
Joyce Ann 253 Lena
Madeline Bennett Totty
257 Lottie May Perkins
24 253 257 Lucille
Herndon 257 Mable
Lorraine 253 Madelyn
257 Margaret 253 Marian
May 258 Marie 258 Mary
257 Mary Ann 255 Mary
A.Elizabeth Simpson 256
Mary Diane 253 Mary Ida
253 Mary Margaret Poe
also Poh 256 258 Mary
Margaret Virginia 253
Minnie 258 Minor
Davidson 257 Nancy 255
Nancy Ann Ellis 255 256
Nancy Lorraine 253
Nancy McCarthy 258
Nettie M.Blair 253 Pearl
Estelle Gerhardt 258
Peter Lynn 254 Robert
Earl 253 Robert G.258
Rosa Alice 258 Rose
Edith 253 Rosetta 256

TREXLER, cont.,
Ruth S.Bowles 257 Ruth
Virginia Pastora 253 Sara
B.258 Susie B.Davis 258
Violet 257 Walter Ignatius
Edward 253 Walter
Warren 253 William 255
256 258 William E.258
TRIBBLE, Andrew J.39
Elizabeth Thomas Halley
39
TRIPLETT, Isabella 34 Sarah
Harrison 34 Thomas 34
207
TRUSSEL, John 27 114 212
Mr.114
TUCKER, Com.236 Mrs.H.B.
258 William 237
TURNER, Almenda 30 Mrs.
Clement 31 corner
boundary 146 Dan 23
Deed Transfer 145 147
Edward 31 32 197 203
Elizabeth 204 F.dec'd.
184 Fielding 5 109 210
Frank A.23 Irene
R.Hawley 23 James 110
127 145 146 208 James
Hawley 5 109 110 John
96 97 109 110 147 210
Lewis 109 147 210 Major
210 Mary 204 Samuel
204 Thomas 204 Turner
vs. Turner 109 unborn
child 210 Williiam 101
Winifred 4 210
TURPIN, Betsey 48 George
W.230
TYLER, James 106 JoAne 99

332

INDEX

INDEX

WATERS, cont.,
William 243
WATKINS, Lucy 254 Robert
166
WATSON, Ephraim 204
Capt.James 255 Peter
204
WATTS, Rev.Jacob 230
Nancy 230
WEB, William 156
WEBB, Addie 258 Elizabeth
94 Joan 118 John 118
120 Thomas 94
WEBSTER, Adam L.143
William L.143
WEEDON, George 158
WEEKES, also Weeks,
Delores Noel 251
Elizabeth 196 Francis
196
WELCH, Caroline 42
Caroline Welch Halley 42
David Hamilton 42 Dora
D.14 Elizabeth Elinor 42
Emily 42 George W.42
John H.42 John Samuel
6 Laura 42 Margaret
Hawley 6 Mary 42 Nancy
Jane 42 Robert D.42
Robert Yocum 42 William
Hunt 42
WELLS, Anthony 151
Fontaine 142
WERH, James L.42
WEST, Col.Hugh 34 John
153 Sybil Harrison 34
William 47 164
WESTHORPE Maj.Jo.206
WEST INDIES 90 195

WESTMINISTER, Chapel 160
place name 92
WHALEY, Edward 29 Nancy
Halley 29
WHARTON, Francis 204
Richard 131
WHEALAND, Mary 163
WHEELER, Elizabeth 234
Hezekia 173 Ignatius 201
202
WHESTON, Ann 213 John
213
WHISLER, Judy 218
WHIT, Enis 119
WHITBYE, Rebecca 86
WHITE, Canya 100 Elizabeth
143 James 38 195
Roland 100 Thomas 143
William 195
WHITEHALL, 91 92
WHITEHEAD, Richard 129
WICKERS, Henry 152
WIGFIELD, Martha 165
WIGGLEWORTH, Nellie
Colvin 226
WILCOXEN, Frances Halley
DeBell 31
WILKERSON, Elizabeth 43
Elizabeth Betsey Halley
42 Hiram 42 John H.42
Moses 43 Nancy D.42
Nimrod A.42 Sarah 43
Sarah Sallie 29 Sedona
C.43 William 29
WILLIAMS, Carolyn 42
Catherine 201 Elizabeth
Jane 42 Emily Halley 42
George Lincol 42 James
113 197

334

INDEX

RESEARCH UNITS INDEX

RESEARCH UNITS INDEX